Using

Windows NT™ Workstation 4.0

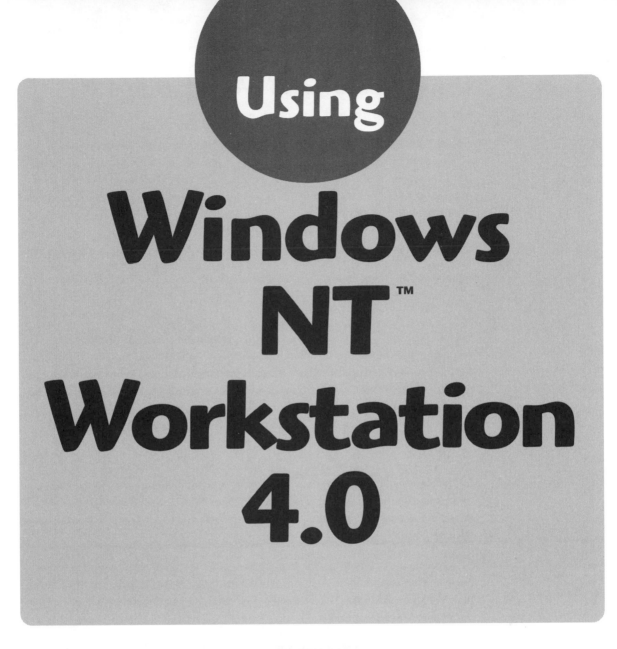

Using

Windows NT™ Workstation 4.0

Ed Bott

Using Windows NT Workstation 4.0

Library of Congress Catalog No.: 96-68982

ISBN: 0-7897-0674-1

97 96 95   6 5 4 3 2 1

Interpretation of the printing code: the rightmost double-digit number is the year of the book's printing; the rightmost single-digit number, the number of the book's printing. For example, a printing code of 96-1 shows that the first printing of the book occurred in 1996.

Screen reproductions in this book were created using Collage Plus from Inner Media, Inc., Hollis, NH.

Composed in *ITC Century, ITC Highlander,* and *MCPdigital* by Que Corporation.

Credits

President
Roland Elgey

Publishing Manager
Lynn E. Zingraf

Editorial Services Director
Elizabeth Keaffaber

Managing Editor
Michael Cunningham

Director of Marketing
Lynn E. Zingraf

Acquisitions Editor
Martha O'Sullivan

Technical Specialist
Nadeem Muhammed

Product Develpomant Specialists
Lorna Gentry and John Gosney

Production Editor
Kathryn Purdum

Editor
Tom Lamoureux

Assistant Product Marketing Manager
Christy M. Miller

Strategic Marketing Manager
Barry Pruett

Technical Editor
Discovery Computing, Inc.

Software Relations Coordinator
Patty Brooks

Editorial Assistant
Mark Kane

Book Designer
Ruth Harvey

Cover Designer
Jay Corpus

Production Team
Stephen Adams
Debra Bolhuis
Jason Carr
Jason Hand
Daniel Harris
Bob LaRoche
Steph Mineart
Laura Robbins
Bobbi Satterfield
Staci Somers

Indexer
Chris Barrick

About the Author

Ed Bott, the author of Using Windows NT 4.0, is senior contributing editor of *PC Computing* magazine, where he is responsible for the magazine's extensive coverage of Windows 95, Windows NT, and Microsoft Office. From 1991 until 1993, he was editor of *PC Computing*, following three years as managing editor of *PC World* magazine.

Ed is a two-time winner of the Computer Press Award, most recently for *PC Computing*'s annual Windows SuperGuide, a collection of tips, tricks, and advice for users of Windows 95 and Windows NT. He lives in Redmond, Washington, with his wife, Judy Merrill, and their two Himalayan cats, Winston and Spencer.

To Judy, with all my love.

Acknowledgments

It took a hardworking team of professionals to bring this book together. Literally dozens of people—editors, designers, proofreaders, technical reviewers, and others—had a hand in the making of this book. It's impossible to thank them all personally, but I would like to mention a few whose efforts were truly noteworthy.

I had a tag team of Product Development Specialists to rely on—Lori Cates, Lorna Gentry, and John Gosney. Their comments and suggestions helped make this book easier to understand.

Acquisitions Editor Martha O'Sullivan came back from maternity leave in time to make sure the project stayed on track.

Discovery Computing, Inc., checked the manuscript for technical accuracy and offered several invaluable suggestions.

And a very special thank you to Publishing Director Lynn Zingraf for his unwavering support.

We'd Like to Hear from You!

As part of our continuing effort to produce books of the highest possible quality, Que would like to hear your comments. To stay competitive, we *really* want you, as a computer book reader and user, to let us know what you like or dislike most about this book or other Que products.

You can mail comments, ideas, or suggestions for improving future editions to the address below, or send us a fax at (317) 581-4663. For the online inclined, Macmillan Computer Publishing has a forum on CompuServe (type **GO QUEBOOKS** at any prompt) through which our staff and authors are available for questions and comments. The address of our Internet site is **http://www.mcp.com/que** (World Wide Web).

In addition to exploring our forum, please feel free to contact me personally to discuss your opinions of this book: I'm **John Gosney, 104436,2300** on CompuServe, and I'm **jgosney@que.mcp.com** on the Internet.

Thanks in advance—your comments will help us to continue publishing the best books available on computer topics in today's market.

John Gosney
Product Development Specialist
Que Corporation
201 W. 103rd Street
Indianapolis, Indiana 46290
USA

Contents at a Glance

Table of Contents

Part II: Controlling Windows

5 My Computer and Everything Inside It   63

Part IV: Making Windows Work the Way You Do

14 Putting Your Favorite Things Where You Want Them   219

Part V: Out of the PC, Onto the Page: Printing and Fonts

Part VI: Beyond the Basic PC

17 The Amazing, Talking, Singing, Exploding PC   279

18 CD-ROMs   293

Part VII: Communicating with the Rest of the World

Introduction

For nearly a decade, I've been helping people learn how Windows works—and how to make it work better for them. During that time I've written four books, hundreds of magazine articles, and countless e-mail messages to friends, family, and complete strangers, all with the single-minded goal of helping people become more productive with computers.

When I installed the very first version of Windows back in 1986, Windows fit on a single floppy disk, and the entire installation process took about five minutes. Windows NT, version 4.0, takes an hour or more to install, and it uses up more than 100 times as much space, or the equivalent of *six* of the hard drives in that original 1986 computer.

I wish I could say that Windows has become 100 times easier to use during the past decade, but I can't. In fact, hardly a day goes by that I don't get a frantic phone call or e-mail from a friend or a relative—or even a total stranger. Invariably, they say the same thing: "I wish I were smart enough to figure this stuff out for myself." And invariably I give them this message:

It's not you, it's the computer.

If you can't get your work done, it's because Windows isn't smart enough to understand what you really want it to do. It's not your fault.

Microsoft has literally hundreds of smart people working on ways to make computers in general—and Windows in particular—easier to use. You'll see some of their work in Windows NT 4.0, but they've got a lot more to do before computers are as easy to use as a TV or a microwave oven—or even a VCR.

Someday, the rocket scientists and behavioral psychologists at Microsoft will create a version of Windows that can read your mind, organize your thoughts, balance your checkbook, and pick up the dry cleaning, all at the touch of a key. (Maybe they could even create a special Do What I Mean key for the next version of the Microsoft Natural keyboard!)

Until that day, though, we'll have to continue communicating with our computers by pulling down menus and clicking buttons. Which is why I've written this book.

Is this book for you?

I hope you won't mind, but I've made a few assumptions about you as I was organizing and writing this book.

I assume that you're using Windows NT on a computer at the office, where your company expects you to get too much work done in too little time.

You've probably been using Windows 3.1 for the past few years, and you've organized all your favorite programs into groups in the Program Manager.

You're really, really busy. You're not the least bit interested in becoming a computer expert. And you'd like me to tell you the one best way to get your work done.

Oh, and you have little patience for computer jargon and technical mumbo-jumbo.

What makes this book different?

You don't need an advanced degree in engineering or computer science to read this book. If you can tell the difference between the left and right mouse buttons, you've got all the technical background you need.

It's written in plain English, too. I promise not to bury you in detailed explanations and three-letter acronyms (TLAs). After all, you're not studying for a degree in computer science—you're trying to get some work done, with the help of some incredibly powerful and occasionally baffling computer programs.

With Windows NT 4.0 programs, there are always at least four different ways to do everything. If you were planning to become a computer expert, you'd expect a computer book to give you step-by-step instructions for each of them. Not this book.

In this book, I focus on results. That means I'll tell you the best way to get each job done. There might be three other ways to do the same thing, but for most people, most of the time, the technique I describe is the one that will get results most quickly.

Oh, and there won't be a quiz.

How do I use this book

This isn't a textbook. You don't have to start at page 1 and read all the way to the end. It's not a mystery novel, either, so if you want to skip to the last chapter first, be my guest.

You'll probably be surprised at some of the things that Windows NT 4.0 can do for you. That's why, if you have the time, it's worth flipping through the chapters, looking at the headings, and searching out the references to the things you do at work. The people who published this book went to a lot of trouble to make sure that those interesting ideas would leap off the page and catch your attention as you browse.

This book will come in handy when you're not sure where to begin. And if you get stuck, you'll more than likely find the way out somewhere within these pages.

Part I: Getting Started with Windows

1

What Is Windows NT?

● In this chapter:

- What is Windows NT, what can it do for me, and why should I care?

- How can Windows NT help me organize my work?

- How can I make Windows NT work the way I work?

- Where do I start?

Windows NT makes your life easier—well, at least the part that can be handled by a computer. . . . . ▶

Unless you've been living in a cave for the past six years, you've heard of Windows. If you've had a computer on your desk anytime in the 1990s, chances are you used Windows 3.1. If you bought a new computer for home or work in the past year, it probably came with Windows 95 preinstalled. Now you're face-to-face with Windows NT 4.0, the latest member of the family of computer operating systems called Windows.

So what is Windows NT? The two letters tacked onto the end of the name stand for *New Technology*. As that bold label suggests, this is not the Windows that most people have been using for the past few years. Yes, Windows NT 4.0 can run most of your old MS-DOS and Windows programs, but the software that's actually doing the work is very different.

Windows NT was designed for use by big corporations, so it does some things very well: password protection that would have Tom Clancy taking notes for his next novel, for example, and the ability to run for weeks on end without crashing. Not surprisingly, the things it doesn't do so well—games and multimedia, for example—are distinctly *un*-businesslike.

Despite these fundamental differences, though, this is still Windows. Windows NT, like MS-DOS and Windows 95, is a computer operating system—a complex program that helps you organize the work you do with your PC every day.

What can Windows NT do for me?

The most obvious part of Windows is the graphical user interface—the colorful screen and those small, sometimes puzzling pictures referred to as *icons*. Once you learn how to move the mouse pointer around the screen, Windows lets you do just about anything by pointing at an icon and clicking a button on the mouse. Those clicks tell Windows to get to work on your behalf. Behind the scenes, beneath the surface and just out of sight, Windows acts as your personal executive staff, complete with the PC equivalent of file clerks, messengers, security guards, administrative assistants, and a full-time maintenance crew. Best of all, you're the boss. Every time you tap a key on your keyboard or click the mouse, this staff swings into action to carry out your requests.

The Windows NT desktop

Where do you begin? The most important pieces of Windows are right where you can see them, on the Windows desktop. This desktop works just like the one in your office. You keep the most important work right on top, where you can get to it quickly. Less urgent things get tucked away in folders and filing cabinets.

My Computer
Mission Control for your PC and any hardware that's connected to it. Double-click this icon to see the files, folders, programs, and hardware on your PC.

Network Neighborhood
Every networked PC and printer you're connected to shows up here—whether it's just across the hallway or halfway around the world.

Inbox (Microsoft Exchange)
Just like the inbox on your real desk, this is where you can expect to find e-mail messages from other people.

Internet Explorer
Use this program to browse through files on the World Wide Web. Like pages in a magazine, these documents may contain text and graphics, but they can also include sounds, snippets of video, and links that you click to jump to different pages containing related data.

The Windows Explorer
With this application, you get a more complicated view of your files and folders. On one side, there's a list of all the drives and folders on your computer and on the network, arranged like an outline. On the other, there is a list of files in the selected folder.

The Windows desktop
This is the blank workspace where you spread out your favorite tools and anything you're working on now. Windows puts a few icons (small pictures that represent documents and programs) here to get you started; you can keep the desktop uncluttered or drag other icons onto it. (You'll learn how to do this in Chapter 13.)

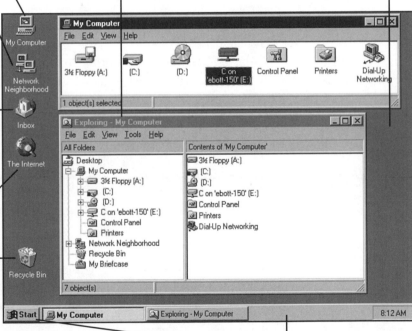

Recycle Bin
When you use Windows NT to delete a file, it doesn't go away immediately. Instead, your deleted files pile up here until you empty the trash or until it gets full.

Start button
Click here to start. When you do, you'll pop up a menu that contains virtually every common task you can perform in Windows NT.

Taskbar
You'll use the three parts of the taskbar often: the Start menu to launch programs; buttons to switch quickly between them; and various status icons on the right side to tell you what Windows is up to.

When you're ready to continue working on that letter you started writing yesterday, just tell Windows the name of the file the letter is stored in, and the letter will pop up, ready for you to start typing. Are you ready to toss out some old files? Just dump them into the Recycle Bin and the housekeeping staff will take care of the rest. When you need to connect a new modem or a laser printer to your computer, it's no problem—there's a Wizard on the premises to handle most of the hard work. Windows can find a lost file for you, help you keep your company's books, even send a message to a co-worker in the next office or a friend halfway around the world, assuming you're connected to some sort of e-mail system.

Windows makes your life easier—well, at least the part that can be handled by a computer. Inside, it has a collection of specialized programs that work together to keep you as organized as you want to be:

- It's an **operating system**. That means it tells your computer what to do and when to do it.

- It includes a **file system** so you can organize your work.

- **Networking and communications** capabilities are second nature to Windows NT, which means your computer can share programs and storage space with other computers in your company.

- It handles the process of **printing** your documents, and it even has built-in **electronic-mail** capabilities. You can share your work with other people by putting it on paper or using a variety of e-mail systems.

- There's a **consistent look and feel** to everything, thanks to a work-shop full of boxes, buttons, toolbars, gizmos, and widgets that other programs can use. The net result? Programs look a lot alike and work in a similar fashion, so when you learn how to use one program, you can use that knowledge to use other programs, too. That allows you to get more work finished.

- It lets you do **several things at once**. (If you're easily distracted, this may not be good news!)

- There's some **productivity software**, including a simple word processor, a calculator, communications programs, and a program you can use to draw or paint pictures.

- There's even some **anti-productivity software**, in the form of games like Solitaire and Freecell.

Why do I need an operating system?

Imagine how chaotic your office would be if your office manager quit tomorrow. The FedEx driver would be wandering the halls looking for someone to sign for all those packages. Telephones would be ringing off the hook. You'd be out of coffee by 9:30.

Without an operating system, things inside your PC would get just as discombobulated, just as fast. Fortunately, the Windows NT operating system is there to act as a ruthlessly efficient office manager. Windows knows every part of your PC, inside and out, so it can send your work to the right place. (When you ask your PC to print a file, you want it to go to the printer and not the trash can, right? That's the operating system's job.) It also knows all the rules for storing and retrieving files, so you can find your work without a hassle.

The icons and menus in Windows make it easy for you to ask your PC to do some work. The operating system is the part that actually does the work. One without the other would be nearly useless, but together they're an unbeatable combination.

How do I use the Windows desktop?

If you could sweep all the clutter off your desk and spread the computer screen out in front of you, it would be easy to see why the Windows user interface is called the **desktop**. It's a smooth, flat surface that works a lot like the top of your real desk. It's where you'll keep the tools you need to work with your computer—not a stapler and scissors, but your word processor and spreadsheet programs, plus the folders full of files created by such programs. Any projects you're working on right now—letters, proposals, budgets, and so on—can sit on the desktop if you'd like, or you can tuck them back into their folders and put them neatly away when you're done.

Thanks to the graphical user interface, you don't have to memorize complicated commands (and you don't have to deal with surly error messages when you accidentally mistype a command). Instead, you point to a picture or an entry on a plain-English list, click the mouse once, and let Windows handle the details.

Things you need to know about Windows

Where do you start? Well, assuming Windows NT is already installed on your PC, you just turn on your computer. When you press that power switch, a complicated sequence of events starts up.

Windows 95? Windows NT? What's the difference?

On August 24, 1995, Microsoft threw a pull-out-all-the-stops party to introduce Windows 95. If you were anywhere near a TV or read a newspaper that week, you couldn't miss it. And you probably heard that Rolling Stones song, "Start Me Up," a bazillion times.

Windows NT may look a lot like Windows 95, but there are some important differences. And Windows 3.1, which was around long before either of these newcomers, is dramatically different from both. Here's a thumbnail sketch of all three Windows versions.

You'll still find **Windows 3.1** in use in a lot of places, perhaps even in your own company. Before you can run Windows 3.1, you have to run MS-DOS. When naming files and directories, you're limited to eight letters, plus a period and three more letters at the end. Getting Windows 3.1 to work on networks is like trying to herd cats. Installing new hardware works best if you have a computer expert and a witch doctor handy.

Windows 95 was designed especially for home users and for people in small offices. It works great on notebook (portable) computers, it's easy to connect with networks, and the Plug and Play features make it a lot easier to add a new piece of hardware. It's not very secure, though; anyone who can get his hands on your keyboard can poke around on the hard disk without too much trouble. And Windows 95, like Windows 3.1, sometimes just stops working, usually when you can least afford it.

At first glance, **Windows NT** looks just like Windows 95. The Start button works the same way, for example, and the My Computer and Network Neighborhood icons perform the same functions. Windows programs have an identical look and feel, although it takes more memory and more disk space to accomplish the same tasks with Windows NT than with Windows 95.

If your network administrator set up Windows NT on your PC, chances are it's more protected from intruders than it would be if you were using Windows 95. You can lock up your computer so that no one can snoop around on your hard disk unless they know the password. And Windows NT is much less likely to crash than any version of Windows before it.

Depending on the kind of hardware you have, it might take a minute or two for Windows to start up. You'll hear some noises from your hard drive, you'll enter your name and a password to prove you are who you say you are, and if all goes well, you'll see the Windows NT logo flash on the screen soon enough. Eventually, you'll see the Windows desktop, but there are many processes that occur under the hood first.

What happens when I start up Windows?

Starting up Windows is like opening your office in the morning. You have to go in and turn on the lights, make a fresh pot of coffee, and get the copy machine warmed up before you can do any real work. Windows has a lot of the same sort of housekeeping to do. There's a long, long checklist that Windows goes through before it lets you get to work, so it's normal for startup to take a little while. Here's what's going on:

1 The BIOS check is your PC's version of opening its eyes, stretching, and yawning. The computer checks to make sure that all its senses are intact. Is my memory all here? Is there a hard disk in the house? Any CD-ROMs? OK, next?

66 *Plain English, please!*

BIOS stands for **Basic Input/Output System**. There are a few essential chores that your computer has learned, like how to store a bit of information in a place where it can be found again. The BIOS holds the instructions that tell the PC how to perform crucial tasks like this. On most PCs, the first thing you see after turning on your PC is the copyright information about the BIOS. 99

2 Once your PC finds its hard disk, it searches for the simplest Windows startup files. These allow the PC to find other pieces of hardware, such as printers, modems, network cables, and CD-ROM drives, then load the software that lets Windows work with these pieces of hardware.

3 Assuming everything's okay (and it usually is), your PC begins loading the rest of Windows at this point. Before you can open a file or run a program, though, you'll have to press the Ctrl, Alt, and Del keys simultaneously, popping up a dialog box in which you type your user name and password.

4 If the name and password you type match the entries in the official Windows NT password list, your personalized startup files load now. Windows keeps track of everything you've asked it to do, including what color you want the background to be and where you want all your icons to sit.

5 Now that Windows NT is running, it loads any programs that are in your **StartUp folder**. When you put a program in this folder, you're telling Windows you want it to automatically start up whenever Windows starts up. (Look in Chapter 14 for more details on how to start up your own favorite programs along with Windows.)

6 That wasn't so hard, and it probably didn't take much time, either. At this point, Windows hands the whole thing over to you.

 Q&A   *What if my computer won't start up properly?*

It *is* plugged in, isn't it? The monitor's turned on, too, and you've checked the brightness and contrast controls? If you pass those checkpoints, try to restart your computer by pressing the on–off switch. When you see the startup menu, press the spacebar to have Windows use the settings that worked the last time you started the computer. If you still can't get things started, it's time to call in a computer expert.

Why does Windows use pictures instead of words?

These days, we're surrounded by pictures and graphic images. Everywhere you look—on road signs, on bottles and cans, even in newspapers and magazines—we're replacing words with pictures. Because Windows is **graphical**—that is, it relies on pictures rather than words—it's chock-full of tiny images, called **icons**, which are intended to make it easier to use.

Icons are used absolutely *everywhere* in Windows NT, so it pays to learn what the different types of icons mean. The contents of an icon might be just about anything—a letter to the IRS, a digitized picture of the Mona Lisa, even a recording of Arnold Schwarzenegger saying "I'll be back!" Once you learn what an icon means, it really can act as a quick and easy way to start a program or perform a task. Just as in the real world, some symbols are instantly recognizable (a skull and crossbones means poison, a red circle and line through a cigarette means "no smoking," a wheelchair means this parking space is reserved for the handicapped). The meaning of many Windows icons, like the printer and calculator, will be obvious at a glance.

Different icons mean different things

If you compare your Windows desktop to the real one in your office, it's easy to find things that work the same way.

Officially, the small pictures you see are called **icons**. We'll discuss each one in more detail in the next section.

Anything that could go on paper—letters, budgets, presentations, and so on—can be stored as a **file** on your PC.

Windows lets you organize your files—everything from quick notes to formal reports—inside the PC equivalent of manila **folders**.

What's a GUI?

It's pronounced "gooey," and the acronym stands for the most obvious part of Windows—its **graphical user interface**.

A user interface is simply the way you communicate with a machine. Your microwave oven has a simple user interface. The 12 buttons on your telephone are the interface between you and your voice-mail system. And *nobody* can figure out the interface of the average VCR.

Some computers use a **command-line interface**, where you type commands at the computer's keyboard (and it beeps back at you when you type a command wrong). Windows is much easier to use because it lets you tell the computer what to do by pointing at pictures on the screen. You don't have to memorize a whole manual full of commands—you just point at what you want on the screen and push a button on your mouse.

When you put it all together, you get a graphical user interface. The pictures on the screen are the *graphics*, you're the *user*, and Windows provides the *interface* between you and the computer.

Why do we need a user interface, graphical or otherwise? Because something has to control the computer's operating system, which actually runs the commands and does the work. You don't really need to know much about your computer's operating system, as long as you know where all the controls are. Think of how your car works: You probably know nothing about how your transmission works, but you tell it what to do when you use the shift lever.

Computer experts can do dazzling tricks with command-line interfaces, but they're almost impossible for average people to use. That's why GUIs are rapidly showing up everywhere—on cable TV boxes, in cars, even on refrigerators and washing machines.

Folders and files are stored on **disks**, which act just like file cabinets (and seem to fill up just as quickly).

Your office equipment claims a few icons here as well. **Printers** and **modems**, for example, get special icons that let you adjust their settings.

What's going on inside My Computer?

I don't know about you, but I'd rather give my PC a friendly name like Calvin, Hobbes, or Jean-Luc. I might prefer an informative name like "Ed's Notebook PC." Unfortunately, someone at Microsoft decided that my computer (and your computer and, in fact, everyone's computer) would start out with the same dull, generic name: My Computer...sigh.

We'll figure out how to change your computer's name later. For now, let's look at the useful tasks you can accomplish when you double-click the My Computer icon. This is your window on the most important pieces of your system—the disk drives, the printers, and all the knobs and levers that make it run smoothly. What can you do here? Plenty.

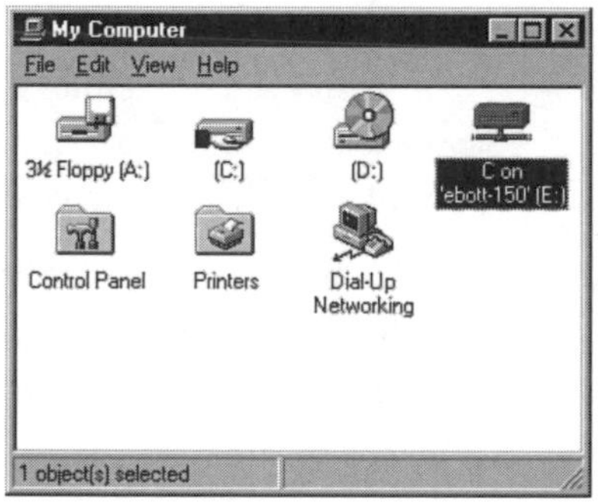

Fig. 1.1
This is My Computer, the place to turn when you want to find a file, set up a printer, or change your PC's settings.

Get the inside story on disks of every kind

How much free space is left on your hard disk? Find out with My Computer. This is the place where you can ask Windows to attach an electronic "label" to your disks, as well, so that the next time you insert a floppy disk you know it contains budget data before you even open it. From here, you can turn on file sharing, so that someone else on the network can use the files on your hard disk. It's also where you turn *off* sharing so that Bob in Accounting can't poke around in your hard disk ("No way, pal. Uh-uh. You're not sharing *this* hard disk.") And it's one of many places in Windows where you can find a file, copy a file, or delete a file.

Ask the Wizard to set up a printer!

Imagine how awkward life would be if you had to schlep your monitor down the hall every time you wanted to show someone this quarter's budget spreadsheet. That's why printers are the most important pieces of computer hardware, next to your PC, and that's why they get their own folder in the My Computer window. There's a built-in wizard that walks you, step-by-step, through the process of setting up a new printer. After it's been set up, this is the place you'll change the settings (maybe you added a new paper tray or moved it down the hall). With a few clicks here, you can share your printer with other people on a network; if they're not suitably grateful, you can stop sharing, too. Windows lists the names of all the files you've sent to the printer (each file listed is considered a "print job"); from here, you can cancel backed-up jobs before they ever make it to the printer (in case you change your mind about printing a particular file).

What's under my PC's hood?

The icon called Control Panel might look like a folder, but it's really more like the hood of your car. Pop open the Control Panel by double-clicking its icon, and you can fine-tune just about anything in your PC. Some of the options are incredibly useful. For example, this is where you set the clock your computer uses to keep track of what time you saved a file or sent a message.

You might never look at all the Control Panel options, but it's nice to know that Windows has a round-the-clock maintenance crew.

Fig. 1.2
This is where you'll turn for the simplest of tasks, like resetting your computer's clock. You might have the tougher jobs, such as installing a new piece of hardware.

Here are just a few of the simple, useful tasks you can perform from here:

- Change the date and time, and tell Windows whether you prefer to see dates displayed in the American or European style.

- Slow down your mouse pointer and keyboard (or zoom them to Warp Factor 9).

- Configure a modem or adjust settings to make Windows easier for users with physical disabilities.

- If you want your sound card to bark every time you get an error message, you've come to the right place. (You'll find the step-by-step procedures in Chapter 17.)

- If you want your desktop to look like a hot-dog stand, with a bright yellow and orange background that's so bright you have to pass out Ray-Bans to anyone who passes within five feet, step right this way.

You really want a command line?

If you learned to use a PC with MS-DOS on it, you might feel temporarily disoriented when you first dive into Windows NT. That's normal—the feeling will pass. There are Windows equivalents for all those old DOS commands.

But if you really want to return to the familiar DOS environment, Windows gives you a choice of two command lines. Both are accessible directly from the Start menu.

The first looks just like the familiar DOS prompt. Click the Start button, then click on Programs and choose Command Prompt from the menu. The C:\ prompt in this window does everything a DOS user would expect, and then some. Unlike old-fashioned DOS, which insists on filling up your entire screen, the Windows NT Command Prompt shows up in a window that you can resize and move to fit your screen. You can type the name of any program—DOS or Windows—and it will start right up. You can also run some of your older DOS programs, although some of them won't work properly with Windows NT.

The other option for anyone who wants to just type a DOS command is the Run command, also found on the Start menu. The Run command gives you a tiny box, big enough to hold a single command, plus a Browse button that lets you search for a specific file to run.

For some tasks, a command prompt is genuinely the fastest way to get the job done. But if you're like most people, the longer you use Windows, the less you'll find yourself craving the comfort of a C:\ prompt.

Network Neighborhood? What's that all about?

If you're connected to a local area network (and most Windows NT users are on a network when they're in the office), all the computers you're allowed to use get their own icons in your Network Neighborhood.

Whoever runs your company network has designated certain computers as **file servers**. These PCs have been set aside to store files and run programs that groups of people on the network can use and share. Icons for each of these computers show up in your Network Neighborhood.

In the Network Neighborhood, you'll also find icons for all the computers in your workgroup, including yours. Dig a little deeper and you can see whether the owner of a PC has put a "Share Me" sign on any folders or printers. For example, if Bob in Accounting wants you to look over this month's payroll report, he could put the report in a folder, call it "Payroll Reports," and tell Windows that it's OK if you look at it. Now, when you explore the icon for Bob's PC in the Network Neighborhood, you'll see that shared folder.

You can share things, too. If you have a laser printer hooked to your PC and you want your assistant to use it, you tell Windows that it's fine for other people to use it and your PC and printer will show up in *their* Network Neighborhoods.

There's even more at the bottom of the screen

You'd have to be in a coma to miss the Start button. You turn on your PC, and there's the word Start, as big as life, all alone on the bottom of the screen. We'll get to the Start button later, in Chapter 8. For now, though, let's move over a few inches.

The Start button sits on the **taskbar**, which runs along the entire bottom of the screen and works a lot like a handyman's tool belt. When you're doing a home improvement project, that belt saves you a lot of steps. After you've finished using a hammer or screwdriver, you don't put it back in the toolbox—you hang it on the belt so you can get to it quickly the next time you need it.

The Windows taskbar works the same way: As you work, you open folders to find files, then start programs to work with those files. As you set one program or folder aside to work with a new window, Windows doesn't put the old window away immediately. Instead, Windows adds a button to the taskbar for each program or folder you're using. When you need to reuse a folder or a program, just check the taskbar to find it fast. We'll look at the taskbar in more detail in Chapter 8.

 **TIP**   **Because it's possible to move or hide the taskbar, yours may** appear somewhere other than the bottom of the screen; it may even seem to be missing. Don't worry about it. If you want to move it or make it visible again, look at the tip near the end of Chapter 7.

Windows helps you organize your work

When you're trying to keep track of a complicated project, you use every organizational trick in the book. All your loose papers go into manila folders. You rubber-band thick reports together so they won't be accidentally separated. If the paperwork gets thick enough, you stuff the whole mess into a filing cabinet drawer.

Windows lets you do the exact same thing—only much neater and much faster.

With Windows, it's easy to stay organized. When you write a new letter, for example, you give it a plain-English name, like **Thank-you letter to Bill Karow, April 15**. Each letter goes in the appropriate folder, which also has a plain-English name like `April Letters`.

And like a great executive assistant, Windows is smart enough to be able to find items that *you* lost. As long as you know some detail, no matter how small, about the file or folder you've lost, Windows can help you find it. Even if you accidentally threw the file into the Recycle Bin (no trash cans here!), there's a fighting chance you can get it back.

CAUTION   **If you've thrown away a file by mistake and you want it back,** stop! Before you do anything else, double-click the Recycle Bin. See Chapter 7 for step-by-step instructions on what to do to retrieve the file.

Shutting down your computer

To turn off your computer, first click the Start button, then choose Sh<u>u</u>t Down from the menu. If you have any files you've been working on that haven't been saved yet, Windows will ask you if you want to save them. Just like the startup process, shutting down takes some time, but eventually you'll reach a screen that says it's OK to turn your PC off and quit for the day.

Q&A *I usually shut down my computer by just pressing the power switch. Is that OK?*

No, it's never OK to press the Off button unless you've first used the Sh<u>u</u>t Down command (found on the Start menu). Windows keeps track of all sorts of important information in the background while you work. When you use the Sh<u>u</u>t Down command, Windows makes sure that that information is saved properly. If you turn off the power before shutting down, you risk losing data.

How can I make Windows work the way I work?

Everybody has a unique way of organizing offices and desktops. Some people like to be surrounded by four-foot stacks of paper; others can't get a thing done unless their desktop is clean enough to eat off of. You can set up your Windows desktop to look and feel just like the one in your real office.

On the Windows desktop, you can rearrange objects to your heart's content. As long as there's free space, you can set a new object down on the desktop (or even on top of another object). Unlike your real desktop, you can even change the colors and put different labels on most of the objects on this desktop. You can throw away almost anything, too, if you don't need it and don't want it cluttering up your desktop.

" Plain English, please!

Computer gurus (and guru-wannabes) like to talk about **objects**, because that word sounds so much better than **things**. It doesn't matter what you call them, though; if you can see something on the screen, it's an object. The most important fact is that objects that look similar usually act alike, too. So once you learn how one part of Windows works, you can apply that same knowledge later to another, similar object. **"**

If you just started Windows for the first time, your Windows desktop is sparkling clean right now. Whether it stays that way is up to you. If you thrive on a little chaos in your working life, go ahead and make this desktop as cluttered as your real desk.

How Windows Works

● **In this chapter:**

● **Do I have to use a mouse? (Yes, but it's easy.)**

● **Opening windows with a double-click**

● **Where do I point? How do I click?**

● **In Windows, every icon has a plain-English name**

● **You can store icons in folders**

Windows NT uses folders and icons and plain–English names. But most of all, it uses the mouse . . . . ●

I f you've never used a computer before, you'll need to learn a few things before Windows NT makes sense. If you have used a computer before, you'll need to *unlearn* a few things before Windows NT makes sense.

Your old computer probably used Microsoft DOS and Windows 3.1 (or maybe 3.11), which means you had to learn how to think like a computer to get even the simplest jobs done. It's hard to imagine anything more complicated and frustrating than good ol' DOS. Most sensible people would rather program a VCR while blindfolded than struggle with a DOS prompt.

With Windows NT, you don't have to look at that ugly old C:\ prompt anymore (as in Fig. 2.1—try not to shudder as you view it). Once you learn to maneuver the mouse, you don't have to type complicated commands to get even the simplest job done, and you don't have to wrack your brain coming up with eight-character names for your files. In fact, you don't even have to think about files anymore.

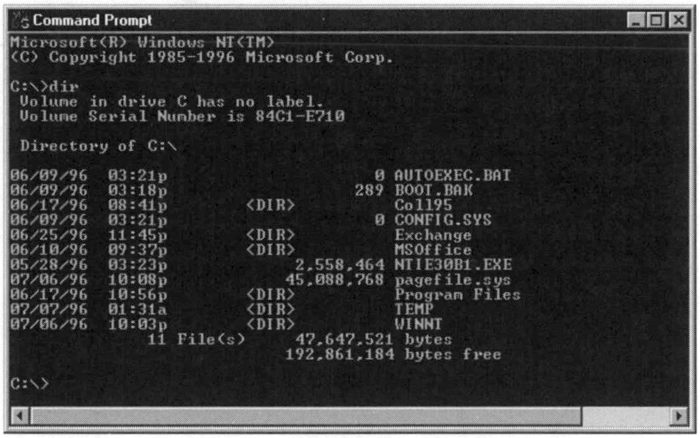

Fig. 2.1
Goodbye, DOS!
Windows uses icons
and folders and plain-
English names instead
of this unfriendly DOS
prompt.

Do I have to use a mouse?

Trying to use Windows without a mouse is like trying to drive your car backward while using only the rear-view mirror. You could probably do it, but it would take forever to get where you're going, and you'd have a horrible headache when you got there.

Mastering a mouse isn't that difficult. It may seem unnatural at first, but once you learn the basic techniques, you'll be able to move things around on your Windows desktop as easily as you shuffle papers on your real desktop.

The secret is to learn a handful of basic techniques that you'll use over and over in Windows, by themselves and in combination. Most of them are easy, especially after a little practice. In fact, one of the best ways to master mouse maneuvering is to use the Solitaire game (see Fig. 2.2).

Fig. 2.2
The Solitaire program is included with Windows to help you learn to work with a mouse. At least, that's what you can tell anyone who catches you playing when you should be working.

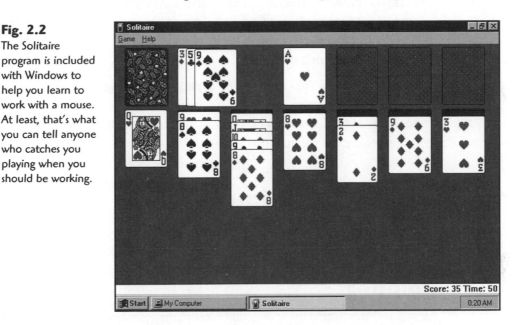

Really important mouse factoids

Here are some things you'll need to know before you start messing with the mouse:

- Most mice have just two buttons, but some have three. If yours has an extra button in the middle, you can safely ignore it—Windows only uses the left and right buttons.

- The cord goes out the back, away from your hand. If you try to use your mouse the other way, the pointer will zig when you expect it to zag, and you'll get hopelessly confused.

- Your mouse has to be plugged into the back of your PC. If it suddenly stops working, follow the cord to the back of your PC and make sure it's firmly connected.

- A mouse works a lot better if you use a **mouse pad** (a thin, soft, rubbery pad, often with a fairly slick surface, that you can run your mouse around on). You can get one for a few dollars at any computer store.

- If you run out of room on your mouse pad or your desk, pick up the mouse and move it to a better position. As long as the mouse is in the air, the pointer won't move. When you start rolling again, it'll pick up right where you left off.

- As your mouse rolls around, it can pick up anything: dirt, dust, muffin crumbs, stray hairs, and little bits of cheese. So keep the mouse pad clean, and clean the mouse occasionally by turning it over, taking out the roller, and wiping off any junk.

Essential mouse techniques

As you get more comfortable with Windows, you'll find yourself using the same mouse techniques over and over. Let's review the entire list right now.

Pointing

As you roll the mouse up, down, and around on your desk or mouse pad, the **mouse pointer** (often called just the **pointer**—it's the arrow you see on the screen) moves up, down, and around, too. When you aim it at one thing in particular, that's called "pointing."

Most of the time, nothing happens when you simply point to a Windows icon. It's just like moving your finger over the buttons on your VCR. Until you actually *push* one, nothing happens.

One exception is the help you get from the taskbar. Point to any button (including the Start button), and just leave the arrow there for a few seconds. Then watch as a small label pops up to tell you the purpose of that button. You didn't click—all you had to do was point.

A field guide to mouse pointers

Under normal circumstances, your mouse pointer looks like a white arrow. But as you do different things and move the pointer to different spots, its appearance changes. Here are some of the most common mutations:

Plain old pointer
Windows is waiting for you to click something.

 Pointer with trails
Windows is still waiting, but at least you've found the pointer and moved it a little.

Pointers for resizing windows
Use these pointers to make a window bigger or smaller.

Hourglass
Windows is working. You can move the pointer, but you can't do anything else.

Pointer with hourglass
Windows is working, but you're free to do something else if you'd like.

I-beam—insertion point
Type some letters or numbers here.

No! pointer
Whatever you're dragging, you can't drop it here.

Help pointers
Find more help about this item by clicking here.

Point, select, act

You and your mouse will get along just fine if you remember the most fundamental principle of Windows: First you point, then you select, and then you act.

Think of Windows as a furniture mover. You'll get great results if you say this: "See these chairs? This one, that one, and those two over there? I want them out of here." You point, you select, and you say the magic words. Poof! They're gone.

But what happens if you try it the other way around? You say, "I want you to move some chairs." With no further direction, the mover has no idea what to do next. Move them all? Just these three over here?

Repeat after me: First you point, then you select, and then you act.

CAUTION

When you hit the edge of the screen, Windows just ignores the messages coming up the wire from the mouse. "Move up? Sorry, I've reached the edge here. You'll have to head in another direction."

TIP

What do you do if the pointer seems to disappear every time you turn your head? Make it bigger. Make it darker. Make it leave a trail so you can spot it the instant it moves. To do any or all of these things, double-click on My Computer, open the Control Panel folder, and double-click on the Mouse icon. Experiment with the options till you find the settings that work best for you.

Clicking (and its mirror image, right-clicking)

If you actually want to *do* something with whatever you're pointing at, you'll have to click it. Point at the Start button, for example, and click once on the left mouse button to pop up a menu of choices. In Solitaire, each time you point at the deck and tap the left mouse button, three cards flip off the deck and onto the face-up stack at the right.

But some tasks require you to use the right mouse button rather than the left one. Most of the time, clicking once on the right mouse button pops up a menu that's tailor-made for whatever you're pointing at. Right-clicking the My Computer icon, for example, pops up a menu that includes an option to rename the icon. Whenever you're not sure what you can do with an icon, just point at it and right-click. The popup menu will tell you what's possible.

❝ *Plain English, please!*

Pushing the right button is called **right-clicking**, but no one ever says "left-clicking." When you see the word **click** by itself, in this book or anywhere in Windows, you can safely assume that you're supposed to push the left mouse button. **❞**

Opening a window by double-clicking

Double-click an icon and something happens: Programs start, folder windows open, a printer pops up a list of all the jobs it's waiting to do. To see an example, aim the mouse pointer at the My Computer icon, and give the left mouse button two quick clicks, one right after another. (That's called a double-click.) If you double-clicked correctly, the My Computer window will open. If it didn't work, try again.

TIP **Double-clicking can be tricky. Don't let the mouse move between** clicks, or Windows will interpret your actions as two single clicks instead of a double-click. If you have trouble keeping the mouse steady, try resting your wrist on the flat surface behind the mouse. Press gently. If you jab too hard at the button, the whole mouse is likely to flinch from the shock. If you still can't get it, and you're ready to fling the mouse into the next room, just click the *right* mouse button and choose Open. Most of the time, that has the same effect as double-clicking.

How do you know when to click and when to double-click? Just remember the difference between buttons and icons.

With buttons, a single click does the trick

It's easy to spot a **button**. Look for the 3-D effect, with a small shadow along the right side and the bottom. It takes a single click to work the following buttons:

- The Start menu

- Any open programs or folders stored on the taskbar

- Minimize, Maximize, Restore, and Close buttons found at the right end of a window's title bar (see Chapter 6 for an explanation of what these do).

- The Yes, No, OK, and Cancel buttons in dialog boxes, like the ones you see in the dialog box when you shut down Windows NT.

With icons, it takes a double-click to do something

How can you spot an icon? Just look for a picture with a label underneath. These icons, for example, demand a double-click before they'll open into a window:

- My Computer and Network Neighborhood

- The Recycle Bin

- Every program, file, folder, or drive icon

TIP **When you double-click, Windows expects that the clicks will come** one right after the other, as fast as lightning. But you can slow down the double-click rate so that Windows will wait a little longer for that second click. To retrain the mouse, open the Control Panel window and double-click on the Mouse icon. Slide the <u>D</u>ouble-click speed lever all the way to the left, and test the new settings by double-clicking the jack-in-the-box. There—isn't that better?

Q&A *I'm left-handed. Is there an easier way to use this mouse?*

Windows lets you reverse your mouse settings, so that the right button does the jobs normally handled by the left button, and vice versa. To switch mouse buttons, double-click on the Control Panel's Mouse icon and follow the instructions. It's a handy trick for left-handers. If you try it, though, remember to do a mental translation from now on: every time we talk about clicking and right-clicking, just reverse the directions.

Dragging-and-dropping

Before you can move something, you first have to pick it up. Imagine that the mouse is controlling a robotic arm on your computer's screen. Point at an icon, click and hold down the left mouse button, and the claws at the end of the arm clamp on just as if you had grabbed the icon in your hand. As you move the object around on the screen, you can see it move with the pointer.

As long as you keep the button down, the claws stay clamped on and you can move the icon around. But you can only carry something around for so long before it starts to seem kind of, well, pointless. When you've dragged something far enough, release the pressure on the mouse button and the object drops at the pointer's current location.

You'll move objects from one place to another all the time in Windows. I've moved the Recycle Bin, for example, from its place on the left edge of the screen to the lower right corner of my desktop. And whenever it's time to clean out old files I no longer need, I pick them up and drag them into the Recycle Bin.

TIP **Remember this sequence of events anytime you want to move** something from here to there: Point. Click and hold the left mouse button down. Drag the object. Let go of the mouse button to drop it.

Dropping something on something else

Most of the time, you'll simply want to move an object from point A to point B. But, in special cases, you can drop it on top of something else and actually cause something to happen. Here are a few things you can do with this trick:

- *Drop an icon onto a folder* to copy or move the icon into the folder.

- *Drop a file icon on a printer icon;* Windows will send the file straight to your printer (unless something goes wrong, in which case you'll need to look for help in chapter 15).

- *Drop a program icon on the desktop* to create a special kind of icon called a **shortcut**, which you can use to start that program in a hurry. (More about shortcuts a little later in this chapter.)

- *Drop a program icon on the Start menu;* Windows will add it to the top of the Start menu.

- *Drop a file icon onto a drive icon;* Windows will copy the file to that drive if it can (you'll get an error message if there's no floppy disk in the drive or if you're not connected to the network).

Right-dragging for total control

Here's something that's guaranteed to confuse everybody. When you drag a file onto a folder, what happens? That depends. If the file you're dragging and the folder you're dropping it onto are both on the hard drive in your computer, then the file will move. But if the folder is on another drive (like a file server on your network, or someone else's drive, or even a floppy disk drive on your own PC), then the file will be copied rather than moved. Unless it's a program file, in which case…. Well, the rules are confusing. Fortunately, you don't need to memorize them; instead, use this foolproof alternative.

Whenever you want to move something, or copy something, or create a shortcut, click with the *right* mouse button and drag it. When you release the button, you'll see a list of choices like the one in Figure 2.3. You can decide whether you want to move the file, make another copy of it, or cancel the whole thing.

Fig. 2.3
Windows lets
you right-drag
just about
anything and
drop it just
about anywhere.

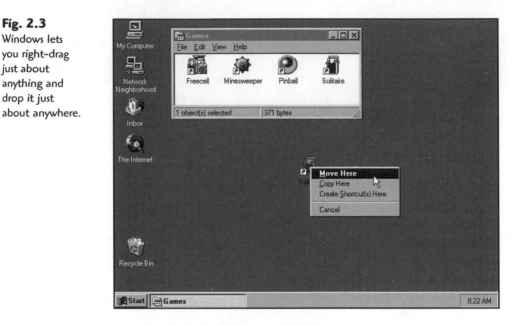

Selecting objects

When you're packing up your household possessions, you can help the
movers work faster and more efficiently by labeling all the furniture in the
house with signs saying "Take this" and "Leave this." This method works
well with the mouse, too. When you tag one or more objects you want to do
something with, it's called **selecting**.

As I emphasized a few pages back, first you point, then you select, and then
you act. Up until now, we've been using the mouse to do one thing at a time:
move an icon or delete a file. But you can save time and energy by doing the
same thing with more than one object at a time. Instead of moving a bunch
of files one by one, for example, you can pick out a group of icons and drag
them all to a new folder. It's just two steps:

1 Mark all the icons you want to work with.

2 Do something with whatever you selected.

How can you tell when you've selected something? Watch the way the
highlighting changes. Click on the Start button and move the mouse pointer
up to Settings. Move the pointer to the right until a new menu pops out that
side. Slide the pointer over to Control Panel and click to open the Control
Panel window. Let's try highlighting some icons.

- **To select one icon**, just click it once (don't double-click it).

- **To select a group of adjacent icons**, use the mouse pointer to "lasso" them. Imagine that the icons you want to select can be contained in a box. Point to one of the corners of that imaginary box, click the left mouse button (make sure you haven't clicked on a specific icon, just the area next to one), and hold it down as you begin to drag the outlines of the box. A dotted line appears as you drag, and each icon inside the box takes on a dark shading to show that you've selected it (see Fig. 2.4). When you've successfully highlighted all the items, release the button.

Fig. 2.4

Drag an imaginary box around a group of icons to select them all. Icons inside the box take on a dark shading to show that you've successfully selected them.

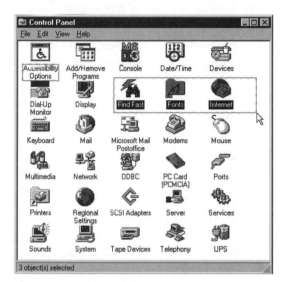

- **To select a group of icons** when they're right next to one another, click on the first one, then hold down the Shift key and click on the last one. All the icons in between will be highlighted, too.

- **To select a group of icons when they're not next to one another,** click on the first one, then hold down the Ctrl key and click on the second, the third, the fourth, and so on.

 TIP   **Anytime you have to simultaneously hold down a key (or keys)**
and click a mouse button, remember to press the keys first and then click.

CAUTION   **Be careful when double-clicking an icon, or you might acciden-**
tally rename a file! Watch what happens when you click the name of an
icon twice, slowly. The highlighting changes and Windows assumes you want
to start typing a new name. To avoid this possibility, always aim at the
picture, not the label. (Press Esc to quit renaming this time.) And practice
double-clicking until you can do it flawlessly.

What happened to my files?

If you've been using DOS or Windows 3.1 for the past few years, you've
grown accustomed to seeing lists of files—either in the Windows File
Manager or in a DOS directory. With Windows 95, all your files are still
there—don't worry about that. And you can see all those icons in a list, if you
prefer, just as you do in the File Manager. (I'll describe how to do that later in
this chapter.) The biggest difference with Windows NT is that you don't have
to deal with files and directories. Instead, start learning how to work with
icons, because in Windows NT, *everything* is an icon.

So, what exactly *is* an icon?

Those small pictures scattered all over your Windows desktop are called
icons. (There's one in Figure 2.5, for instance.) Every icon consists of a
picture and (usually) a text description, like "My Computer" or "Program
Files" or "Interoffice Memo."

Fig. 2.5
Look closely at an
icon (like this one
for a CD-ROM
drive). You'll see
that it's made out
of square dots—32
of them on each
side.

Think of each icon as the label on a box that holds something inside your
computer. You may have the world's messiest office, but Windows is fussier
than Felix Unger. Windows makes sure that everything inside your computer
is contained inside one of these icon/boxes. And not just any icon/box, either.

There are five distinct types of icons, and each one is reserved for a special kind of data. (After all, it wouldn't do to have your dress shirts and muddy old work boots just shoved into the same drawer, would it?)

Don't let the tiny size fool you, either; Windows can pack an amazing amount of data inside each one of these boxes.

TIP   **If you pick up a magnifying glass and look really closely, you'll see** that each icon is composed of square dots called **pixels**—normal icons have 32 pixels on each side. Look in the top left corner of each window, and you'll see miniature versions of the same icons—these scaled-down icons are a mere 16 pixels on each side.

The Five Basic Icon Types

Everything inside your computer is contained inside one of five distinct types of icons. , The type of icon gives you an important clue about what you can expect to find inside; for example, document icons often combine a picture of a piece of paper with the icon for the program you use to work with that document type.

The Icon	What it's called...	What it really means...
![document icon]	Document	A document is the basic unit of Windows, the equivalent of one or more pieces of paper. A document might consist of words or numbers or pictures, or all of them combined.
![program icon]	Program	Programs are the parts of Windows that actually do the work of putting words, numbers, and pictures into documents. They get the coolest icons, too.
![folder icon]	Folder	Folders are special places where you can organize a bunch of icons of any kind. If you're the fussy sort, you can even put folders inside of folders inside of folders.

continues

The Icon	What it's called...	What it really means...
	Device	Each piece of your PC—hard drive, printer, mouse, and the like—gets its own icon. Inside, there are knobs and levers to help you fiddle with the device.
	Shortcut	A shortcut is a special sort of icon that helps you organize icons. The icon you're looking for isn't really stored here, but double-clicking on the shortcut will open the original program or folder anyway.

How do I make an icon do something?

There's one surefire way to open an icon, and that's to double-click it. When you do, the icon opens into a **window**, which is simply another view of what's inside that icon. Depending on the type of icon you double-clicked, you might see a *folder* full of documents, a *program* like Word for Windows, a *document* like an Excel spreadsheet, or a collection of *controls* for all the hardware in and around your PC.

I wonder what this icon does

It's easy to find out: Click the right mouse button and choose Properties from the pull-down menu. This lets you look at the icon's Properties sheet (see Fig. 2.6). No, it has nothing to do with Donald Trump, and you won't have to pay any taxes on these Properties. Instead, it's Windows' way of providing you with detailed information about the contents of each icon.

The label underneath an icon is useful, but a bit limited—especially because you fill it out yourself. You've probably had the same experience in your own garage or attic. You wrote "Christmas Ornaments" on the outside of five different boxes. Next December, when you're trying to find the one with the angel for the top of the tree, you'll have to pry each one open and look inside. Unless, of course, you were fussy enough to make a list of each box's contents and tape it to the outside.

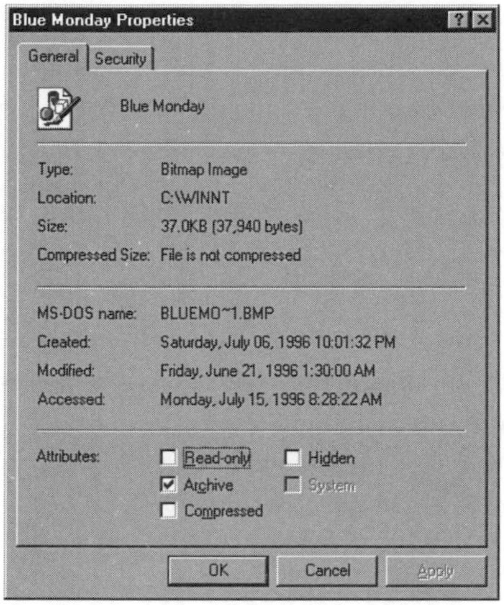

Fig. 2.6
What's underneath that icon? Click the right mouse button and look at the Properties sheet to see for yourself.

Blue Monday Properties

General | Security

Blue Monday

Type:	Bitmap Image
Location:	C:\WINNT
Size:	37.0KB (37,940 bytes)
Compressed Size:	File is not compressed

MS-DOS name:	BLUEMO~1.BMP
Created:	Saturday, July 06, 1996 10:01:32 PM
Modified:	Friday, June 21, 1996 1:30:00 AM
Accessed:	Monday, July 15, 1996 8:28:22 AM

Attributes: ☐ Read-only   ☐ Hidden
☑ Archive   ☐ System
☐ Compressed

OK   Cancel   Apply

Well, Windows *is* that fussy. You can scribble whatever you want underneath the icon, but Windows assigns an inventory clerk to follow along behind you, so that later, when you click the right mouse button, it can hand over a detailed report summarizing the contents of the icon you just clicked, in the form of the Properties sheet.

TIP To quickly change an icon's label, press F2 and then start typing the new name.

What's on each Properties sheet? That depends:

- For a **document**, the Properties sheet gives you all the details you'd expect from DOS's DIR (directory) command, which include name, size, date created, and so on. (See the example in Fig. 2.6.)

- For a **folder**, you can see at a glance how many items are inside; you can also use the Properties sheet to share a folder with someone else on your network.

- For a **Windows program**, the Properties sheet looks nearly the same as the one associated with a document, with the addition of a Version tab.

- For a **DOS program**, the Properties sheet lets you tinker with all sorts of technical settings. Don't even think of looking here unless you're really a DOS expert!

- For a **device**, the pop-up Properties menu lets you adjust the way Windows works with your hardware. For example, you can turn down the volume on your modem's speaker if that screeching is bugging you or your coworkers.

- For a **shortcut**, clicking the right mouse button displays details about the shortcut and about the original file that it refers to.

CAUTION **Windows hides things from you, including a lot of the files it needs** to run. With the help of a few DOS tricks, you can easily find these hidden files. But you're better off just leaving them alone. They're hidden for a good reason, and if you accidentally mess with them, you could get your PC so thoroughly confused that it won't run.

What does that arrow in the corner of this icon mean?

The little arrow in the lower left corner of an icon means it's a **shortcut** to an original file. If you've grown accustomed to DOS and Windows 3.1, you've never seen anything like shortcuts before. But once you learn what they do, you'll find yourself using them everywhere.

Shortcuts work like small pushbuttons that let you jump straight to a particular file, called the **target file**, stored somewhere else. When you double-click a shortcut, Windows looks inside the shortcut for instructions on where to go next. (Those instructions will probably look a lot like those in Fig. 2.7.) In this case, the target file is the program called Calc, stored in the System32 folder inside the Winnt folder. Windows scurries off in search of Calc and opens it up, just as if you had opened all those folders yourself and then double-clicked the icon. But a lot faster.

Q&A *Hey! That target file thing looks a lot like a DOS command! Didn't you say I wouldn't have to type in DOS commands anymore?*

Yes, I did. And no, you don't. You can create a shortcut by simply dragging a file or folder icon to the desktop, or you can have Windows automatically fill in the blanks for you with the Create Shortcut Wizard (right-click on the desktop or in a folder, then choose New, Shortcut). You can type in commands if you want, but you never have to.

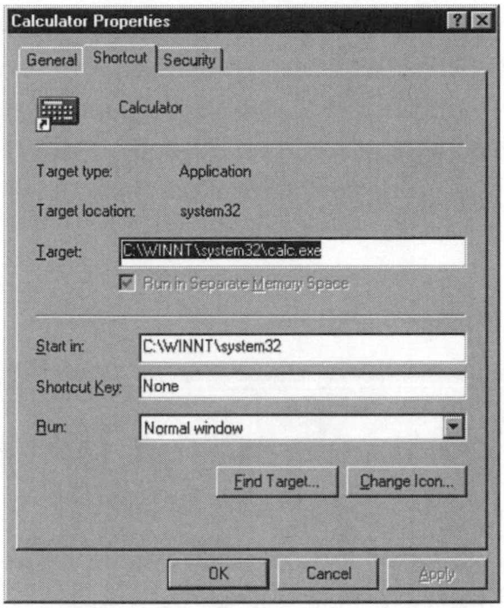

Fig. 2.7

When you create a shortcut, Windows fills in these blanks on its Properties sheet. Later, when you double-click the shortcut, Windows finds the target file and opens it up instead.

Why are shortcuts useful? Well, let's say you crunch numbers for a living. The fastest, easiest way to crunch all those numbers is with the help of the Windows Calculator, but you don't like poking and clicking through all those menus and folders looking for it. No problem—just create a shortcut on your Windows desktop.

Every icon has a plain-English name

Let's say you're moving across the country, and all of your worldly goods are packed in cardboard boxes. You've got a Magic Marker, but someone just told you that you can only use eight letters (although you can have an extra three letters if you separate it from the eight letters with a dot). "That's ridiculous!" you'd complain. And you'd be right. But that's exactly how MS-DOS (and previous versions of Windows that required MS-DOS) worked for more than a decade.

If you've used MS-DOS, you've learned to compress complex thoughts into ridiculously compact spaces. All the letters you wrote last June, for example, went into a directory called LETTER06, with names like BILLTHX1.DOC and WLDPRC11.DOC. Who knows what those names meant?

Well, with Windows NT, you don't need to create cryptic eight-letter file names anymore, because Windows replaces your folders and documents with icons and lets you label each one with a plain-English name of up to 255 characters. (You'll run out of room on the screen before you'll use that many characters.) And won't it be easy to find documents when they have names like Thank you letter to Bill Karow, 6-30?

The long and the short of Windows file names

Windows lets you use up to 255 characters to name each icon on your screen; that's more room than you get on the average postcard. But when it comes to storing data on your hard disk, Windows still uses the old-fashioned DOS filing system, which is limited to an eight-character name, plus a period and three more letters. You rarely have to worry about the short names, though, because Windows handles the confusing details behind the scenes.

As far as you're concerned, that WordPad file you just finished is called "Letter to the IRS, begging for a four-month extension." But as soon as you saved it, Windows converted the long icon name into a short file name that follows the DOS rules. First, it trimmed away all the spaces inside (spaces are a no-no for DOS files, but they're A-OK for you to use in Windows NT). It also whacked away everything after the first six characters, and then added a tilde (~   a squiggly character you'll recognize from high school Spanish classes), the number 1, a period, and the letters DOC at the end. So your letter's real name, known only to Windows, is LETTER~1.DOC.

Whenever you ask for the file, you double-click an icon labeled with an easy-to-understand name. When Windows gets your message, it looks through its list of short file names to find the one that matches the icon you asked for.

Now, let's say you used your word processor to create another letter in the same folder. This one's called "Letter to our accountant demanding a pretty good explanation!" Windows might try to save this file under the name LETTER~1.DOC, but it won't work—there's already a file by that name, and duplicates aren't allowed. So Windows reaches into its bag of file-naming tricks to come up with a unique name. Add a character here and chop one off there, and you wind up with the next name in the series, LETTER~2.DOC. That name may be meaningless to you and me, but we don't care, because we use the icon's long name.

So far, so good. But what happens when you save a file with a long name to a network folder so that other people in your company can share it? Well, if the other person is using Windows NT or Windows 95, then there's no problem. They'll see the long file name just as you created it. But if the person at the other end is using DOS or Windows 3.1, then they can't see the long file name; all they can see is a file called LETTER~1.DOC.

TIP   **You can make an icon's name up to 255 characters long, and**
you can even use some punctuation marks: periods, commas, semicolons,
ampersands, parentheses, and dollar signs. There are a handful of characters
you can't use to name a file or folder, though. Here are the characters that
you're not allowed to use in an icon's name:

> : " \ / * ? | < >

What happened to the three-letter file extensions, like .TXT, that you used to
tack onto the end of files when you used DOS and old versions of Windows?
Windows NT still keeps a record of these (and you can change settings
to make them appear on-screen, if you like). Whenever possible, though,
Windows hides the extensions and gives you a more meaningful explanation.
Instead of .TXT, Windows labels those files as Text Documents.

You store information in folders

One of the most confusing parts of the good ol' DOS file system is the way it
forces you to use complicated directory names. If you wanted to stay organized, the only way to store your data (and then find it again) was to type a
mind-boggling path name like C:\WALDO\DATA\LETTERS\JAN95\AARRGGH!

With Windows, you don't need to type in complicated path names because all
your files are icons, remember? And they're arranged neatly inside folder
icons. Even the Desktop, the place where you see My Computer and the
Network Neighborhood, is really just a folder that's always open.

Deep down inside, there's not much difference between a folder and a DOS
directory, except for the fact that one is easy to use and the other is nearly
impossible.

What can I put inside a folder?

Folders hold icons. Most of the folders you'll work with every day will hold
icons representing your program files and documents. But folders can also
hold other folders. If you want all your work filed in one place, for example,
you might create a folder called Projects and fill it with other folders, one for
each iron you and your fellow workers have in the fire right now.

This folder-in-a-folder idea isn't difficult to understand. Just think of a typical
filing cabinet. Let's say our imaginary cabinet has four drawers, and in the

top drawer there's a divider where we keep manila folders full of blank expense report forms. When you need a fresh form, you march over to the file cabinet, open the top drawer, flip through folders to find the one you want, and finally look in the folder. Windows works the same way.

If you're the sort who puts each paper in its own color-coded folder in separate drawers, you can put folders inside of folders inside of still other folders, until they're buried so deeply you'll need a backhoe to dig them out. Windows makes it easy to find folders within folders by arranging folders at the top, ahead of any other icons it finds, whenever you open a window.

How do I look inside a folder?

To open a folder, just double-click it. By default, you'll see the contents of the folder displayed as large icons, like the ones in figure 2.8. You can change the way the icons appear (known as their **view**) by selecting a different choice from the View menu, or by clicking one of the View buttons in the top right corner of the window.

*To see this **Large Icons** view, click here.*

*To see more icons in the same space, click on **Small Icons**. The icons in the folder will still be arranged from left to right.*

*If you want to see small icons arranged from top to bottom in columns, click the **List** button.*

Fig. 2.8
Four ways to look at your work: Large icons or Small, in List form, or in Details view (which gives you more information about the files).

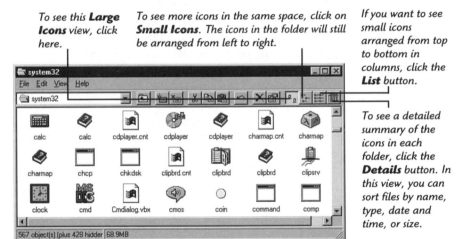

*To see a detailed summary of the icons in each folder, click the **Details** button. In this view, you can sort files by name, type, date and time, or size.*

Your programs all work about the same

Of course, you didn't get a computer so that you could simply move files from folder to folder. Your computer is a tool that lets you get work done. That means you need **programs** to get that work done. (We'll talk more about programs in Chapter 10.) After work—or whenever the boss is away—you can also use it to relax with a game of Solitaire or Pinball.

❝ *Plain English, please!*

A program (also referred to as an **application**) is a piece of software that helps you do a wide range of business tasks. Your word processor is a program; so is your spreadsheet and your e-mail access software. Tiny application programs that do a simple job are sometimes called **applets**. ❞

The advantage of Windows software is that when you learn how to use one program, you've learned the basics of every Windows program. They all use windows and icons and menus and mouse pointers. Windows also gives you a special tool called the **Clipboard**—with its help, you can copy information (a list of names, perhaps, or a column of numbers) from one place and paste it into another, even if the two programs are completely different.

Finally, Windows lets you work with different programs at the same time. And inside each program you can handle many different data files, also at the same time. As long as you're not overwhelmed by all those windows, it's a great way to get a lot of work done.

3

Windows NT and Your Office

In this chapter:

- Learn what you can—and can't—do with your PC

- How your administrator defines your role in the company

- Connecting to the company network

- Using (and losing) your password

You have rights—plenty of them. But before you can use your computer or connect to your company's network, you'll have to identify yourself to Windows NT . . . .

When you own your own business, you get to make all the decisions on your own. You decide when to open the doors and when to shut down. You choose who has a key to the front door and who has to sign in with the security guard. To keep phone costs down, you might set things up so only a few key employees have the right to make overseas phone calls—and only if they punch in a secret access code first.

If you're an employee, you're on the other end of all those decisions. It may be inconvenient to use an electronic card key just to enter the front door, but you tolerate the nuisance in exchange for the security of knowing that total strangers can't wander through your company's hallways. Likewise, when your company uses Windows NT, you'll face a similar set of restrictions—a long, usually logical list of do's and don'ts designed to safeguard the computer on your desktop, other computers on your company's network, the programs you use, and the data files you and your coworkers create.

It all starts with you

Have you used a personal computer before? If you're using Windows NT for the first time, be prepared to adjust your thinking—and your ways of working. Your old computer probably used a different operating system, such as MS-DOS or Windows 3.1. With these and other operating systems, you're free to do just about anything you want on your own computer, even installing your own application software and adding new hardware if you wish.

Now that you're using Windows NT, things are very different. This operating system is designed with the same sort of protective services you'd find at a security-conscious office building. Before you can get past the guard's desk, you have to sign in, and you'd better have proof that you are who you say you are. Even after you've gotten into Windows NT, you'll discover that some doors—well, OK, windows—are locked, and you don't have the key.

An administrator manages your PC

In my office, there are locks everywhere you turn. I have a key to the front door and another one that unlocks my office door. A few people who can be trusted not to steal all the pens have a key to the office supplies closet. Sensitive personnel files are kept in locked file cabinets, and only the president and the human resources director have keys. Of course, the cleaning crew has a master key that gets them in practically anywhere.

That's roughly how Windows NT works as well. The person who installed the software on your computer is called the **system administrator**, and that person has the equivalent of a master key that opens every lock on your PC. The administrator can read your data files, install and remove programs, even erase your entire hard disk! Most important of all, though, the system administrator determines what you can and can't do with your computer and the rest of the computers in your company.

The system administrator assigns **user names and passwords**, and decides who can use a given computer or printer. Typically the administrator will create a set of folders where you can store files you create and edit; other users won't be allowed to snoop in those folders. He or she also creates **groups** of users with common permissions; by adding your user name to the Accounting group, for example, the administrator could tell Windows it's OK for you to use the laser printer outside Bob's office and to look at files in the Budget folder.

If you try to do something with your PC that you don't have permission to do, you'll see an error message like the one in Figure 3.1.

Fig. 3.1
Certain tasks are reserved only for administrators. Windows won't let other users install a new hardware driver, for example.

> **Driver Error**
>
> ⚠ You have insufficient privilege to add or remove a driver
>
> OK

TIP **Don't be surprised if your system has more than one administrator.** In most companies, several people have the right to act as administrator on a given PC; that way, someone's always available to help with a problem, even if the regular system administrator is out sick or on vacation.

Know your (user) rights

The administrator uses a special program called the User Manager to track which users and groups have which permissions (see Fig. 3.2). Based on your company's policies, the system administrator has decided which of the following things you can do:

- **Log on locally.** If this is your computer, you certainly have this right. Coworkers and assistants may also have the right to log onto your machine, with a different set of permissions.

- **Access this computer from the network.** You'll have this right if you're expected to "roam" from place to place and still be able to connect with the data stored here. Other users may also have this right if you expect to share files with them.

- **Back up and restore files and directories.** This is a special sort of permission intended just for people who operate backup devices like tape drives. They can't read your files, but they can make copies of your data to protect it in case of disaster.

- **Shut down the system.** Most users have this right automatically. If your PC contains files that other people need to access, or if a shared printer is connected to your PC, the administrator may set things up so the Shut Down menu choice doesn't work.

- **Change the system time.** If you share lots of files with coworkers, it's crucial that the time stamp be correct on each one. E-mail programs are also picky about this setting. The administrator may choose to set each PC's clock from a central location and not allow users to adjust it.

- **Perform special system tasks**, such as loading device drivers or managing a security log. Typically these tasks are reserved for administrators only.

- **Take ownership of files or other objects.** This setting lets you bypass the lock that a user has put on a file or folder. You have to be very well trusted to earn this right.

Fig. 3.2
Administrators and Power Users can organize users into groups and give them specific rights with the help of the User Manager.

User Manager

Username	Full Name	Description
Administrator		Built-in account for administering t
Ebott-150	Ed Bott	Ebott-150
Ebott-2	Ed Bott (AST)	
ed	Ed Bott	Production system
Faxguy	Fax Server	
Guest		Built-in account for guest access t
Jmerrill	Judy Merrill	

Groups	Description
Accounting	
Administrators	Members can fully administer the computer/domain
Backup Operators	Members can bypass file security to back up files
Guests	Users granted guest access to the computer/domain
Power Users	Members can share directories and printers
Replicator	Supports file replication in a domain
Users	Ordinary users

Find your place in the big picture

As I said earlier, it's a lot of work to assign one right at a time to each user. It's more convenient to create groups of users, each with its own "package" of user rights, and then add users to that group, where they will automatically have the same rights as all the others in the group.

Windows NT includes the following predefined groups, and chances are you already belong to one of them:

- The **Administrators** group includes everyone who has the right to log on and act as an administrator. Some administrators keep two accounts—one in this group, which they can use when they need to do system maintenance, and another account, for everyday use, that has more restricted user rights.

- **Everyone** is the least exclusive group of all. Typically users in this group get the right to log on to a specific machine and shut it down, and that's all.

- **Users** have restricted rights, not because they're not trusted, but because administrators want to keep them from accidentally deleting important files or stumbling into areas where they don't belong.

- **Power Users** are assumed to be more experienced (like you, after you've read this book!) and are allowed to share files and folders with other users, and to create new user accounts on their own computers.

- **Guests**, as the name implies, are allowed to log on to a machine and use it temporarily. A guest account might be created to allow visitors to log on and use a few application programs and a shared printer, storing their files in a special folder not shared by anyone else.

- **Backup Operators** are allowed to get around file and folder security, but only for the purpose of making backup copies of important data files.

Halt! Who goes there?

In gangster movies from the 1930s, heroes and bad guys alike had to use a special knock and say the secret word before they could get past the front door. You'll have to go through the same process—although with considerably less melodrama—to start Windows NT each day. After your system has gone through its startup routine, you'll see the dialog box shown in Figure 3.3.

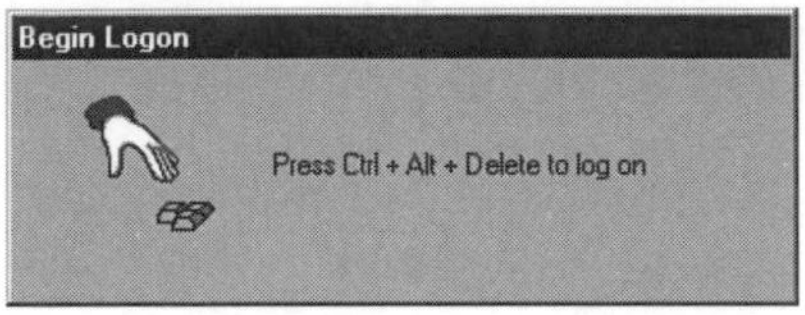

Fig. 3.3

Before you can get started with Windows NT, you have to press the Ctrl, Alt, and Del keys, all at the same time.

Begin Logon
Press Ctrl + Alt + Delete to log on

Instead of a secret knock, you have to press a particular key combination: Ctrl-Alt-Del. When you do, you'll see a logon screen like the one in Figure 3.4. Type your password and press Enter.

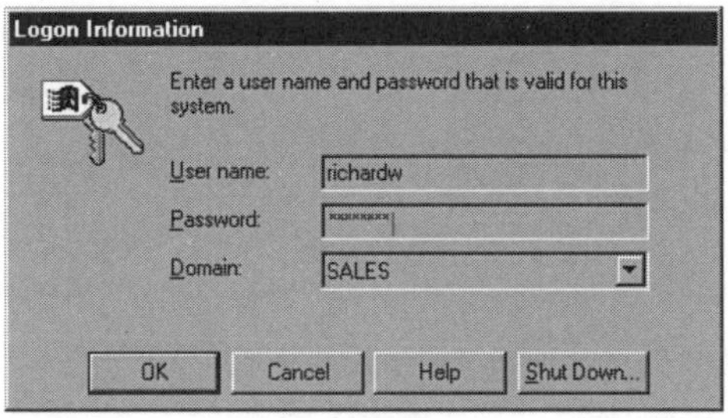

Fig. 3.4

Windows needs your user name and password to verify that you really are who you say you are.

Logon Information
Enter a user name and password that is valid for this system.
User name: richardw
Password: ********
Domain: SALES
OK   Cancel   Help   Shut Down...

The basic concept of logging on is simple: Windows acts like a no-nonsense security guard. You have to show your identification, and then Windows has to check the list of names to make sure it's OK for you to come in. The password, which only you should know, is as good as a photo ID. When the system administrator first created an account for you, he or she added your name to the list of authorized users and gave you a password.

TIP   **Why did Microsoft choose Ctrl-Alt-Del to start up Windows NT?**
For security's sake, naturally. With most other PC operating systems, that combination of keys restarts the computer. If the Windows NT logon box appears instead, you can be certain that Windows NT is really running.

Connecting to the Network

Once you've logged on, the Windows NT security system lets you see the files on your own computer. It also allows you to do things with other computers and printers on the network. Exactly what you can do is determined by the permissions you've been granted. We'll talk more about networking in Chapter 20.

 Q&A *Help—I've forgotten my password! How do I get to my files?*

Ask your administrator. He or she can't tell you what your password is, but the administrator can do the next best thing, by deleting the old one and giving you a brand–new password.

Changing your password

Every so often, just on general principle, you should change your password. And if you ever even *suspect* that someone has learned your password, change it right away. It's not difficult: Just press Ctrl-Alt-Del and click the button labeled Change Password. You'll see a dialog box like the one in Figure 3.5.

Open Sesame...

You use passwords all the time, although you might not think of them that way. The PIN number that coaxes cash out of your ATM? That's a password. The numbers you have to push before you can listen to your voice mail? Password. Your Social Security number and mother's maiden name? If the bank makes you recite both before they'll talk about your balance, that's a password. Although as we'll see, it's not a very good one.

The reason you use a password in the first place is to protect your privacy. The more people who know that password, the less secure you can expect your data to be. If you write your password on a Post-It note and stick it on your monitor, you're practically rolling out the red carpet for meddlers and thieves.

Here are some time-tested rules for making sure that your passwords remain your little secret.

- Make the password long enough to resist random guessing by a stranger—at least 8 characters.

- Avoid the obvious—don't use your birthday or your Social Security number or the names of your kids as a password.

- Mix numbers, letters, and symbols; nonsensical combinations are much harder to guess.

- If you must use a real word, use something that you won't forget and no one else could possibly guess, like the name of the sled you had when you were a child.

- Change your password regularly—at least as often as you change the oil in your car. Your system administrator may require that you change passwords every 6 weeks or so.

- Don't forget: A good lock is sometimes more effective than any password.

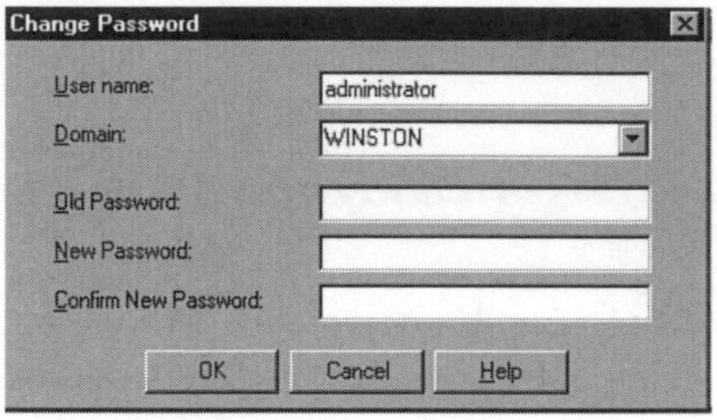

Fig. 3.5
To change your password, you first have to enter your old password. Then type the new one, and type it again to make sure you didn't make a mistake the first time.

Change Password	✕
User name:	administrator
Domain:	WINSTON ▼
Old Password:	
New Password:	
Confirm New Password:	

[OK] [Cancel] [Help]

What do you do if you can't change your password? Your system administrator may have placed additional restrictions on your account. For example, she may have told Windows that your password has to be at least 10 characters, or that you can't reuse any of the last four passwords you've used. If you have trouble, ask your system administrator whether any of these restrictions apply to you.

4

Help! Fast Answers Straight from the Source

● **In this chapter:**

- **Where to start looking for help**

- **I know what I want to do, but how do I look it up?**

- **If the computer isn't working right, try looking here**

- **Help can serve up shortcuts and tips, too!**

- **I'm tired of looking this up every other day. Can't I print it out?**

Sometimes you just need directions. Other times you need a search–and–rescue party. . . . . ❯

There are two ways to ask for help. There's "Excuse me, I seem to be a bit turned around here. I wonder if you could help me find my way back to the folder I was just in." And then there's "HELP!!!!!"

No matter where you're lost, Windows has a built-in information system that can give you the quick answer you need, when you need it.

Now what do I do?

That's the big question, isn't it? Windows does so many different things that it's impossible to cover them all in a book like this one. In a week-long training course, you'd barely scratch the surface. In fact, even if you could convince someone to pay you to become a Windows expert, it would be months of full-time work before you covered everything, much less figured it all out.

Fortunately, you don't need to convince your boss to rewrite your job description. Because so many parts of Windows work the same way, it's possible to figure a lot of things out by simply guessing what to do next.

The answer when you're not sure how something works is to ask for Help. Don't worry, there's plenty to go around.

How does Help work?

There's an extensive library of helpful reference material in Windows, mostly stored in a group of files in the Help folder, which is inside the Windows folder. Although these files are organized like books, they actually work more like videotapes. Without a VCR to use as a player, your videotapes are just big hunks of black plastic. Likewise, without a Help "player," your Help files are just digital gibberish.

When you ask for help, Windows starts up its version of a VCR, running a program called WINHELP.EXE. Then it pops in the tape, loading the most appropriate volume for what you're trying to do right now. If you click the Start button and choose Help, you'll open the master Help file, a huge document that gives you a close-up view of everything in Windows.

Using Windows' built-in instruction book

Open Windows Help, and you'll see one of these three views. In Windows, Help works just like a shelf full of well-organized books.

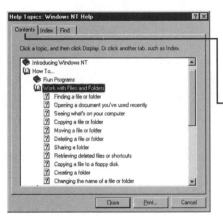

The **Contents** tab helps you see what main topics are covered in each Help file. This tab divides the Help "book" into sections, chapters, and individual pages and paragraphs.

Use the **Index** tab to find a specific section or page and jump straight to it. This approach works best when you know exactly what you're looking for and you're in a hurry.

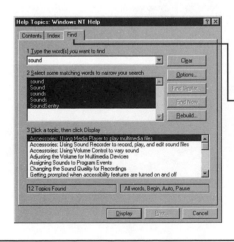

The **Find** tab scans through every word of the Help book to help you find a particular word or phrase, no matter where it is, even if the author didn't think it was important enough to include in the table of contents or the index.

TIP **It sounds strange, but there's even help for using Help. To get** more information, choose Help from the Start menu. Click the Contents tab, double-click How To, and then Use Help to see the specifics.

How do I ask for help?

If you're on the bridge of the U.S.S. Enterprise, you can just say, "Computer!" Here on earth, though, there are four ways to signal Windows that you need a little assistance:

- Click the **Start button** and choose Help from the menu. That opens the help system for all of Windows.

What to do when you're not sure what to do next...

Most of the manuals that came with my software are covered with a thick layer of dust because the answers I need are usually easier to find with a couple of mouse clicks. There's no magic in-volved—just a little common sense. The next time you're feeling stuck, follow these suggestions to get unstuck in a hurry:

- Pull down all the menus, open all the dialog boxes,and push all the buttons. The feature you're looking for may be hidden underneath a button that says Advanced or Setup. Don't worry, you can't break anything just by looking. (But do pay attention to any warning labels you see!)

- Right-click everywhere. The Windows NT shortcut menus that appear when you

right-click are supposed to offer only the choices you need, when you need them. So try right-clicking buttons, words, icons, and boxes. Maybe you'll get lucky.

- Press F1. For years, this has been the universal software Help signal, as recogniz-able as SOS or 911. It doesn't work every-where in Windows, but it pays off often enough that it's worth a try when all else fails.

Most Windows programs use this built-in help system, so after you learn how to use it, you're well on your way toward being able to find Help in any program.

- Look on the **Help menu** in most programs (Help is usually the last choice on the right). You'll probably open a help file created especially for that program. The last entry in the Help menu is typically About.... Choose this one to find out the name and version number of the program you're using right now.

- Click the **Help button**, if there is one. (You'll find them most often in dialog boxes). In the Modem Properties dialog box, for example, the Help button takes you straight to the Modem Troubleshooting Wizard.

- Click the **Question mark button** in the top right corner of some dialog boxes (such as the dialog box you see when you right-click on the desktop and choose Properties). The mouse pointer changes to a combined arrow-and-question mark. Aim that arrow at any part of the box and click for a pop-up explanation of what that aspect of Windows really does.

Where am I now?

The best kind of help is the sort that's right there when you need it. In Windows, this is called **context-sensitive help**. Think of it as a way to get specific directions. Opening the main Windows Help system is a bit like unrolling a map of the United States—interesting, but not very detailed. Context-sensitive help gives you a close-up map of the neighborhood you're standing in right now.

For example, let's say you're having trouble hearing the sounds coming out of your multimedia PC. You've found the Multimedia icon in the Control Panel window. You click the icon. Now what? If you need an explanation for any of the terms in the Multimedia Properties dialog box that appears, just point to the label that has you baffled, then right-click. You'll see the words What's This? pop up. Click again to see an explanation like the one in Figure 4.1.

There's a profound difference between context-sensitive help and the more general variety. Most of the time, Help takes you to the front of the book, where you have to start searching. But context-sensitive help looks around, tries to figure out where you might be stuck, then puts up detailed information about what you're doing right now.

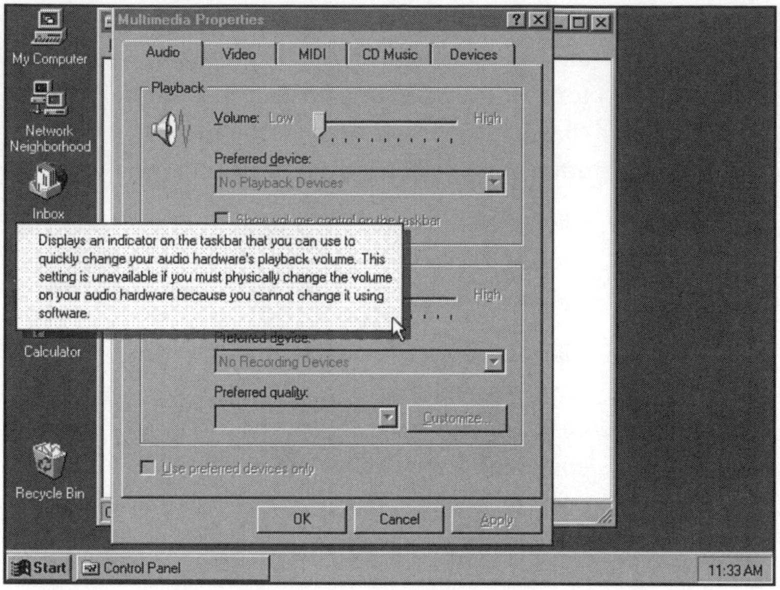

Fig. 4.1
Can't figure out what that button does? Right–click anywhere in a dialog box to get "What's this?" help. The information that pops up is usually a slightly more detailed explanation than the simple label.

What are all these colors and buttons for?

Inside a Windows Help file, there are all sorts of secret passageways to extra information. When you see any of these special buttons or type treatments, you can click for more information or jump directly to where you want to go.

- A **dotted-underlined word** means there's a definition waiting behind it; click the word to pop up a definition (see Fig. 4.2).

- A **Jump button** (a button with an arrow on it) means you can jump quickly to a particular folder or feature in Windows (see Fig. 4.3).

- If there is related information for the topic, or a cross-referenced subject, you'll see a **plain button** like that shown in Figure 4.3. Click it for a list of other topics that may help you out.

Fig. 4.2
You can pop up quick definitions of unfamiliar terms. On most computers, these links appear in green underlined text. When the pointer turns to a finger, it's OK to click.

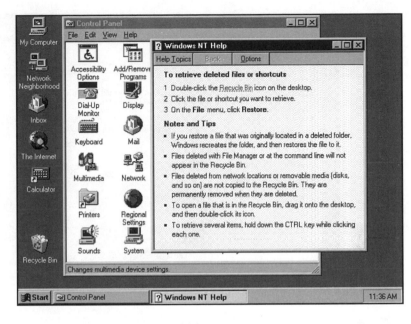

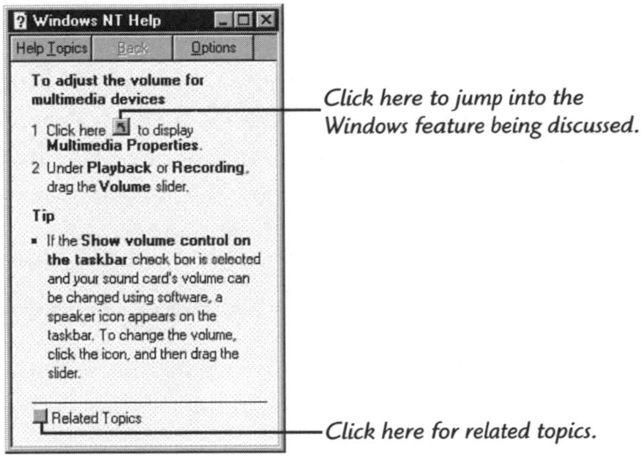

Fig. 4.3
Jump buttons let you open the dialog box or run the program you're reading about, with a single mouse click.

Click here to jump into the Windows feature being discussed.

Click here for related topics.

- Some key topics have their own full-blown graphical displays, complete with buttons and bright red arrows (see Fig. 4.4).

Fig. 4.4
Other buttons and
demos illustrate key
tasks or point you to
other parts of the Help
system.

*These buttons let you
choose which topic you
want to learn about.*

*A graphical
display appears
here for the
selected topic.*

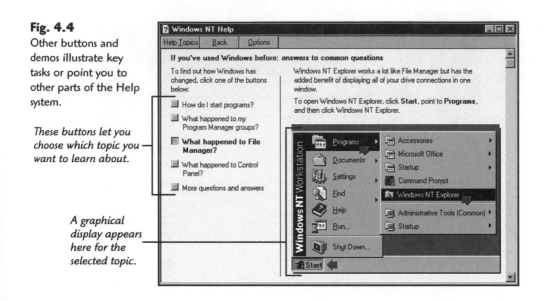

I can't remember how to...

Let's say you created a folder called "Hot! Income Tax Files," where you
kept all of last year's financial records. It's April 16 and you've filed your tax
return; now you want to rename the folder "Last Year's Tax Files" and copy
it to a floppy disk, but you can't remember exactly how to do it. Try these
steps, and remember: you can follow the same general path to find the
answers to any how-to question about Windows.

Start with the Table of Contents

The Windows Help file starts out with a handful of broad sections. Click the
Start button, choose Help, and select the Contents tab. By double-clicking
How To, then Work with Files and Folders, we eventually drill down to a list
of topics that includes Changing the name of a file or folder and Moving a file
or folder. That sounds promising, doesn't it? But it's not the only way to get
the answers.

TIP **When you open a Help "book" for the first time, each section has**
an icon to its left that looks like a closed book. When you double-click a
topic, the icon changes to an open book, and you'll see additional icons,
for books and pages, just below it.

Try the Index next

Click the Index tab and type a word. Let's try **move**. You don't even need to type all the letters—as you hit each key, the selection bar in the Help list jumps to the first entry that begins with what you've typed so far. After three characters, you've reached moving, files or folders. When you double-click here, you get more choices, including an option to learn how to accomplish the same task by dragging and dropping. Pick an item from the list and click the <u>D</u>isplay button to read the Help topic. If that screen doesn't have the answer you were looking for, click the Help <u>T</u>opics button and try it again.

Search the whole book, if you need to

Both the Table of Contents and the Index depend on someone else to organize the Help book. Murphy's Law of Help predicts that the question that has you stumped won't be covered in either place. This is when you'll be grateful that Windows Help can find a word or a phrase anywhere in the Help file.

The first time you click on the Find tab, you'll see a dialog box like the one in Figure 4.5. Don't be alarmed. Before Windows can find the word or phrase you type, it has to rearrange every word in the file into an alphabetical list called an index. You choose whether to create a simple index or a thorough one.

Fig. 4.5
Before you can find a word or phrase in a Help file, Windows asks you to choose the type of index you want to use.

- Choose **Minimize database size** if you want to save space on your hard disk. Windows creates a list from which you can find only one word or phrase at a time.

- If you have lots of hard disk space, choose **Maximize search capabilities**. Windows Help creates an index three times bigger, allowing you to search for words and phrases even if they're not part of the ready-made Help index.

- The last choice, **Customize search capabilities**, takes you through a series of picky options. Don't bother.

After you've created the index, just start typing in the box at the top of the Find tab. Topics that match the words you enter will appear in the list at the bottom. Highlight the topic that looks most promising and click the Display button to read the Help text.

Search tips

When you're having trouble finding the help you need, follow this list of handy tips:

- Try to think of synonyms. If "sound" doesn't work, maybe "audio" or "multimedia" will.

- Open a dialog box that looks like it might be related to your topic, then press F1 for context-sensitive help.

- Look for cross-references to similar topics. At the bottom of some Help windows, you'll see a button and label like the ones in Figure 4.6.

Fig. 4.6
When you see a button labeled Related Topics, click to see a list of answers to similar questions.

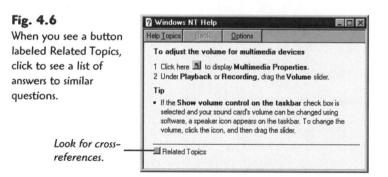

Look for cross-references.

My computer isn't working the way it's supposed to...

Sometimes when you're working with Windows, things go wrong—and the solution isn't always obvious. If you're experiencing real problems with Windows, you don't need advice, you need step-by-step troubleshooting assistance. There are two places to look: Troubleshooting Tips (look on the Contents tab of the main Windows Help file), and in the ReadMe files, which are used extensively in Windows and Windows programs.

> ## 66 *Plain English, please!*
>
> Why are they called **ReadMe files**? It's a time-honored tradition in the software industry. The folks who made the manuals had to finish before the folks who made the program, and sometimes there were last-minute changes in the program that didn't match the printed manuals. To include a file called Readme (or README.TXT) was the answer, with last-minute changes noted here. 99

TIP **Look for Readme files, not just for Windows, but for everything.** Try clicking the Start button and using Find Files to search for files anywhere on your hard drive that have the letters READ in their names.

There must be an easier way!

There usually is. Sometimes you find yourself doing the same thing over and over again, and it drives you crazy. For example, if you regularly send print jobs to a laser printer somewhere on your company's network, you'll understand how useful it can be to check your place in the print queue.

You *could* open My Computer, then open the Printers Folder, then open a window on the printer you want to check. But if you look in the Printing chapter of the Windows Help book, it suggests a faster, easier way: Drag the printer icon to your desktop and create a copy there. Now when you want to see whether your print job is done, you can just double-click the icon.

Most of the Windows Help files have a Tips and Tricks section. Look here for other time-saving suggestions.

TIP **How do you follow along with a complicated set of instructions?**
Click the Keep Help On Top option (it appears whenever you press the Options button). When this feature is turned on, the Help instructions will "float" over whatever you're doing until you close the window or uncheck the Keep Help on Top option.

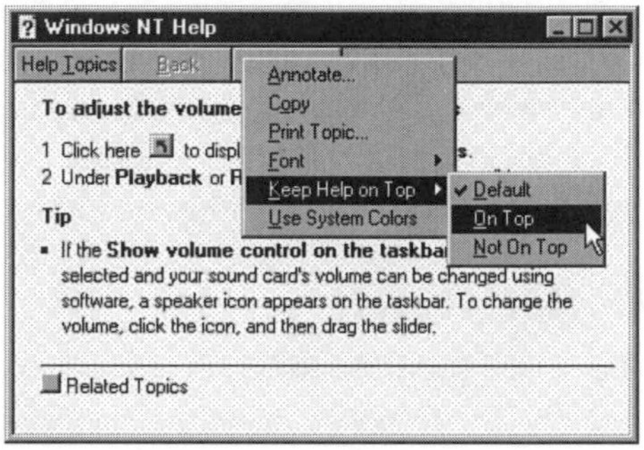

Fig. 4.7
To avoid covering up Help screens, use the Keep Help on Top option.

Q&A *I keep looking up the same things over and over. Isn't there an easier way to find the info I need repeatedly?*

Don't reinvent the wheel! When you learn something that isn't in Help, use **annotations** to save your comments. It's especially useful if someone else (like a PC support person at your company) modifies your system. Press the Options button, then choose Annotate. You'll see a small window where you can type a note to yourself or to anyone else who uses your PC. When you see a green paper-clip icon in a Help screen, click it to read the annotation.

Printing out those helpful hints

If you're having a hard time learning something, you can print out the help topic and keep it alongside your PC until you get the hang of it. When you see a particularly helpful Help screen, click the Options button and choose Print topic from the pop-up menu. If you'd rather incorporate the instructions into your own note, use the mouse to highlight the helpful material, then right-click and choose Copy. Now you can paste the copied material from the Windows Clipboard into your document or into a mail message.

Part II: Controlling Windows

5

My Computer and Everything Inside It

● **In this chapter:**

● **What are all these icons doing in My Computer?**

● **How filing cabinets and folders keep you organized**

● **An ounce of backup is worth a pound of lost data**

● **What you can—and can't—do with floppy disks**

● **How are CD-ROMs different?**

● **How can I tell one dialog box from another?**

Files go in folders, and folders go in drives. After you learn your way around the My Computer window, you'll get organized in a hurry! . . . . **>**

There are 7,917 separate data files on my computer's hard drive. If you were to print all those documents and pile them on my desk, they'd punch right through the ceiling and probably interfere with low-flying aircraft. Of course, I'd never be able to find a single letter or report if it was part of a mile-high stack of paper. Instead, on my desktop and on my PC, I use a logical filing system so that I can find documents when I need them.

I don't just toss all my paper reports into one extra-large filing cabinet. So why should I just throw all those data files into a single folder on my hard disk? In my office, all the paper files go into manila folders, and all the files on my computer go into Windows folders. Folders with similar topics go into bigger folders, and I stash everything in my neatly alphabetized file drawers. So no matter which desktop I'm dealing with—the one that's covered with paper or the Windows desktop—I can put my hands on the right file fast.

If you expect Windows to help you organize your work the same way, you have to understand two of its most important building blocks—drives and folders.

 TIP   **You can choose from four different ways to arrange the drives in** the My Computer window. Pull down the View menu and choose Arrange Icons. Now you can sort the entries in the window by drive letter, type, size, or amount of available free space.

Working with hard disks

Your disk drives work just like filing cabinets, and to keep your files organized you use the computer equivalent of manila folders. So far, so good. But just like the filing cabinets in your office, you have to do a little prep work before you dump your data into folders.

Before you can use any disk—hard or floppy—it has to be formatted. If your computer is running right now, your hard disk is already formatted just fine. (We'll get to floppy disks in a moment.) The next challenge is to make sure there's enough free space on the disk and that the files are organized properly.

Fast facts about disks

In your office, you have all sorts of storage spaces— ranging in size from shoe boxes to file cabinets to warehouses. On your PC, you have all sorts of storage spaces, too, and each one works in its own unique way. When you double-click the My Computer icon, it opens into a window filled with icons for each disk drive you have access to. Double-click any drive icon, and it opens into a drive window. The menus that appear when you right-click a drive icon contain choices that let you work with each type of drive, like Eject for a CD or Disconnect for a network drive.

The different drives within "My Computer"

CD-ROM
Don't be startled if a window pops open on its own when you put certain CD-ROMs (or even audio CDs) into your drive. Right-click here to choose the Eject command from a menu (no, Windows won't put the CD back in its box). If you have a sound card, audio CDs will play automatically when you insert them.

Floppy disks
They don't hold much data, but they're portable. Your first floppy drive is A:, and if you have a second drive it gets the letter B:. Right-click here to format a disk or give it a descriptive label; drop a file on this icon to copy it to a floppy.

Hard disk
Most of your everyday files go here. Your main hard disk is almost always called C:. The right-click menu includes tools for making sure your files are stored safely.

Network drive
If there's a drive or a folder somewhere else on the network, you or your network administrator can tell Windows to give it a drive letter (but not A:, B:, or C:). Once you've done that, this icon appears. If Windows can't connect to the network drive, the icon gets a big red X.

Shared volume
The outstretched hand appears if you've told Windows that it's OK for other people on your network to share one of your drives or folders.

Labels
In addition to its drive letter, every disk can have a plain-English name, also known as a label. Labels, which are strictly for informational purposes, can have as many as 11 characters, including spaces.

Drive letters
It's as easy as ABC. Every disk drive has a single letter, followed by a colon, for a name. Floppies are always A: and B:. Your main hard drive is almost always C:. If you have a second hard drive, it's probably D:. If there's a CD-ROM attached to your computer, it might be D: or E: or F: or anything up to Z:. Look in My Computer to see for yourself.

Plain English, please!

A blank, freshly manufactured disk is about as useful as a half-acre of dirt and weeds. **Formatting** prepares the magnetic surface of a disk so your PC can store data there, in much the same way that you'd pave the vacant lot and paint white lines so you could use it as a parking lot. You format a disk the first time you use it, and the only time you reformat it is when you want to erase the disk and start all over again.

CAUTION   **Formatting a hard drive is a job for a computer expert. Don't** even *think* about doing it yourself, and that goes double if you're connected to a network. Fortunately, Windows NT makes it nearly impossible for you to accidentally format your C: drive.

NTFS and FAT

I don't mean to get too personal, but is your disk FAT? The acronym has nothing to do with calories. It stands for **File Allocation Table**, and it's one of two alternative file systems for storing information on computers running Windows NT. The other is called NTFS—short for **NT File System**.

File systems are simply sets of rules that your computer uses to keep track of the information on a hard disk. Think of your hard disk as a warehouse containing many, many small boxes, each one the same size. To keep track of everything, the file system creates a label for the outside of each box, spelling out exactly what's inside.

Most of the time, you won't have any reason to care which file system is installed on your computer. In fact, whoever runs your company's computer network probably will decide which file system is used on your computer. But there are differences in the ways FAT and NTFS handle files, and in certain situations the differences are

important. Here's a quick rundown on the differences between FAT and NTFS disks.

Disks formatted FAT-style are compatible with old versions of MS-DOS and Windows. You can even run Windows 95 and Windows NT on the same PC (but not at the same time) as long as the main hard disk uses FAT. FAT disks can't be compressed.

NTFS has complicated security and compression options on its Properties sheets. (Right-click the icon for an NTFS disk and you'll see what I'm talking about.) Because it writes information in more efficient ways, you can store more bits and bytes on an NTFS disk than on a disk that uses FAT. And NTFS disks can actually clean up errors before your data gets corrupted.

Floppy disks use the FAT format only. CD-ROMs use a completely different format called CDFS. And for network disks, it doesn't matter what file system the other disk is using, as long as the two computers can talk with each other over the network—and as long as you have permission to use the other machine's hard disk.

How much space do I have left?

Every time you save a file to a hard disk, it gobbles some of the empty space on that disk (which is measured in **megabytes**), and sooner or later you'll fill up every square inch of space. As the disk gets fuller, your computer starts running more and more slowly, and eventually you won't be able to open or save new documents. That's why you should keep an eye on free disk space. It's especially important to check how much space is left on a disk if you're planning to install a new program. Here's how:

1 Double-click the My Computer icon on your desktop to open My Computer.

2 Click the icon for the drive you want to check. The total disk capacity and free space appear in the status bar at the bottom of the My Computer window. (If the status bar isn't visible, pull down the View menu and select Status Bar.)

3 To see a graphical display of free disk space, right-click the hard drive icon, then choose Properties from the popup menu (see Fig. 5.1). Above the pie chart, you can see exactly how many free megabytes are left, and how many total megabytes your hard disk has.

Fig. 5.1
Right-click your hard drive icon and choose Properties to see how much space is left.

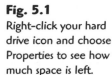

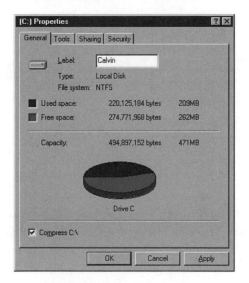

4 To give your hard drive an informative label to accompany the letter, right-click the drive icon and choose Properties. Then select the General tab and type a name (up to 32 characters) in the Label box·

66 *Plain English, please!*

A **byte** is one character, and **mega** means million. So a megabyte is a million characters, right? Not exactly. Your PC can only count in twos, so a megabyte is actually 2 to the 20th power, or 1,048,576 bytes. For anyone but an accountant, it's accurate enough to round off that precise number to an even million. **99**

Whoops—I'm almost out of room!

It's one of the unpleasant realities of the universe, right up there with those laws that Newton and Murphy discovered. Sooner or later (usually sooner), you'll have more files than your hard disk can hold. If you've been checking your free disk space regularly, you'll get some advance warning. Otherwise, you'll just get a rude error message when you try to save a file. Either way, you have three choices:

- **Clean some files off your hard disk.** The cheapest solution to an overstuffed hard disk is to delete files you don't need. Of course, that's about as much fun as sorting your socks by color.

- **Get a new hard disk.** That assumes you have a few hundred dollars in the budget; you'll also need to find someone who'll install it for you. If you plan to replace your existing hard disk, you might also have to reinstall all your software, including Windows.

- **Stuff it.** Or "compress" it, if you'd prefer to use the technical term. Assuming your hard disk is formatted with the NTFS file system, you can tell Windows to pack one or more files, a folder, or even an entire drive so that they take up less space. After Windows gets through squeezing your data files, you might find you have twice as much room. (See the section "How does disk compression work" for more information.)

TIP **You might have more free disk space than you think—maybe all** you have to do is take out the trash. Check the Recycle Bin first. If it's filled with files, simply emptying it might clear enough room to let you finish whatever you're doing. (You can do so by right-clicking the Recycle Bin icon and selecting Empty Recycle Bin from the pop-up menu.) To read all about the Recycle Bin, skip ahead to Chapter 9.

How does disk compression work?

Imagine that your hard disk is a plastic bag, and each document is a potato chip. Even when it's full, that bag doesn't feel heavy; but it sure takes up a lot of shelf space, thanks to all the air between the chips. You could squeeze the entire bag into a Pringles can if you could rearrange every chip into the same shape. The weight of the chips wouldn't diminish, but the amount of volume they took up sure would. Disk compression works the same way, squeezing the air—in this case, empty spaces and repetitious data—out of your files, then packing them tightly onto the disk.

When you compress a file, Windows replaces the repetitious characters with shorthand symbols. When you ask Windows to open a file, it grabs the compressed file and quickly expands the shorthand into plain English before handing you the file. On most computers, the process happens so fast you wouldn't even realize it's happening.

The method you use to compress files depends on whether you have an NTFS disk or a FAT disk.

 TIP **To see whether your disk is FAT or NTFS, right-click the disk** icon in My Computer and check its Properties. The name of the file system is listed on the General tab.

If you have an NTFS disk...

If your hard disk is formatted using NTFS, it's easy to compress a file or group of files, an entire folder, even an entire drive.

- **To compress your C: drive**, right-click its icon in the My Computer window, choose Properties, and check the Compress C:\ box at the bottom of the General tab, as shown in Figure 5.2.

- **To compress a file, a group of files, or one or more folders**, open a folder window or the Windows Explorer (described in detail in Chapter 9) and select one or more icons. Right-click and choose Properties, then click to add a check mark in the box labeled Compress. To squeeze the contents of every file, even those in folders inside the selected folder, check "Also compress subfolders" in the next dialog box, then click OK and watch as Windows squeezes the selected files.

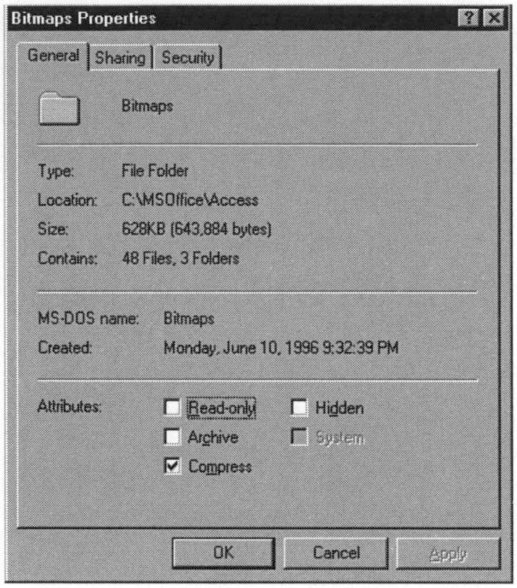

Fig. 5.2
Check this box and watch as Windows squeezes your files and folders, or even an entire disk, so that you can store more data in the same space.

Bitmaps Properties

General | Sharing | Security

Bitmaps

Type: File Folder
Location: C:\MSOffice\Access
Size: 628KB (643,884 bytes)
Contains: 48 Files, 3 Folders

MS-DOS name: Bitmaps
Created: Monday, June 10, 1996 9:32:39 PM

Attributes: ☐ Read-only ☐ Hidden
☐ Archive ☐ System
☑ Compress

OK   Cancel   Apply

- **To restore a compressed file** to its original format, just right-click the icon or icons for the compressed files or folders, choose Properties, and remove the check mark from the Compress box..

- **To see how much space you've saved** by compressing, select one icon at a time, right-click, and choose Properties.

- **To see which files are compressed**, open any folder window, choose View, Options, and click on the View tab, then check the box labeled "Display compressed files and folders with alternate color." Click OK, and the next time you open a folder you'll see compressed files in blue instead of the usual black.

If you have a FAT disk...

If your hard disk was formatted using the FAT file system, you have no compression option. Unlike the built-in compression that NTFS disks can use, the DriveSpace disk-compression program included with previous versions of MS-DOS and Windows cannot be used with Windows NT.

Network drives are a little different

Most of the time, you'll probably store files on the hard disk in your own PC. On a network in your office, though, you can also choose from other hard disks in other computers connected with yours by a network cable. Typically, these shared hard disks have names that you need to know before you can use them. On my company network, for example, the network administrator named all the file servers after Greek gods, so I save my work on hard disks named Bacchus, Eros, and Athena. A friend of mine works for a company that has three file servers—Larry, Moe, and Curly. Nyuk, nyuk.

Do network drives have to have drive letters like other drives? Not necessarily. You can always track down a file by typing its full name: `\\Curly\Data\Letters`, for example. But some people find it easier to **map** a shared hard disk to an unused drive letter. And some old programs insist that you use letters to refer to network drives. In these cases, you can work out a deal with Windows to go to that place on the network whenever you refer to a certain drive letter.

On your own computer, you can count on using C: (and maybe D:) most of the time. On networks, you'll typically find every letter from A: to F:. If your network uses the Novell NetWare operating system on some file servers, you'll probably have an X:, Y:, and Z:, too.

> **❝ Plain English, please!**
>
> A **file server** is a computer that's been set aside for people on the network to use for storing files. A **share** (also called a **volume**) is the name of the area that's available for network users to put files. To store files on a network drive, then, you'll need to enter its name as `\\server\share`. See figure 5.3 for an example. **❞**

To compress, or not to compress?

Some people just don't trust disk compression. I understand why they feel that way. There's something almost magical about the way this stuffing and unstuffing works, and it takes a giant leap of faith to trust Windows to do it all safely and reliably.

Basically, disk compression takes your files—one at a time or in groups of hundreds or even thousands—and translates them into a shorthand language only it can understand. The good news is you can get hundreds of megabytes of free disk space without any additional cost. The bad news? If something happens to that file...

If you choose to use disk compression, be smart. Keep backup copies of your important data files, and store them in a safe place, preferably away from your computer.

Come to think of it, that's good advice even if you *don't* use disk compression.

To map a shared network drive to a drive letter, just look in the Network Neighborhood. Double-click a computer icon and select the name of the **share** you want to connect to from the list that appears, then choose Map Network Drive. . . from the popup menu. The dialog box that appears is simple: You pick a free drive letter from the list, click OK, and from now on, you can get to that place on the network by using the new drive letter. To tell Windows that you want to use this mapped drive letter every time you log on to your computer, check the Reconnect at Logon box.

To see a list of all the shared folders and drives available on your network, right-click the Network Neighborhood, then choose Map Network Drive. You'll see a dialog box like the one in Figure 5.3. Choose a share (shown by a folder-and-hand icon) and a drive letter in the Drive box. Click OK and your drive mapping is complete.

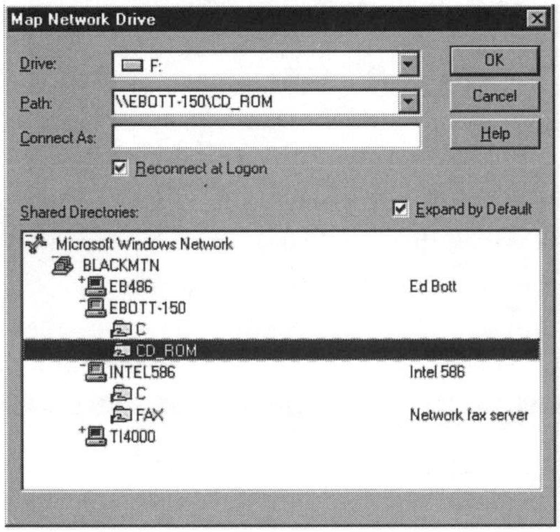

Fig. 5.3
Right–click the Network Neighborhood and choose Map Network Drive to see this list of shared network folders. The Path box includes the drive letter's full legal name.

To disconnect a drive mapping and to stop using that drive letter, right-click My Computer, select the mapped drive and right-click it, then choose Disconnect from the pop-up menu.

Back up those files!

I don't like dental checkups, and I hate waiting around while my car gets an oil change. You probably don't look forward to these chores, either. But we do them both, because the consequences of not doing these simple tasks are too unpleasant to imagine. Likewise, the data files on your hard disk will be a lot safer with a little preventive maintenance. What would you do if all your data files disappeared overnight? (After you stopped crying, I mean.) You might never be able to reconstruct all that work from scratch.

The solution is to regularly copy your files to a safe place: onto floppy disks, to a magnetic tape if you have a tape backup drive, or even to a network file server. Which strategy should you follow? It doesn't matter. Just make sure your files are stored somewhere safe!

If your irreplaceable files are small enough, you can use floppy disks to store them. But it's usually easier and safer to copy them to a network drive—as long as your network administrator says it's OK. Just open a folder window or the Windows Explorer and copy your important files from your hard disk to the network.

If you have a tape backup drive installed in your computer, use the Windows NT backup program to save all or some of the files on your drive. To start the Backup program, right-click on a drive icon, choose Properties, then click the Backup Now button. (If there's no tape drive installed, the Backup program will run, but every time you try to do anything with it it will pop up an error message.) If you need detailed instructions for using the Backup program, check the online Help.

Using floppy disks to move files around

Your hard drive probably has room for hundreds of megabytes' worth of files—and, if you're like me, your free disk space is shrinking every day. Floppy disks (sometimes called **diskettes**) hold far less data; the most common size has a capacity of 1.44 megabytes, which means you'd need about 350 of them to hold the data on a 500 MB hard disk.

Still, the mere fact that they're small doesn't mean floppies are useless. Floppy disks come in handy when you need to share files with other people, or when you want to take work home, or when you want to make backup copies of a small number of valuable data files.

How do I copy files to a floppy disk?

You can always use side-by-side folder windows to copy files from your hard disk to a floppy disk, but Windows gives you two better ways.

What is the easiest way to move files from your hard disk to your floppy disk drive? Point to the file you want to copy, right-click it, select File, Send To, and choose the floppy drive, as shown in Figure 5.4.

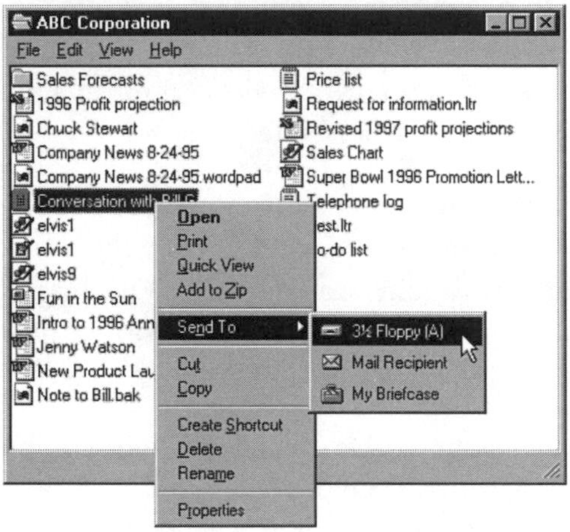

Fig. 5.4
Make sure there's a floppy disk in the drive before you try sending a file there! If you've passed that test, it's the easiest way to copy a file from your PC to a diskette.

If you regularly carry files around on floppies, put a shortcut to your floppy disk drive right on the Desktop. Open My Computer, and drag the drive icon to the Desktop. Windows will warn you that it can't move or copy your floppy drive icon and will ask if you want to create a shortcut here. Answer yes. Now you can simply drag files out of other windows and drop them right on the floppy disk shortcut to copy them to a floppy disk.

CAUTION Remember: **When you use the left mouse button to drag an icon** out of a folder window and drop it onto a floppy, you'll end up with a copy. To move a file (or files) from your hard disk to a floppy, use the *right* mouse button as you drag. The pop-up menu lets you choose to move, copy, or create a shortcut.

Why do I have to format floppies?

Before you can use a floppy disk for the first time, it has to be *formatted*—that is, Windows has to prepare the disk surface with special markings that define where the data goes. Even after a disk has been formatted, you can reuse the disk-formatting tools to quickly erase all the files from it. To format a floppy disk, first make sure it's in the drive, then right-click its icon in the My Computer window and choose Format. You'll see the dialog box shown in Figure 5.5.

Fig. 5.5
Formatting floppies is
simply a matter of
filling in the blanks.

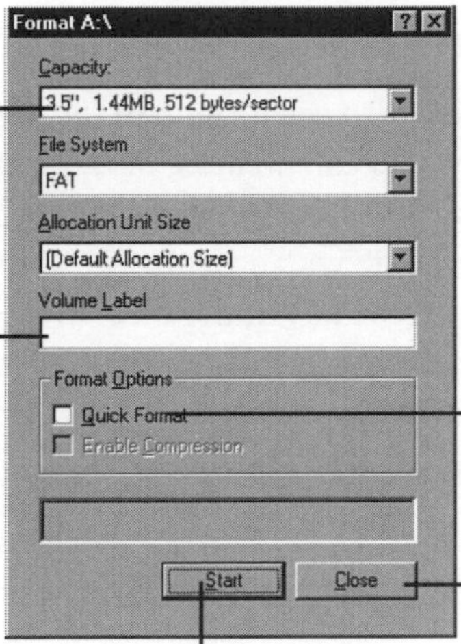

> *Pick a disk capacity.
> If you're not sure
> which is the right
> size, just use the
> default value that
> Windows suggests.*

> *Give the disk a
> label of up to 11
> characters, if you
> want.*

Format A:

Capacity:
3.5", 1.44MB, 512 bytes/sector

File System
FAT

Allocation Unit Size
[Default Allocation Size]

Volume Label

Format Options
☐ Quick Format
☐ Enable Compression

[Start] [Close]

> *To reformat an already-formatted disk,
> choose the Quick option. To format a new
> disk that's never been used, uncheck this
> box.*

> *After formatting a disk, you can format
> another by swapping diskettes and repeating
> the process. Click here to put away the
> Format dialog box.*

> *Click here to start
> formatting. You can do
> other work while Windows
> is busy formatting disks.*

I want a copy of the whole disk

If you have a floppy disk full of files, it's easy to make an identical copy of the
floppy. Put the original disk in your floppy drive, then right-click the drive
icon in the My Computer window. Choose Copy Disk from the popup menu,
and follow the on-screen instructions, as in Figure 5.6. You'll need a blank
floppy for the copy, of course, but you don't need a second floppy drive.
Windows is smart enough to tell you when it's time to remove the original
disk and put in the new one.

Fig. 5.6
To copy a floppy,
right-click the drive
icon, select the drive
types from this dialog
box, and follow the
on-screen instructions.

Copy Disk

Copy from: Copy to:
3½ Floppy (A:)   3½ Floppy (A:)

[Start] [Close]

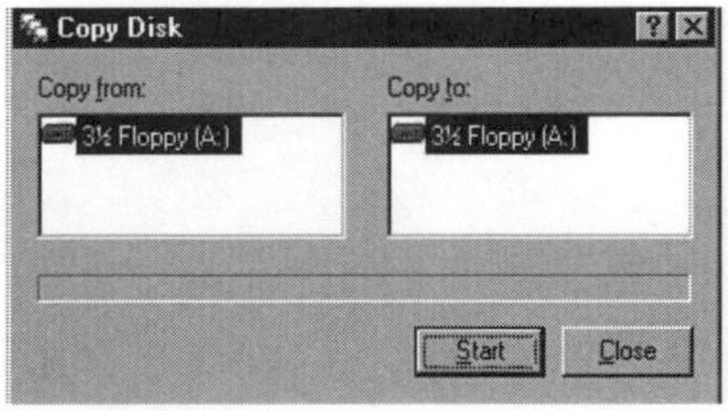

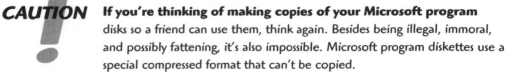

CAUTION **If you're thinking of making copies of your Microsoft program**
disks so a friend can use them, think again. Besides being illegal, immoral,
and possibly fattening, it's also impossible. Microsoft program diskettes use a
special compressed format that can't be copied.

Can I copy from a CD-ROM?

If you have a CD-ROM drive, you'll see its icon in the My Computer window. When it comes to CD-ROMs, you can do most of the same things you do with other types of drives—look at files, run programs, copy files from the CD to your hard disk. What can't you do with a CD-ROM? You can't add your own files to the disk. You can't rename any of the files on the CD. And you can't delete files. (The RO stands for Read Only, after all.) For more information about how to work with CD-ROM disks, see Chapter 18.

6

Organizing Your Files and Keeping Them Neat

● In this chapter:

- Getting around with the Windows Explorer

- Where do I put this file so I can find it when I need it?

- Creating, renaming, moving, and deleting folders

- Why you should *always* drag icons with the right mouse button

- Oops—I didn't mean to delete that file!

When you're buried under a mountain of paper, you grab manila folders and sort everything. Do the same with your computer files . . . . >

Everything in your computer—every program, every document, every little scrap of information that Windows lets you save— winds up on a hard disk somewhere. I have 8,722 files and folders on my hard disk. Even if you have only a fraction of that number, how do you keep things straight? With the help of folders, Windows lets you keep things as neat as you want them to be.

Use folders to get organized in the first place. Make as many copies of your documents as you like, and put them anywhere you want. If a folder starts to get too crowded, tidy up by moving files to another folder, or creating new folders inside the existing folder. When your hard disk gets too cramped, reclaim real estate by deleting old files and folders you don't need anymore. Windows lets you clean up as much as you'd like, and it also gives you some tools in case you throw out too much. (Did you really mean to toss *those* files? Don't worry—you can probably find them in the Recycle Bin.)

In this chapter, we'll also look at the many ways you can find any file, any-where, even when you can't for the life of you remember what you named it. If you can't figure out what's underneath that icon, you can always sneak a peek inside with the help of the built-in Quick Viewer.

How do I keep my files organized?

When you're buried under a mountain of paper, the first thing you do to get things under control is grab a stack of manila folders and start sorting things out. Do the same with Windows to get all those files on your hard disk under control. The first step is to open the root folder of your hard drive and create the main folders you'll use.

Double-click a drive icon and you'll go straight to the root folder.

❝ *Plain English, please!*

When you double-click a drive icon, you start out in a special folder called the **root**. If you think of your hard disk as a filing cabinet and each folder as one of its drawers, then the root folder acts like the frame that holds the drawers in place. The root folder has no name, just a backslash. Thus, to refer to the root of drive C:, you'd type **C:**. You can put files in the root folder if you'd like (and most people do), but the real purpose of this area is to hold the main folders you plan to use. **❞**

Windows does some of this filing and sorting for you. You don't have to look far to find examples of folders. Even if you haven't installed any software other than Windows NT, you'll have a whole stack of folders—including, naturally, a WinNT folder stuffed with files and folders. (When I open my WinNT folder, I can see 18 more folders, and I know there are three more that Windows hides from me so I can't tamper with them. If I keep clicking, one of those subfolders, System32, has another *nine* folders inside it!) Back in the root folder, there's a Program Files folder, a hidden Recycler folder, and a few more devoted exclusively to Windows NT tasks.

How do I use folders?

There's nothing complicated about folders. Used properly, they help you keep similar files together in a place where you can find them when you need them. If your bedroom was organized this way, you'd be able to track down a clean pair of socks in seconds, just by looking at storage areas inside of other storage areas: \bedroom\dresser\top drawer\box of underwear\white socks. The socks are in the box, which in turn is in the drawer, which is ... well, you get the idea.

Windows lets you put folders inside of folders so they fall into the same sort of hierarchy. For example, you might create a folder called "1997 Budget;" then, inside that folder, you'd create additional folders called "P&L Statements," "Forecasts," and so on. You might create a "Sales Reports" folder and then, inside that folder, add a separate folder for each member of the sales staff.

For a graphic display of how this folder-in-a-folder routine works, just look at the outline-style Explorer view in Figure 6.1.

 TIP **Do you think the Windows Desktop is something special? Nope,** it's just another folder. You might not recognize it as such, because the icons inside this folder are arranged differently from any other folder you'll see. Nonetheless, it acts just like a folder, as you can see if you open the Windows Explorer and look at it. (In the Explorer, you'll find the Desktop in the left-hand pane, at the very top of the tree—see Fig. 6.1.)

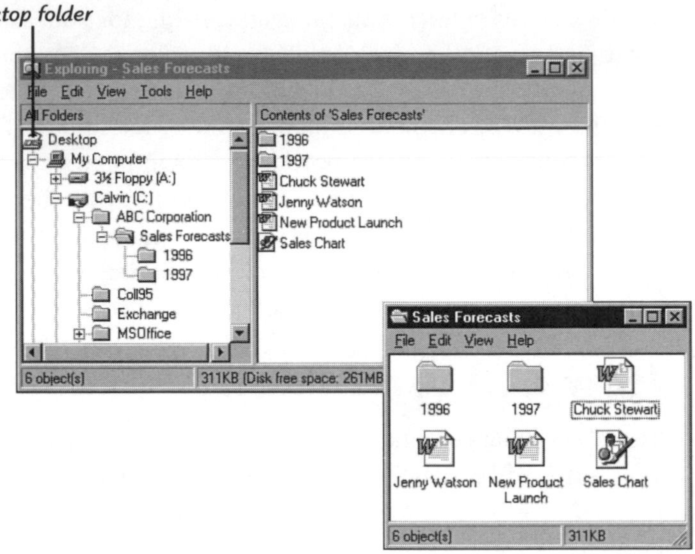

Desktop folder

Fig. 6.1
Use folders inside of other folders to keep your files organized. The Explorer view (left) lets you see the "tree" of folders; if you prefer, you can open a folder window (for example, by double-clicking My Computer) (right) and look at a simpler display of the same icons.

I want to create a new folder

Let's say you've just been promoted to sales manager. Congratulations! Now what are you going to do with all those sales forecasts that the folks in your department keep sending you via e-mail? For starters, open your C: drive and create a folder called Sales Forecasts in the root folder. You can throw all those sales forecasts in that folder if you'd like, or create a set of new folders, one for each of your salespeople, in that folder.

Sometimes you'll save files directly into these folders from your application programs. Other times, you'll get files from other people and you'll need to do your filing after the fact. Either way, the technique is the same.

To create a new folder, just follow these steps:

1 Double-click the My Computer icon and keep double-clicking folders until you've opened the one where you want to create a new folder.

2 Right-click any empty spot in this folder window and click New. Choose Folder from the cascading menu (see Fig. 6.2).

3 A new folder will appear, with a suitably generic label in place. To give it a more meaningful name, just start typing (see Fig. 6.3).

Fig. 6.2
Right-click any folder window to create a new folder from the pop-up menus.

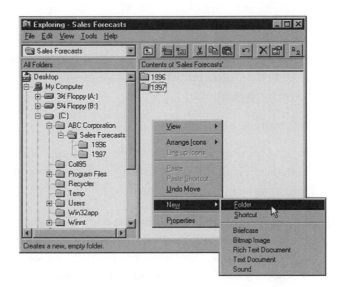

Fig. 6.3
The generic label New Folder isn't very helpful, is it? Just start typing to give it a more descriptive name.

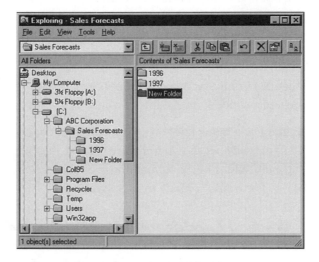

I want to get rid of a folder

It's easy to get rid of a folder. Just point at the folder, click once to select it, then right-click and choose Delete from the pop-up menu.

This desktop is too cluttered!

When it's time to move or copy files from one place to another, you'll want to open two windows—one for the original location of the files in question, the other for the place where you want to move them. Trouble is, all that double-clicking can open a lot of windows on your screen, which makes it difficult to find the two you want to use. Before you can move or copy files, you need to sweep aside the clutter and arrange both folders on the screen so you can see them clearly. Here's how:

1 Minimize or close all open windows.

2 Open My Computer and double-click the appropriate drive icon. Keep double-clicking folders until you've opened the window where the files you want to move are stored.

 TIP **Do you get a new window (and a bunch of unwanted clutter)** every time you double-click a folder? It's easy to keep things neat and avoid window clutter. Open a window for My Computer (or any folder), and choose <u>V</u>iew, <u>O</u>ptions. On the dialog tab labeled Folder, make sure there's a dot next to the choice that reads, Browse folders by using a single window that changes as you open each folder. Click OK, and from that point on, whenever you open a new window, it will automatically close the previous window.

3 Open My Computer again and double-click some more until you've opened a window on the folder where you want the files to end up.

4 Right-click a blank spot on the taskbar and choose Tile <u>H</u>orizontally or Tile <u>V</u>ertically, as shown in Figure 6.4. Presto! Both windows will automatically zoom to fill half the available space, either one over the other (horizontal) or side by side (vertical).

Q&A ***Whoops! I accidentally had three windows open when I chose the Tile command, and now all three windows are tiled on the screen. What do I do now?***

Right-click the taskbar and choose Undo, then minimize the stray window and try again.

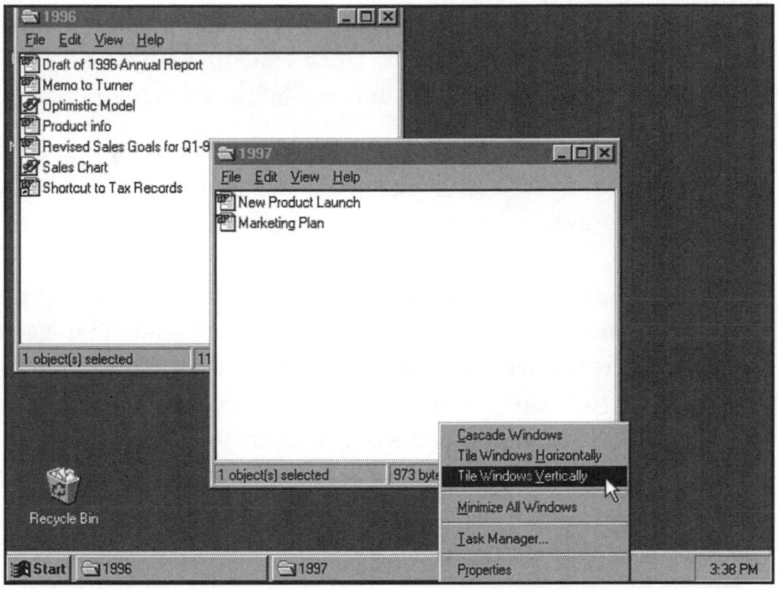

Fig. 6.4
Use one of the Tile commands to arrange these two windows on the desktop.

Moving files and folders around

As we saw in Chapter 5, you can use the mouse to drag just about anything from one place to another. Most of the time, that's how you'll move or copy files and folders. You could simply hold down the left mouse button and start dragging things around, but you'd be in for some very confusing times.

Dragging-and-dropping with the left mouse button, you see, has completely different effects, depending on what kind of object you're dragging and where you're dropping it. When you drag with the right mouse button, on the other hand, dragging-and-dropping always works the same way.

You never know what will happen when you use the left mouse button...

When you select an object, hold down the left mouse button, and drag, one of three things happens when you let go of the mouse button:

- **If you're moving to another folder on the same drive,** Windows will move the files to the destination folder. They no longer exist in their original location.

- **If you're moving to another folder on a different drive,** Windows will copy the files. You'll wind up with duplicate files—one in the original location and one in the destination folder.

- **If any of the files you're moving are programs,** Windows will create a **shortcut** in the destination folder. The file itself remains in the original folder.

Confused? You should be. Even certified Windows experts get befuddled sometimes by this now-you-see-it-now-you-don't nonsense. Fortunately, there's a better way: Just hold down the *right* mouse button and drag. When you release the button to drop the object in its new location, you'll see a shortcut menu like the one in Figure 6.5. *You* decide whether you want to move the file, copy it, or create a shortcut in the new location.

Fig. 6.5
When you hold down the right mouse button and drag an object—file, folder, whatever—you get to choose what happens next from this pop-up menu.

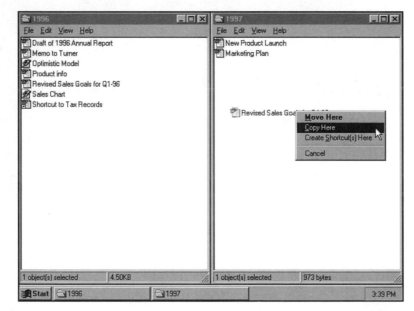

I don't *want* to drag all those icons around!

Some people never get used to the idea of dragging and dropping files. If this description fits you, use the other technique for moving and copying files. The trick is to *cut* or *copy* the original files and *paste* them into their new home. You'll still need to open two folder windows: one for the folder that holds the files you want to move, the other for the destination folder. Once you've done that, it's a simple process:

1 Select the file or files from the original folder.

2 Right-click one of the selected files to pop up a shortcut file menu.

3 Choose Copy if you want to leave the original files where they are and make identical copies in the destination folder. Choose Cut to delete the original files, essentially moving them to the new location.

4 Switch to the destination folder window, and right-click an empty area. Choose Paste to finish the job.

I want to move a bunch of files

It's easy to select one file for moving or copying. Just point and click. But what happens when you want to move or copy or delete a whole bunch of files? You can handle each file by itself, but there's a much easier way to select a group of files.

- **To select every file or object in a folder,** look on the menu bar and choose Edit, Select All.

- **To select a group of files that are right next to one another,** use the mouse to select the first file in the group. Hold down the Shift key and then click the last file in the group. Voilá! All the files between the two points are highlighted and ready for you to tell Windows what to do with them.

- **To select a large group of adjacent files,** use the mouse to draw an imaginary box around them. Pick one of the corners of this "box," hold down the left mouse button, and drag the selection to the opposite corner of the group you want to select. As you drag, you'll see the selected icons change color to let you know you were successful.

 TIP If you're having trouble selecting a group of files, try switching to List view instead (choose View, List from the pull-down menus). The neat columnar display and smaller typeface make it easier to grab a flock of files.

- **To select a file here and a file there,** hold down the Ctrl key as you click one file after another. Without that special keystroke, Windows won't let you select more than one thing at a time. With that help, though, you can select as many files as you want, even when they're not adjacent to one another.

- **To actually move or copy the files** takes a little bit of practice. With a single file, it's easy— just watch the icon as it moves from one window to the other. When you've selected a group of files, though, the Windows pointer shows you a "ghosted" image as you drag. The outlines of the selected files let you know which files you successfully selected, but they also make it difficult to tell where you're supposed to drop the files. If you're confused, there's an easy way out: Just keep your eye on the arrow pointer. When it's aimed directly at the destination folder or drive, the target changes color (as it has in Fig. 6.6). When you see this signal, let go of the button. If it doesn't work, right-click, choose Undo Move or Undo Copy, and try it again.

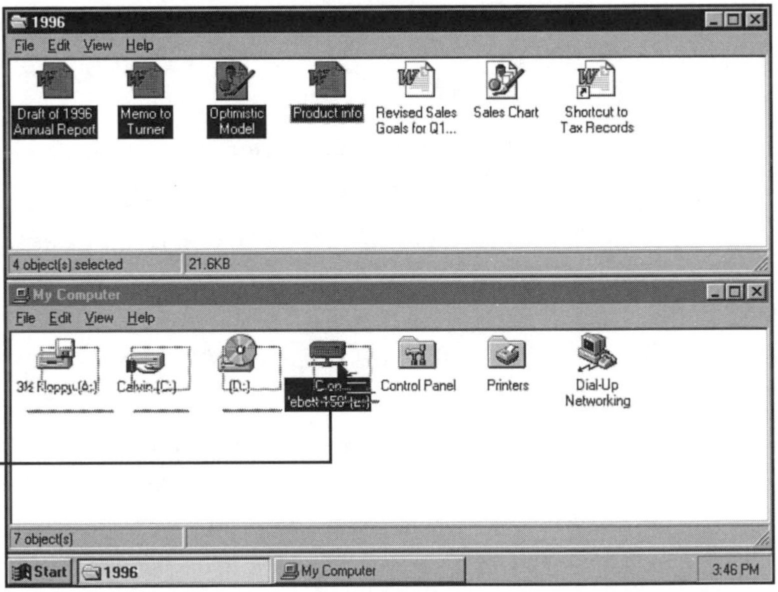

Fig. 6.6
Dragging a group of files (like the four in the top window) is easy, but where do you drop them? Keep your eye on the tip of the arrow in the bottom window.

The ghostly image of the files you're dragging may be distracting. Ignore it and concentrate on where this pointer is aimed.

What happens when I try to copy a file with the same name?

Let's say you have a file called LETTER1 (everyone who uses computers eventually has a few files with dopey names like these). You want to make a copy of that file, so you right-click and choose <u>C</u>opy. Here's what happens when you choose <u>P</u>aste:

- If you make a copy in the same folder, your new file will be called Copy of LETTER1.

- If you point to another folder, and there isn't a file with that name there, you'll get another file called LETTER1.

- If you point to another folder, and there's already a file with that name, you'll see a dialog box like the one in Figure 6.7. Use the file dates to decide whether to replace the existing file.

Fig. 6.7
Windows won't allow two files in the same place with the same name. Do you want to replace the old file?

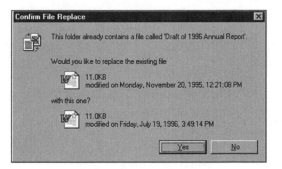

Using the Windows Explorer

For simple tasks, a simple folder window is usually sufficient. But there will be times when you want to do some major maintenance with your computer's file system—the PC equivalent of spring cleaning. For those instances, you need a way to move files from folder to folder with just a few clicks. That's where the Windows Explorer comes in.

When you double-click a drive or folder icon, you get a window filled with icons. When you right-click an icon and choose Explore, though, you get a window with a split personality. On the right, it looks just like an ordinary folder window. On the left, you'll see an outline view that shows all the drives and folders on your desktop, your computer, and even other computers (if you're hooked up to a network).

The Windows Explorer, up close and personal

Use the Windows Explorer to do industrial-strength clean-up jobs with the files on your computer. The tree window on the left lets you move from folder to folder (and even to different computers on a network) with a minimum of mouse clicks. The window on the right acts like an ordinary folder window whose contents correspond to the icon you've selected on the left side.

When you click a folder in the left pane, its icon changes to an open folder and the contents appear in the right pane, just as if you'd opened a folder window.

You can collapse and expand the outline on the left to make it easier to see. A plus sign next to a folder means there are more folders inside.

Click a minus sign to collapse the outline again.

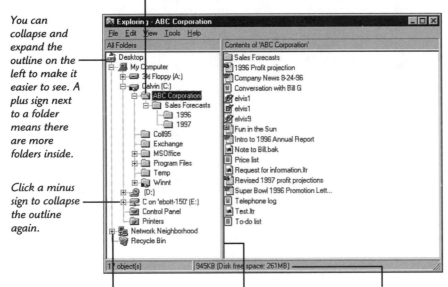

Click a plus sign to see all the folders inside the current folder or drive.

Want to make the panes narrower or wider? Point to the vertical bar between the two halves of the window until it turns to a two-headed arrow. Now, click the left mouse button and drag it in either direction.

Look in this status bar to see information about the files in the current folder and a running tally of everything you've already selected. If the toolbar and status bar are not visible, pull down the View menu and check the appropriate entries.

TIP **No matter what kind of window you use, you can sort files in any** order you like. Choose <u>V</u>iew, <u>D</u>etails, and then sort the list by clicking the column headings. Click the headings again to sort in reverse order. This is especially useful when you want to sort by size or date.

What's in that file? Use the Quick Viewer

One reason not to use names like LETTER1.DOC is that they don't tell you anything about what's in the file. It's especially confusing if Windows finds a bunch of files that share the same name but are stored in different folders. How do you tell what's inside? Try using Quick View. It works like an airport X-ray machine to peek inside the file and display its contents. The resulting display might not look the way it would if you were to open the file with a fancy application, but it only takes a few seconds.

Point to the file you're curious about and right-click. If Windows recognizes the file format, one of the choices available to you is <u>Q</u>uick View. Click to pop up a window like the one in Figure 6.8, showing you the contents of the file.

Fig. 6.8
Use Quick View to peek inside a file without starting up the program that created it.

Click here to open the file for editing. The icon tells you which program Windows will use.

Click here to make the typeface in the window bigger or smaller.

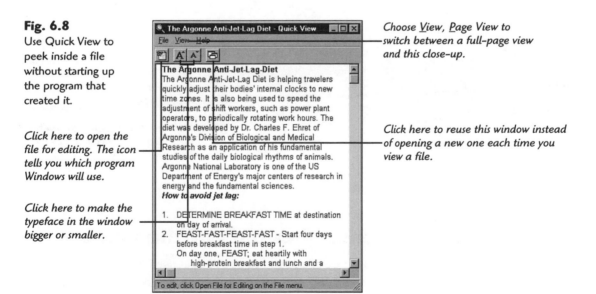

Choose <u>V</u>iew, <u>P</u>age View to switch between a full-page view and this close-up.

Click here to reuse this window instead of opening a new one each time you view a file.

The foolproof way to find any file, anywhere, anytime

Like I said, there are 8,722 files on my hard disk—give or take a few hundred—and the number gets bigger every day. How do I find the one I need right now? It used to be that you had to open all the files and look through them to see which one had the data you were looking for. With Windows NT, though, you can search through an entire hard disk to find any file, any time—even if you only remember a tiny scrap of information about it.

To set the Windows bloodhound on the trail, click the Start button and choose Find, Files or Folders. Use the Find Files command. You'll see a dialog box like the one in Figure 6.9. What do you do next? That depends on how much you remember about the file in question.

Fig. 6.9
Can't remember where you put that file? Fill in the blanks in this dialog box to ask Windows to look for it.

First, tell Windows what to look for. Enter any part of the name here; use the other tabs to enter information about the file's date and time, size, or any text inside.

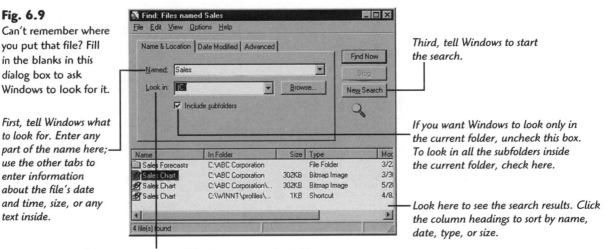

Third, tell Windows to start the search.

If you want Windows to look only in the current folder, uncheck this box. To look in all the subfolders inside the current folder, check here.

Look here to see the search results. Click the column headings to sort by name, date, type, or size.

Second, tell Windows where to look. You can choose any drive, any folder, or a single file.

I think I remember part of the name

If you know a word (or even a few letters) that you used in the file name, enter it in the box labeled Named. Windows will search for those letters at any position within a file name. For example, if you enter **LET**, the search results windows will show Letter to the President and Collette's Report because both have those three letters somewhere within the name.

TIP **You can sort the search results in four different ways. Click the** Name heading, for example, to sort by name, sorted in alphabetical (A-to-Z) order. Click again to sort in reverse (Z-to-A) order. The date, size, and folder headings work the same way.

I don't remember the name, but I remember when I saved it last

If you're sure you last saved the file sometime in the past month, click the Date Modified tab, and choose the option During the previous 1 month(s). You can also specify a range of dates here—for example, between March 15, 1996 and April 15, 1996.

I think I know which folder it's in

You can help Windows narrow down the search by specifying that folder (and only that folder) in the box labeled Look in. You can enter the folder name (**C:\Letters**) yourself, or click the Browse button to choose it from an Explorer-style list.

I remember a few words that were in the file

Obviously, it won't do you much good to search for common words like "the," but if you remember a specific phrase, you can have Windows track down all files containing that phrase. If you're looking for a letter you sent to President Clinton, for example, click the Advanced tab and enter **Clinton** in the box labeled **Containing text**. Then click the Find Now button to start searching.

How do I delete a file?

There are several ways to delete a file, or a folder, or any combination of the two. Depending on what you're doing, you'll probably wind up using them all at one time or another.

- From a folder window, select the icon or icons you want to delete, right-click, and choose Delete.

- Select the icon, then pull down the File menu and select Delete.

- Easier still, select one or more icons and press the Del key.

- If you can see the Recycle Bin on the desktop, you can also drag the selected files and/or folders and drop them on top of the icon. (I keep the Recycle Bin in the lower right corner of my screen just to make it easier to drag things there.)

No matter which way you choose, you'll see a dialog box like the one in Figure 6.10. If you'd rather skip that extra step every time, right-click the Recycle Bin, open its Properties sheet, and remove the check mark from the box labeled Display delete confirmation dialog.

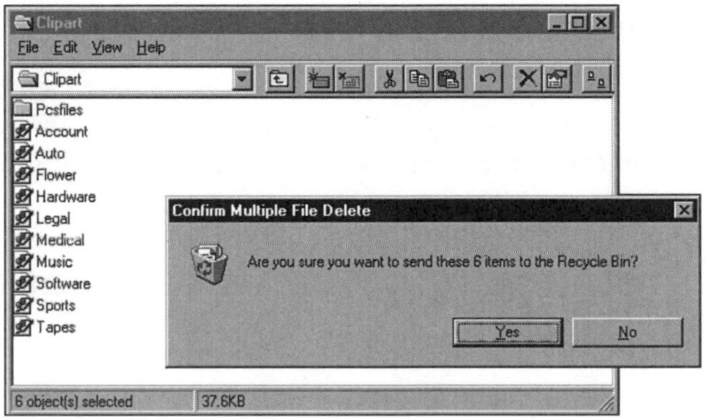

Fig. 6.10
Do you really want to delete these files? By default, Windows asks you to say OK every time you zap a file or folder.

![Clipart window screenshot showing a Confirm Multiple File Delete dialog box with the message "Are you sure you want to send these 6 items to the Recycle Bin?" and Yes and No buttons. The file list shows Pcsfiles, Account, Auto, Flower, Hardware, Legal, Medical, Music, Software, Sports, Tapes. Status bar reads "6 object(s) selected" and "37.6KB".]

Oops! The foolproof way to bring back a file you just deleted

Have you ever accidentally thrown away an important piece of paper? Uma Thurman's phone number, perhaps, or a sweepstakes check? If you really had won that publisher's sweepstakes, you'd root through old coffee grounds and eggshells to find that check. Fortunately, it's a lot less messy to recover lost files, thanks to the Windows Recycle Bin.

 TIP **What if you're absolutely, positively certain you want to get rid of** an icon once and for all? Right-click it, then hold down the Shift key as you choose Delete. When you use this trick, you'll bypass the Recycle Bin completely and simply vaporize the rascal.

How do I get my files back?

It's easy to tell when there's something in the trash—the Recycle Bin icon changes from empty to this full version. If you discover you need to resurrect a file you deleted earlier, double-click here. The window that opens up will look a lot like the one in Figure 6.11. Select the files or folders you want to bring back, then choose File, Restore. Unzap! It's just as if the files never went away.

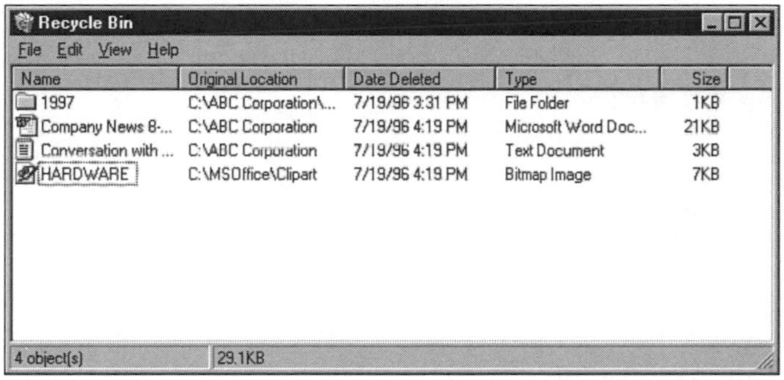

Fig. 6.11

To restore any of these deleted files, open the Recycle Bin, select the file or files to bring back, and choose File, Restore from the menu.

Name	Original Location	Date Deleted	Type	Size
1997	C:\ABC Corporation\...	7/19/96 3:31 PM	File Folder	1KB
Company News 8-...	C:\ABC Corporation	7/19/96 4:19 PM	Microsoft Word Doc...	21KB
Conversation with ...	C:\ABC Corporation	7/19/96 4:19 PM	Text Document	3KB
HARDWARE	C:\MSOffice\Clipart	7/19/96 4:19 PM	Bitmap Image	7KB

4 object(s) 29.1KB

What happens when the bin gets full?

The Recycle Bin isn't a bottomless pit. Sooner or later (probably sooner) you'll fill it up. When that happens, Windows automatically deletes files to make room for the freshly deleted ones. Of course, you can always tell Windows to take out the trash. Right-click the Recycle Bin, then choose Empty Recycle Bin.

CAUTION **When you're trying to make room on your hard disk to install a** new program, the Recycle Bin can drive you crazy. You delete some old files thinking that you're clearing space. Instead of freeing up room, though, Windows just moves the deleted files to the Recycle Bin, where they still gobble up the same amount of space. The moral: When space is at a premium, always remember to empty the Recycle Bin.

How can I cut down the Recycle Bin's appetite?

If you're running tight on hard disk space, you might want to restrict the amount of space that Windows sets aside for the Recycle Bin. To adjust this setting, right-click the Recycle Bin, choose Properties, and move the slider control left or right. If you have two (or more) hard drives in your computer, you can tell Windows to leave a different amount of Recycle Bin space for each one.

Using the controls here, you can even turn off the Recycle Bin completely, although you can't remove its icon from your desktop. Beware, though—if you take this drastic step, you lose the comforting ability to retrieve deleted files!

Using shortcuts

Sometimes a copy is better than the real thing. If you don't believe me, consider this scenario:

You, Ms. Sales Manager, have three rich and demanding customers. You keep each customer's sales records in a separate manila folder. You also have a product catalog the size of a phone book that you use, no matter which customer you're working with. If you make three copies of that catalog, and put one in each client folder, you've created a big problem the next time you revise your catalog. You have to remember to put a new copy in all three client folders, or you might wind up sending the wrong merchandise or charging the wrong price.

The solution is to store the catalog in its own folder, then store a note in each client folder that tells you where to find the catalog. That's how shortcuts work. They act like little notes that tell Windows to find something stored elsewhere on the disk, or even on another computer, and open it—right now. Shortcuts use only a small amount of disk space, and they can point to just about anything, just about anywhere: programs, documents, printers, and drives—even a location on The Microsoft Network.

How do I create a shortcut?

One of the most useful places to create a shortcut is right on the Windows desktop. For a program you use every day, like the Windows Calculator, why should you have to rummage through the Start menu? You don't want to move the program out of its home in the Windows folder, but you would like to be able to start it up by just double-clicking an icon. Here's how:

- If you already know where the program is stored, just open its folder or highlight it in the Windows Explorer. Drag the icon using the right mouse button, then drop it onto the desktop, choosing Create Shortcut(s) Here from the menu that pops up.

TIP **When you drag-and-drop a program to create a shortcut,** Windows calls the new icon Shortcut to ... the program's original name. You can delete the two extra words if you like, or even completely rename the shortcut. Word, for example, takes up a lot less screen than Shortcut to Microsoft Word for Windows.

- If you're not sure where the program is located, use the Create Shortcut wizard. Right-click the spot where you want the new shortcut to appear, and choose New, Shortcut. In the first step (see Fig. 6.12), you can browse through folders to find the program file; in the second step, you give your shortcut a name.

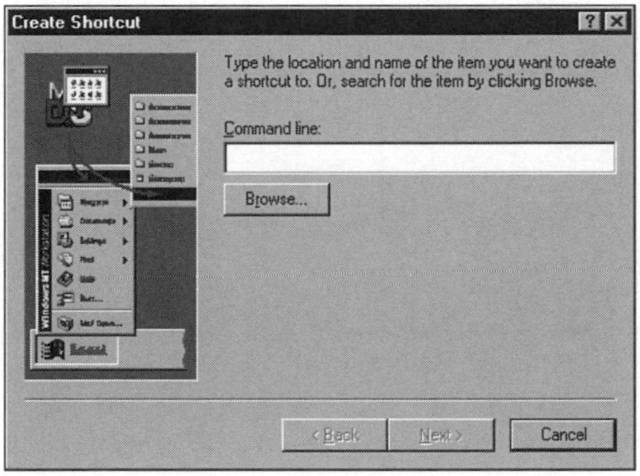

Fig. 6.12
The Create Shortcut Wizard lets you create a shortcut and name it in two easy steps.

How do I use a shortcut?

Just double-click it. Windows looks inside the icon, finds the shortcut note, and goes off to find the original file. If you've changed the name of the target file, or moved it to a new folder, it might take a few seconds.

Q&A *My shortcut isn't working. What's wrong?*
Right-click the shortcut icon, click Properties, and look at what's in the box labeled Start in. You might have to tell Windows to start in a different folder—the one where your data files are stored, for example.

Why is this DOS shortcut different?

When you start a program that was designed to run under MS-DOS, Windows needs to rush around like a nervous headwaiter getting things ready first. All those details are stored in the program's Properties.

With the help of the DOS program properties, you can control the amount of memory your DOS program gets, tell Windows whether to let it take over the whole screen or just run in a small window, and set dozens of technical options (see Fig. 6.13). Most of the time, you won't want to mess with these settings. If you have a DOS program that's giving you trouble, look in Chapter 11 for more details about how to get it working.

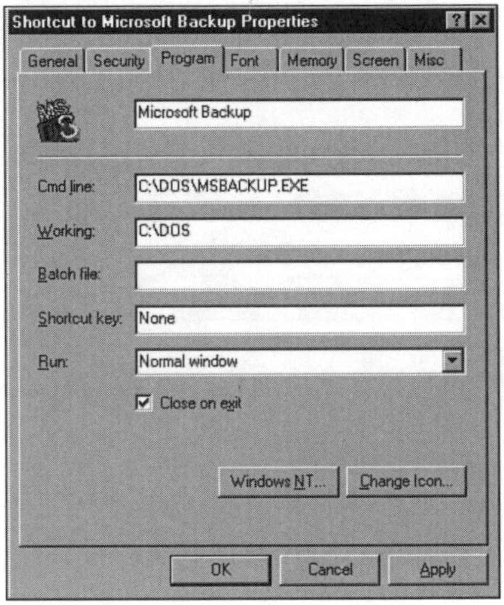

Fig. 6.13
DOS shortcuts are different. Look at all these confusing options!

7

Opening and Closing Windows

● **In this chapter:**

● **The whats, wheres, and whys of windows**

● **How do I open a window?**

● **You can—and should—run more than one program at a time.**

● **Want that window out of the way? Minimize it!**

● **OK, I'm through with this window. Now what?**

With a name like Windows NT, it only figures that the program's main building blocks are—you guessed it—windows . . . . ➤

Windows (with a big W) uses lots of individual windows (with a small w) to hold all the different things you're trying to juggle at once. One window might contain a memo to your boss, while another one might have a spreadsheet with the numbers you're supposed to put in that important memo. At the same time, you might have four or five folder windows open while you search for the memo you wrote last month. That's at least six windows already, and we haven't even counted that Solitaire game you've been playing while you thought no one was looking.

Sound complicated? It's not, really. Keeping track of five or ten windows and switching from one to another is no more difficult than zapping from CBS to NBC to HBO to the Home Shopping Network on your 163-channel cable TV system.

Of course, whether you're sitting in your living room or sitting in front of your PC, it helps to have a good remote control. And working with Windows' remote control (the taskbar) is a snap, once you know which buttons to push.

So what exactly is a window, anyway?

Whenever you double-click a folder, Windows draws a neat little rectangle on the screen and arranges the contents of the folder inside. That rectangle is a window. The same thing happens when you double-click a program icon—the program opens in a window. Think of a window as an enclosed patch of land where your data can roam freely. The outside edges of the window, called **borders**, act like fences to keep the window's contents from wandering onto the desktop or into another window by accident.

What's in a window?

Windows are incredibly versatile spaces that hold data, programs, lists of files…you name it. You can move them around on the screen, arrange them side by side, make them bigger or smaller, or expand them to fill the entire screen. When you want to move a window out of the way, you can even stuff it into a box and store it (temporarily) on the taskbar at the bottom of the screen.

No matter what you do with a window, though, the contents always stay inside the window's borders.

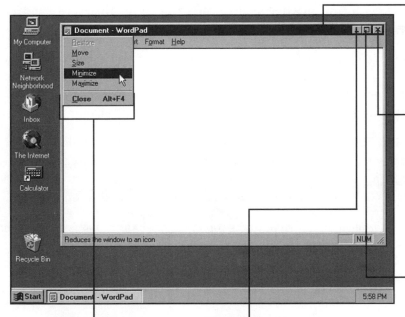

Title bar
Each window has its own name badge to help you figure out what's inside. Double-click any empty space here to maximize or restore the window.

Close button
X marks the spot when it's time to put a window away for good. Click here to close a window.

Maximize button
Want to give one window your full attention? Click here to "explode" a window to full size, covering up everything on the screen except the taskbar. This button changes to a Restore button after the window is maximized.

Control menu
The one-stop shopping center for people who don't like to push buttons. Click the tiny icon just to the left of the window's label to make this list appear.

Minimize button
You want the window out of sight, but you might need it again. Click here to stuff the entire window into a tiny box and store it on the taskbar.

I want to start a program

Before we tackle the hard scenario—juggling a whole screen full of windows—let's try something simple: working with a single window.

1 First, make sure no programs are running. (You'll see any running programs in the taskbar.)

2 Click the Start button, and click Programs.

3 Follow the cascading menu to the right, and click Accessories to bring up yet another cascading menu.

4 Now, click WordPad to start up Windows' built-in word processor.

You'll notice that it takes a few seconds before WordPad appears; that's because Windows has to go find the program on your hard drive and load it into your computer's memory.

When WordPad started up, it opened into a timid little window that only used part of the screen. Hmmm, that's not exactly what we wanted, is it? We want to devote our full attention to WordPad, and we don't need to see any other distractions on the screen. So let's **maximize** WordPad.

Look at Figure 7.1. See the three buttons at the far right of the WordPad window's title bar? The one in the center (it looks like a box with a thick border along the top) is the Maximize button. Click that button and stand back as the WordPad window zooms out to take over the entire screen.

The buttons at the far right of the top of each window change, depending on whether you've maximized the window or not. The Maximize button is in the center of the bottom set; once the window's maximized, Windows puts the Restore button there instead (top set), so you can switch back to a smaller window when you're ready.

That's much better, isn't it? The effect is just the same as if we'd clicked Channel 2 on our TV's remote control to watch David Letterman. The WordPad window now occupies the full screen, covering up everything except the taskbar down below.

When you **maximize** a window, it takes over the entire screen. As long as the window is maximized, there are a few things you can't do:

- You can't move the window around.

- You can't make it any bigger.

- You can't see its borders. For all intents and purposes, the edges of your monitor serve as the window's borders.

- You can't see anything on the desktop except the taskbar. If you want to open the My Computer window, you're out of luck until you figure out how to get this window out of the way (don't worry, it's not hard).

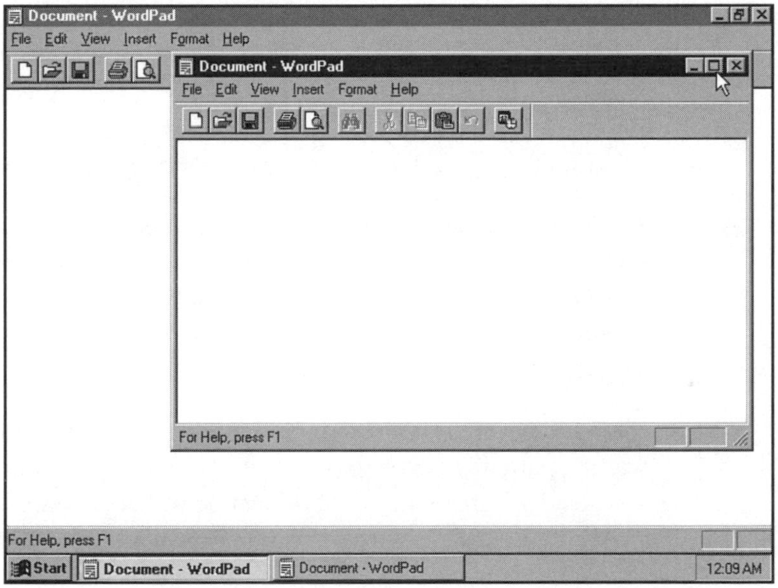

Fig. 7.1
To enlarge a window so it takes up the entire screen, click the Maximize button.

TIP **Are those tiny buttons too small to hit without squinting?**
Make the little suckers bigger:

1 Click the Start button and choose Settings, Control Panel.

2 Double-click the icon labeled Display.

3 Click on the tab labeled Appearance and watch the contents of the window change. Aha! Now click any of those pesky tiny buttons. If the box labeled Item contains the words Caption Buttons, you succeeded; otherwise, try again.

4 Now click the number in the box labeled Size, then press the up and down arrows to make the buttons grow and shrink.

5 When you're happy with your new, extra-large buttons, click OK.

There are more goodies you can change to make Windows your own—check out Chapters 13 and 14 for details.

I want to start another program

To open a second window, we don't need to do anything with WordPad. Let's just leave it there, and use the Start menu to run Paint, Windows' built-in drawing program. Click the Programs menu, then Accessories, then Paint. Here, too, we'll have to wait a few seconds while Windows reads the Paint program from your hard drive and loads it into the computer's memory.

Just like WordPad did, Paint starts in a small window, which means we can still see Wordpad in the background. Since we don't want any distractions, let's click the Maximize button to zoom Paint to full size, too. Now it's occupying the entire screen, just as if we'd switched to Channel 4 to watch Jay Leno.

What happened to WordPad? Nothing. It's still there in the background, waiting patiently for us to pay attention to it again. But the only thing we can see besides Paint is the taskbar, just below the maximized Paint window. If we wanted to, we could start another program right now. For now, though, let's stick with just two windows.

66 *Plain English, please!*

You can use Windows to do two, three, five, even twenty things—all at the same time—on your PC. Sometimes one or more of the windows in the background are actually working, doing things like formatting a floppy diskette, downloading a file from the Internet, or crunching a big batch of numbers. This frenzied, everything-happening-at-once activity is called **multitasking**. If there's nothing going on in the background windows, you're simply **task-switching** when you move from one program to another. 99

TIP   **The taskbar is anchored to the bottom of the screen when you** start Windows, but you can move it if you'd like. Aim the mouse pointer at the taskbar, click and hold the left mouse button, and then drag the taskbar to any side of the screen you'd like. It'll "stick" to the top, bottom, or either side.

I want to switch between two windows

Now that both programs are running, it's time to start zapping back and forth between them. For that, we'll need to use the taskbar.

The taskbar works just like your TV's remote control. Each time you press a button on the remote control, the entire contents of the screen change. Click! There's David Letterman! Click! There's Jay Leno! Click! There's Dave again! Each time you click a button on the taskbar, one (and only one) program comes to the foreground, and everything else seems to disappear. You know you can switch between programs any time, but as long as Dave is on the screen there's no sign of Jay, and as long as WordPad is showing, there's no sign of Paint.

3-D, without the funny glasses

How can you tell when a button on the taskbar (or anywhere else, for that matter) is "pushed"? The trick is to recognize some of the special effects that Windows uses to fake a three-dimensional look. And unlike those cheesy 3-D science fiction movies that were popular in the '50s and '60s, you don't need special glasses to see them.

When you look carefully at the Maximize, Minimize, and Close buttons in any window, you'll notice a thin white line that runs along the left and top edges of each button, and a corresponding thin black line that runs on the right and bottom.

The effect of these matching lines is to create the illusion that the button is sitting on top of the title bar, catching rays from a light that shines from the top left corner of the screen.

When you "push" a button, the lines reverse, with the left and top edges turning dark, and the bottom and right edges turning light. The image on the button's face also shifts slightly to the right. To your eye, which still thinks the imaginary light source is shining from the top left, it looks just as if the button is now depressed below the surface of the title bar.

Along the taskbar, the effect is more noticeable and a bit more dramatic, thanks to the lighter background behind the "pushed" button.

I want to switch between windows the fast way

There's an ultra-cool way to switch from one window to another without using the mouse or the taskbar. (In fact, it's so cool that the official Microsoft name for this little trick is Coolswitch.)

When you have more than one window open, hold down the Alt key and press the Tab key. Keep holding the Alt key down, but take your finger off the Tab key. A box will pop up in the center of the screen with the icons and labels for all your open windows (see Fig. 7.2 for details). To switch programs, hold down the Alt key and just keep hitting the Tab key until the icon that represents the program you're looking for is highlighted. Once you let go of the Alt key, the Coolswitch box will go away and your window will pop instantly into view.

Fig. 7.2
Bet your TV's remote control can't do this! Hold down Alt and press the Tab key repeatedly to zap among every window you have open.

The Argonne Anti-Jet-Lag Diet - WordPad

Can I move one window out of the way?

When you want to switch away from one window and start working on something else, Windows lets you set the first window aside temporarily. It's out of sight, but not out of memory. When you **minimize** a window, it's just as though you've taken the contents of that window, stuffed them into a box, and placed the box down on the taskbar. Everything in that window is still on call; you just need to push a button to bring it back.

Let's minimize both WordPad and Paint. To get Paint out of the way, push the Minimize button in the top right corner of the Paint window (it's the one with the small horizontal line along the button—the design is supposed to remind you of the taskbar). Do the same with WordPad.

Now press either button on the taskbar, and watch the same effect in reverse, as the window instantly zooms back up to its previous position.

What's the difference between minimizing and closing a window?

There's a critical distinction between minimizing a program and closing it. Remember how it took a few seconds for WordPad and Paint to load from the hard drive? In contrast, reloading either minimized application by pushing its taskbar button was nearly instantaneous.

When you **close** a window, you unload it from your computer's memory. In effect, you're telling it to go home and relax. If you decide you need it again, you'll have to wait while it wakes up, gets dressed, has a cup of coffee, and drives back to work. With a bigger program (like Microsoft Word or Excel, for example) it could take a minute or even longer for the program to go through all the rigmarole it requires to get up and running.

When you minimize a window, on the other hand, you leave it in memory. You're telling the program to go sit on the taskbar and take a quick coffee break. The next time you call, the program is still wide awake, fully dressed, and ready to get right back to work. Whatever documents you were working with are right there where you left them. If you had shut down the program, you'd have to find your file again, open it, and scroll down to the place you were working.

 TIP **You've probably had it drilled into you since you were a kid:** Clean up after yourself. Well, don't do it here. As long as your computer has enough RAM, don't close programs—instead, get in the habit of minimizing them. You'll save time, and as long as you have enough memory you have nothing to lose. How do you know when you're running low on memory? If Windows tells you it's run out of memory or system resources, or if you hear the hard disk chugging away continually, and there's a long delay every time you try to switch between programs, it's time to close a few windows (see "How do I close a window?" for more information). Of course, eventually you'll have to close those windows and save any open files before you shut down your computer.

TIP **When you've got a lot of windows open, the buttons on the** taskbar become unreadable. No problem—just point to any button and let the pointer sit there for a few seconds. Eventually, a little label called a ToolTip will pop up, telling you the full name of that button, including the name of the program and the document you were working on within the program (see Fig. 7.3 for an example). After the first tip appears, you can slide the pointer from button to button, and the remaining ToolTips will appear instantaneously.

Another fix for a full taskbar is to increase its height. Point to the top border of the taskbar, until you see a double-headed arrow. Then click and drag the edge of the taskbar upward to make the taskbar tall enough for two rows of minimized programs.

Fig. 7.3
Let the mouse pointer sit on top of any button for a few seconds, until the ToolTip label pops up; now you can slide the pointer from side to side to see what's what.

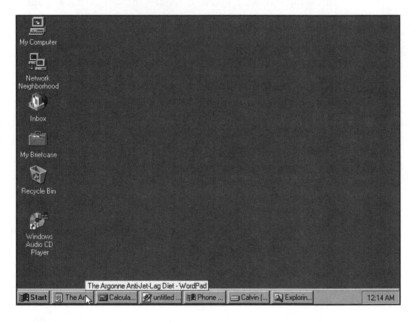

How do I close a window?

When you're absolutely, positively sure you're all done with a window, it's OK to close it. To make it disappear, press the Close button, which is the one labeled with a big X. The X means "go away." All done. Cross it off your list.

You can't get into trouble by pressing the Close button. If you've got unsaved work in the window you're planning to zap, Windows will give you the opportunity to save it before it goes away.

If you prefer to use the keyboard instead of the mouse, you can almost always use the keyboard shortcut Alt+F4 to close a window, too.

TIP **There's another way to minimize, maximize, or close a window:** Every window has a Control menu that you can pull down by clicking the small icon at the far left of the title bar. Frankly, it's easier to use the buttons on the right side, but there is one time when it helps to know about the Control menu: If your mouse stops working, you can open the Control menu with Alt+spacebar.

CAUTION **There's one last way to close a window, but it's strictly for** emergencies. If a program just stops, with no explanation, and won't go away, here's how to shut it down—losing all your data along with it, unfortunately. Press the Ctrl, Alt, and Delete keys simultaneously, then click the button labeled Task Manager. Choose the name of the "stuck" window from the pop-up list of Applications and click End Task. Don't even think of selecting an item on the Processes tab, though! The Task Manager should only be used as a last resort, when you're absolutely sure it's stopped working.

8

Moving Windows Around (and Moving Around in Windows)

● **In this chapter:**

- ● **Resizing a window for a perfect fit**

- ● **Picking a window to work with**

- ● **Are there different types of windows?**

- ● **Taking a scroll with the scroll bar**

- ● **Too many windows? Clean up with a couple of clicks**

Take advantage of Windows NT's everything-at-once capabilities. Once you know how to switch from one window to another, you'll never get lost. . . . . ●

S o far, we've been treating each window as though it were a
television screen where we can watch only one program at a
time. But suppose we replace our tired old TV set with a state-of-the-art,
501-channel, fully fiber-optic on-ramp to the Information Superhighway.
On the main screen, we might watch Jay Leno's monologue; but we'd use
the picture-in-picture feature to keep an eye on Dave Letterman, so we can
switch back when he gets to the Top 10 list. In fact, if we get a really hot
model, we can put CNN, The Disney Channel, and MTV on the screen all at
once, although even Larry King would have a hard time making sense of it all.

That's how Windows works when you really start to take advantage of its
everything-at-once capabilities. You can shrink a window so it occupies a
fraction of the screen, leaving you a clear view of the desktop—and other
windows—in the background. You can stack windows up like so many
"While You Were Out" message slips, and shuffle through them just as easily.
If a window is in the way, you can pick it up and move it somewhere else.

It's a great way to stay on top of all the demands of a typical workday. It's an
even better way to get thoroughly lost on the desktop, unless you know the
secret techniques for putting the right-sized window right where you want it.

How do I see what's behind this window?

The difference between maximizing and minimizing is an all-or-nothing
proposition. A window either takes up the full screen or it's stuffed into one
of those buttons on the taskbar. But as you saw when you started up the
WordPad and Paint programs, there *is* a middle ground between maximize
and minimize. From either state, you can **restore** a program or folder to a
window. As the name implies, restoring a window means putting it right back
where it was before, in the exact same position and trimmed to the exact
same size it was last time.

Unlike maximized applications, which hog every square inch of the screen,
once a program has been restored to a window, you can resize the window or
move it around. You'd pay hundreds of dollars extra to get this feature on
your TV set, but it's built right into Windows.

Windows hot spots

The Argonne Anti-Jet-Lag Diet - WordPad

File   Edit   View   Insert   Format   Help

The Argonne Anti-Jet-Lag-Diet

The Argonne Anti-Jet-Lag Diet is helping travelers quickly adjust their bodies' internal clocks to new time zones. It is also being used to speed the adjustment of shift workers, such as power plant operators, to periodically rotating work hours. The diet was developed by Dr. Charles F. Ehret of Argonne's Division of Biological and Medical Research as an application of his fundamental studies of the daily biological rhythms of animals. Argonne National Laboratory is one of the US Department of Energy's major centers of research in energy and the fundamental sciences.

How to avoid jet lag:

	Day 1 FEAST	Day 2 FAST	Day 3 FEAST	Day 4 FAST
Breakfast	high protein	light foods	high protein	light foods
Lunch	high protein	light foods	high protein	light foods
Supper	high carbo	light foods	high carbo	light foods

BREAK FINAL FAST
Westbound: If you drink caffeinated beverages, take them morning before departure.
Eastbound: take them between 6 and 11 p.m. If flight is long enough, sleep until destination breakfast time. Wake up and FEAST beginning with a high protein breakfast. Lights on. Stay active.

For Help, press F1

Title bar
Every window has a handle you can grab—this is it. Click anywhere on the title bar, hold down the mouse button, and drag the entire window to move it; let go of the left mouse button to drop it in its new location.

Maximize/Restore button
Zooms a window to take up the entire screen, or shrinks a maximized (full-screen) program or folder back to a window. The picture on this button changes, depending on whether the program or folder is maximized.

Window border
To make a window wider or narrower, taller or shorter, aim the tip of the mouse pointer at the edge of the window until the pointer changes into a two-headed arrow. Then click the left mouse button and drag the border; let go of the mouse button when the window is the right size.

Scroll bars
When there's more data inside the window than you can see at once, scroll bars appear. Grab the box in the center and drag it down to move the contents of the window up; drag it up to shift the window's contents back down. A horizontal scroll bar (which appears along the bottom of a window) works the same way, moving things from left to right.

Corner
Want to change a window's width and height with one smooth motion? Point to any corner and watch the cursor change to a two-headed diagonal arrow; then drag the window to its new size.

How do I put a program or folder back into a window?

How you restore a window depends on whether it's minimized or maximized at the moment.

If it's maximized—if you can't see anything else on the screen—look to the right of the title bar for the Restore button. It's supposed to look like two windows arranged one on top of the other, but I think it looks more like a coffeepot. Look at Figure 8.1 and judge for yourself.

Fig. 8.1
The Restore button. Click here to transform a maximized program or folder back into a window.

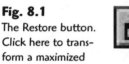

If WordPad isn't already open, start it up by using the Start button. Maximize the WordPad window, then push the Restore button to send it back into a window. Did you notice that the window returned to the exact size and position it was in when you started it up? Now press the Minimize button to temporarily stow WordPad on the taskbar.

Now that the WordPad window is off the main screen, there's no Restore button—but we can still make it return to a window with two swift clicks. Aim the pointer at the WordPad button on the taskbar and right-click. There, at the top of the popup menu, is the Restore command. Click it, and WordPad snaps back into its familiar window on the desktop.

TIP   **This is yet another illustration of a fundamental Windows NT** principle: When in doubt, right-click. You'll be amazed at the sheer number and variety of menus you'll see when you right-click seemingly random objects such as taskbar buttons, as shown in Figure 8.2, and those little icons at the right of the taskbar!

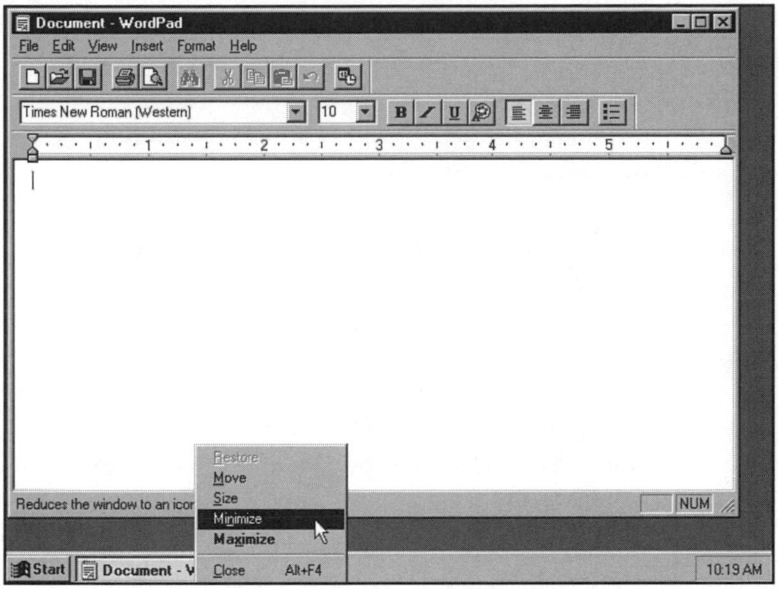

Fig. 8.2
Right-click any taskbar button to display this shortcut menu. From here, click to restore a program to a window, maximize it, or kiss it goodbye.

TIP **When it's time to close a few windows, use this popup menu to** quickly get rid of the ones you no longer need. Right-click the window's taskbar button, and choose Close.

How do I know which window I'm working with?

You can have hundreds of windows open simultaneously, but Windows can only focus on one window at a time. You use the mouse pointer like a spotlight to tell Windows which one you want to work with. No matter how many windows you can see on the screen, only the window you select can be in the foreground; all the rest stay in the background, waiting for their turn in the spotlight.

Windows uses the terms **active** and **inactive** to distinguish between a window in the foreground and one in the background. The term's pretty stupid when you stop to think about it, though. When you click in a window, it doesn't suddenly become active. It just sits there, waiting for you to start typing or clicking. If you want something to happen, *you* have to do it! Harrumph....

Anyway, there are two cues you can use to tell which window is active. First, it usually won't be covered by any other window. Second, the title bar changes color. Unless you've fiddled with your desktop colors, Windows uses a dull gray for the title bar of a background (inactive) window, and bright blue for a foreground (active) window.

Why do some of my windows look different?

Most program or folder windows look and act alike, but you'll notice a big difference when you work with a window inside another window. These **document windows**, found in programs like Microsoft Word for Windows and WordPerfect for Windows, are generally pretty similar to program windows, but there are a few subtle differences. When you minimize a document window, for example, it doesn't plop down on the taskbar; instead, it shrinks into a miniature box, complete with its own Restore, Maximize, and Close buttons, at the bottom of the program window.

 TIP   With any window—even a window inside another window—there's an easier way to maximize and restore. You don't need to hit that tiny button at the right of the title bar. Just aim anywhere in the title bar, and double-click to switch back and forth between a window and a maximized program.

It doesn't matter what's inside—most windows work exactly the same way

- Most windows "remember" the size and shape they were in the last time you used them.

- Most windows remember their position on the desktop, too.

- It's easy to move a window almost completely off the screen. This is a little disturbing the first time you see it, but it's perfectly normal.

- Some windows can't be resized. The Windows Calculator, for example, is always the same size.

- A few special windows have an "Always on Top" option. Windows Help lets you do this, for example, so that you can follow step-by-step instructions in another window without losing your place. But most windows move meekly into the background when you click another window.

Q&A ***I accidentally made a window so small I can't see the menus anymore. What do I do now?***

No problem. It may not look like a window, but it still acts like one. Aim the mouse pointer at any corner of the window until it turns to a diagonal, two-headed arrow. Now click the left mouse button and drag the window's borders out until the window is a more useful size.

This window is too big!

There are plenty of reasons why you might want to adjust the size of a window. The number one reason is so you can see another window or the desktop. Unlike our picture-in-a-picture TV, you're not limited to a single size and shape, either; you can make one of these windows tall and narrow, or short and wide. It's up to you.

Resizing a window sounds easy, but it takes a little practice. Most people have trouble the first few times they try it. The secret? You have to hit the ultra-slim border *just right*—you'll know you've succeeded when the pointer turns into the two-headed arrow you use to resize the window. It's not easy. If your hand trembles ever so slightly, the pointer slips and you have to start over again.

When you're aiming at a window's border, the tip of the arrow is the only part that counts. That end consists of one tiny dot, and you're trying to use that dot to hit a window border that's as thin as a piece of thread. If you're having trouble resizing windows, why not make the borders a little bigger? Right-click anywhere on the desktop, choose Properties from the popup menu, and when the Display Properties dialog box appears, click on the tab labeled Appearance. Click inside the box labeled Item, then click on the arrow at the right of the drop-down list and select the `Active Window Border` entry. Now click in the box labeled Size and use the up arrow to increase the setting from a measly 1 to a wider 3 or 4. Click OK and try again. There—isn't that easier?

How small can I make a window?

The correct answer is "Ridiculously small." Just for fun, let's make the WordPad window as small as possible. Aim the mouse pointer at the window's lower right corner until it turns to a two-headed diagonal arrow.

Now drag the window border up and to the left until there's nothing left but a title bar and a couple of buttons (see Fig. 8.3). That's pretty useless, isn't it?

Fig. 8.3
Click here, drag there. If you go too far when you're resizing a window, this is what you'll wind up with. Not very useful, is it?

How big can I make a window?

Let's try the other extreme. Grab the lower right corner of our microscopic Wordpad window and drag the two-headed arrow as far as possible toward the lower right corner of the screen. Whoa! It looks almost like a maximized window, and it's nearly impossible to find the borders. This type of too-big window isn't very useful, either.

What's the right size for a window?

When you're working with individual windows, follow the Goldilocks principle: The perfect window is not too big, and it's not too small. What's just right? Well, the window should be just big enough to show you what you need to see inside, yet small enough to let you see the rest of the desktop and any other windows you need to work with.

Grab the lower right corner of the WordPad window (if it's truly at the edge of the screen, you may only be able to see half of the two-headed arrow) and drag to the top left until the window is a reasonable size.

CAUTION Remember, some windows, like the Windows Calculator, are a fixed size and can't be resized.

I want this window out of the way

When you click in a window to make it active, the window will always cover up anything underneath it, including the desktop and other windows. To see what's underneath, move a window out of the way by using its built-in "handle"—the **title bar**. It's an easy, four-step process:

1   Click anywhere in the window you want to move, to make sure it's in the foreground.

2   Click anywhere on the title bar, and hold down the left mouse button.

3   Drag the window wherever you like.

4   Let go of the mouse button to drop the window in its new location.

Q&A   ***Hey! I can move the window off the screen! What's going on here?***

That's perfectly normal; in fact, it's a convenient way to take a quick look at the rest of the desktop without minimizing the window you're working with. If the window moves so far off the screen that you can't get it back, here's the secret fix: Don't switch to another window. Instead, hold down the Alt key and press the spacebar. That will pull down the window's Control menu. Press the letter **M** (for Move), and then use the arrow keys to slide the window back toward the main screen. When you can see enough of the title bar to grab, press Enter, and move the window using the mouse.

Help! My document won't fit in the window! Now what?

At the end of every television program, a list of credits appears on our super-duper state-of-the-art set. If David and Jay could handle their shows with a staff of 10 or 12 people, all those credits would fit on a single screen. In Hollywood, of course, even the guy who drives the catering truck gets his name in the closing credits. They could squeeze all the names onto one screen by printing them in type so small you'd need the Hubble Space Telescope to read it. Instead, the director displays the credits on a long list that rolls up from the bottom of the screen and disappears into the top as new lines force their way up from underneath.

Windows does exactly the same thing when there are more words or numbers or icons than you can see in a window. To see all the data in a window like this involves **scrolling** through the window. When you scroll through a window, you move up, down, left, and right to bring the hidden contents into view.

How to scroll a document

Let's fill our WordPad window with more data than we can see at one time. Type a few words, press Enter, and repeat until you've forced a few lines off the top of the screen. As the first line disappears, you'll see a thin vertical bar appear along the right side of the window. There's an up arrow at the top of the bar, a down arrow at the bottom, and a rectangular gizmo in the middle, as shown in figure 8.4.

66 *Plain English, please!*

Believe it or not, the box within the scroll bar is called a **thumb**, and sometimes a **handle**. In previous versions of Windows, the thumb was always one size; in Windows NT 4.0 and Windows 95, however, the thumb becomes larger or smaller to reflect the percentage of the document you can see in the window. (A big thumb means you can see almost the entire document in the visible portion of the window; a small thumb means you'll have to do a lot of scrolling to see the entire document.) This feature is called a **proportional thumb**. 99

Fig. 8.4

When there's more in your document or folder than the window can hold, a vertical scroll bar appears along the right edge of the window. Grab the button in the middle of the scroll bar, and drag it up and down to see the window's full contents.

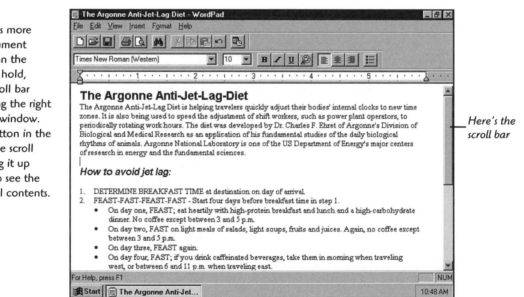

Here's the scroll bar

Imagine that the contents of the window are printed on a long piece of paper, and that you can see a portion of it through the window. The button in the middle of the scroll bar—the thumb—acts like a handle attached to the rope that pulls the piece of paper up and down, so you can see different sections of the paper. When the handle is up, you're seeing the top part of the paper. When it's down, you're seeing the bottom part.

When the scroll handle hits the top or the bottom of the scroll bar, you've gone as far as you can go. There's nothing more to see in the direction you've been scrolling.

 TIP **You can move the scrolling list up and down in two other ways as** well: click the arrows at the top and bottom of the scroll bar. With each click, the list will move a short distance. To move in giant steps through the window, click in the middle of the scroll bar, above or below the handle. The contents of the window will jump a full window at a time.

How much data is there?

In most windows, the size of the scroll handle tells you how much (or how little) is hidden from view. The bigger the handle, the less there is in the rest of your window, and vice versa. If you were looking at the file that contains this book, for example—all 90,000 words of it—you could probably scroll through 900 screens before you read every word. In this case the scroll handle would be a tiny square floating in a big empty scroll bar. On the other hand, with a file that's just one line longer than your screen, you'd get a scroll bar with a jumbo-sized handle.

I can't see the right side of the screen, either

Scrolling a window horizontally is a little less common, but the principle is exactly the same. If the contents of your window stretch to the right or left, and your window isn't wide enough to show it all, a horizontal scroll bar will appear. Drag the handle to the left or right to pan through the entire window.

These windows are a mess!

Sooner or later, despite all the resizing, reshaping, moving, and manipulating, you'll wind up with too many windows on the screen. You can't concentrate, and you can't find *anything*. How do you clean up the mess? That depends on what you really want to do. In every case, the secret is to point to an empty space on the taskbar and right-click. The pop-up menu that appears (see Fig. 8.5) gives you three basic options, explained in just a second.

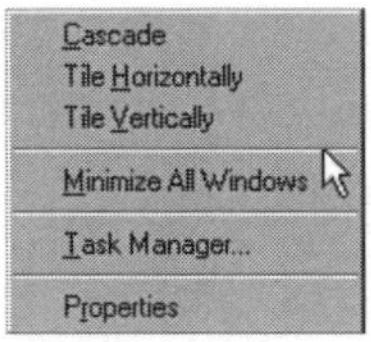

Fig. 8.5
Use the taskbar's pop-up menu to rearrange windows with precision. Right-click any free space in the taskbar to make it appear.

I want to focus on one window, but see all the rest

Then choose Cascade from the taskbar's pop-up menu. This option stacks all the windows one on top of the other (**cascades** them), fanned out like a poker hand, with just enough room to see the title bar and left edge of each window beneath the active window on top. (Fig. 8.6 shows an example of several cascaded windows.)

TIP If the Tile menu didn't produce the results you expected, don't despair. Right-click the taskbar again, and you'll see a menu choice that wasn't there before. Choose Undo Tile to put everything back the way it was, then rearrange windows and try it again.

Fig. 8.6
The Cascade option lets you fan out every open window, like a poker hand.

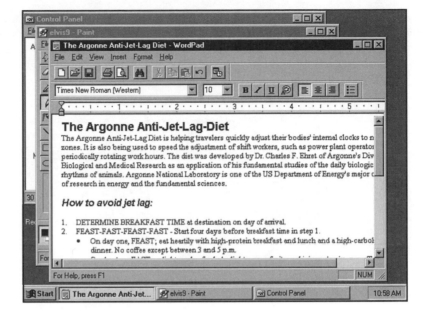

I want to see several windows at one time

Then choose either of the **Tile** options from the taskbar's pop-up menu, and stack the open windows alongside one another. Tile Vertically resizes every open window, and lays them out edge-to-edge, side-by-side, as if you were laying tile on the kitchen floor. Tile Horizontally arranges the open windows, edge to edge, from the top to the bottom of your screen. Either way, unless you have a jumbo monitor, you're better off trying this trick with two or three windows only; any more, and every window becomes too small to use comfortably.

Fig. 8.7
The Tile option arranges two or more windows alongside one another, either horizontally (as in this example) or vertically.

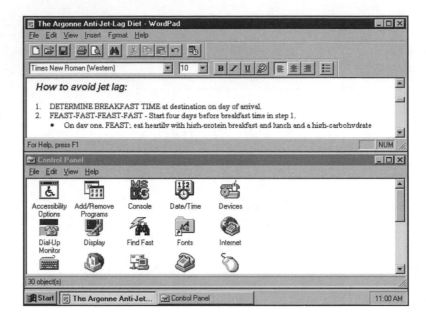

I want all these windows off my desktop. Now!

Then right-click the taskbar, choose <u>M</u>inimize All Windows, and watch each window shrink down onto the taskbar, one after another. When the job's all done, you're back at a sparkling clean desktop, with no annoying windows.

 TIP **Want a little extra room on the screen? Then "hide" the taskbar.**
Right-click in any empty space on the taskbar, and choose Properties from the popup menu to give yourself a little extra room on the screen. Click the tab labeled Taskbar Options, and find the box that says A<u>u</u>to hide. Click in the box to make a check mark appear, then click OK to close the dialog box. The taskbar disappears, giving you a little more working room. To make it reappear, just bump the mouse pointer into the bottom edge of the screen. Shazam! Up pops the taskbar.

CAUTION **Be careful you don't accidentally open two copies of the same** document at the same time! With some programs and most folders, when you click the icon and the window is already open, Windows just switches you to that window. But other programs (including WordPad) let you open a new copy of the program in a new window, without warning you that another window is open. If you're not careful, you might forget that you opened your document a while ago and made some changes without saving them. If you open the same file in a new window, make some more changes, and save that file, you might accidentally overwrite the changes you made in the first one. The only cure is to keep an eye on the taskbar and watch out for duplicate windows.

9

Working with Windows: Mice, Menus, and Dialog Boxes

● In this chapter:

- The function you're looking for is on the menu

- Making menu selections

- Where can I find menus?

- Providing more info with a dialog box

- How to use every button and gizmo in a dialog box

They may not be flashy, but menus and dialog boxes are your key to controlling Windows' every move . . . . ➤

ommunicating with a computer is a tricky business. For all its speed and power, your PC is actually the strong, silent type: it has a limited vocabulary, it doesn't understand English, and you definitely can't talk to it. So how do you tell Windows exactly what you want to do—no ifs, ands, or buts? Simple. You ask Windows for a list of all the things your PC is capable of doing right now; then pick one.

These plain-English lists are called **menus**. After you make your selection from the list, Windows passes the instructions along to your PC in a way it's guaranteed to understand. If Windows needs more information—for example, if you ask it to save a file and it needs to know what you want to name the file—it will pop up a fill-in-the-blanks form called a **dialog box** to make the process a little easier.

Menus and dialog boxes are the most common ways to communicate with Windows and Windows applications. And here's the good news: They look and act the same no matter where you are in Windows. Once you master a few simple concepts, you're well on your way to telling your computer exactly what you want it to do.

What do I do with these menus?

A menu is simply a list of choices. You use menus all the time in your every-day life. When you drive up to the order window at McDonald's, you pick your lunch from a menu. When you withdraw cash from your ATM, you touch a menu on the screen to tell the bank's computer to hand over a few $20 bills. Menus are always tailor-made for the circumstances: You can't get a burger and fries at the bank, and there's no way Ronald McDonald will fork over forty bucks. The same is true of Windows menus: the actual choices you see will be different, depending on the kind of window with which you're work-ing; only the choices that make sense will be on the list.

When you choose something from a Windows menu, you're telling Windows you want it to do something. Whatever you click might perform an action, or it might pop up a box asking you for more information. Or it might do nothing at all.

Mastering menus and deciphering dialog boxes

Menus and dialog boxes help you and Windows communicate without any misunderstandings.

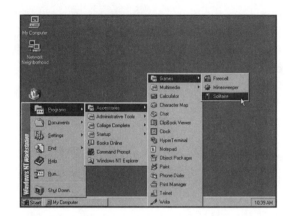

Start menu: *Windows' home base. Click the Start button to see a list of all the things you can do with Windows*

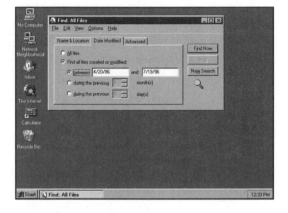

Dialog boxes: *just fill in the blanks and go. When Windows needs detailed information from you, it will pop up one of these handy fill-in-the-blanks forms.*

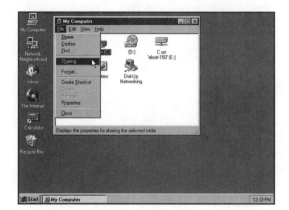

Pull-down menus: *command central for Windows programs. Whenever you want to do something in a window, these handy lists are the first place to look.*

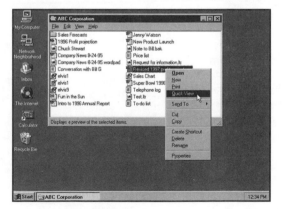

Pop-up menus: *quick shortcuts for common commands. Point to an item and right-click to get a list of options you're most likely to need for that item.*

The Start menu: Click here to begin...

OK, you've wandered into the Windows desktop and you're not exactly sure where to go next. When you want to know where you can go, it's time for a visit to the Start menu, which pops up when you press the Start button at the bottom-left corner of your desktop.

No other menu, anywhere else in Windows, is quite like this one. What's different? For one thing, you push a button to get to it; with other menus, you click a word or an object. For another, the Start menu extends upward from the bottom of the screen, unlike other Windows menus, which follow a more conventional top-down organization. It's more colorful, with icons for each entry instead of simple lines of text. You'll also notice that the Start menu uses cascading menus, in which one menu choice leads to a brand-new menu (follow the small black arrowheads in Figure 9.1 to pick up the trail of cascading menus).

66 *Plain English, please!*

Cascading menus get their name from the same effect you'll notice if you watch a waterfall as it rushes down a cliff. Each time the stream of water hits a rock, it splashes off to the side to form a new waterfall. If you can't remember what a cascading waterfall looks like, it's time to get up from that computer and take a vacation! 99

Fig. 9.1
The Start menu is the first place to look when you're not sure where to go next. Cascading menus lead you automatically to other programs and other places in Windows.

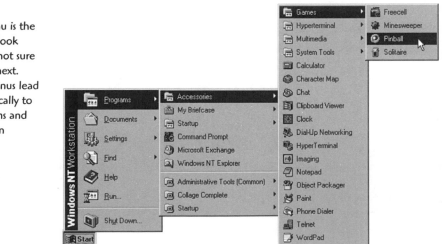

You'll use the Start menu every time you fire up Windows, but you'll use the two other kinds of menus—pull-downs and pop-ups—much more often.

Why is there an arrow next to some menu choices?

With cascading menus, one thing leads to another. When you rest your mouse pointer on a menu choice with one of those small black arrows, another menu pops out, usually to the right. After you see the new menu, you're free to move your mouse pointer to one of the choices on that menu, where you may find even more cascading menus.

TIP   **Sometimes, menus cascade in a different direction than you** expect. If Windows sees that it's run out of room on the right side, it will pop up the new cascading menu to the left. If there's no room below, the new menu may shift up on your screen.

Suppose, for example, that you want to open WordPad so you can write a short report. Here's how it's done:

1 Click the Start button.

2 Move the mouse pointer to Programs. When you do this, a **pop-out menu** cascades off to the right.

TIP   **Cascading menus take some getting used to. If you find that they** disappear before you can make your choice, try slowing down a little. When the menu appears to the right, move the cursor slowly, in a straight line, to the new menu. Now you can move up or down as fast as you like.

3 Move the mouse pointer to Accessories. When you do this, a second pop-out menu cascades off to the right, and displays the names and icons of all the Windows accessories.

4 Move the mouse pointer to the WordPad choice, and click once to open WordPad.

Pull-down menus: open-and-shut cases

Pull-down menus are *everywhere* in Windows. With a few rare exceptions, everything you can do in any Windows program is available underneath one of these main menu choices. (Sometimes your choices are buried under two or three cascading menus, but they're almost all in there somewhere.)

To find a pull-down menu, just look for the **menu bar**, right underneath a window's title bar. Think of the menu bar as a long curtain rod, with each individual menu hanging from it in a neat line. Each menu unrolls like an old-fashioned window shade to reveal the list of choices printed on it (see Fig. 9.2). Getting to a pull-down menu is easy: just point to one of the keywords on the menu bar, and click the left mouse button to unfurl it.

Generally, your choice of pull-down menus is **fixed**; that is, the selections on the menu bar remain the same, no matter what you're doing in the program. Double-click My Computer, for example, and you'll see the same menus—File, Edit, View, and Help—every time, without fail. Sometimes, however, the choices on a pull-down menu vary, depending on what icon you have selected or what kind of file is open.

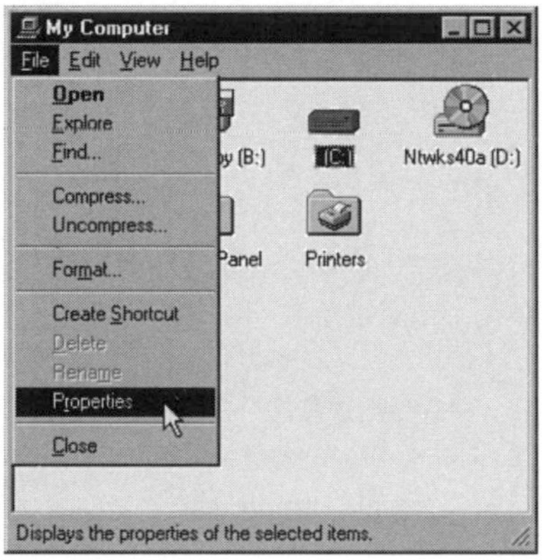

Fig. 9.2

Everything you could possibly want to do in Windows, you can do from a pull-down menu. Use the File menu in the My Computer window, for example, to open or close a file, or even to find a file or folder when you're not sure where you put it.

Q&A *My mouse works, but I prefer the keyboard. How can I make menu choices without a mouse?*

Press the Alt key and the underlined letter of a menu name to open a menu or highlight a command. Press the down arrow to move the highlight down the list of commands in a menu. Press Enter to choose the command, or Esc to close a menu and say "Never mind, I don't want any of these."

Pop-up menus: shortcuts and settings

To uncover the last menu type, we'll have to go on the Windows version of a treasure hunt, because pop-up menus (sometimes called shortcut menus) are literally hidden throughout Windows. Revealing these buried treasures doesn't take a pick and a shovel, though—just a click with the right mouse button (see Fig. 9.3).

Fig. 9.3
Position the mouse pointer, click the right mouse button, and pop goes the menu. To pick a menu selection, point to your choice and click the left mouse button once.

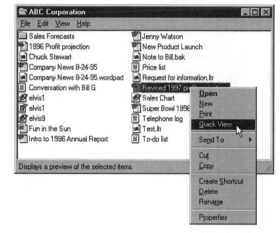

TIP **Besides being hidden, pop-up menus are unlike pull-downs in** another way: the choices available from a pop-up menu change, depending on what you're pointing to. But you'll almost always see a choice called Properties, which will give you detailed information about whatever you're pointing to.

What can I do with pop-up menus?

You'll use pop-up menus for two main reasons: as shortcuts and to adjust the settings of nearly everything within Windows. The shortcut part is easy: when you click the icon for your hard drive, notice how the first three choices on the pop-up menu are the same as the first three choices on the pull-down File menu. To adjust settings for a particular piece of hardware or a specific part of Windows, you'll use the Properties menu choice to pop up a properties sheet; you'll find references to these properties sheets nearly everywhere in this book.

I use the pop-up Properties menu all the time to make sure there's enough room on my hard disk before I copy a large file there. It's a simple process:

1 Double-click the My Computer icon to open a window showing all the drives on your computer.

2 Point to the icon for your hard drive (drive C:), and click the right mouse button once.

3 Move the mouse pointer to Properties (at the very bottom of the menu), and click with the left button.

4 Check out the colorful pie chart Windows draws to show you how much of your hard disk has been used and how much is free. If you see only a tiny sliver of free space, it's time to put that disk on a diet! (For tips on how to slim that disk down, see Chapter 5.)

5 Click the Cancel button to make the Properties sheet disappear.

TIP   **How do you know when a pop-up menu is available? You don't.**
So, anytime you're not sure what to do, just point at something and click the right mouse button. Trust me: There's no way you can hurt your system just by popping up a menu, so click away.

Pop-up menus can be extremely useful, and sometimes the only way you'll find out about them is by accident. Suppose, for example, that you've been trying to find a file on your hard drive, and you've cluttered up the entire screen with stray windows. You'd like nothing more than to sweep them all out of the way in one motion. You don't know whether the taskbar has a pop-up menu, but you can find out by aiming the mouse pointer at the taskbar and clicking the right button. Yep, there's a pop-up menu, all right, and one of the choices is Minimize All Windows. Click there and voilà, your screen is clean again.

TIP   **I'm constantly amazed at the things I discover when I right-click**
some objects. For example, if you have a CD-ROM drive like mine, you can right-click its icon, choose Eject from the pop-up menu, and watch the CD slide out of the drive without any human intervention.

Selecting from the menu

Anything you can do in Windows, you can do with the help of a menu. It might not always be the fastest way, but it's guaranteed to work. If you're ever stumped at how to get a particular job done with a Windows program, your best bet is to look on every menu you can find—sooner or later, the command you're looking for will turn up.

Don't forget the basic principle of Windows: First select, then act. Before you can pick something from the menu, you have to point at it.

What are my choices?

Remember, pull-down menus work just like window shades. When you pull down the shade, it stays down. And when you click a pull-down menu, the menu stays down, too, even if you lift your finger from the mouse button. That makes it easy to move through the menu searching for the right choice. Once you've found the menu choice you're looking for, just point at it and click again.

The whole point of pull-down menus is to make Windows easier to use, so it's reassuring to know that there are a few widely accepted conventions you can count on. The first two menu choices on the left are almost always File and Edit, and the last menu on the right is usually Help (see Fig. 9.4). What's in-between is different for every program.

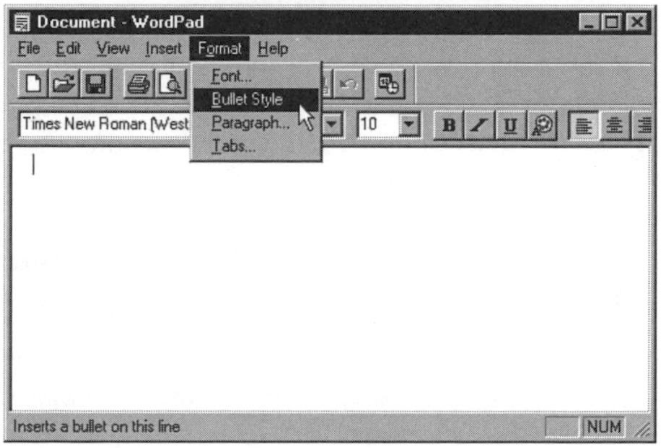

Fig. 9.4
Most Windows programs follow common conventions for the main menu. WordPad's main menu, for example, features the familiar File, Edit, and Help menus. Specialized menus like Format are displayed in the middle.

TIP You can almost always close a program by choosing E**x**it from the bottom of the **F**ile menu. You can almost always get information about a program by choosing **H**elp, **A**bout.

How do I move to the next menu?

Notice how the mouse pointer is "sticky"—even when you take your finger off the mouse button, it keeps tracking through the menu choices as you move the mouse—left and right, up and down. To see all the main menus, just move the pointer along the keywords in each menu bar.

Why don't some menu commands work?

Sometimes choosing a menu item does something right away. If you choose **F**ile, **S**ave, for example, and you've already given your file a name, a program like WordPad will simply save your most recent work using the existing file name, and return you to what you were doing.

But sometimes a menu choice does nothing at all. You can point and click until your finger falls off and nothing happens. What's going on? You've stumbled on a menu choice that's temporarily unavailable. Maybe you were working on a word processing document, and tried to use the **P**aste command without first cutting or copying something to the Clipboard.

Windows could simply remove the **P**aste choice from the **E**dit menu, but then you'd be left scratching your head. "I know it was there a minute ago," you'd say, as you scrambled through all the other pull-down menus to find the missing command. And you'd be right. So instead of leaving you to guess whether or not you can do something, Windows **grays out** the command (see Fig. 9.5 for an example), to let you know that it's still there—it's just not available for you to use right now.

Q&A *I chose a command, but nothing seemed to happen.* *It wasn't grayed out, but it isn't working. What's up?*

Is there a check mark next to the command you think is not working? If there is, click the command again. Now is it doing what you expect?

Some commands are like on/off switches. A check mark means it's "on"; the lack of a check mark means it's "off."

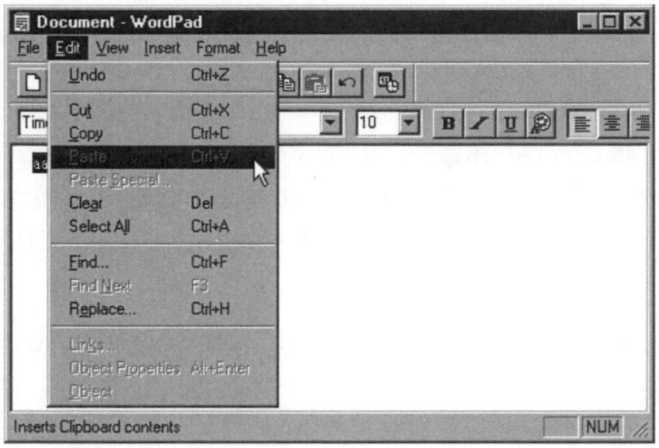

Fig. 9.5
When a menu choice is temporarily unavailable or inappropriate, it doesn't disappear from the menu. Instead, Windows "grays out" that choice so you'll know it isn't working right now.

How do I get rid of this menu?

When you want to roll a window shade back up again, you've got to give it a snap. A Windows menu works in much the same way. If you decide you don't want to choose anything from the menu, just give a quick click anywhere in the window *except* on the menu itself to make the menu roll up again.

Can we talk? Windows and dialog boxes

Sometimes, a simple menu choice isn't enough to get what you want. If you're sitting at a sidewalk cafe in the rue de Dialog and you use your high-school French to order *le Big Mac*, your waiter will know that you want a burger, but he won't know *how* you want it. Medium rare or burnt? Do you want lettuce and tomatoes? How about catsup? And would *monsieur* or *madame* care for some *pommes des frites* on the side? Sigh .... Wouldn't it be convenient if you could just point to all your choices at once?

Well, that's precisely what Windows lets you do. Instead of bombarding you with one question after another, Windows puts together a simple fill-in-the-blanks form and hands it to you. You check a box here, pick an item off a list there, fill in the empty spaces, and hand it back by clicking the OK button. These interactive forms are called **dialog boxes**, and you'll use them constantly when you work in Windows.

Why do I have to deal with dialog boxes, anyway?

Windows is constantly asking you for more information. When you print a document, for example, you'll have to answer a few questions: Where's the printer? How many copies do you want? Do you want to skip any pages? What kind of paper? And so on.

Fortunately, you'll find the same kind of gizmos and widgets in all of Windows' dialog boxes.

For example, let's say you've just created a file using WordPad, Windows' built-in word processor, and now you want to save it. You get the ball rolling by doing the following:

1 Choose File, Save. Windows displays the File Save As dialog box shown in Figure 9.6.

Fig. 9.6
To save a file in WordPad, you use a dialog box to tell Windows exactly where and how you want it to store your work.

You tell Windows what you want to call the file.

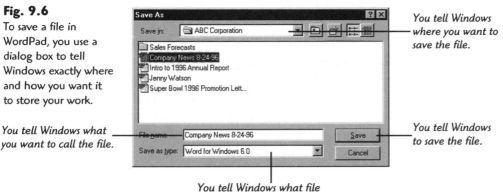

You tell Windows where you want to save the file.

You tell Windows to save the file.

You tell Windows what file format you want to save it as.

2 Give the file a name.

3 Press OK if you want to save the file to the default directory.

The conversation can be as short and sweet as that, or you can get more elaborate: Which file format would you like to use? Which folder do you want to store the new document in? Windows will take its best guess, but you'll need to make the final decisions.

Dialog boxes look like program windows, but they behave a little differently. Generally, you can't change the size of a dialog box, although you can move it around on the screen. And they're as persistent as a door-to-door salesman— in most cases, when a dialog box pops up on your screen, you've got to deal with it before you can do anything else.

> **TIP** **Sometimes, a dialog box gets in the way of the very thing you** need to see to answer one of its questions. Although you can't resize dialog boxes, you *can* move them around the screen and out of the way. Put the mouse pointer on the title bar, click and hold down the left button, and drag the box to another location. That way, you can deal with those persistent questions without losing sight of your work.

Dialog boxes come in all shapes and sizes. Fortunately, they're made out of interchangeable parts, so once you learn to recognize the pieces, you'll know how to deal with any dialog box.

Different types of dialog boxes...

When you see a dialog box, odds are it popped up for one of three reasons:

- **Windows has a message for you.** It could be an error message ("I can't find that file"). Or it could be a more benign bit of information ("Congratulations! You've successfully installed WonderWord Pro! Please be sure to send in your registration card today!"). In any case, your only option when you see a message box is usually OK (although there might also be a Help or Details button to choose, which would provide more information about the message).

- **Windows wants you to make a choice.** If Windows were a close-up magician, it would ask you to pick a card—any card. You'll see this option when your choices are limited.

- **Windows needs more information.** Sometimes, *you* hold all the cards; for example, when you want to save a file, you can usually give it any name you'd like. In this case, Windows simply presents an empty box and says, "Type something here, please."

Dealing with dialog boxes

When you're faced with a new dialog box, don't panic—it may look different, but it works just like every other dialog box in Windows. Table 9.1 is your secret decoder ring.

Table 9.1   Dialog box controls and buttons

What's it called?	What does it look like?	What do you do with it?
Button. When you're done with a dialog box, your main choice will be the OK button. Other popular buttons include Cancel ("Oops! I didn't mean to open this dialog box!"), Help, and Close. If you see an ellipsis (...) following the label on a button, you can expect to see another dialog box when you press that button.		Press the OK button to send your input on to Windows. Press the Cancel button to back out without doing anything. Press Help if you're not sure what to do next.
Input box. When Windows wants you to type something and doesn't have a suggestion, it shows you an empty box.	*Containing text:*	Click inside the box and start typing.
Drop-down list. Sometimes, Windows knows what you want to do, but wants to make sure you can choose another option if you wish. In file boxes, for example, Windows assumes you'll want to use drive C:, but lets you pick a floppy drive or CD-ROM if you prefer. A drop-down list looks a lot like an input box, except that it offers you multiple choices.	[C:] ▼ My Computer 3½ Floppy (A:) 5¼ Floppy (B:) [C:] Ntwks40a (D:) C on 'Ebott-150' (E:)	Type in your choice (even if it's not on the list). Click the arrow just to the right of the box to view the other choices on the list.
Scrolling list. When Windows is pretty certain that you'll want to pick one item from a long list, it uses a scrolling list. The scroll bars look and act just like the ones you'll find elsewhere in Windows.	Wallpaper cars castle chitz egypt honey	Pick an entry from the list. Windows won't let you type in anything that isn't already on the list.
Check box. These tiny boxes come in handy when you need to make a simple yes-no decision. Sometimes a section of a dialog box will contain a number of check boxes arranged together.	☑ Password protected	Click the box to add a check mark; click again to remove the check mark.

What's it called?	What does it look like?	What do you do with it?
Radio button. Sorry, you can't get news, sports, or weather on your PC. But if you think of the buttons on an old-fashioned car radio, you'll understand how this control works—and how it got its name. Since you can't listen to more than one station at a time, when you push one button, the one that had been depressed pops out. (The one that's currently "pushed" has a black mark inside the circle.)	Display: ⊙ Tile ○ Center	When you see a dialog box that contains two or more choices with a circular button in front of each entry, you have to choose one and only one of the options.
Spinner. Spinners work like the numbers on a safe—the number in the box goes up and down when you click the matching arrow.	Wait: 15 ⏶ minutes	Click the up or down arrow to make the value in the box higher or lower, respectively.
Slider. Have you ever stood on a doctor's scale? Then you know how this control works. You drag the indicator to change the value.	10%	Slide the indicator to the right or left to make the value bigger or smaller.

Getting around in dialog boxes

If you've ever filled out a census form or taken part in an opinion poll, you'll feel right at home with dialog boxes. It's not a test; it's simply a convenient way for Windows to gather a lot of information in a very small space.

Most of the choices you'll make in a dialog box are simple and straightforward. Check boxes, for example, are easy—a check means yes, and a blank box means no. Radio buttons and drop-down lists are equally easy, as long as you're careful to click in the right place.

Scrolling lists can be trickier to work with, especially when they're used to keep track of files and folders. To see an example of how to move through a scrolling list, right-click any blank space on the Windows desktop and choose Properties. Click the index tab labeled Background (you'll find it at the top of the box). You'll see the dialog box shown in Figure 9.7. Now look at the matched pair of scrolling lists: one for patterns, the other for wallpaper. Use the up and down arrows to move through the lists. When you see an entry you like, click it.

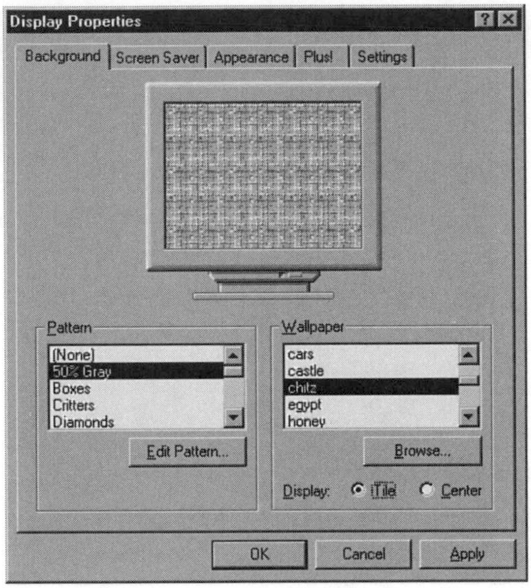

Fig. 9.7
Scroll through the list
to select the back-
ground you want on
your Windows desktop.
You can use the arrow
keys, the mouse, or the
keyboard to move
from one entry to the
next.

TIP   **This one's a real time-saver: When a drop-down list or a scrolling** list contains lots of files, a simple shortcut lets you jump quickly through the list. Just press the first letter of the item you're looking for. For instance, if you're looking for a file named Sales Report, just press **S** to skip straight to the first entry that begins with that letter. In a long list, you can type the first few letters very quickly. In a folder window, for example, if you want to jump to the Sales Report file, you can type the letters **SAL** in quick succession; Windows will take you there.

It's easiest to work with the mouse, of course, but a few keys serve crucial functions when it comes to getting around in dialog boxes—especially crowded ones. The Tab key, for example, moves you from one section to the next, and the cursor keys (the up and down arrows) move between different options within each section. To set a check mark without using the mouse, just hit the spacebar.

TIP   **If a dialog box still has you stumped and leaves you speechless,** remember that you can press F1 (or the Help button, if there is one) for help written just for that dialog box. Help will pop up in its own box on-screen to explain what's in the dialog box and what you're supposed to do.

66 *Plain English, please!*

When you get help that's specifically designed for the task or box you're working with right now, it's called **context-sensitive help**. Pressing F1 will often get you context-sensitive help, no matter what you're working on. 99

Q&A *Hey—this dialog box won't let me do anything! What's up?*

It must be either inappropriate or impossible for Windows to do what's in that section of the dialog box. When that happens, you'll usually see that section grayed out.

OK? Cancel? You make the call

When you click OK, you're sending your message to Windows, and it's going to do exactly what you asked it to do. If you decide that's not what you want, don't click OK—instead, back out gracefully by clicking the Cancel button that appears in many dialog boxes. If there's no Cancel button, you still may be able to back out by pressing the Esc key. If you click OK and don't like the results, you can sometimes reverse what you've done by choosing Undo.

Q&A *My mouse isn't working. How do I get around in a dialog box without it?*

When you press the Tab key, you move forward to the next option in the tabbing order of a dialog box. As you move, the option that is currently chosen has a dotted line around it, or is highlighted. (Sometimes the highlight can be hard to see. If you're not sure which option is highlighted, press the Tab key repeatedly until you're sure where it's ended up.)

Press Shift+Tab to return to the previous option in the tabbing order. Press Enter to carry out the options you have chosen.

If one of the letters in a button or a label is underlined, you can use that letter to move directly to an option. Press Alt and the underlined letter at the same time. For example, to move to the File <u>N</u>ame option in the above example, press Alt+N.

How Common Dialog Boxes Work

Pick the folder to look in or save from the tree-style list here. Your desktop is always at the top of the tree—it's a handy place to set temporary files where you won't forget them. Or click the drop-down arrow at the right, pick drive C: under the My Computer icon, and keep double-clicking until you find the folder you're looking for. Or double-click the Network Neighborhood icon on your desktop to find a folder on a computer elsewhere on the network.

Switch between icon view (easy to read) and a details view (fewer objects visible, but more information, including date and size).

Move back up the tree to the folder the current folder is stored in.

Create a new folder.

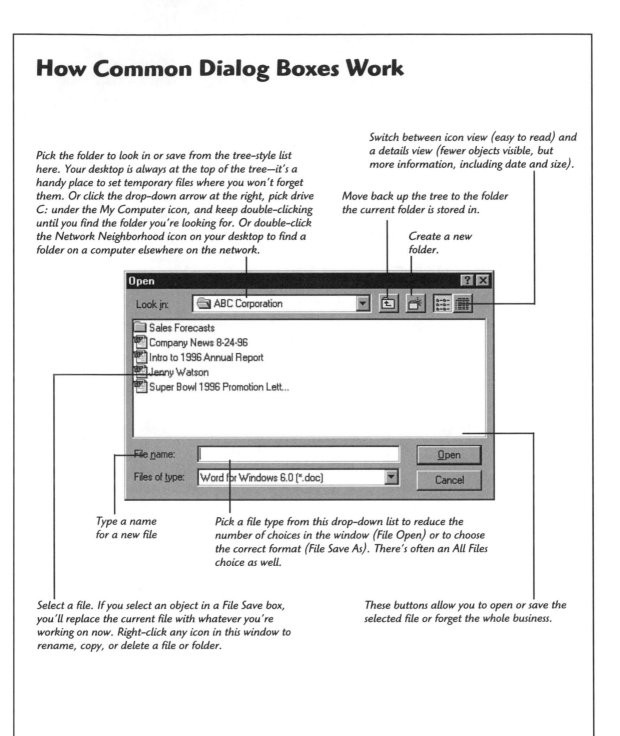

Type a name for a new file

Pick a file type from this drop-down list to reduce the number of choices in the window (File Open) or to choose the correct format (File Save As). There's often an All Files choice as well.

Select a file. If you select an object in a File Save box, you'll replace the current file with whatever you're working on now. Right-click any icon in this window to rename, copy, or delete a file or folder.

These buttons allow you to open or save the selected file or forget the whole business.

Common dialog boxes

Most dialog boxes look and act very similar, but some are absolutely identical. When you tell any Windows program to open or save a document, you'll see one of these **common dialog boxes.**

With virtually all Windows programs, the dialog boxes you see when you choose File Open, File Save, and File Save As are exactly alike. In fact, these dialog boxes are just another variation of the Windows Explorer, which we'll cover in more detail in Chapter 10.

Part III: Working with Applications

10

Setting Up New Programs (DOS and Windows)

● In this chapter:

- Easy installation with the Add/Remove Programs Wizard

- How to respond when Windows begins asking technical questions

- What to do when a program doesn't run right

- Tips and tricks for making DOS programs behave

You can do more with Windows than play Solitaire (most days, anyway). Here's how to set up new programs—and your old favorites, too . . . . ➤

When you add a new program to your PC, it has to go through a short getting-acquainted drill with the rest of your computer. The whole process is not that different from what you would do during the new-employee orientation program your first day on a new job. You'll meet the folks in the mail room, someone will issue you a phone number and a badge, and you'll pick up an armload of office supplies. After that, the boss will show you your new cubicle and your old computer (unless you landed a really great job, that is, in which case you'll get a corner office and a shiny new Pentium PC).

So, how does orientation work for a new application program? First, it has to check in with Windows, and then, if necessary, it introduces itself to other programs you use. It has to find a home folder, and it has to make a note of any special instructions that you give it. Sound like a lot of administrative overhead? It needn't be. A good installation program takes care of all those details behind the scenes.

How do I install a new Windows program?

The nice thing about Windows programs is that they all work pretty much alike, starting with the installation. Most of the time, setting up a new application is a simple point-and-click proposition. But you can speed up the process if you know how to add a new piece of Windows software to your system.

Start with Setup...

 These days, most software arrives on a handful of floppy disks or a CD-ROM. The most popular way to get started is to put a disk in your drive and run an installation program—usually called Setup. It's so easy, in fact, that Windows can do the process automatically: click the Start button and choose Settings, Control Panel; then double-click the Add/Remove Programs icon. You'll see a dialog box like the one in Figure 10.1. Click the Install button, and follow the wizard's instructions, clicking Next and then Finish as you complete each step.

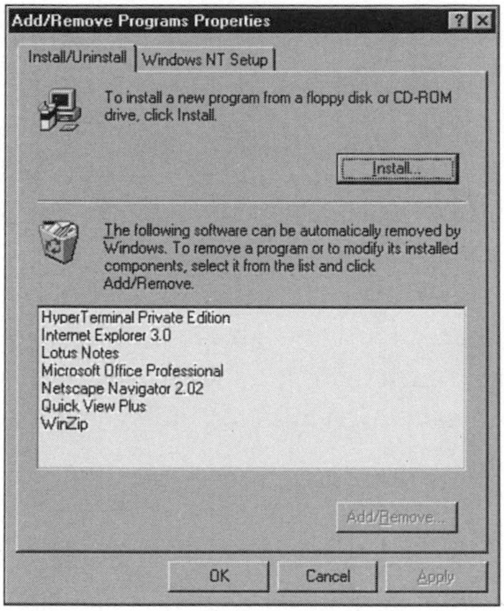

Fig. 10.1
To set up a new Windows program (or get rid of one you don't want anymore), use the Add/Remove Programs utility in the Windows Control Panel.

Add/Remove Programs Properties

Install/Uninstall | Windows NT Setup |

To install a new program from a floppy disk or CD-ROM drive, click Install.

Install...

The following software can be automatically removed by Windows. To remove a program or to modify its installed components, select it from the list and click Add/Remove.

HyperTerminal Private Edition
Internet Explorer 3.0
Lotus Notes
Microsoft Office Professional
Netscape Navigator 2.02
Quick View Plus
WinZip

Add/Remove...

OK | Cancel | Apply

TIP **Some programs have taken the idea of automatic installation to** an extreme. With some AutoPlay CD-ROMs, for example, all you have to do is insert the CD into your drive and click a button. Other programs, especially updated software that you download from Microsoft's World Wide Web site, offers to install itself automatically if you give Windows the OK. When Windows makes this kind of offer, just say yes.

Answer a few questions...

Almost all Windows Setup programs ask the same questions over and over again: In which folder would you like the program files to be stored? Do you want to install all of the program, or just parts of it? Do you want to create a new group of icons cascading out from the Programs entry on the Start menu? Once you've answered all the questions, you're ready for the tedious work of swapping floppy disks. (Unless your software came on a CD-ROM, of course, in which case all you need to do is sit back and watch—once you see the Setup program start to copy files to your hard disk.)

TIP **Just say yes! Windows and Windows programs that use SETUP will** almost always suggest the best place to store files. These preferences are called **defaults**, and you're less likely to get into trouble if you simply accept the defaults. If Microsoft Office wants to create a folder called C:\MSOFFICE, let it.

Make your preferences known...

Occasionally, the Windows Setup program will ask you some more detailed questions. For example, a word processor might ask you if you'd like to install its built-in grammar-checking module, or it might ask for your name and address so it can add that information automatically to your letters and envelopes. In some cases, the program will even order you to shut down Windows and restart so that it can be sure that all the changes it made actually go into effect. Answer the questions as best you can, but don't worry too much: There's no such thing as a failing grade, and you can always run the Setup program again if you miss something important the first time around.

Try it!

If everything went well, the new program probably added itself to the Start menu. To find the program icon, click the Start button, select <u>P</u>rograms, and look for the folder that contains the new icon. When you find it, click and hold your breath. If it starts and runs properly, congratulations! You've successfully installed the new program.

New software? It's not as easy as you think ...

Why does Setup have to be so complicated? Why can't you just copy a bunch of files to your hard disk and get to work? Well, with a few programs you can, but those efficient little marvels are few and far between.

There are good reasons for using the official installation routine, not the least of which is consistency: You can be sure you won't miss an important step.

The Setup routine typically copies all the program files and stores their locations, a description of the data files the application uses, any personal preferences you enter, and all the technical information the program needs to communicate properly with Windows. By the time Setup is done, you might have files scattered all over your hard disk: Besides the application's own folder, you can sometimes find new files in a special Windows NT folder called System32 and in the place where you store your data.

If even one of those pieces is missing, your new application probably won't work. And that's why it pays to follow the standard operating procedure, even if it seems a bit overcomplicated.

Q&A *I just added a new program, and now I can't find it. What should I do?*

Click the Start button and choose Find, Files or Folders. In the box labeled Named, type part of the name you're looking for. Click the Find Now button, and if you're lucky the shortcut to your program will appear in the list below. If you still can't find it, choose View, Arrange Icons, by Date. The most recent files will float to the top, and your new program may be there. Once you find it, drag its icon onto the Start menu to add it to the top of the list.

The Wizard didn't work. Now what?

The Add/Remove Programs Wizard is convenient, but it isn't actually that smart. It does nothing more than search your floppy disk and CD-ROM for a file called Setup (or Install). What happens when it can't find that file? You'll see a dialog box like the one in Figure 10.2.

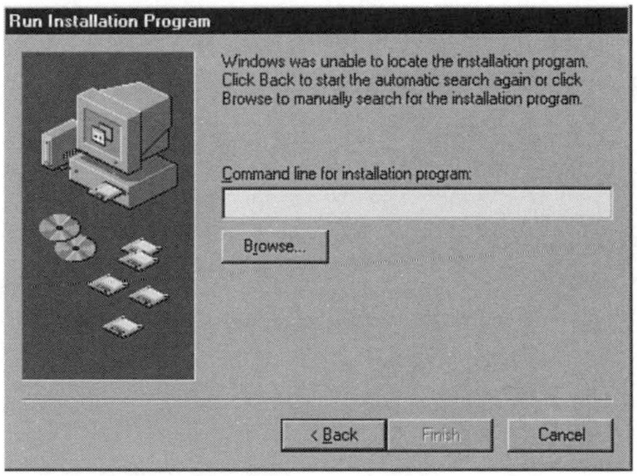

Fig. 10.2
Oops! If the Wizard can't finish the job, you'll have to step in and do it yourself. Click the Browse button to start.

Run Installation Program

Windows was unable to locate the installation program. Click Back to start the automatic search again or click Browse to manually search for the installation program.

Command line for installation program:

[   ]

[Browse...]

[< Back] [Finish] [Cancel]

What happened? One of two things, probably. Here's what to do in either case:

- Windows might have had trouble finding the Setup program. Maybe it had a different name, like Wsetup. Or maybe the Setup program is in a subfolder where Windows doesn't know to look. The solution is to click the Browse button and look on the floppy disk or CD-ROM for the Setup program, then double-click it yourself.

- Windows might expect you to install the program using a special type of file called a Setup Information file. These files are easy to see: They have an icon that looks like a piece of paper with a gear on it, similar to the one in Figure 10.3. If you can't find another Setup option, right-click this icon and look for Install on the pop-up menu. Clicking that choice starts the Setup process.

Fig. 10.3
When the Wizard can't find a Setup program, look for a Setup Information icon like this one, then right-click and choose Install.

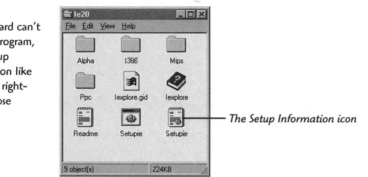

——— *The Setup Information icon*

![Q&A] **Windows told me that some of the files I'm trying to install are older than the ones I already have. What's that all about?**

When you use the Setup program that comes with some Windows programs (especially older ones), watch carefully as status messages flash by on the screen. Windows will warn you when a program tries to add files to the System or System32 folder on your computer. Now, if the files were from 1993 and you were using a version of Windows that was produced in 1992, this would probably be the right thing to do. But it's definitely a no-no to put those 1993 files in the 1996 version of Windows NT.

Fortunately, Windows anticipates this possibility and asks your permission before it replaces a shiny new file with an out-of-date one. Just keep the newer files and you'll be OK.

Why doesn't this program work right?

When is a Windows program not a Windows program? When it's an old Windows program that doesn't understand how to work with Windows NT 4.0, of course.

Now, there's nothing wrong with being old—sooner or later it happens to all of us. But the single biggest problem with Windows programs that were developed before mid-1995 is that they don't understand how to deal with long file names. If you use one of these older programs, any files you use with that program will be limited to eight characters and a three-character extension.

For a graphic example of the problem, look at Figure 10.4. On the top is the up-to-date Windows NT version of Notepad. Go ahead and open a file—it's not hard to tell what's inside each one. But now look at the old Notepad from Windows 3.1, below. The same files show up with cryptic, confusing names like TO-DOL~1.TXT. Is that your to-do list? Probably, but who can be sure?

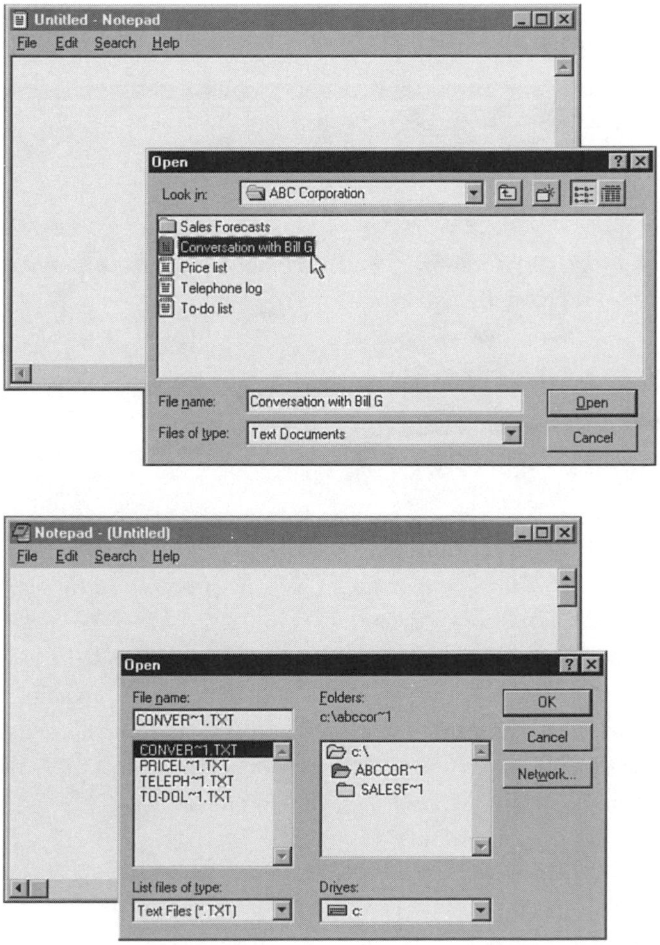

Fig. 10.4

One great reason to insist on new, 32-bit versions of your programs. The new Notepad (above) shows you plain-English file names; the old version (below) keeps you guessing.

It's not you, it's a bug!

When you walk into a computer superstore, you'll see aisle after aisle of Windows software. All told, you can take your choice of thousands of programs. Is that good news? Well, that depends. People have been writing Windows programs for years. Some are good programmers, some aren't. Some programs that worked just fine under old versions of Windows will do all sorts of screwy things when you try to use them with Windows NT.

If you've installed a program successfully but encounter odd behavior when you try to run it, don't assume you're doing something wrong. You could be looking at a **bug**—simply put, whoever wrote the program made a mistake. Sometimes you can work around bugs; other times you can't. But it helps to know what you're up against.

Getting your 32 bits' worth

What kind of software should you feed Windows NT? Well, it can digest almost any Windows programs, even those 16-bit programs that were originally designed years ago for Windows 3.1. But Windows NT runs best on a steady diet of new 32-bit software.

What's the difference? Why should you care whether your software is 16 bits or 32?

Each bit represents a digit in Windows' binary counting system, and the total defines how much working room a program has in memory. Programs written in 16 bits can work with a puny 64 kilobytes of memory at a time, or roughly as much as you'll find in a pocket calculator. By contrast, 32-bit software means Windows NT programs can use up to 4 *gigabytes* of memory, which is a lot of breathing room. The old programs spend all their time moving data through this tiny block of memory (a process called paging), while you wait.

All that memory is what makes it possible for Windows NT to keep track of long filenames and to keep multiple programs going without getting confused.

How can you be sure your software is up-to-date? One surefire way is to look on the box. If the box says it's compatible with Windows NT 4.0, you'll have no problems. If the box has the Windows 95 logo on it, it's a 32-bit program and will probably work well with Windows NT (although there are some Windows 95 programs that don't). And if it's an old 16-bit program (designed for use with Windows 3.1), don't be surprised if you encounter some problems.

Here are a few of the puzzling symptoms you might see when you run into a bug in a program.

- Your application simply disappears—now you see it, now you don't. The program attempted to save some data in a protected portion of the computer's memory. Windows NT won't allow a program to do this because it might cause problems with other software, so it simply killed the program. (You'll lose any unsaved work, unfortunately.)

- Your system freezes up. You might be able to move the mouse, but nothing happens when you tap the keys or click the mouse button. Just wait—most often the system will return in a minute or two. If it doesn't, press Ctrl-Alt-Del to pop up the Windows NT Security box and click the button labeled T̲ask Manager. Now you can select the one that isn't responding and click End Task. In the rare cases when this tactic doesn't work, the only cure is to turn the PC off and then back on again.

- Everything begins to move at a glacial pace. It might not be a bug: When your PC begins to sllllooooowwwwww dooooooooooooown like this, you might just be running low on memory. Close some other windows and see if performance improves. If the problem persists, though, save what you're working on and try closing all open programs, then restarting your computer.

- You see a bright blue screen filled with white error messages and lengthy lists of numbers. That generally means there was an error within Windows itself. You'll have to restart your computer. If it happens more than once in a blue moon, ask your system administrator for help.

- You see a Windows dialog box telling you your application has caused a general protection fault (see Fig. 10.5). Click OK, and see if you can get back to work. You'll probably lose anything you haven't saved lately.

66 *Plain English, please!*

Protection? Is this some kind of racket? Nope. Windows is talking about memory. Every program you run should have its own chunk of memory that no other program can touch. If another program's data accidentally gets mixed into that space, there's no telling what can happen. But it's usually not good.

Suppose your office building has a well-organized team of messengers whose job is to carry packages from one suite to another, all day long. Each time a messenger picks up a package, he checks the address label and delivers it to its destination. But what happens if a package is mislabeled? Maybe the freshly ground coffee goes to the person who changes the toner in the copy machine, while the toner ends up in the coffee room. (Bleccchh.)

Windows has built-in protection against this sort of thing, designed to keep your other programs from being damaged by a buggy program. The usual cure is to shut down the guilty program, no questions asked. The moral? Save your data regularly! 99

Fig. 10.5
Here's what a General Protection Fault error message looks like. It's a warning that something's gone wrong, and displays some techno-babble for any programmer who might be looking over your shoulder.

If your computer consistently acts up when you try to run one particular program, contact the company that made the software (or ask your network administrator to contact them) and ask if they know about the problem. They might have a new, fixed version they can send you. If they don't, ask them when they're going to fix the bug.

TIP **What should you do if your computer crashes? Don't kick the** computer; instead, close any open files (if you can) and restart your computer. Windows NT has a special program that repairs any damaged files on the hard disk each time you start up. This extra step will make sure you don't have any serious problems that will get worse later.

What do I do with these old DOS programs?

You might have a collection of DOS programs that you've been using for years, and when you upgraded to Windows NT, they remained on your computer. Surprisingly, Windows NT makes it very easy to deal with old DOS programs, the kind that don't use windows, icons, and—in some cases—even the mouse. If you have one of these programs, the easiest way to set it up is to drag its icon onto the Start button; then, to launch it, click its entry in the Start menu.

Most DOS programs work just fine under Windows NT. But some need a bit of special treatment, and the first place to look when you're having trouble is on the program's Properties page. Right-click the program icon, then choose Properties. You'll see a dialog box with six tabbed sheets, each one filled with complicated options. You can find a few helpful things among all that mumbo-jumbo.

 TIP **Windows stores all the technical details about how to run a DOS** program in a special type of shortcut called a **Program Information File**. The extension attached to is DOS name is the same as its abbreviation—**PIF**. When you use the DOS Properties sheet, you're actually making changes to this PIF shortcut. Don't be confused when you see the original program and this shortcut in the same folder—clicking either one will start your program just fine.

Here's some hard-won advice on whether and when to mess with the shortcuts for your DOS programs:

- If it ain't broke, don't fix it.

- Use context-sensitive help to learn what each item in the dialog box is. (See Chapter 4 for more details about Help.)

- If you're having a lot of problems with DOS programs, start up the Windows NT Help file and look on the Index tab for "optimizing, MS-DOS programs," as shown in Figure 10.6.

Setting up a DOS program

If you absolutely must fiddle with DOS applications, here's where to look.

General
Strictly informational. There's almost nothing you can change here.

Security
You can check the restrictions on a file here, but these settings probably won't affect your DOS programs.

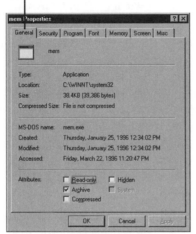

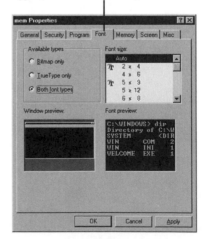

Program
If you have trouble starting the program, try setting the Working folder to be the same as the one in which the program is stored. You can also click in the Shortcut key box and define a Ctrl- or Alt-key combination that will pop up the program in a hurry. The Windows NT button is strictly for experts.

Font
Scroll through the list of fonts to make the text in the window bigger (and more readable) or smaller.

Setting up a DOS program (continued)

Memory
Most of these options are strictly for propellerheads, but if your program is causing trouble, check the Protected box and try again. Also try setting the EMS and XMS memory options to Auto. (But don't ask what those abbreviations stand for!)

Screen
Do you want the program to run in a window or puff up to fill the entire screen? You make the call. You can also have a DOS toolbar on a window, if you'd like.

Misc
More technical mumbo–jumbo, except for the Allow Screen Saver check box. Some DOS programs freeze at the mere mention of screen savers. If your program is like that, uncheck the Allow screen saver box here so that your screen saver won't start while you're using this program.

Fig. 10.6
Working out the kinks in an MS-DOS program. Windows can offer detailed help if you're having problems getting a DOS program to work properly.

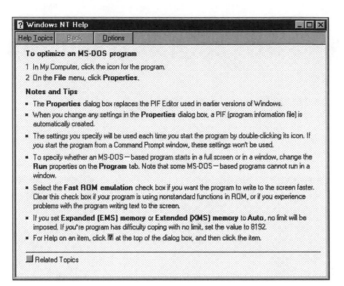

How does Windows know what kind of file this is?

To start a program, you don't have to click its icon. If you've found a file that was created by that program, you can double-click that file's icon and launch the program instantly, with the file you clicked already loaded.

How does it work? Well, Windows knows that every file on your PC has a first name and a last name. The first names have to be unique, but the last name (also known as the **file extension**) works just like your family name to identify a family of files that look and act somewhat alike. When you double-click one of these files, Windows looks up its file type and says, "OK, the DOC extension means this is a document, and I need to use WordPad to open it."

Here are a few important facts about this whole process:

- File types are based on file extensions.

- Extensions have to be "registered" with Windows before your applications can automatically start up when you double-click a document.

❝ *Plain English, please!*

How does a file type get **registered**? When you first set up a program, part of the process includes telling Windows which file types it can open and save. For instance, when you install Microsoft Word, the Setup program tells Windows to reserve the .RTF and .DOC extensions for its use. These extensions are "registered"—that is, added to a master list of extensions that Windows knows about. When you double-click a data file to open it, Windows looks in this list to see which program to use. ❞

- Registered extensions are usually hidden from you when you view files in the Windows NT Explorer or a folder window. This prevents you from accidentally changing the file extension and breaking the link between the document and the program.

- You can tell Windows that you don't want those extensions hidden—open a folder window and choose <u>V</u>iew, <u>O</u>ptions, click the View tab, and remove the check from the box labeled Hide file <u>e</u>xtensions for known file types.

Why is this important? Because you can double-click a file and it will start up the program that recognizes it. You save time and effort because you don't have to start the program, then go looking for the file, then load it. Windows does it all in one smooth operation.

 Q&A ***I have two files in the same folder with the same name. How can that be?***

They have the same first name, but their last names are different, and because the extensions are hidden, you can't see the differences. One might be called Windows.exe, while the other is Windows.ini. You can tell them apart in one of two ways: by the icon that the files use; or by right-clicking and looking on each file's P<u>r</u>operties sheet to see its file type.

Working with file types isn't hard. Here's how to train Windows to open WordPad whenever you double-click a file with the extension .LTR.

1 Use WordPad to create a file, and save it using any name you like, as long as the name ends with .LTR. When you save the file, be sure to enclose its full name in quotes ("Congratulations.Ltr").

2 Open My Computer and navigate through the folders until you find the file you just created. Right-click the file icon, and choose Open With from the popup menu. You'll see a dialog box like the one in Figure 10.7.

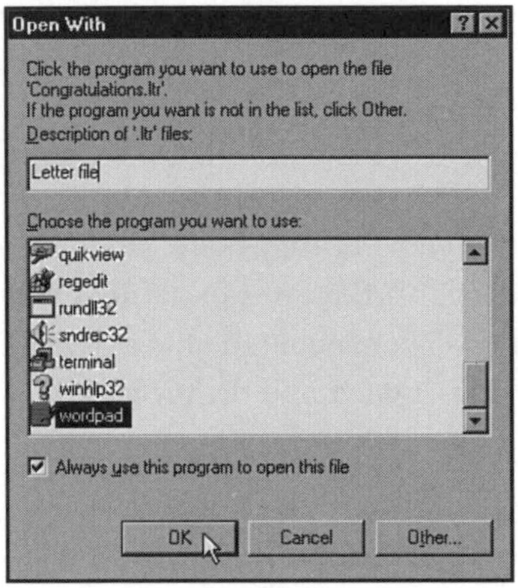

Fig. 10.7
Teaching Windows how to associate a file extension with an application.

3 Enter a description of the type of file. Then choose WordPad from the list of applications in the middle. (If the program you want to use isn't in this list, click the Other button and browse through your hard disk to find it.) Finally, make sure the box that reads Always use this program to open this file is checked. Click OK.

4 To make sure the extension was properly registered, open any folder window (My Computer works just fine) and choose View, Options. Click the File Types tab. You'll see a dialog box like the one in Figure 10.8. As you move the pointer through the list, the details below change to tell you about the file type and the application it's associated with. To change an existing entry, click the Edit button. To remove an entry completely, click on Remove.

Fig. 10.8
Does this file go with
that program? Here's
where to find out.

  TIP   **Hold down the Shift key and then right-click a file to see the**
Open With menu instead of the Open menu. This technique can come in
very handy if you have two programs (like Microsoft Word and WordPad, for
example) that you might want to use at different times to open up .DOC
files. Only one of the applications can be associated with .DOC files, but
the Open With menu lets you pick either one.

11

What Do All These Free Programs Do?

● **In this chapter:**

- **How do I edit a simple text file?**

- **What can I do with WordPad?**

- **Not for artists only: creating a masterpiece with Paint**

- **Two ways to crunch numbers with the Windows Calculator**

- **FreeCell, Pinball, and Minesweeper: the other games**

Write a letter, paint a picture, crunch some numbers, or waste some time. Windows has lots of tiny, free programs (and games) . . . . **>**

Windows NT is stuffed full of little programs designed to handle odd jobs. There's a Calculator and a Phone Dialer, a scratch pad for taking notes, and a word processor for writing letters. There's even a CD player that can coax music out of your multimedia PC.

In other chapters, we'll look at some of the more specialized accessories, like the ones that help you keep coworkers from getting annoyed about your CD's volume (Chapter 17), or the one that lets you chat with your coworkers without using the telephone (Chapter 20).

In this chapter, we'll focus on the bread-and-butter mini-programs that help you keep track of words, numbers, and the occasional picture. We'll also look at the three games that complement Solitaire in Windows.

Field guide to the free accessories in Windows NT

Windows NT is stuffed to the gills with programs that do all sorts of interesting odd jobs. (If you've used any version of Windows before, many of these programs will be familiar or even identical.) Here's a quick rundown on what you can do with these free add-ins. To find the complete collection, click the Start button, choose Programs, and look in the Accessories folder.

Icon	Name	What it does...
	Calculator	You won't want to use this ten-key calculator to figure your mortgage payments, but it's perfectly good for 2+2=4.
	CD Player	Play the *Lion King* soundtrack (or any audio CD) on a multimedia PC. This little program is surprisingly powerful and fun. See Chapter 18 for more details.

Icon	Name	What it does...
	Character Map	Pick a symbol, any symbol, from any font. Copy it to the Clipboard. Paste it into your document. Useful if you're trying to write in a language other than English.
	Clipboard Viewer	A small, simple program that lets you make sure what you cut or copy winds up on the Clipboard.
Clock	Clock	You say the tiny clock in the corner of the Taskbar is too small to see? This replacement lets you choose digital or big-hand/little-hand versions.
	FreeCell	A strategy-oriented solo card game. Highly addictive. You've been warned.
	HyperTerminal	This easy-to-use communications program lets you dial up other PCs and online services. Useful enough for simple tasks. See Chapter 24 for more information.
Imaging	Imaging	Do you work with scanned images? This tiny program lets you view, edit, organize, and annotate your graphic files.
	Minesweeper	A game of logic and strategy. Guess right and you win; guess wrong and—kaboom!—you lose.
	Notepad	This simple text editor is OK for jotting down a few words or sentences, but if you want your words to look good you'll choose WordPad instead.

continues

continued

Icon	Name	What it does...
	Paint	For the Van Gogh in you. Use the shapes, text tools, different brushes, and spray cans to create colorful images.
	Phone Dialer	Speed-dial up to eight of your favorite phone numbers. Requires a modem. See Chapter 24 for more information.
Games	Pinball	Not a real Pinball game, but an amazing simulation, complete with sound effects, flashing lights, and even special keys that let you "tilt" the table.
	Solitaire	The original Windows time-waster. Certified platinum: over 2 billion hours of productivity lost since 1990.
	Sound Recorder	If you've got a microphone and sound card, you've got a studio. See Chapter 17 for more information.
	WordPad	A surprisingly useful little word processor. Handles simple formatting, and it reads and writes files in the same format as Microsoft Word for Windows.

That program isn't on my PC!

I know, I know—some of the programs in that list aren't on your computer. So what happened? Do we have different versions of Windows?

Probably not. The more likely explanation is that the little programs you're looking for were never installed on your PC. Fortunately, we can take care of that in a flash, as long as your system administrator has given you permission to add programs. If he hasn't, you'll need to convince him to help you add these extras.

Let's get serious for a second. When you install Windows NT and choose the Typical option, it doesn't put the FreeCell, Pinball, and Minesweeper games on your system. What a horrifying oversight! To add these crucial missing pieces, first make sure you have your Windows NT CD-ROM. Then click the Start button and choose Settings, Control Panel. Double-click the icon labeled Add/Remove Programs, then click the Windows Setup tab. The programs you're looking for are discreetly hidden; highlight the Games entry and click the Details button. You'll see a dialog box like the one in Figure 11.1.

Fig. 11.1

Is there something missing from your PC? Use Control Panel to add these important Windows programs.

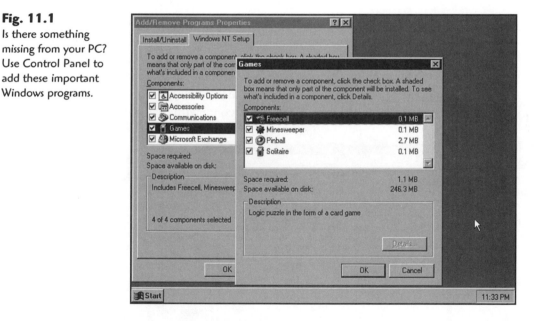

Scroll through the list, and click in the empty box next to any item you want to add. (If the box is already checked, it means that piece is already installed on your computer.) After you've finished with the list, click OK twice to start the ball rolling. Windows may ask you for the drive letter of your CD-ROM and the folder in which the program files are stored; after it finishes chugging away, you can get back to, um, work.

CAUTION The Add/Remove Programs utility can be a little confusing until you learn how it works. A check mark means the item is already on your PC. If a box is empty, clicking to add the check mark tells Windows to add the program. Clicking to remove a check mark removes the program, too. Don't touch those check marks unless you want to take a program off your computer!

I need to jot down some notes

Windows includes a program that works just like the pad of scratch paper next to your telephone. It's called Notepad, and you can see it in Figure 11.2. It's perfect for jotting down simple notes and lists. It's easy to find, easy to use, and the files are generally smaller than the files your word processor creates, so you can save space on your hard disk.

Notepad has one big advantage over more powerful word processors—it's fast. On my PC, for example, I'll stare at the Windows hourglass for about 10 seconds while I wait for WordPad to start up. The Notepad window, on the other hand, opens up in a fraction of a second after I click its icon. You'll use Notepad all the time, especially for the little informational files (usually called something like README) that come with new software packages.

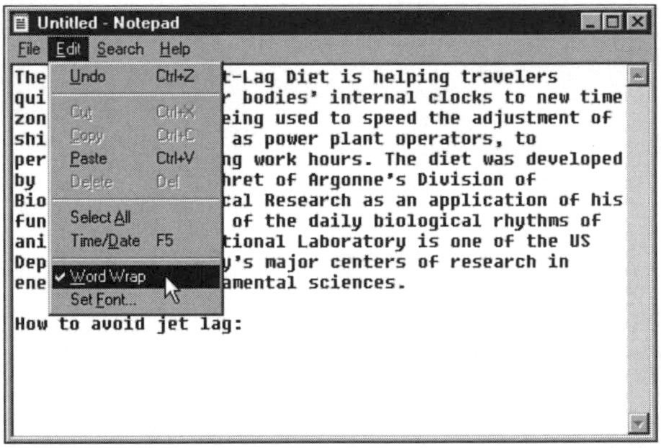

Fig. 11.2
Use Notepad to jot down simple notes and lists. The Word Wrap option makes sure your words fit neatly in the Notepad window.

TIP You can use Notepad to open files that contain things other than text, such as programs and bitmap images. When you do that, you'll see a lot of characters that look like gibberish. Don't worry—you can't hurt a file just by peeking at it in Notepad. Just make sure you don't save or change the file!

I want to write a good-looking letter

You might jot down a phone number on any old scrap of paper, but if you're writing a letter to your boss, you'll probably want to use a professional piece of stationery. That's the difference between Notepad and WordPad. For more formal documents, where you want to make some of your words stand out with special formatting, you'll use Windows' built-in word processor, WordPad.

How can I make this document look great?

If you prefer, you can use WordPad as nothing more than a souped-up scratch pad. But its real strength is its ability to help you use different fonts, colors, and other word processing tricks that make your simple letters and reports get noticed. It can't do the tricks you might expect of a heavy-duty word processor like Microsoft Word or WordPerfect, but it's got enough oomph to produce a document like the one in Figure 11.3.

Fig. 11.3
WordPad lets you choose different type styles, sizes, and colors—even add bullets to set off lists.

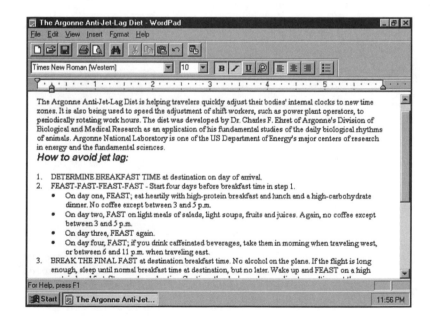

You can use WordPad's menus to apply special formats to the words you type, but it's easier just to use the tools on the bar at the top of the WordPad window.

Close-Up: the WordPad Toolbar

Use WordPad's collection of toolbars to make great-looking letters and short reports.

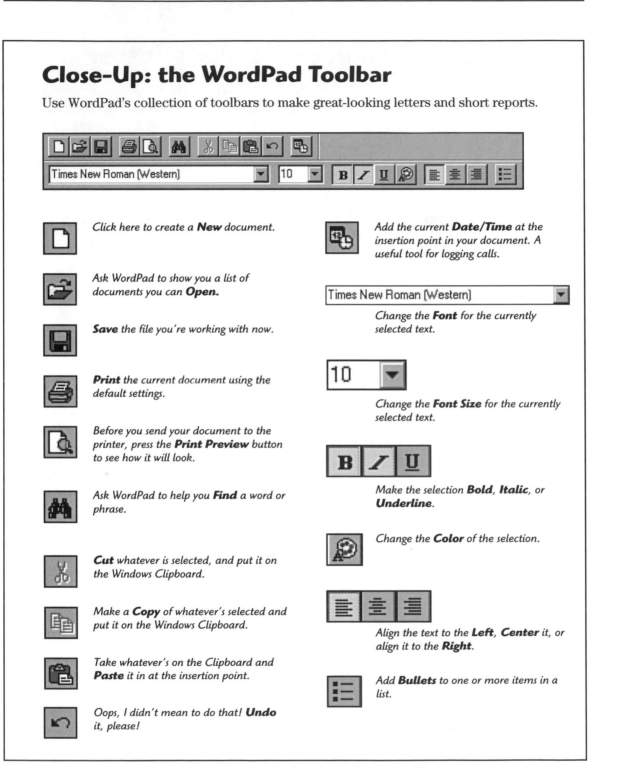

*Click here to create a **New** document.*

*Ask WordPad to show you a list of documents you can **Open.***

***Save** the file you're working with now.*

***Print** the current document using the default settings.*

*Before you send your document to the printer, press the **Print Preview** button to see how it will look.*

*Ask WordPad to help you **Find** a word or phrase.*

***Cut** whatever is selected, and put it on the Windows Clipboard.*

*Make a **Copy** of whatever's selected and put it on the Windows Clipboard.*

*Take whatever's on the Clipboard and **Paste** it in at the insertion point.*

*Oops, I didn't mean to do that! **Undo** it, please!*

*Add the current **Date/Time** at the insertion point in your document. A useful tool for logging calls.*

*Change the **Font** for the currently selected text.*

*Change the **Font Size** for the currently selected text.*

*Make the selection **Bold**, **Italic**, or **Underline**.*

*Change the **Color** of the selection.*

*Align the text to the **Left**, **Center** it, or align it to the **Right**.*

*Add **Bullets** to one or more items in a list.*

Most of my words are disappearing into the right side of the window. What's going on?

You need to set the **word wrap** option. When you do that, WordPad puts up a solid wall along the right edge of the document, and when the text gets there it has to turn and run into the next line instead. Most of the time you'll wrap to the window so you can read your writing more easily, but sometimes you'll want to wrap to the ruler, especially when you want to see what your document will look like when printed.

I'm ready to print now

 To send a WordPad document directly to the printer, just click the Print button. Because I hate to waste paper, I usually go through one extra step, choosing File, Print Preview to look at what Windows is planning to give me. To choose a different paper size or a different printer, select File, Page Setup. To specify any special printing options (extra copies or only selected pages, for example) choose File, Print.

How do I save this letter for later?

 Most of the time, you can save a document for retrieval later. The technique is simple: Click the Save button, or pull down the File menu, then click Save. If you haven't saved the current file, Windows will ask you to give the file a name.

Which document type should I use?

You'll see the same dialog box whenever you choose File, Save for a new document or File, Save As to store a previously saved document under a new name. (See Fig. 11.4.) Choose a folder in which to store the document, give it a name, and then click OK. The only important option in this dialog box is the file format, which you can specify using the drop-down list at the bottom of the dialog box.

- Select **Word for Windows 6.0** if you want to see every last bit of formatting. This is the same file format that Microsoft Word and Microsoft Office use.

- Choose **Rich Text Format (RTF)** when you're not sure whether the person to whom you're sending the file can read a file in Word format. RTF is a standard way for Windows word processors to exchange formatted documents.

- Select **Text Document** if you don't care about the formatting but simply want to save the letters, numbers, and other characters in your file.

- Select **Text Document—MS-DOS format** when you expect non-Windows users will also use the file.

I want to create a picture

If you have any artistic talent at all (unlike me) you'll want to try the Paint program.

Its drawing tools aren't sophisticated enough to turn you into another Michelangelo, but there's certainly enough to help you create a simple sketch to use in a letter or report. To launch the Paint program, click the Start button and follow the cascading menus from Programs to Accessories. The Paint window consists of an image area, plus a color palette and a tool box, as laid out in Figure 11.5.

Fig. 11.5
The pieces of Paint. The image window is your canvas, the tool box contains your brushes, pens, and other drawing implements; your palette lets you draw with different colors.

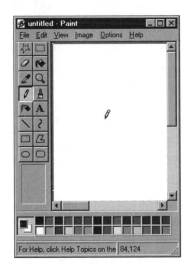

How do these tools work?

All of the drawing tools in Paint work the same way. Click the tool button to pick up the tool (the mouse pointer will usually change shape to show you what you can do right now). If there are any options available for the tool, you can select them from the bottom of the tool bar. For example, the

Close-Up: the Paint tools

 Take your choice of 12 tips for the **Brush** tool and achieve a variety of cool artistic effects.

 The **Airbrush** adds a mottled mix of the foreground color (left mouse button) or background color (right mouse button) to the screen. Choose the thick option and drag slowly to create a graffiti-style effect.

 Add words to your drawing with the **Text** tool.

 Draw a straight line with the **Line** tool. The line starts where you first click and stops where you release the button.

 Use the **Free-Form Select** tool to highlight an irregular shape so you can drag it elsewhere.
Hold down Ctrl to copy the selection instead of moving it.

 The **Curve** tool is tricky to describe but not hard to use: Click and drag to define the beginning and end points of the line, release the mouse button, and then click and drag again to define the curve of the line.

The **Select** tool highlights a rectangular shape for you to move or reuse.

Draw a **Rectangle** with this tool's help. Tool options let you automatically fill it with a color and add a border.

To rub out part of your image and replace that part with background or foreground color, use the **Eraser** tool.

The **Polygon** tool lets you draw irregular shapes with a straight side. Click and drag to draw one edge, then click each corner of your shape. Double-click when you're done.

Fill With Color pours the current color into the selected region. Use the left button for the foreground color and the right button for the background color.

The **Ellipse** tool draws round shapes, centered on the place where you click and begin dragging. Hold down the Shift key to create a perfect circle.

 Use the **Pick Color** tool to select a color from one region and use it for the foreground or background color.

 The **Magnifier** lets you zoom in for a close-up view of your image so you can do fine editing.

Use the **Rounded Rectangle** to create a rectangle with rounded corners.

 Do free-hand drawing—or just doodle— with the **Pencil**.

Magnifier gives you a choice of four different zoom levels, from actual size to eight times normal, while the Line tool lets you select one of four thicknesses. Finally, click and drag to use the tool (most allow you to do something slightly different with the right mouse button).

How do I work with colors?

If you've ever seen the Hollywood portrayal of a great artist (Charlton Heston as Michelangelo, for example), you know that every painter uses a **palette** to mix colors for use on the canvas. When you use Paint, your palette of colors appears at the bottom of the screen. You can choose from as many colors as your hardware will let you see—literally millions, if you have a really good video adapter. But you can only work with two colors at a time—one for the foreground and one for the background.

To change the default colors temporarily, click the appropriate square in the color palette. Use the left mouse button to change the foreground color; the right button controls the background. Watch as the two squares at the left edge of the palette change to show you which colors are active right now.

You can even add a new color from among the thousands or millions available to you—just choose Options, Edit Colors, then press the Define Custom Colors button. Move the pointer through the color matrix at right to choose a new color, and use the vertical slider at far right to control its brightness. The color you've selected appears in the Color|Solid box. To save the color in your palette, click an empty square in the Custom colors area and then click the Add to Custom Colors button.

Remember, these colors affect everything you do—from drawing a line to creating colorful boxes and circles. Always check the colors before you use any of the Paint tools.

TIP **You can anchor the toolbox and color palette to any edge of the** Paint window, or you can drag either one so it floats in the window. To drag the color palette, point to any empty space just above the little color squares. Moving the toolbox is trickier: you have to double-click the little area beneath the tools without releasing the mouse button after the second click. When you do it correctly, you'll see a thick, shaded box appear around the box, signaling you that it's ready to be moved. To snap either piece back into position, drag it to the edge and watch it go.

How do I add text to a drawing?

I sometimes use Paint to create combinations of text and graphics that I can insert into reports to help mark the beginning of a new section. You can, too. Our goal is to create a graphic that looks like Figure 11.6.

Fig. 11.6
Use Paint's Text and Rounded Rectangle tools to create this graphic for use in a report.

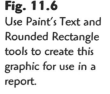

1 Start by clicking the Text tool, then click and drag to define a rectangle where you want your letters to appear. When you release the mouse button, the insertion point (a thin vertical line) will appear.

2 Choose a typeface, size, and any text attributes such as bold or italic. If you don't see the Text Toolbar, choose <u>V</u>iew T<u>e</u>xt Toolbar choice to make it visible.

3 Start typing. Don't worry if your text doesn't fit perfectly in the box. When you're through typing, you can use the sizing handles on each corner and in the center of each edge to stretch the text box to fit the type.

4 When you're satisfied with the look of the text, it's time to add a border. First, click the Line tool and select a line thickness. In this case, we'll use the third choice. Next, click the Rounded Rectangle tool; make sure the top shape is chosen in the area at the bottom of the tool box.

5 Click a spot just above and to the left of the type where you want the border to begin, then drag the shape to the right and down to complete it. Release when you reach the lower right corner. (You could hold down the Shift key as you drag to create a perfect square. Use the same trick with the Ellipse tool for a perfect circle, or with the Line tool for a perfect horizontal or vertical line.)

6 To create the interesting 3-D effect, go back to the Line tool and choose the thinnest line, then click the Rounded Rectangle tool and draw another border around the original shape. It might take several tries to get it just right; use Undo if you want to start over.

TIP **If you don't like the results of anything you do in Paint, use Edit,** Undo immediately. Don't be afraid to experiment a little: Paint lets you undo the last three things you did.

7 To add the 3-D shading between the inner and outer borders, use the Fill With Color tool. Click the gray square in the palette, then on the Fill With Color tool. The cursor will change to a bucket with a dribble of paint coming out. Aim the end of that dribble at a spot between the borders. (If you can't see it clearly, use the Magnifier tool to zoom in closer.) Click to fill in the color.

8 Finally, save the image you've just created. You could just choose File, Save, but there's a much more efficient way to make sure you just save the portion you want. Click the Select tool, and use the right mouse button to drag a rectangle around the graphic. When you release the button, a shortcut menu will pop up. Choose Copy To; Paint will let you choose a location and a name for your graphic.

I need to add up some numbers

Windows includes a handy accessory you can pop up whenever you need to crunch a few numbers. I use the Windows Calculator every month to help when I reconcile my checking statement, but it can do much more than that.

You can view the Windows Calculator in either of two modes, as shown in Figure 11.7.

- By default, it acts like a ten-key adding machine. You can use the numbers on the keyboard or click the buttons using the mouse. Use the Edit menu to copy and paste numbers to and from the Calculator.

- If you want to do scientific and statistical calculations, you can switch the Calculator into genius mode by choosing View, Scientific. I don't have much use for these functions, but if you do, you can get instant help on how to use them by right-clicking any button. To return to the simple view, choose View, Standard.

Fig. 11.7
Simple or scientific? The two faces of the Windows calculator. If you know what all those buttons are for, you're a full-fledged rocket scientist.

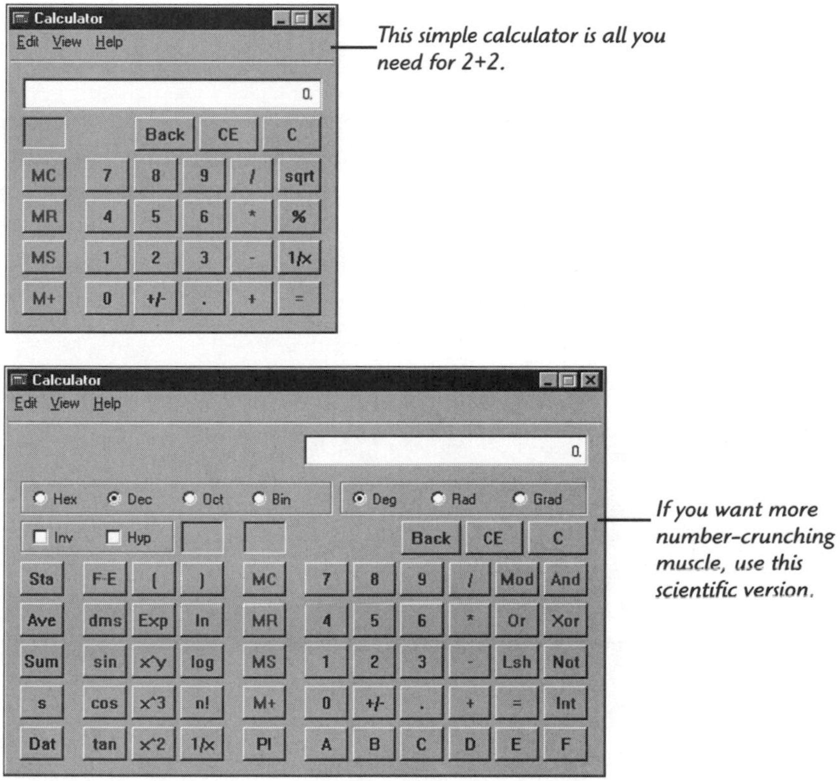

This simple calculator is all you need for 2+2.

If you want more number-crunching muscle, use this scientific version.

I just want to relax!

Who says Windows is all work? Your boss might not want you to know about them, but Windows includes a collection of four cool games. We've already seen and worked with Solitaire at length. Now it's time to look at the other three games. (Remember, Windows doesn't make it easy to find them; click the Start button, then Programs, Accessories, and Games.)

Minesweeper

The object of the game is to clear away every square on the screen without stepping on a mine. It's tougher than it looks! Each time you click on a square, one of two things will happen: Either you'll clear one or more squares and reveal some numbers, or you'll click on a bomb, and the game is over. The numbers tell you how many bombs are adjacent to that square, and you can use this information to make educated guesses or definitive decisions about which squares contain bombs.

When you're sure you know where a bomb is hidden, right-click to mark the square with a flag. Once you've found all the mines around a numbered square, click both mouse buttons simultaneously to clear all the squares around the one you're pointing to. Figure 11.8 shows a game I just lost. (Notice the unhappy face just above the playing area? Click that button to start a new game.)

Fig. 11.8
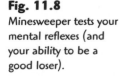
Minesweeper tests your mental reflexes (and your ability to be a good loser).

Pinball

In my youth, I used to spend days at a time pumping quarters into pinball machines when I should have been studying. The Space Cadet 3-D Pinball game in Windows NT lets me goof off just as though I were back in school—and it never asks for quarters!

To start a game, click the Pinball menu choice, then choose Game, New Game. To set up for two, three, or four players, choose Options, Select Players. To launch the ball, hold down the spacebar for a second or two and then let it go. By default, the "flippers" are the two keys just inside the Shift keys on your keyboard—for most of us, that's the z and / keys. The x and > keys just inside those two keys let you bump the table to the left or right, respectively. (Be careful not to bump too hard or you'll tilt and lose the ball in play!)

For a summary of the rules and a quick reference to keyboard shortcuts, look in online Help. Figure 11.9 shows a game I'm playing when I should be writing the rest of this book.

Fig. 11.9
The 3D Pinball game uses impressive sound effects. Keep the sound turned down if you want your co-workers to think you're working.

FreeCell

Bored with Solitaire? This is another solo game that uses one deck of cards. The object of the game is to move all the cards into the four home cells at the top right, each in a stack of its own suit, starting with the ace. You shuffle cards from stack to stack on the bottom using alternating colors in descending order (a black queen on a red king, for example, or a red 7 on a black 8). The four cells at the top left are the free cells, where you can temporarily store cards while you move others around. Figure 11.10 shows a game in progress.

Supposedly, it's possible to win every game of FreeCell. To check your win-loss record, choose Options, Statistics. For complete rules and strategy tips, use the Help menu. Bet you can't play just one game!

Fig. 11.10
After you've mastered
Solitaire, check out the
nearly endless display
of possibilities in
FreeCell, the *other*
solo card game.

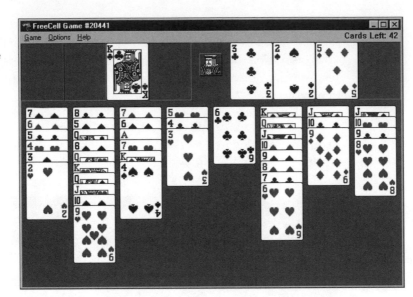

Using Windows to Tie it All Together

● **In this chapter:**

● Easy sharing with the old cut-and-paste routine

● Special tricks for cutting and pasting in a DOS program

● What's so special about Paste Special?

● Linking, embedding, and other sophisticated tricks

With Windows, you can combine text, graphics, charts, tables—whatever—into magnificent, attention-getting documents . . . . ▶

When you're ready for a great meal at a great restaurant, you certainly don't expect that one person will prepare the whole thing. There's a crew of assistant chefs who slice, dice, and chop all the different ingredients. The vegetables are over there, the meat and seafood are over here, and the pastry chef is in a world of her own. If the master chef is running things right, though, all those pieces come together to form a perfect presentation on your plate.

Windows lets you work the same way—with Windows playing master chef to all those assistant chef programs. You might have a formatted report in your word processor, a set of charts and pictures in your graphics program, and a stack of numbers in a spreadsheet program. When it's time to blend all the ingredients into one good-looking document, Windows makes it easy. The secret? Learning how to cut, copy, and paste.

Cut, copy, and paste: the easy way to move things around

When you want to take a little data from here and put it over there, the technique is the same, no matter where you are in Windows. It doesn't matter whether you're moving between two different places in the same window or between two completely different applications—thanks to Windows, you'll always follow exactly the same procedure.

If you managed a warehouse, you'd probably carry around a clipboard, big enough to securely hold a few sheets of letter-sized paper. To manage the process of transferring data, Windows uses a similar holding area called the **Clipboard**. As you move from place to place in Windows, the Clipboard stays discreetly alongside you. Most of the time, you don't even notice that it's there. When you want to move something from one place to another, though, it's right at your fingertips: You pick up the thing you want to move and fasten it to the Clipboard. Whatever you placed on the Clipboard stays there as you move to your next destination. When you're ready to set the copied object down in its new home, just unfasten it, and put it where you want it.

Using the Clipboard to cut, copy, and paste is simple, as long as you remember the universal rule of Windows: first you select, then you act:

1 Select the thing you want to copy or move. It could be anything: a word or sentence, a few cells from a spreadsheet, some or all of a picture. Use the technique that works for the application you're in. For example, in WordPad, hold down the left mouse button as you drag across the words you want to highlight.

2 Right-click the highlighted section, and then choose Cut or Copy. You'll see a menu like the one in Figure 12.1. (If your application doesn't use popup menus, look for Edit on the pull-down menus.) Windows takes a snapshot of whatever is highlighted and places it in the Clipboard. If you chose Copy, your document remains just as it was; if you chose Cut, whatever was highlighted is now gone.

3 Move the mouse to the place where you want to paste the copied material. This could be in the same document, or in a completely different document in another application. Click to be sure the insertion point is where you want it to be.

4 Right-click at the spot where you want to insert the data from the Clipboard, and then choose Paste. Whatever is on the Clipboard will appear at the insertion point.

Fig. 12.1
To put the selection from this WordPad document onto the Clipboard, use the right mouse button to pop up this menu. Use the same menu to paste it into its new location.

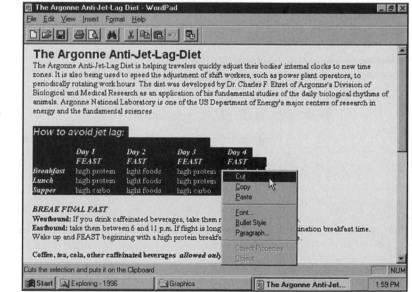

CAUTION

The Clipboard can hold only one thing at a time. If you've copied or cut something, it will wipe out anything that's currently being stored on the Clipboard. That's why, if you're shuffling a lot of data around, it's always a good idea to paste it into its new home *immediately* after you've cut or copied it to the Clipboard.

What happens when I paste data?

When you paste something from the Clipboard, Windows tries to figure out the most appropriate action to take with the specific type of data you've put there. It's easiest when the type of data you're pasting is exactly the same as the surrounding data in the place where you intend to paste it. Results are less predictable when the data types are very different; for example, when you have a paragraph of text on the Clipboard and you're thinking of pasting it into a bitmap picture in Paint. Here's a sampling of what you can expect:

- **Words and numbers** usually move easily from one place to another. The formatting may or may not survive the trip, though. For example, if you copy a fat, bold headline from a WordPad document and paste it into a Notepad file, the words appear; but because Notepad doesn't allow fancy formatting, the text loses its "boldness."

- **Pictures** can move from one place to another in a variety of formats. Most of them are simple bitmaps, which means you have to paste them in at exactly the same size and shape as the original, unless you want them to be distorted.

66 *Plain English, please!*

A **bitmap** image is one that consists of different-colored dots (bits) that the eye sees as a single image. (If you look closely at a newspaper photo you can actually see these dots.) Bitmaps are useful for simple pictures, but the dots can't be stretched; so when you try to change the size or shape of the image, the results will usually be ugly. For those kinds of tasks, graphics artists use sophisticated **vector** formats that tell Windows how to draw the picture at any size and shape. The Windows Paint program uses only bitmaps. 99

- You can even use the Cut, Copy, and Paste commands to move **files** from one place to another. Open My Computer and keep double-clicking until you reach the folder window that contains the file or files you want to move. Highlight one or more files, right-click, and choose

Cut or Copy from the popup menu. Now you can move to another folder window, right-click, and use the Paste command to insert the files in that folder.

Can I cut and copy with a DOS program?

It's easiest to move things between Windows programs, but there's a special set of procedures for copying text to and from MS-DOS programs. Here's how:

1 Open your MS-DOS program in a window. If it opens in full-screen mode (where it takes over the entire screen, with no taskbar, no title bar—no evidence of Windows anywhere), force it into a window by holding down the Alt key while you press Enter.

2 Click the icon at the far left edge of the DOS program's title bar to unfurl the pull-down control menu. (See Fig. 12.2 for an example.)

Fig. 12.2
Run any DOS application in a window and you can cut, copy, and paste text between it and Windows applications.

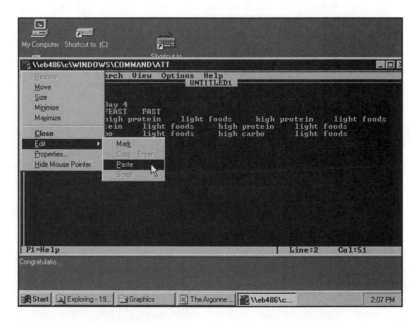

3 Choose the Edit command; a cascading menu will appear to the right.

4 To copy part or all of the screen, choose Mark. This switches the mouse into marker mode, which allows you to swipe it across any portion of the DOS screen to highlight a rectangle. When you've marked the section you want to copy, press Enter. Whatever you marked is now available on the Windows Clipboard, and you can paste it anywhere you want.

5 To paste text from the Clipboard into your DOS program, make sure the insertion point is at the right spot in your DOS screen. Next, use the same pull-down menu to choose Edit, Paste.

What's so special about Paste Special?

When you highlight part of a document and right-click on it, you'll almost always see the same three choices: Cut, Copy, and Paste. But when you use the pull-down Edit menu instead, you'll sometimes see a fourth option as well: Paste Special. What's so special?

The plain old Paste command acts instantly. But when you choose Paste Special, Windows waits for more instructions from you before it actually inserts the contents of the Clipboard. The options it presents to you are context-sensitive; your exact choices depend on the format of the data you've placed on the Clipboard.

Why would you want to do this? It's a good way to save time if you want to choose a different format for whatever you're pasting, or if you want to get rid of any formatting completely. For example, you might want to copy some text from a report you wrote in WordPad or Microsoft Word, then paste it into a letter. If you used Paste, the text you added to the letter would retain the formatting of the report text. To make the newly pasted text blend in properly, you'd have to fuss with fonts and margins.

Instead, copy the section to the Clipboard as usual, then move to the second document and Select Edit, Paste Special. You'll see four choices, as shown in Figure 12.3.

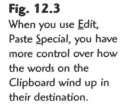

Fig. 12.3
When you use Edit, Paste Special, you have more control over how the words on the Clipboard wind up in their destination.

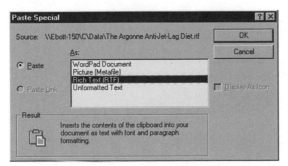

There are two options you'll use most often. The first is Rich Text, which lets you transfer the words and the formatting together. The other useful option, Unformatted Text, simply pastes in the words, which then pick up whatever format is already in your document.

TIP **Are you tired of constantly shifting your hands between the** keyboard and the mouse? Try these universal shortcuts instead: Ctrl+C copies the current selection to the Clipboard; Ctrl+X cuts it; Ctrl+V pastes the contents of the Clipboard to the current insertion point.

All about OLE

You can't pick up a new Windows program without hearing the term **OLE** (it's generally pronounced oh-lay, like the shout you might hear at a bullfight, although you can also refer to it by spelling out the letters). What's it all about? OLE stands for **Object Linking and Embedding**, which is an extremely technical term for the act of working with two types of data in one place.

You've already seen how copy-and-paste (or cut-and-paste) works. When you select some data and paste it into a different document, it becomes part of the second document. You can make changes to the original document from which it came, but those changes won't be reflected in the fragment that you pasted somewhere else. If you make a lot of changes, you could spend days or weeks recopying and repasting the same data to all the places you pasted copies!

Linking and embedding are two ways to avoid doing all that rework. I'll talk about each of them in detail, later in this chapter. For now, it's sufficient to know that when you link two documents, or when you embed information from one document in another, Windows stores information about the *connection* between the two documents. This technique lets you edit information in an original document and guarantee that your changes will show up wherever there's a reference to this document.

Using different types of data in one file

Let's say you've written a report in WordPad. You know what you want to say, but you need to add a sketch or a map to make it easy for your coworkers to see what you're talking about. So you fire up the Windows Paint program and create your own work of art. Those are two completely different kinds of data. Can you really mix words and pictures together?

Yes, you can. In fact, you have several choices for how to mix and match different types of data in a single document.

You can **paste** the picture into your document, using one of several formats. You can **embed** the picture in the document, or you can **link** the picture to the document. The technique you choose will dictate what you can do with the document later.

What's the difference between pasting, linking, and embedding? To understand the distinction, let's imagine that we're in a fancy restaurant—the kind where there's more silverware in front of your plate than you'll use at home in an entire month. You've asked the waiter to bring you some oil-and-vinegar dressing for your salad. Instead of going into the kitchen, though, he goes into the back office and uses his Microsoft Salad Dressing for Windows software. What happens next?

I want these two kinds of data mixed into one document

Our waiter could just pour a little bit of oil into a big bottle of vinegar and bring the whole bottle to the table. He might have to shake things up to get it to look good, but for all practical purposes, you see one big bottle of salad dressing in a bottle labeled "Vinegar." (If our waiter is smart, he'll relabel the bottle "Oil-and-vinegar" before he brings it to our table.)

In Windows terms, that's exactly what happens when you simply paste one type of data into a document that contains another type of data—for example, when you insert a picture into a WordPad document. The data that you're pasting (the oil) gets added to the original document (the vinegar) in a format that the original document can recognize. For all practical purposes, the drawings and words mix together to form a single document that you can use without any fuss. The label on the outside says that it's a WordPad document, but you know there's a drawing mixed in with it. Most importantly, there's no easy way to take the pasted picture back out, any more than you could extract that oil from the vinegar and start all over again.

I want two kinds of data to travel together without being mixed

Let's say that our waiter isn't certain how much oil you want with that vinegar. So, instead of mixing it up for you he brings two bottles to the table—a large bottle of vinegar and a small one filled with oil. He doesn't want the two bottles to get separated, so he fastens the smaller bottle to the side of the larger bottle and brings it to the table. You can see what's in each bottle without any work at all, but to put the dressing on your salad, you have to open each bottle separately.

In Windows terms, the big bottle is the **container**, the smaller bottle attached to it is the **embedded object**, and the complete package is called a **compound document**. The second document is literally stored right alongside the first so that the two types of data never mix. When you embed one piece of data in a file that contains another kind of data, they're not mixed together, so you can edit either one separately. Just as you could replace the olive oil with canola oil, you could change the picture without having to start all over.

Even though they travel together and can be looked at together, the data types in a compound document (words and pictures in the case of our document, oil and vinegar in the case of the salad) remain completely separate. If someone across the table asks you for the salad dressing, you hand them the complete package. Likewise, if you send your two-in-one document to someone else, you don't have to worry about them getting separated. And best of all, you can click on the embedded document to edit it using the program that you originally used to create it.

I want to use two kinds of data together but store them separately

OK, let's say this restaurant is fancy, but not very well-stocked. There's a bottle of vinegar on every table, but there's only one bottle of oil. Attached to each big bottle of vinegar, there's a picture of the bottle of oil, along with a note that tells you to ask the waiter when you want to add dressing to your salad. Just ask, and the waiter will bring the bottle of oil from the pantry, stand there while you use it, and return it to the pantry when you're done.

Why on earth would you want to do something this complicated with your data? Well, imagine that the picture is your company's logo. If you embed a separate copy of the logo into all your documents, you'll have a heap of work ahead of you if your company logo changes—you'll have to find each document and change the embedded logo in each one. A better solution is to keep the logo art in a central file and include instructions for finding the **linked object**—in this case, the logo file stored on your company's network.

Links always contain both a picture and a set of instructions for finding the original. So if you send a file with the linked logo to someone else, she can see what the logo looks like. She can even print it out. But if she wants to change the logo, her application will have to follow the instructions in the link to find the original logo and the application that created it.

How do I recognize an embedded or linked object?

Most of the time, when you've pasted one object into another, the document you end up with will look smooth and seamless, with no evidence of the pasting you've done. But you will notice a difference if you click on an embedded or linked object. When you do, you'll see a dark line that forms a box around the object. In each corner, and in the middle of each side of this box, you'll see black squares called **sizing handles**. (See Fig. 12.4 for an example.) You can drag these handles in any direction to change the size and shape of the object. (But remember, if that's a bitmap image, you probably won't like what happens when you start tugging and stretching!)

Fig. 12.4
The dark box and square handles around this object are your visual cues that this is an embedded object. Right-click on it for more information about what it is and what you can do with it.

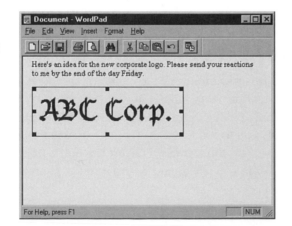

What am I supposed to do with an embedded object?

To select an embedded or linked object, just click it. Like any object anywhere in Windows, the best way to find out more information about what it is and what you can do with it is to right-click it.

If you've embedded or linked an object from one program into a document created by another program, you don't necessarily have to do anything special with it.

- To **view** the document, just open it. All the information you need to see is already there, so you'll see exactly what you expect to see.

- To **print** the document, just choose the print command as you normally would.

- To **edit** the inserted object, double-click on it. To see all your options, right-click on the object, then choose the appropriate command from the bottom of the menu. (See Fig. 12.5 for an example of what you might see.) You can also change any of the options for an inserted object by using this menu.

Fig. 12.5
Right-click an embedded object, and choose Properties to see what you can do with it. The same popup menu also includes the option to edit the picture.

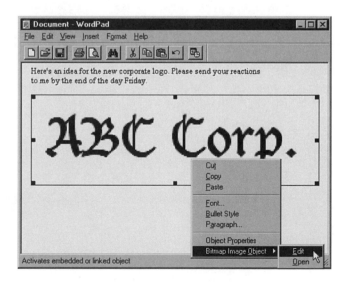

TIP **Remember, the menus that pop up when you right-click on an** object change to reflect what Windows can do with that object. So, if you're not sure what an object is, use the right mouse button!

Do I really need to worry about OLE?

Most of the time, you don't really need to be concerned about how you're cutting and pasting between two different places. Windows looks at the different types of data you're trying to mix together, makes a few assumptions about what you probably want to do, and then takes care of the details.

When you're not sure what will happen, try the Paste command first. If you're not satisfied with the results, undo what you just did and try again with Paste Special.

Q&A *I pasted something into a document, and now there's a box around it. What's that all about?*

Congratulations! You just embedded one type of data inside another without even realizing it. If that's not what you wanted to do, you'll have to tell Windows to do the paste differently. Go to the Edit menu and choose Paste Special. This time, you'll see a dialog box with a list of the options available to you. As you highlight each option in the list, look in the Results area at the bottom of the dialog box to see what will happen, then choose the one that matches what you want.

Part IV: Making Windows Work the Way You Do

13

Changing the Way Windows Looks

● **In this chapter:**

- **I can't see all the windows I need at the same time!**

- **Want to put your favorite picture on the desktop? Here's how**

- **This screen is boring**

- **Keep other people from snooping when you go to lunch**

- **Help—I can't find my mouse pointer!**

I want my Windows desktop to be just as comfortable and personal as my office. Don't you? Fortunately, Windows lets you do just that · **>**

Your office probably started out looking just like mine: white walls, a cork-covered bulletin board, an empty desk, and some bookshelves—oh, yes, a computer, too. Pretty boring, huh? That's why I've added all sorts of personal touches to the environment. Step into my office and you'll find family pictures, a couple of Dilbert cartoons, a wall calendar, a bunch of framed pictures (I'm partial to racehorses), and a coffee mug that says, "You want it WHEN?????"

It's no problem to personalize your Windows environment, just as you can redecorate your office to make it more comfortable. Replace that boring green background with your favorite picture, change the colors and fonts, even shrink the whole display so you can see more details at once. A few of these changes can actually make you more comfortable and productive. Most, though, are strictly for fun and visual relief.

Put more data on the desktop—here's how...

How much do you want to see on the screen at one time? Well, how sharp is your eyesight? When you first started Windows, it most likely came up using the normal video settings, where everything on the screen is big and easy to see. If you have the right combination of video card and monitor, though, you can change the resolution (Windows calls it the **desktop area**) and put more pixels on the screen. Is this the right option for you? You'll have to make a trade-off between your eyesight and the convenience of seeing more of your work on the screen.

> **“ Plain English, please!**
>
> **Pixels** are the small dots of color that make up the image on your screen, and **resolution** is simply a fancy term for the number of dots that Windows displays on a single screen. Resolution is usually expressed as a measurement—when we refer to 640×480 resolution (pronounce it *six-forty-by-four-eighty*), that means a display with room for 640 dots from side to side, and 480 dots from top to bottom. Increasing the resolution while using the same monitor means that everything on the screen appears smaller, so you can see more words, numbers, pictures...whatever data you're working with. **”**

Decorating the desktop

Does this screen look familiar? Windows NT lets you personalize practically every part of the workspace, just for fun. If your hardware allows it, you can change the screen **resolution** (increasing the number of dots on the screen means you can see more details at once) and the **color palette** (to make photographic images look more realistic). You can also tell Windows to use a **screen saver** that puts something else on the screen if you haven't touched a key or used the mouse for a while.

*You can adjust the **colors** for every part of the Windows environment, from the desktop background to the labels under each icon.*

***Wallpaper** consists of graphic images that fill all or part of the desktop.*

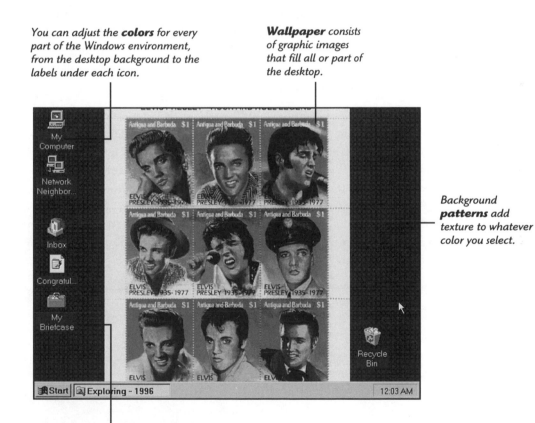

*Background **patterns** add texture to whatever color you select.*

*Having trouble reading the labels in windows and on icons? Try using different **fonts** at larger sizes.*

What happens when I change resolution?

If you've ever looked through the viewfinder of a camera, you understand everything you need to know about screen resolution. Let's say you're taking a group photograph at a family reunion; the photograph you get back from the Fotomat is always the same size (just as your computer screen stays a constant size). But depending on where you stand, the image on the photo might be very different.

Stand close to the group and look through the camera—you can only get two or three people in the picture. Take a step back and now Uncle Bill shows up in the frame, but everyone looks a little smaller. Go back a few more steps, and you can squeeze in everyone in the family, including all those cousins and even the family dog, but you'll need a magnifying glass to tell whether that's Uncle Bill or Aunt Hillary in the back row.

Each time you increase the resolution of your Windows screen, it's exactly like stepping back to get more into the picture. Eventually, the image will be so small that it won't be usable. See Figure 13.1 for a graphic illustration of how much more room you have on-screen when you increase the display resolution. Note that at a low resolution the Solitaire window takes up the entire screen, while at a higher resolution there's plenty of room to see more data on the screen. If this were a spreadsheet instead of a card game, you'd be able to see many more rows and columns of data, simply by adjusting the screen resolution.

Table 13.1 describes the four most common choices of screen resolution.

Table 13.1 The four most common screen resolutions, in plain English

Number of pixels	How it looks	Use this setting if you...
640×480	Normal	...have average eyesight and work with uncomplicated documents.
800×600	Wide angle	...regularly cut and paste information between two applications.
1024×768	Extra-wide angle	...have a big monitor, and have lots of windows open at once.
1280×1024	View from the Space Shuttle	...have a *really* big monitor, and the eyesight of a red-tailed hawk.

Fig. 13.1
If your eyesight is 20/20, you can make everything on the Windows desktop smaller—which lets you see more data on the screen.

How to adjust the screen resolution

Right-click any empty spot on the desktop, and choose Properties. Click the Settings tab (see Fig. 13.2) to reveal all the controls for adjusting the image size and number of colors you can see at once.

CAUTION **Be very careful with the box labeled Refresh Frequency! On some** monitors, if you specify the wrong number in here, you could end up sending a signal to the monitor that causes some of its innards to *literally* go up in a puff of smoke. Windows will probably set up the monitor correctly the first time. Unless you're sure you know what you're doing, don't touch this setting.

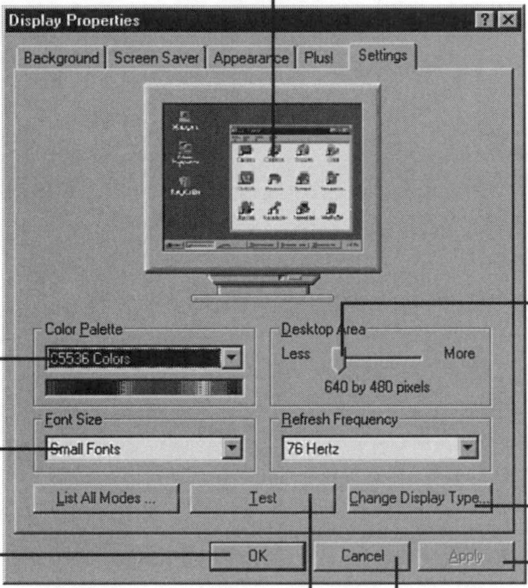
Display Properties
Background
Screen Saver
Appearance
Plus!
Settings
Color Palette
65536 Colors
Desktop Area
Less
More
640 by 480 pixels
Font Size
Small Fonts
Refresh Frequency
76 Hertz
List All Modes ...
Test
Change Display Type...
OK
Cancel
Apply
Choose a color palette. (See the section called "How many colors do you need?" for an explanation of which setting you should choose—and why.) Depending on the video driver you have, the colors might be listed as High Color instead of 65536 Colors.
Look here to see a preview of what your changes will look like.
Slide this lever left to make all the objects on the screen larger and easier to see. Slide it to the right to put more objects on the screen by making everything smaller.
Click here to change the settings that tell Windows which video adapter you're using and how many times per second it can redraw the image on the monitor. A faster refresh rate is easier on the eye, but if the setting is too high you can damage your monitor. Don't touch this unless you're sure you know what you're doing.
Choose a font size for Windows objects like icons and menus. Small is neater and lets you pack more pixels on the screen. Large fonts are easier to read. Custom fonts are more trouble than they're worth. Your call.
Click OK to accept the changes and close the dialog box.
Click here to see a test pattern that will let you know whether the settings you've selected will display properly on the screen.
Click Cancel to stop fooling around and get back to work.
Click Apply to change your display settings and leave this dialog box open.

Fig. 13.2
Use this dialog box to adjust the settings for your screen. Want to see more of what you're working with? Slide the lever to the right. Too small? Slide it back to the left.

How many colors do you need?

Setting the Windows color palette is like shopping for paint to redo your living room. At the lowest setting in the Display properties sheet, you might get your choice of **16 colors** that can appear on the screen at once (some video cards won't even offer this paltry choice). That's like doing the walls, the trim, and all the furniture and decorations using only the colors on the sale shelf at the Sherwin-Williams store. It's not a heck of a lot of choices, but you can probably find something you'll like.

When you boost the level to **256 colors**, you can take your choice of any combination of colors from the ready-mixed selection in the paint store. In practice, because you're doing the walls and the trim and the furniture and decorations, that means tens of thousands of combinations. Surely you'll find *something* you like in there.

If you have an expensive video card and monitor, you can boost the color resolution to **High Color** (65,536 colors) or even **True Color** (16.7 million colors). That's the equivalent of bringing in your own swatches of color and asking the paint store to match them molecule for molecule.

Why not choose the highest number? Because it might slow down your screen. It's as if Windows has to search through the entire list of colors and calculate all those bits for every dot on the screen; that uses a tremendous amount of computing power. And while Windows is getting a headache sorting through all those colors, it can't do anything else. Most video cards can do just fine at 256 colors or even higher, but if you notice a difference, feel free to change the settings.

For most people, a setting of 256 colors is good enough. That's enough color options to handle the needs of most applications, but not so many that Windows will neglect the rest of its work while it's sorting through the color palette. The option for 65,536 colors will produce more realistic-looking images while possibly slowing down your system slightly.

Unless you're a professional graphic artist, skip the higher palettes. Can you *really* put 16.7 million colors on the screen? Do they all have names? (Hey, the Crayola Company had to use strange names like Burnt Umber when it got up to 64 crayons, so what could it possibly come up with for the box with 16.7 million crayons inside?) The only time you'll really *need* to use a lot of colors is when you're working with **digital images** (like the photographs found on Photo CDs); then you'll appreciate the smoother, sharper, more realistic images. For people who work with a word processor or spreadsheet all day long, 256 is puh-lenty of colors.

 Q&A ***When I changed the resolution, the color palette changed, too! Why?***

Your video card doesn't have enough memory on it to handle all those colors at all resolutions. If you want to see photos in True Color, you may have to choose the smallest desktop area—640 × 480. If you want to pack more pixels on the screen—at 1024 × 768, for example—you'll have to settle for fewer colors.

Decking the walls

I don't like wallpaper. If I bought a new house, and discovered that the kitchen walls had been covered with quaint country scenes, I'd spend days scraping it off and repainting. Fortunately, changing the wallpaper in Windows doesn't require a belt sander. Just right-click the Desktop, choose Properties, click the Background tab (see Fig. 13.3), and you can redecorate in a few seconds.

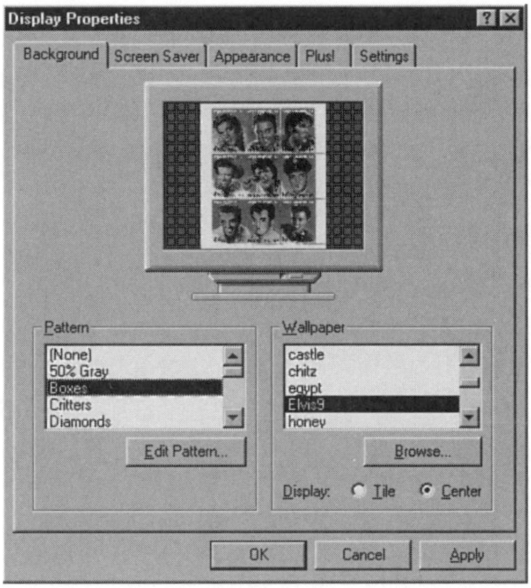

Fig. 13.3
Use the Display Properties dialog box to change the background pattern.

Wallpaper? Patterns? What's the difference?

When it's time to redecorate your Windows desktop, you have the same choices you have in your house. You can use a single color for the background, just as you might paint the walls canary yellow. Or you can add artwork—images or patterns—to make the background more interesting.

Windows gives you two choices for images. Background **patterns** are simple, repeating arrangements of black pixels that create a design when viewed together—like a fancy tile pattern for a kitchen countertop or floor. Your background color shows through behind the pattern (right now it's a dull teal, but you'll see how to change this later in the chapter).

Wallpaper, on the other hand, is an actual graphic image, such as a photograph or drawing, that covers the background color and pattern you've chosen. You can center a single image on your desktop, just as you would hang a large painting on the living room wall; or you can choose a smaller image and let Windows duplicate it to cover the entire surface of the desktop.

Wallpaper is always a separate image file, stored in a format that Windows can recognize. Typically, this is a **Bitmap image format** file.

CAUTION **Wallpaper and background patterns can make your screen look** as sophisticated as the Museum of Modern Art, but they also can make it difficult or impossible to see icons on the desktop. If you choose an intricate wallpaper pattern, be prepared to squint.

I want a nice clean screen...

That's easy. Just make sure that (None) is selected in both list boxes in the Display Properties dialog box. You'll see a plain background with only the colors you've selected—no patterns or pictures.

I want to break up this boring color

Then use one of the Windows background patterns. These work just like a decorative pattern on a kitchen tile. The base color of the tile may be different (depending on what desktop background color you've chosen), but the pattern itself is always black. Choose a pattern from the list, then look in the preview screen above to see what it will look like. Or you can take a close-up look at the pattern (and even make changes to it) by clicking the Edit Pattern button. When you do, you'll see a dialog box like the one in Figure 13.4.

 Q&A *I selected a pattern and clicked OK, but I don't see it.*
Make sure that you don't have any wallpaper selected. Wallpaper always covers up the desktop pattern, which in turn covers up the background color. To clear the selection, highlight the (None) entry in the wallpaper list.

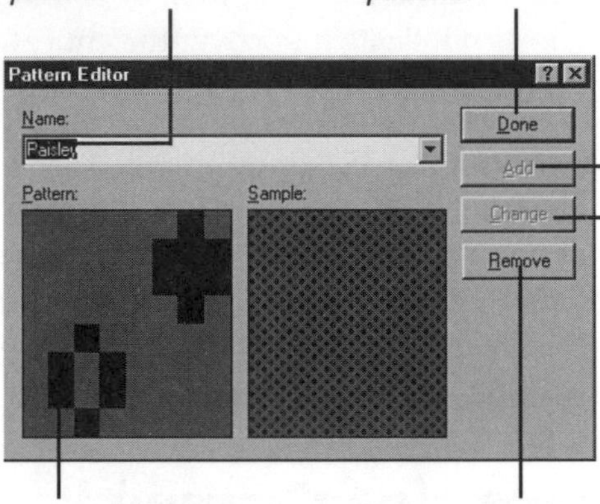

Enter a new name here.
If you don't, Windows
assumes you want to
replace the existing
pattern.

Click here when you're
through editing
patterns.

Fig. 13.4
Click the Edit Pattern
button to create your
own desktop look.

Click here to add the new
pattern to the list.

Click here to replace the
existing pattern with the
one you just changed.

Each big block is a pixel.
Click once to turn the pixel
to black; click again to
restore it to the default
background color.

Click here to delete
the pattern from the
list. Zap, it's gone!

I want to see the big picture...

When you have a favorite image stored in the right (bitmap) format, why not use it as the Windows wallpaper? If the image is big enough to take over the screen, then check the Center option in the Wallpaper box. Windows will neatly position the image so it's perfectly centered on your screen, as in Figure 13.5. Unless you've had the foresight to store the image in the Winnt folder, though, you'll need to click the Browse button and track down your work of art.

Some people like to use an image that's slightly smaller than the full screen, as shown in this figure. That way, they can arrange desktop icons like My Computer and the Recycle Bin without having to squint to pick them out against the background image. On the other hand, if you'd like to see the entire image from edge to edge, you can click the Plus! tab and check the box labeled Stretch desktop wallpaper to fit the screen.

Q&A ***I have an image that I'd like to use as wallpaper, but it's not a bitmap. What do I do?***

There's nothing Windows can do to help you, unfortunately. You'll need an image editing program (CorelDRAW! and Paint Shop Pro are two popular choices) that can open the image file and save it using the bitmap format.

Fig. 13.5
When you ask Windows to center an image as wallpaper, it positions it right smack in the center of the screen. If the image is smaller than your desktop area, you'll see some of the background color and pattern as well.

The tiled look: bricks and boxes

Take your favorite postage stamp, put it in a frame measuring two feet on each side, and hang it on your living room wall. What happens? The stamp practically disappears, of course. The same thing happens if you take a small bitmap image, just 20 or 30 pixels on each side, and try centering it on your screen. The tiny image is overwhelmed by that big desktop.

To make the framed image stand out on your wall, you could use an entire sheet of stamps instead of just one. You can do the same with a bitmap wallpaper image. When you check the <u>T</u>ile option, Windows copies your original image and uses the copies to fill the entire screen, as shown in Figure 13.6. The repetition makes a much better visual impact, because the image gets to fill a proper amount of space.

 TIP When you're experimenting with different desktop options, use the Apply button instead of the OK button. That way, you can check out different looks without constantly clicking to reopen the Display properties box.

Where to find wallpaper

If you're looking for wallpaper, you can find interesting images just about anywhere. Windows comes with some of its own, including my personal favorites, Greenstone and Santa Fe Stucco, which look great as tiled backgrounds. For a bright full-screen image that's especially effective on a gray winter's day, check out the Swimming Pool file. All three, plus a lot more, can be found in the Winnt folder.

Fig. 13.6
A small image can look lonely when it's centered on the screen

TIP **Can't find the wallpaper files? They probably aren't installed on** your PC. To put them on your hard disk, you'll need the Windows NT CD-ROM, and then you've got to go through the following steps. Click the Start button, choose Settings, and click the Add/Remove Programs icon. Select the Windows NT Setup tab, highlight Accessories, click the Details button, and (finally!) check the Desktop Wallpaper box. Click OK to copy the desktop wallpaper to your hard disk.

You can find other images, everything from animals to space shots, in art and photo collections available from a variety of sources: on CD-ROMs, from online services like CompuServe and The Microsoft Network, or even from the Internet. (That's where I discovered those hip Elvis postage stamps.)

You can even make your own wallpaper, if you have a little artistic talent and the Windows Paint program. (See Chapter 11 for more information on how Paint works.) After you've created and saved the Paint image, look on the File menu for the two Set as wallpaper options.

Redoing the color (and font) schemes

The Windows default colors are pretty boring. Dark green. Blue. White. Yawn. It's almost as bad as a model house, which is designed to be safe and bland so as not to offend anyone.

Want a different look and feel? A purple background? Lime-green title bars? Red letters? Hey, it's your computer. You can use any colors you like, and you can even replace the fonts Windows uses for the labels on icons and folders.

Windows comes with a predefined collection of desktop arrangements, with different coordinated colors and fonts. These collections are called **schemes**, and you can find them in the Display properties dialog box. If you find a scheme that has some elements you like, use it as the base for your own desktop. Start with the ready-made choices, then add your own options and save the edited scheme under a new name of your choosing, as shown in Figure 13.7.

 TIP **If you're not sure what a part of the desktop is called, look in the** preview window. All the parts of this window are "live"; if you click the menu bar here, for example, it selects the Menu option in the Item list below so you can adjust its size, color, and associated font.

Fig. 13.7

As you work, watch the example screen change to reflect how your options will look. If you're not happy with the way it's turning out, just click the Cancel button and start over.

Give the collection of visual effects a name, called a scheme. Next time you want your desktop to adopt this look, don't redo all that work; just select the scheme.

Pick a part of Windows that you would like to see displayed in a different color or with a bigger, bolder font.

Click here to pull down the color list—the small box filled with color squares. Choose a size and a color, where appropriate.

Choose a label font, where appropriate. Remember to specify size and attributes (bold, italic, color) for any fonts.

Where did all my colors go?

It doesn't matter how many colors you've told Windows you want to use. When you pull down the color widget in the Display properties dialog box, you only see 20. What happened to the others? Well, you'll have to mix them by yourself. Here's how:

1 Pull down the Color control, and click the Other button. Right off the bat, you get an expanded list of 48 colors to choose from (see Fig. 13.8 for an example).

2 Still can't find the right one? Click one of the empty squares in the section labeled Custom Colors; this is where you'll store the new color you're about to create.

3 Use the controls at the right to pick your color. Move the black **cross hairs** from side to side in the color matrix to shift along the spectrum from red to yellow to green and blue, and so on. Moving the cross hairs up and down changes the intensity of the color.

4 Having trouble seeing any colors? You might need to adjust the amount of black or white in the image. Drag the slider at the right down to add more black; push it up to add white. Stay somewhere in the middle, though; if you go all the way to the top or bottom all your color will disappear.

5 Preview your color in the box just below the color matrix. When you're happy with the look, click the button labeled Add to Custom Colors, then click OK to exit.

Fig. 13.8
Don't see the precise color you're looking for? Use the custom colors dialog box to mix it yourself.

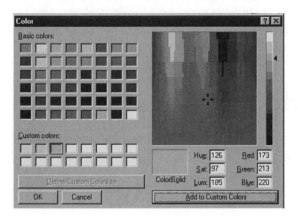

I can't read these labels!

Then change the font size. The normal size for window titles, for example, is 8 point. Try bumping it up to 9 or 10 points to make those labels more readable. (Don't know a point from a pixel? See Chapter 16 for more details about fonts.)

These buttons are too small!

You won't find a setting for adjusting the Minimize, Maximize, and Close buttons. But you can adjust their size just the same: When you change the size of the type in the Active and Inactive Title Bars, the size of the buttons changes, too. To make the buttons bigger, just make the Title Bar font bigger.

Oops—that's *ugly*. How do I get it back to normal?

Don't like that purple and lime-green after all? I don't blame you... Open the Display properties sheet and choose one of the predefined schemes stored there instead. You can always get back to normal by choosing Windows Standard from the list of schemes on the Appearance page.

TIP   **After fiddling with fonts and colors, if you find a group of settings** you really like, save it. Give it a name like **Favorite Colors**. Then, if something happens to your settings, you can always restore the ones you know you like.

CAUTION   **If you accidentally make the background color and the foreground** color the same somewhere in Windows, you won't be able to see what you're doing. To fix it, just go to the Desktop and restore the Windows Standard scheme.

Fine-tuning the look of your desktop

With Windows 95, Microsoft introduced a special add-on product called Plus! (the exclamation point is part of the name). Some of those fancy features are now part of Windows NT 4.0. To take advantage of some of these slick visuals, you'll need a better-than-average video card set to run at High Color or better.

Pop up the Desktop Properties dialog box and click the Plus! Tab. You'll see a dialog box like the one in Figure 13.9.

At the top of the Plus! Tab, you can change the icons that Windows uses for My Computer, the Network Neighborhood, and the Recycle Bin. Click the Change Icon button and browse through the available icons (look inside a file called shell32.dll, in the System32 folder, for a particularly rich assortment).

The other options on the Plus! Tab allow you to enhance the visuals throughout Windows. Personally, I have a lot of trouble working with Windows when the box labeled "Show windows contents while dragging" is unchecked. With this option on, you can actually see where the window and everything inside of it will land when you move it. Go ahead and experiment with the other Plus! Settings.

Fig. 13.9
Some of the settings on the Plus! Tab are subtle, but they add some interesting designer touches to an otherwise drab PC.

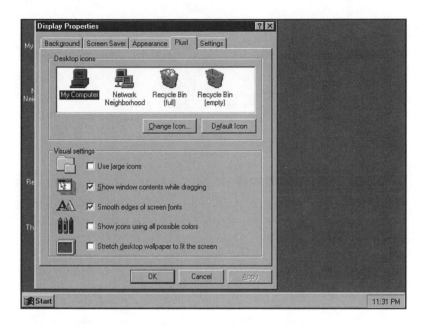

Installing a screen saver

Computer old-timers will tell you that screen savers are necessary to prevent characters from "burning in" to your monitor. That used to be true, but it isn't anymore. Still, there are two reasons to use a screen saver: for fun or for privacy.

The concept behind a **screen saver** is simple. When you tell Windows to use a screen saver, it starts a timer each time you tap a key or click a mouse button. When a predetermined amount of time passes without any action, Windows replaces whatever is on the screen with the screen-saver image, usually something that moves.

The most interesting screen savers are the 3D varieties, which draw fancy looping geometric shapes. To install any of them, click the Screen Saver tab in the Display Properties dialog box, as shown in Figure 13.10.

Fig. 13.10
Watching Windows NT draw intricate 3D pipes can be entertaining—and keep passers-by from snooping at your screen.

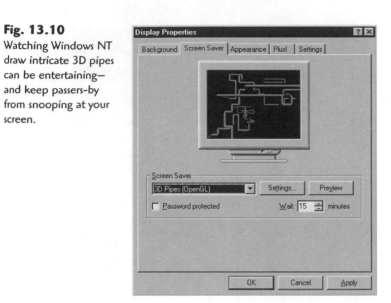

The following table describes what the options do; as usual, the sample screen shows how the various settings will look after you choose OK.

Table 13.2   Screen Saver Options

Choose this option...	...and then adjust this screen saver setting
Screen Saver	Pick the screen saver you want from this list.
Settings	Set preferences here—for example, how fast the image moves and which colors it uses.
Password protected	Once the screen saver kicks in, you'll have to press Ctrl-Alt-Del and enter your Windows NT login password before you can get back to work. This feature is handy if you want to be able to walk away from your desk without worrying about snoopy coworkers.
Wait	Tells Windows how long you want it to wait before turning on the screen saver. The default setting of 1 minute is a little quick. Try 5 or 10 minutes for starters.
Preview	Click to see a full-screen demonstration of the screen saver in action. Move the mouse or tap a key to end the preview.

When you've finished telling Windows how you want your screen saver configured, click OK. From then on, after the specified amount of time passes without your pressing a key or moving a mouse, your screen saver will turn on automatically, covering up whatever's on your screen. As soon as you tap a key or move the mouse, you'll regain control of the screen (although you may also have to enter a password as part of the process).

Fine-tuning the mouse

Most people don't realize that you can also change the mouse pointers that come with Windows. And that's just one of the changes that are possible. If you sometimes have trouble picking out the pointer on your screen, double-click the Mouse icon in the Control Panel. You'll see a dialog box like the one in Figure 13.11.

Fig. 13.11

Master your mouse! Windows lets you adjust all sorts of mouse options to make it easier for you to find that pesky pointer.

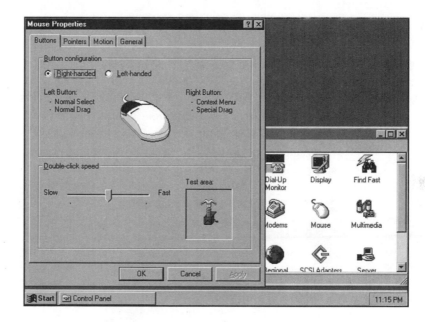

These are some of the options available:

- **If you're a lefty...** click the Buttons tab and tell Windows you want to switch the functions of the left and right mouse buttons.

- **If you have trouble double-clicking...** Tell Windows to be more patient. Look for the Double-click speed control on the Buttons tab. Move the slider to the left to make Windows recognize a double-click even when there's a brief delay between clicks, then test the new double-click rate on the Jack-in-the-box at the right.

- **If you think the mouse pointer is too small...**Pick a new pointer scheme from the list on the Pointers tab. The Dinosaur scheme is amusing, while the Magnified variety is helpful if you sometimes have trouble finding the mouse pointer.

- **If the pointer is moving too fast or too slow...** Click the Motion tab and slide the Pointer speed control in the appropriate direction.

- **If you sometimes lose track of the mouse pointer...** Try adjusting the Pointer trail settings on the Motion tab. If you select the Show pointer trails option, your mouse pointer will leave a noticeable trail on the screen as you use it. This option is especially useful on notebook computers, where the pointer is sometimes difficult to see because of the smaller, less distinct screens.

Changing the date and time

Not every PC keeps perfect time. If you notice that the time on the taskbar isn't quite right, reset it. Right-click the time display and choose Adjust Date/Time. You'll see the dialog box shown in Figure 13.12. Enter a new date or time, if necessary, and Windows will reset the system clock as well as the display.

Fig. 13.12
The Windows clock lets you reset the system date or time without a lot of fuss—if you've been given permission, that is.

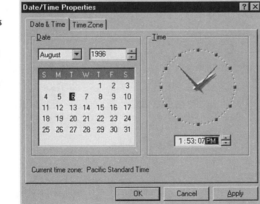

CAUTION **You might not be able to change the time on your system clock.** That privilege has to be granted to you by the Administrator of your system. If you see an error message when you try to open the Date/Time Properties dialog box, it means you'll need to talk to your network administrator before you can change the time or date.

Why does Windows care what time zone you're in? That can be important if you dial into a network that's in another time zone, or if you send e-mail out over the Internet, where the recipient might be in Arizona or Argentina or even Afghanistan. As long as both computers know about time zones, they'll be able to keep track of which file or message came first.

TIP If your PC loses track of the right time at an alarming rate, try this trick: Drag a shortcut of the Date/Time icon from the Control Panel into the Startup folder. That way, every time you turn on your PC, you'll get a chance to reset the clock. (And while you're at it, ask your system administrator to see about changing the battery on your motherboard.)

14

Putting Your Favorite Things Where You Want Them

● **In this chapter:**

- **Tell Windows exactly what to do with your data files**

- **Is your Start menu a mess? Reorganize it!**

- **Make the taskbar bigger—or make it disappear**

- **How to whip up new documents from scratch**

- **Give your desktop a productivity makeover**

Just as there's more than one right way to organize your kitchen, there are plenty of smart ways to organize your Windows desktop to make yourself more productive. . . . . . ⊳

How you use your computer is a matter of personal preference, in much the same way that cooking shows off your individual style. Do you lay out all the cast iron pots and stainless steel mixing bowls before you start preparing that gourmet dinner? Or do you clean and chop every ingredient first, *then* go looking for the utensils? Or do you call Pizza Man to have a pizza delivered?

Everyone has a different style of working, and Windows is nothing if not flexible. In this chapter, I'll show you how to rearrange the programs you use most often and how to group your working documents into efficient folders. In short, how to organize things so you can find them with as little fuss as possible.

It's important to know your working style

Where do you start? Well, it helps if you know how you prefer to work. Some folks tend to create a bunch of new documents, work with them for a few minutes or hours, then move on. Others work with the same set of documents for days or weeks at a time. It also helps to know how you can use Windows to keep your programs and documents close at hand.

How should you organize your work with Windows? Which techniques will make you most productive? That depends on whether you prefer to start with documents or with the programs that create them. Most people will actually do a little of both—sometimes double-clicking on document icons and other times launching programs from the Start menu. Windows responds a little differently in each case, depending on whether you start with a program icon or a document icon.

I know which *program* I want to start with...

Every program on your hard disk has an **executable file.** When you double-click on this file (or when you double-click on a shortcut that points to that file), your program starts. When you work this way, your organizational challenge is to find the program, start it up, and then use the program's File menu to create a new document or look for one you've already used.

66 *Plain English, please!*

An **executable** file is one that starts (or executes) a program when you double-click it. WordPad and Paint are executable files; so are Solitaire and Minesweeper. Contrast these files with simple **containers**, such as the My Computer window or any folder, and **documents** that require you to open a separate program to view or edit them. **99**

Windows organizes your programs into cascading menus that appear when you click the Start button and choose Programs. Once you learn how these shortcuts work, you can reorganize the Start menu to make it easier to use. You can even create new shortcuts to your favorite programs and put them on the desktop for quick access.

I know which *document* I want to start with...

What's in a **document file**? Well, all your data is there—words, numbers, pictures, and so on. The file has a name that, presumably, describes the contents. There's also information in the file that tells Windows about the program that created that data file. Once you find the document, you can usually double-click on it and let Windows figure out which program it needs to run. You may have to do some advance work to make sure that Windows knows which programs go with which documents, though.

Windows knows your (file) type

When you double-click on a file, Windows has to make some fast decisions. What kind of file is it? Which program created it? Is that program running right now? If not, where is it?

To answer all those questions, Windows maintains a list of **file types**, with each entry containing three pieces of information: a friendly description, one or more file extensions that go with that file type, and the name of the program Windows should start up when you want to use that kind of file.

Let's look at what happens after you create a file with Notepad. (Make sure to give it a long file name like Important Notepad Document.) Open a folder window, right-click on the name of the file you just created, and inspect its properties. You'll see plenty of information about its file type. Just below its icon, after the word Type, you'll see the words Text Document. That's the friendly name.

Now look a few lines lower on the properties sheet, next to the entry for the MS-DOS name. You'll see a clipped-off version of your long file name that ends in a period followed by three letters. In this case, those three letters are TXT, which is the file extension that Windows tacks onto the end of every file classified as a Text Document.

Those little three-character stragglers are annoying and confusing most of the time, so Windows hides them from you by default. But it doesn't actually get rid of them because that's how it knows to use Notepad to open these files. To see where that **association** between the file type and program is stored, open a folder window, choose <u>V</u>iew, <u>O</u>ptions, and click on the File Types tab. Scroll through the list until you get to the entry called Text Document, then highlight that entry. You'll see a box like the one in Figure 14.1.

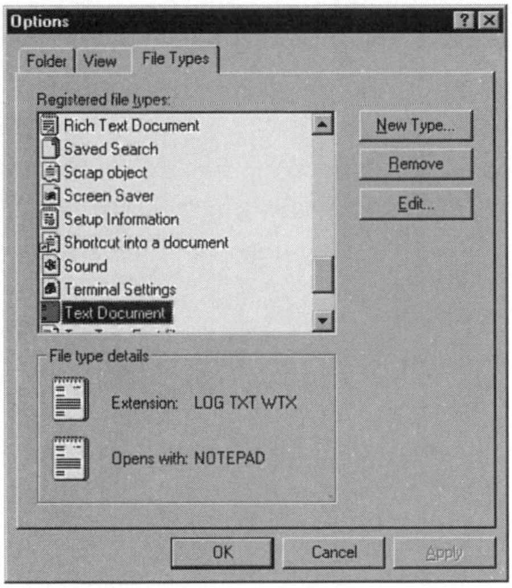

Fig. 14.1

When you double-click a file, Windows looks in this list to see what it's supposed to do next.

When you double-click a file in a folder, Windows checks its list of File Types to see what it's supposed to do next. If it knows how to handle that file type, it starts the program and loads the file. If it doesn't know how to handle the file type, it asks you what to do (see Fig. 14.2).

Fig. 14.2
When you double-click a file and Windows doesn't know what to do with it, Windows asks you for help. Just pick a program from the pop-up list, and you're in business.

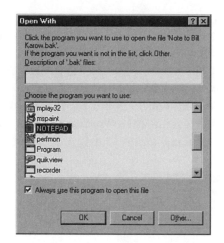

When you see this dialog box, scroll through the list of available programs and pick the one you want to use—Notepad and WordPad are good choices for text files. Make sure the type of data in the file is compatible with the program that you intend to use; it won't do you any good to try to open a graphics file with WordPad!

If you want Windows to always start the program you picked whenever it encounters a file of this type, check the box labeled "Always use this program to open this type of file." If the file has an extension (like .BAK), Windows will let you give the new file type a friendly description, like "Backup files."

Q&A *My program isn't in the list that Windows offered me. What do I do now?*

Click the button labeled O**t**her and find the icon for the program you want to use. Click **O**pen to add that program to the list. Then click OK to associate it with the file you want to edit.

Add a shortcut to get to what you need

Instead of forcing you to search for programs and documents all over your hard disk, Windows lets you create shortcuts to both. A **shortcut**, as we saw in Chapter 9, is a special sort of icon containing instructions that tell Windows exactly where it can find a particular file. And because you can create more than one shortcut for any file, you can have the best of both worlds: Keep your hard disk organized the way you want it, then use shortcuts to temporarily pull together groups of programs and documents into one convenient location.

When you right-click a shortcut and choose Properties, you'll see a dialog box like the one in Figure 14.3. Notice that the name of the shortcut doesn't have to match the name of the file it points to. That makes it easy to label a shortcut with a descriptive name (like Working Copy of Sales Chart) without changing the original file name (Sales Chart).

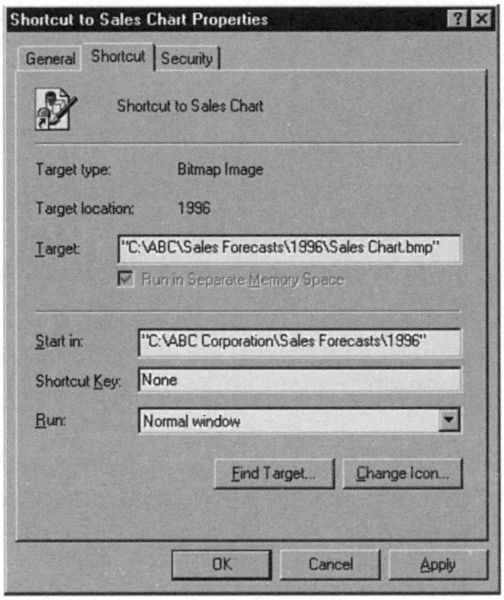

Fig. 14.3
Shortcuts are incredibly useful tools for getting and staying organized.

You can use shortcuts just about anywhere in Windows. They're particularly useful in these places:

- **To add a shortcut to the Start menu...** just drag a file and drop it on the Start button.

- **To put a shortcut on the desktop...** use the right mouse button, drag one or more files out of a folder and onto the desktop, then choose Create Shortcut(s) Here from the pop-up menu shown in Figure 14.4.

- **To add a shortcut to a folder...** right-click one or more files, and choose Copy. Then point to an empty space in the new folder, right-click, and choose Paste Shortcut.

- **You can even put a shortcut inside a Microsoft Exchange e-mail message...** just create the shortcut in a folder and drag it into your new message window.

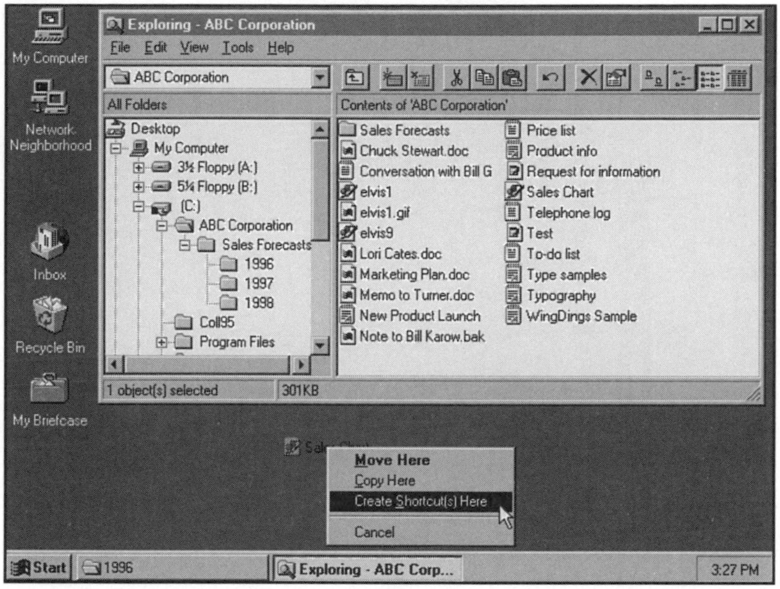

Fig. 14.4
Use the right mouse button to drag a file out of its folder and onto the desktop as a shortcut.

> **TIP** **Shortcuts can come from anywhere, not just your hard drive. If** you've found a noteworthy location on the Internet or on The Microsoft Network, you can create a shortcut to that location and put it on your desktop. You can also drag a file or folder from a shared folder on another networked computer or file server, and make a shortcut out of it. Don't worry—Windows can keep track of where everything came from.

You can even add shortcuts to the Start menu

All your programs should be available in the cascading menus that pop out from the Start menu. But for programs you use every day, that "click, wait, click, wait, click" routine can get pretty annoying. For those programs, why not create shortcuts at the top of the Start menu?

Adding an icon to the Start menu

Putting your favorite icon at the top of the Start menu couldn't be easier. Just open the folder that contains the file you want to add, drag the icon out of the folder, and drop it right smack on top of the Start button. If you drag WordPad from the Accessories folder onto the Start button, for example, it creates an instant shortcut that shows up at the top of the Start menu, as shown in Figure 14.5.

Fig. 14.5
Drag icons out of any folder and drop them onto the Start button, but don't get carried away! Five is enough.

My Start menu is a mess!

Over time, as you add new pieces of software to your system, the Programs section of your Start menu will start to get cluttered. It seems like every program insists on creating its own folder, even if it's only going to put one or two icons in it.

To cut through the clutter, put the programs you use every day at the top of your Start menu, while putting others you use regularly a click away inside the Programs folder. Finally, reorganize all those folders into a smaller number of folders, consolidating and renaming where appropriate. (I've put all my CD-ROM icons into a single folder, for example.) It's easy enough: Just right-click the taskbar, choose Properties, and then click the Start Menu Programs tab.

- Click the Add button to call up a special version of the Create Shortcut Wizard that automatically adds a new entry to the Start menu's Programs list.

- Click the Remove button to bring up a special box that lets you instantly zap a shortcut or folder from anywhere in the Start menu's Programs list.

- Click the Advanced button to call up a special version of the Windows Explorer that lets you manage all the folders and icons in the Programs area of the Start menu (see Fig. 14.6).

Click on any folder name in the
left pane, and you'll see its
contents in the right pane, just as if
you had opened a folder window.

To see folders inside of
other folders, click on the
plus sign to the left of any
icon in the left pane.

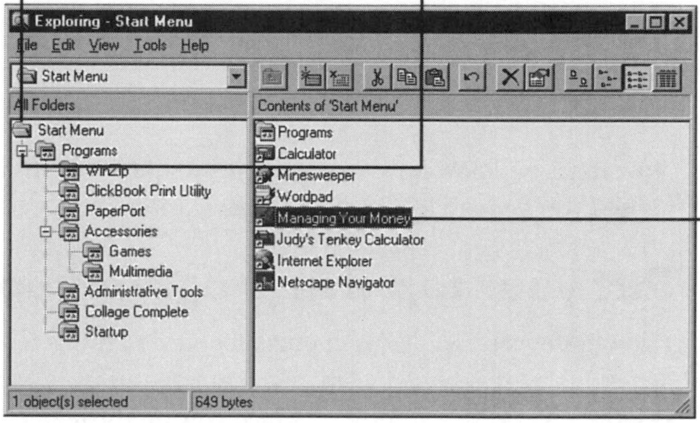

Fig. 14.6
To move a shortcut or
folder, make sure the
icon you want to move
is visible in the right
pane and the folder
you want to move it to
is visible in the left
pane. Then drag the
icon and drop it on
the new location.

To rename a shortcut
or a folder, click on its
name in the right
pane and start typing.
To delete an object,
highlight the entry and
press Delete.

How can I get this program off the Start menu?

The Start menu is just another folder that's found several levels deep inside
the Windows folder. (Each user on a given computer has a separate Start
Menu folder.) To delete, rename, or move icons in the Start Menu folder,
right-click on the Start button and choose Open; you can manage the shortcuts there just as you would those in any other folder. An even easier way to
delete Start menu items is to right-click on the taskbar, choose Properties,
and then click on the Start Menu Programs tab. The Remove button gets rid
of unwanted shortcuts without any fuss.

Why is there a line above some programs?

Your system administrator has the option to install some programs and
put them on the Start menu for every user. In addition, you (or the system
administrator) can install programs that are intended only for you. The icons
for the "All Users" programs appear at the bottom of the Start menu, with a
line separating them from the programs that are just for you. Likewise, on the
Start menu, any icons for All Users appear just above the Programs choice,
and the programs you drag onto the Start menu appear above those icons,
with a line separating the two groups.

Unless you have administrator-level privileges, you can't add, remove, or change any of the programs in the All Users category.

Organize your Start menu to make it efficient

Now that you know how the Programs folder on the Start menu works, what should you do with it? Try these organizational strategies.

Put your top five programs on top

The Windows setup program puts all your programs into folders that you can access using the cascading menus that pop out from the Programs choice. For the programs you use every day, why go through that extra pointing and clicking? Pick the five programs you use most often, and drop them onto the Start menu to put them closer at hand. Why five? Well, OK, maybe six or seven, but any more than that and the top of the Start menu will run out of room at the top of the screen (unless you've set your display to run at a higher resolution).

Reorganize the rest of your shortcuts in the Programs menu

Consolidate all those little groups into a handful of folders. For example, put all your Internet-related programs into a folder named "Internet," and put that folder inside the Programs folder. Take the programs you use once a week and move them straight into the Programs folder; that way they're only one cascading menu away instead of two.

TIP   **Use lots of shortcuts! There's no law that says you can only have** one shortcut for any program or document. If you have a favorite program, scatter shortcuts anyplace where you might want to get to it.

Put a Favorites folder on the Start menu

Do you constantly find yourself going to the same places and doing the same things? I have a few folders that fit that definition, so I've created a special folder filled with shortcuts for each of them. To create your own Favorites folder, right-click on the Start button, choose Open, and right-click any empty space. Choose New, Folder, and immediately type in the folder name you want to use, and then press Enter. Now, open a folder window for drive C: and right-drag the folder icons you use most often into the new folder. Choose the Create Shortcut(s) Here option, and you're done.

> **TIP** **If you use other Microsoft software, you may already have folders** where your favorite documents are stored. Internet Explorer, for example, keeps your World Wide Web shortcuts in a folder called Favorites. Microsoft Office creates a folder called My Documents. Why not add shortcuts to these folders to your Start menu?

Make your Start menu a little leaner

For some reason, Windows insists on using big, clunky icons on the Start menu. That's fine until you start adding your own entries to the Start menu. Oops—once you hit five or so, they start bumping into the top of the screen! To streamline the Start menu, open the Taskbar Properties dialog box (right-click an empty space on the taskbar and select Properties), and put a check mark in the box labeled Show small icons in Start menu. See Figure 14.7 for a before-and-after comparison.

Fig. 14.7
With the default large icons, the Start menu rapidly runs out of room. Turn on the small icons option and it slims down in a hurry.

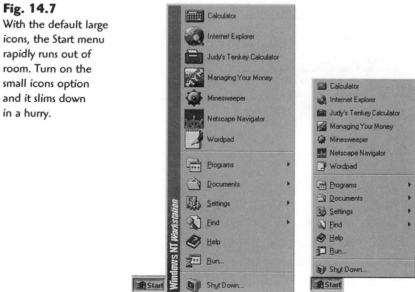

Working directly with documents

The most natural way to get work done with your PC is just to pick up a document and start typing. After all, the alternative—starting up a program—is a little like picking up a frying pan and then trying to decide what to cook. If you constantly find yourself working with the same documents, Windows gives you plenty of ways to quickly pick up where you left off before.

I just worked with that document yesterday!

Whenever you create a new document or open one you saved previously, Windows adds an entry on its built-in document-tracking list. To open one of the 15 documents you've used most recently, just click the Start button and choose <u>D</u>ocuments. A list of names like the one in Figure 14.8 will cascade out from the Start menu.

Fig. 14.8
To resume working with one of the documents on this list, just click its choice on the menu. Windows will launch the program and load the file for you.

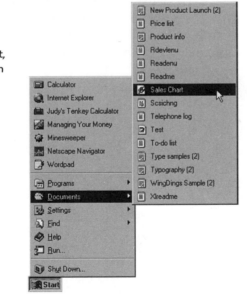

Q&A *I know I worked with a file this morning, but it's not on the Documents menu. What did I do wrong?*

Nothing, probably. Windows can only keep track of files that are opened from a folder window, from the Windows Explorer, or from a program that was designed for Windows 95. If you use the File menu to open or save a document with an older Windows application, it won't be added to the Documents menu.

The Documents menu doesn't go on forever, of course. There's a limit of 15. After you've filled the list, Windows kicks the oldest one off to make room for any new entries.

TIP **To clear the Documents menu, open the taskbar Properties dialog box, and click on the Start Menu Programs tab.** In the bottom half of the dialog box that pops up, you'll see a section devoted to the Documents menu. Click the Clear button to empty the list and start with a clean slate.

Cooking up new documents from scratch

Some people like to whip up an angel food cake without Betty Crocker's help. And when it comes to computers, some people like to create new files without any help from application programs. If that's your style, Windows has a feature you'll love. As long as Windows knows how to create the file type you're looking for, a new document is just a few clicks away. All you have to do is use the New choice on the right-click shortcut menu in any folder—or even on the desktop.

Let's say you're talking with your best client on the phone. You've gotten past the pleasantries, and now it's time to get down to business, which means you need to take some notes. Right-click on any empty spot on the desktop, and choose New, Text Document. Windows instantly adds a new icon to your desktop, with the (boring) default name, New Text Document (see Fig. 14.9).

Just start typing to give the new document a new name; it's already high-lighted for you. Press Enter to make the new name permanent. Press Enter again (or double-click) to start Notepad and load the new document. Now you can begin entering your notes.

When you're finished, save the document just as you normally would. You can leave it on the desktop if you like, or you can move it to another folder by using the right-click shortcut menus and the Cut and Paste commands.

Fig. 14.9
Right–click the desktop and click Ne<u>w</u> to create a text document from scratch. Rename it now or wait until later.

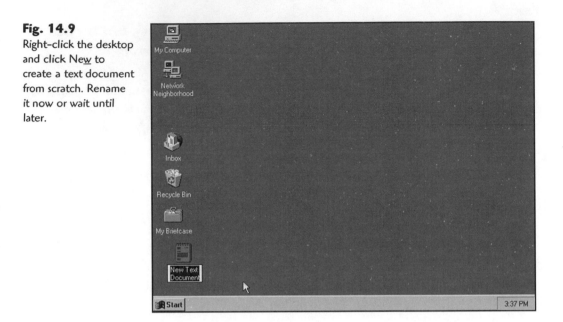

Making the taskbar mind its manners

If you've gotten into the habit of right-clicking on everything in Windows, you've probably already discovered that there are a pack of options for the taskbar as well. That's right—because the taskbar is just another Windows object, it has properties that you can inspect (and change) with a quick click.

Here's a sampling of what you can do.

Hide it, if you like...

Some people, especially those with smaller monitors, don't like having the taskbar take up any space at all at the bottom of the screen. If that's you, no problem—right-click the taskbar, choose P<u>r</u>operties, and check the A<u>u</u>to hide box. From now on, the taskbar will turn to a thin gray line at the edge of the screen whenever you have one or more windows open.

To make it pop up again, just slide your mouse pointer to the edge of the screen where the taskbar normally appears. (That's usually the bottom, but if you've moved the taskbar to another side, as we'll talk about in a few pages, you'll have to adjust accordingly). As soon as the mouse pointer bumps the edge of the screen, the taskbar will pop up.

Make it bigger, if you prefer...

Normally, the taskbar is tall enough to hold one row of buttons—no more, no less. But if you regularly open lots of windows and don't mind losing a chunk of the screen, you can make it taller:

1 Aim the mouse pointer at the top of the taskbar until it turns into a two-headed arrow.

2 Grab the edge of the taskbar and drag it up. You can keep dragging until the taskbar takes over about half the screen, but you'll be better off starting with two rows, as shown in Figure 14.10.

Fig. 14.10
Not enough room on the taskbar? Grab its upper edge and drag upward to make it bigger. This example has room for two rows of buttons, but you can keep dragging till it takes up more than half the screen.

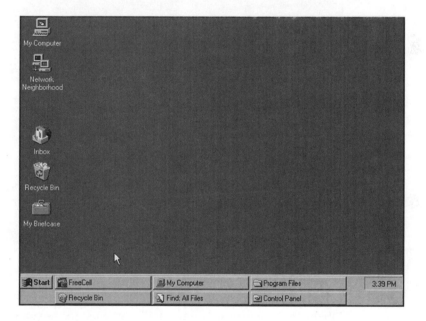

Q&A *My taskbar disappeared, and the **Auto** hide option isn't checked. Where did it go?*

You might have accidentally dragged the taskbar down instead of up, so that it's set to be zero buttons high. To put it back to normal, aim the mouse pointer at the very bottom of the screen (or to the side where you've moved the taskbar) until it turns to a two-headed arrow, then drag the pointer up slightly. The taskbar will pop back into position.

Move it, if you want to...

The taskbar is "sticky"—it fastens itself to the bottom of the screen like a refrigerator magnet. If you don't like it at the bottom of the screen, though, you can stick it to any of the other three edges of the screen. Just aim the mouse pointer at any empty spot on the taskbar, click, then drag it up to the top of the screen and watch it fasten itself there; your new taskbar will look like the one in Figure 14.11.

Fig. 14.11

Don't like the taskbar at the bottom of the screen? Drag it to either edge of the screen or to the top (as in this example), and it will "stick" to the nearest edge.

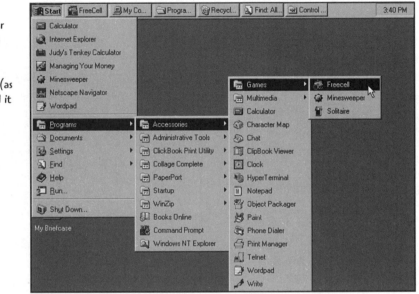

There are actually good reasons to leave the taskbar on the bottom of the screen. When it's positioned on either side, it's nearly impossible to read the labels on the buttons. And when it's fastened to the top edge, its menus end up where I expect my other program's pull-down menus to be. But it's your computer, and if you want your taskbar somewhere else, that's your privilege.

TIP **Some older Windows programs don't communicate well with the** taskbar. The result? Part of a crucial screen or dialog box may be hidden behind the taskbar. If you use an application that behaves this way, try hiding the taskbar so it stays out of your way.

Give your desktop a makeover

Windows puts a few things on the desktop, whether you want them there or not. My Computer, the Recycle Bin, and the Network Neighborhood, for example—you can't get them off the desktop with dynamite. But that still leaves plenty of room on the desktop for the things you use every day. When they're on the desktop, you can get to them with a click or two (see Fig. 14.12).

This is a folder stored directly on the desktop. Open by double-clicking.

This is a shortcut to a folder stored somewhere else. Open it by double-clicking, too.

Put a printer shortcut here, then print files by dropping them right onto the printer icon.

Fig. 14.12
The desktop makeover: You might not want to clutter your desktop with all these shortcuts, but a few are certain to fit comfortably into your working style.

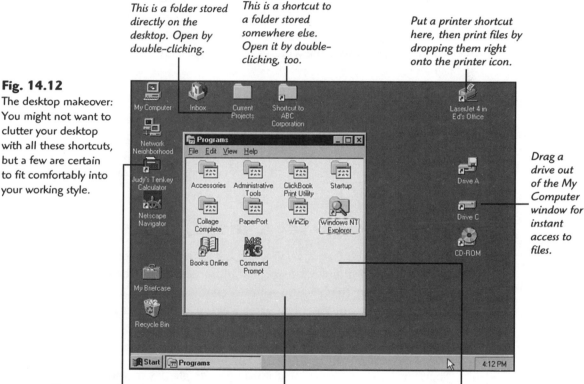

Drag a drive out of the My Computer window for instant access to files.

The arrow in the corner of the icon tells you this is a shortcut, not the real thing.

Keep the Programs folder open if you prefer easy-to-read big icons to the Start button's cascading menu.

Drop shortcuts to your favorite programs here.

Just try to count how many times you click the mouse button every day. A few hundred? Easily. If you keep up with that pace (which isn't all that frantic, really) your mouse fingers will click more than 50,000 times a year. Whew! Interested in a few finger-saving shortcuts? One unbeatable way to let your fingers do a little resting is to put a few strategically selected shortcuts on the desktop.

Drop a drive on the desktop

On my desktop, I have shortcuts that take me straight to two hard drives, a floppy drive, a CD-ROM reader, and a hard drive on another computer across the network. To copy a file, I drop it on the floppy drive icon. I can also poke around on any hard drive without having to detour through the My Computer folder.

It's easy to add these shortcuts to your desktop. Just open the My Computer window and drag one or more drive icons onto the desktop. Windows will protest. You cannot copy or move this item to this location, it will say. Do you want to create a shortcut to the item instead? Yep, that's *exactly* what you want to do. Say yes, and all you need to do is rearrange the icons to your liking.

Put a printer icon there, too

Maybe you need this, maybe you don't. If your print jobs go halfway across the building to a popular networked printer, it's a must-have. With a shortcut to that printer on the desktop, you're never more than a double-click away from checking your document's place in the laser printer line.

Add shortcuts to your favorite programs

There are a few programs that I use every single day, without exception. For those greatest hits, I want instant access, regardless of where I happen to click. I've created shortcuts to my top three programs so I can launch them with a double-click.

Add shortcuts to your favorite folders, for that matter

I don't know about you, but I tend to store most of my stuff in a few special places, and they're not all that easy to get to. My Letters folder, for example, is buried five folders beneath My Computer. I don't want to move those files, but I do want to get to them without 10 mouse clicks. The solution? I right-dragged the icon for the Letters folder onto the desktop and told Windows to create a shortcut. Now, when I want to look through Letters, I just double-click.

Fill a new folder with your favorite shortcuts

At any given time, I might be juggling work for three different clients. The files for all these projects are scattered on every corner of my hard drive. There's no need to move them around, though. Instead, I create a separate folder for each client, put it on the desktop, and fill it with shortcuts to the files I want to access when I'm working on a project for that client. I can have multiple shortcuts to the same document, too, which is a useful way to make sure I can always get to the master copy of documents I share across projects.

Here's a simple illustration of how you can use this technique to save time and energy. Let's say you have two big clients whose happiness is Priority One on your job description. You've got letters, memos, and e-mail about their business stored all over your hard disk. Your company also keeps an online price list stored on a network file server so everyone in the company can get to it quickly.

To make sure you don't lose track of any details, create a folder for each client right on the desktop. Then, make sure your price list is handy, no matter which folder you're using.

1 Find an empty space on the desktop, right-click, then choose Ne<u>w</u>, <u>F</u>older. Give the folder a name, and repeat the process for the second client.

2 Drag shortcuts for all your letters and memos into these folders, or move the documents themselves here.

3 Open the Network Neighborhood, and find the price list on the file server. Select the icon, right-click, then choose <u>C</u>opy.

4 Switch back to one of the folders on the desktop, right-click an empty space, and choose Paste <u>S</u>hortcut. Repeat for the second folder. Now, no matter where you're working, you'll never be more than a couple of clicks from that all-important document.

Keep the Programs folder open

Do you hate the cascading menus that fly out of the Start menu every time you click on Programs? Do you miss the Windows Program Manager? Then you might appreciate this shortcut. It doesn't look or act exactly like the old Program Manager, but the large icons and labels are easier to see than those tiny ones on the Start menu. With the Programs folder open on the desktop, you can always get to it with one click on the taskbar.

Give your folders a new look

When you first open up a folder, you get great big icons with nice readable labels. My Computer, for example, starts out this way. The default view is fine most of the time, but there are specific instances when you'll want to change the look of one or more folders.

The secret to quickly changing views is to turn on the toolbar in your folder window. Choose <u>V</u>iew, <u>T</u>oolbar, then look for the set of four buttons at the far right edge of the toolbar. Each of these buttons changes the icon view in your window. (You can also accomplish the same end by using the pull-down <u>V</u>iew menu and choosing one of the icon-related commands.)

CAUTION   **If you've turned your desktop into a work of art, with every icon** positioned exactly where you want it, DON'T use any of the Arrange Icons options that pop up when you right-click on the Desktop!

I want to see more icons in each window

Try the Small Icons view or the List view. They're nearly identical; the only difference is that the Small Icon view arranges everything in rows, from left to right, while the List view arranges things in columns, from top to bottom. Who thinks of these things?

I want to see as much information as possible

Then you'll want to use the Details view. The advantage here is you can quickly sort a list by clicking the label at the top of the column.

TIP **In Details view, you can sort by date or size with a single click. Just** click the word Modified to sort by date. Click Size to reorder the files by size, from smallest to biggest.

I want those big icons back!

 Large icons are easier to see, and their labels are easier to read, too. For windows where you don't have a lot of objects, the Large Icons view is just fine.

Part V: Out of the PC, Onto the Page: Printing and Fonts

15

Printing Perfect Pages

● **In this chapter:**

- **I have a new printer—now what?**

- **Which port should I use?**

- **How do I know this printer is working right?**

- **Why printing sometimes takes forever**

- **Using Windows NT to share your printer**

PC's and printers go together like ham and eggs as long as they're set up correctly. . . . . ▶

The screen is a great place to create and edit documents, but when it's time to share them with others, you don't want to lug your monitor all over the office. And one of the most important jobs Windows NT does is to make sure that you can capture your work on paper for other people to see.

It's not a small job, either. With the right software, you can create some impressively complex documents—filled with fancy fonts, all manner of lines and boxes, and eye-grabbing graphics using a full palette of colors. If your printer and Windows don't have perfect communication, there's no telling what will wind up on the page.

Best of all, you don't have to have your own printer, because Windows NT lets two or more people share a printer over a network. Your company might not be able to justify an expensive color printer for just one person, but it starts to make a lot more sense when ten people can share it.

Why do I need to worry about printing?

As long as you set up your printer properly and keep it filled with paper and toner, and as long as your documents are relatively simple—letters and memos on plain ol' 8-1/2 by 11 paper—you shouldn't ever have to think about it. But it helps if you have a basic understanding of how Windows NT works with a printer.

The goal of printing, of course, is to be perfectly **WYSIWYG**—which is pronounced *whizzy-wig* and means What You See (on the screen) Is What You Get (on paper). Here's how it works:

After you get your screen looking just right, you tell Windows to print the job. Right away, it looks to see that you have a printer hooked up; then it looks for the driver for that printer.

66 *Plain English, please!*

This printer isn't a car, so why does it have a driver? Ahem. A **driver** is a special piece of software that lets your computer talk intelligently with a piece of hardware. In this case the printer driver acts like a PC-to-printer dictionary for Windows. Your PC is filled with drivers; fortunately, you rarely have to think about them. 99

Inside the Printers folder

All the printer settings are gathered in one folder; to find it, choose Settings on the Start menu.

*Click here to set up a **new printer**. The icon reminds you that adding a new printer is as easy as tearing a new sheet of paper from a scratch pad.*

*You can spot a **shared printer** by the outstretched hand underneath it.*

*Any **installed printers** get their own icons in the Printers folder. Local devices have a simple printer icon.*

*If you've hooked up to a **network printer**, you'll see this cable underneath its icon.*

*Every time you tell Windows NT to print, it adds the document to the **print queue**, which sends jobs to the printer in the order they were received.*

With the right driver, Windows NT can tell your printer exactly which fonts to use, where all the graphics go, and just how to draw those lines and boxes. If your printer has any fonts of its own installed, Windows has to decide whether to use those fonts or substitute the ones that are in your document. As it works, Windows creates a full description of the document, one page at a time, in a language your printer can understand.

This all happens very fast, which is good news for your speedy PC, but lousy news for your printer, which actually has a lot of physical work to do while it handles the paper. There's no way the printer can keep up with the PC, so Windows puts the job in a special holding area called a **print queue**, and dribbles it out, a little bit at a time, to the printer.

Installing a new printer

When you set up a new printer, you're really installing special driver software that tells Windows NT exactly how to turn What You See into What You Get. Fortunately, setting up a new printer ranges from easy to ridiculously easy.

Can my printer install itself?

Sorry, no. That other Microsoft operating system, Windows 95, uses a feature called Plug and Play to automatically sniff out your printer and get it talking to Windows like they were old buddies. But as long as you know the make and model of your printer, installing a printer in Windows NT is no problem if you use the Add Printer Wizard.

To begin the step-by-step process, click the Start button, choose <u>S</u>ettings, and open the <u>P</u>rinters folder. Double-click the Add Printer icon, and you'll see a dialog box like the one in Figure 15.1.

Fig. 15.1
Where's that printer? The first thing Windows needs to know is whether the new printer is plugged into your computer or available elsewhere on your company's network.

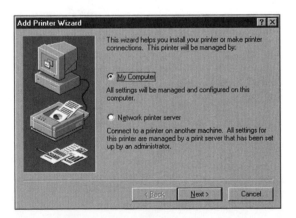

Which port should I use?

Follow the wizard's instructions, which will be slightly different depending on whether the printer is local or out on the network.

- For a **local printer**, tell Windows which port the printer cable is plugged into. Most printers use a parallel port, and most computers have only one of these, called LPT1. If you're sure that's the right port, check the box shown in Figure 15.2.

66 *Plain English, please!*

A **port** is the socket on the back of your computer where you plug in the cable that goes to your printer. You have your choice of parallel ports (also known as printer ports) and serial ports (aka communication ports). Except in very rare cases, the correct choice is a parallel port, usually the one called LPT1. Make sure you have the correct printer cable, then connect it securely to the printer and the back of the PC. 99

Fig. 15.2
Pick a printer port. LPT1 is the most common choice for printers. The COM options identify serial ports, which are more commonly used to hook up modems and mice.

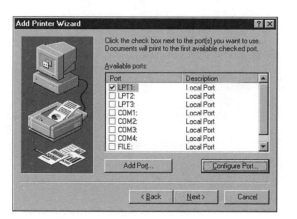

- For a **network printer server**, the procedure is slightly more complicated. As soon as you click the Next button, Windows NT pops up a dialog box like the one in Figure 15.3. Before you can set up your printer, you'll need to identify it, using its name and the name of the computer it's hooked up to. Pick the printer's name from the list of Shared Printers and click OK.

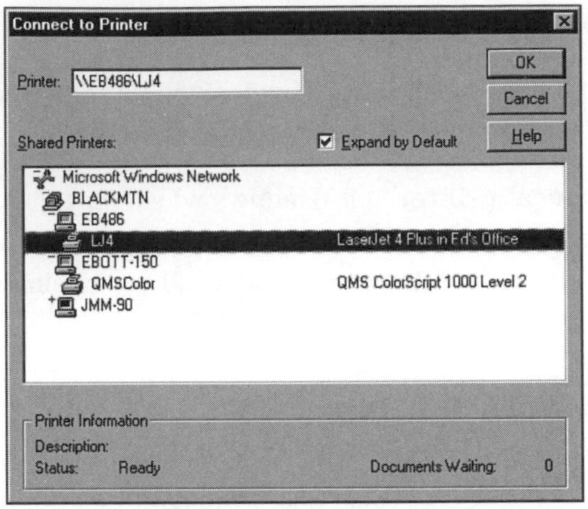

Fig. 15.3
Find the name of the printer and the computer it's attached to. As soon as you select it from this list, Windows NT fills in the box at the top.

- If you're lucky, Windows NT can automatically install a copy of the printer driver stored on the machine to which the printer is attached. If you're not so lucky, you'll see a message like the one in Figure 15.4, and you'll have to track down the Windows NT CD-ROM or another copy of the printer driver before you can continue.

Fig. 15.4
Windows NT can install a printer driver automatically, but this process doesn't always work. If you see this message, you'll need to find your own copy of the printer software.

CAUTION **Be careful to choose the right printer driver. Even subtle** differences in a model name or number can have a big impact on your print jobs. For example, there are 22 different printers whose names include "HP LaserJet 4." Use the wrong driver, and you might not be able to use some of the special features you bought the printer for in the first place!

- Pay particular attention to the last step in the Add Printer Wizard, where you have the chance to do two things on one screen, shown in Figure 15.5.

- Give the printer a **friendly name**. You can call it Fast Eddie or Big Red, if you like, but it might be more useful to add a descriptive name, like "Apple LaserWriter in Art Dept."

- Tell Windows whether you want to make this the **default printer**. Say yes here, and Windows will automatically send all your print jobs to this printer unless you go out of your way to choose another printer.

Fig. 15.5

Make the printer name as descriptive and helpful as possible. Even a temp could probably find this printer...once he found the right office.

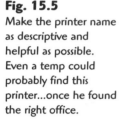

How do I know my printer is installed correctly?

When you first install a new printer, Windows offers to print a test page for you. Just say yes! This is the best way to make sure that the printer works correctly. Later, if you have any problems, come here (see Fig. 15.6) and print another test page to determine whether the problem is with your printer or your application.

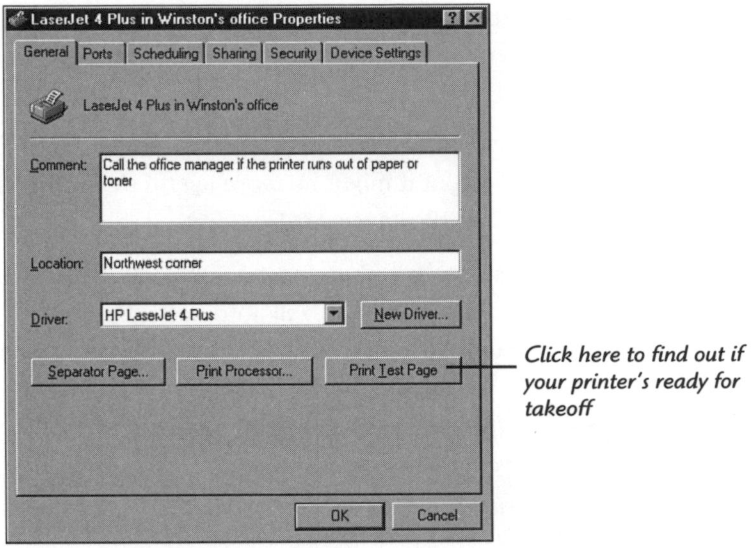

Fig. 15.6
Is your printer hooked up correctly? To find out, right–click on its icon in the Printers folder, choose Properties, then click the Print Test Page button.

Click here to find out if your printer's ready for takeoff

Can my printer do any special tricks?

Hey, this isn't the Late Show with David Letterman. No Stupid Printer Tricks, please!

But it's true that every printer is different, and you may find that your printer is capable of doing some Smart Printer Tricks. The best way to find out is to right-click the printer icon, choose Properties, and click the Device Settings tab. What will you find? Lots and lots of settings, as the dialog box in Figure 15.7 shows.

You'll find all the routine information about your printer here—its name, port, and location, for example. But, depending on the kind of printer, you may also find some surprises.

- Ignore the technical mumbo-jumbo. Do you really care that the Halftone device gamma is 1.2500? (Are they serious?)

- There's an option to print a special sheet of paper called a **separator page** at the start of each new job. The separator page identifies the source of the print job, so that anyone looking at the pages that have come out of the printer won't have to guess who printed what.

- You can fine-tune your font selections here, so that your documents always use either the fonts in your printer or the ones on your PC, whichever you prefer.

- You'll even find **color options** here, if you have a printer that produces color output.

Fig. 15.7
If your printer has more than one paper tray, you can tell Windows NT exactly which size you store in which tray, along with many other options.

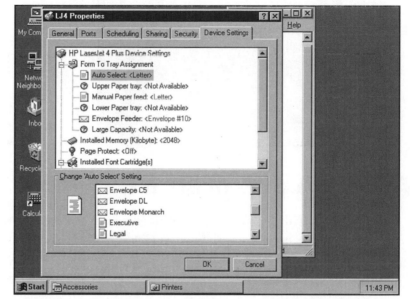

66 *Plain English, please!*

If you look in the printer properties sheet, you'll see references to the **enhanced metafile format**, sometimes abbreviated as **EMF**. That's the ten-dollar name for the temporary file that Windows creates and then sends to your printer. A very small number of printers can't handle EMFs. 99

But wait! There's more. Right-click on the printer icon once again, and this time choose Document Defaults from the pop-up menu. You'll run into another long list of options that help you control the way your printer handles each document. These options, like the ones in Figure 15.8, allow you to specify which resolution you'll use for printing (lower resolutions don't look as sharp, but they save toner); tell the printer to automatically make more than one copy unless you say otherwise; even shrink documents down in size, if that feature is available on your printer.

Fig. 15.8
Save a tree, if your printer will let you. The Default Document Properties dialog box lets you print using both sides of the page on certain laser printers.

Take this job and print it!

Eventually, you get everything looking just the way you want it on your screen, complete with fonts and lines and boxes and margins and pie charts and pictures (not the ones from your vacation, please). Of course, you want everything to look exactly the same on the paper as it did on the screen. What do you do now?

With most applications, you can just choose File, Print, or click the Print button. When you do, you'll see a dialog box like the one in Figure 15.9, taken from WordPad.

 TIP **Many programs offer a Print Preview option. If the program from** which you're trying to print gives you this choice, take advantage of it. You can quickly look at what Windows thinks it's going to send to the printer. If it doesn't look the way you expect it to look, fix the problem before you've wasted paper (and time) printing it out the wrong way.

 CAUTION **Old Windows programs don't use the same dialog boxes as new** ones written especially for Windows 95 and Windows NT, so with these programs you may not be able to set up your pages and printers completely. If you find yourself in this situation, contact the company that made the program and ask it if it has a new version designed for Windows NT.

Fig. 15.9
Choose File, Print;
most applications will
show you a dialog box
like this one.

Check that you're sending the job to the right printer.

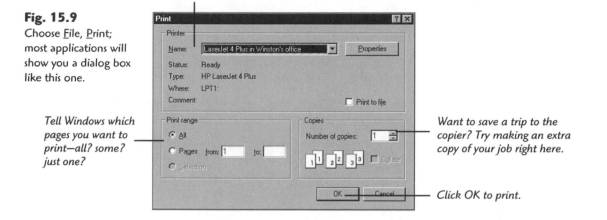

Tell Windows which pages you want to print—all? some? just one?

Want to save a trip to the copier? Try making an extra copy of your job right here.

Click OK to print.

PostScript or LaserJet?

When you buy a new printer, you can choose from literally thousands of different models. But eventually it all comes down to a single choice: Do you want to use the PostScript language? Or will you be more comfortable with the Hewlett-Packard language?

No, you don't have to actually learn a foreign language to use one of these printers. The Windows printer drivers take care of these translations for you. But there are differences between the two types of printers.

PostScript is the most common language among people who do desktop publishing. If anyone you know uses an Apple Macintosh, chances are it's hooked up to an Apple LaserWriter, the best-known PostScript printer. It's not super fast, but a PostScript printer lets you print complex graphics with beautiful results. If you plan to make your own newsletters, this is your choice.

The **Hewlett-Packard Page Control Language (PCL)** is the way that LaserJets and most ink-jet printers talk to Windows. The graphics aren't as good-looking as the ones that come out of a PostScript printer, but these printers are fast and can handle just about any job you can throw at them.

There's a third standard, too, for old, noisy dot-matrix printers, but these are becoming less common. And there's even a fourth standard, for ink-jet printers, although these are more common at home than in the office.

Most printers, no matter who manufactured them, use one or both of these languages. If you can't find your printer on the official list of Windows NT drivers, look at the printer manual and see whether it emulates one of these printers. If it does, you can choose the Apple LaserWriter II NT or the Hewlett-Packard LaserJet III and be very happy with the results.

What happens when I click the Print button?

When you tell Windows NT to print (either by choosing a menu item or clicking a button) it starts a complicated process that would make a rocket scientist proud. And something can go wrong at any of these steps.

What Windows does	What can go wrong	How to fix it
Matches up **fonts**. With non-TrueType fonts, you need both a screen font and printer font. Windows uses the screen font to show you how the document will look, and the printer font to print it.	The fonts you see on the screen don't match the ones on the printed pages.	Replace the fonts that aren't printing properly with TrueType fonts.
Converts **graphics** on the screen into dot patterns that your printer can print.	Graphics are missing or don't look right.	The printer may need more memory to handle complex graphics. Try printing at a lower resolution.
Looks to see whether you've issued any **special instructions**, like extra copies or two-sided printing.	You asked for two-sided printing, but nothing happened.	This feature is only available on some printers when a special hardware option is installed.
Sends the job to the **print queue** at the right speed.	Pages are missing, especially sections with graphics, because Windows waits longer for the printer to finish.	Check the printer properties and increase the timeout setting so printer can't keep up for the with the PC.

66 *Plain English, please!*

A print queue is the name for the line that your print jobs wait in. In a busy office, print jobs stack up like 747s waiting to land at O'Hare Airport. When print jobs are coming from every direction, Windows NT makes like an air traffic controller and keeps each job in a holding pattern until the printer is ready; then it waves the next job through and lets each job in turn make a safe final approach to the printer. The process of doling out print jobs at just the right speed is called spooling. 99

Q&A *My fonts don't look right on the printed page. What went wrong?*

You chose a non-TrueType font that isn't available on your printer. (For more information about TrueType fonts, skip to the next chapter.) When that happens, Windows looks around for another font and tries to print using this font instead. If the results of this substitution process aren't good enough for you, choose a new font, preferably one with the TT (TrueType) symbol next to it.

My page came out sideways!

You wanted zig, but Windows NT set up the printer for zag. It happens, because Windows has at least two settings for each piece of paper. With standard American 8-1/2 by 11-inch paper, you can print in **portrait** mode (with the long edge going from top to bottom, the way letters typically are printed) or in **landscape** mode, which is what happens when you give that same piece of paper a quarter turn so the long edge runs from left to right. (Some printer drivers include a setting called **landscape 2**, in which the paper rotates a quarter-turn in the opposite direction.)

Changing orientation between portrait and landscape is easy with new Windows NT applications (including Paint and WordPad). Just choose File, Page Setup to see a dialog box like the one in Figure 15.10. Can't remember which is portrait and which is landscape? Just click the appropriate button and the graphic at the top of the box shifts to give you the answer.

Fig. 15.10
Choose File, Page Setup to pick a new paper type and orientation. The graphic at the top reminds you that landscape is sideways.

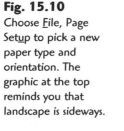

Why is this print job taking so long?

When you print to a shared printer, especially a slow one like a color printer, you sometimes have to wait in line while other jobs work their way through the printer. But sometimes delays are caused by hardware problems: The printer might be out of paper, jammed, or just not turned on. (Don't laugh— it happens.) You won't know exactly why your print job is moving like rush hour traffic on an L.A. freeway unless you check your place in the print queue.

Did I say freeway? Actually, the print queue is more like a one-lane highway. When four or five people try to print at once, only one job gets to actually go to the printer at a time. The others have to slow down, line up single-file, and wait their turns. If you tell Windows to pause one of the jobs, though, traffic doesn't come screeching to a halt. Instead, Windows moves on to the next job in the list if it can.

Double-click on the printer icon in the Printers folder and you'll see a list of all the jobs waiting to be printed, including yours (see Fig. 15.11).

Fig. 15.11
There's no traffic jam here, because the lower documents are able to continue printing even when the top document is paused.

Document Name	Status	Owner	Pages	Size	Submitted	Port
Microsoft Word - Chap15 - Usi	Paused	Ebott-150	19	155KB	11:24:06 PM 6/18/96	
Microsoft Word - Memo to Turn		Ebott-150	1	818 bytes	11:38:15 PM 6/18/96	
Microsoft Word - Company News		Ebott-150	1	10.6KB	11:38:24 PM 6/18/96	
Monthly budget.xls		JMERRILL		2.30KB	11:39:22 PM 6/18/96	
8-31-95 Letter to Tibe		FAXGUY		1.12KB	11:46:30 PM 6/18/96	

LaserJet 4 Plus in Winston's office - Paused

Printer   Document   View   Help

Pause
Resume
Restart
Cancel
Properties

Cancels the selected documents.

Here's what you need to know about print queues:

- Windows NT uses the Priority setting for each job to determine its place in the line. The default priority is the lowest setting, 1. Increasing this number (to a maximum of 99) tells Windows to move the job ahead of others in the queue.

- All priorities being equal, Windows works its way through the list from top to bottom.

- If there are any problems with the printer, you'll see an informative message in the window's title bar.

- The first column shows information about the document being printed—its name, most of the time, although sometimes all you see is the name of the program that printed it.

- To see whether there's a problem with one of the documents, look in the second column to check its status. Out of paper and Paper jam are among the common errors you'll see here.

- The next column shows who sent the job to the printer.

- How far along is this job? Some programs report progress in pages; others use bytes. If you see Now printing page 3 of 457, you can probably guess that it'll be a while before your print job emerges.

- Who was there first? Every job's starting time shows up here.

TIP **Every time you send a job to the printer, Windows NT puts a tiny** printer icon into the notification area at the right of the taskbar. To see all the jobs that are waiting in the queue, double-click on this icon.

Oops—I didn't mean to print that!

Sooner or later, it happens to everyone: You send a big job (40 pages? 100? 400?) to the printer, and the instant you finish clicking the Print button you realize that you left out a paragraph on page 1. You could just let the printer chew through all those pages, then throw everything away and start over. But if you're quick enough, you can jump in right now and stop everything.

You have to be quick, though, because you can only cancel a print job if the job is still in the queue. Open the printer window, select the job, right-click, and choose Cancel Printing from the shortcut menu (see Fig. 15.12). If you don't want to kill the job, but just want to stop it temporarily, choose Pause Printing instead.

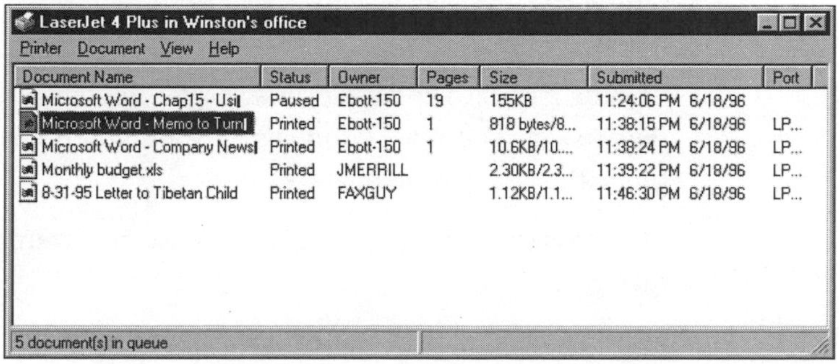

Fig. 15.12
To kill a print job, open the printer window, select the job, right-click, and choose Cancel.

TIP **Want to make sure you can always see where you stand in the line** for the printer? Add the printer icon to your Startup folder. First, open the Printers folder. Then use the Find command on the Start menu to search for and open your StartUp folder. Drag the printer icon from the Printers folder into the StartUp folder and restart Windows NT. Now, every time you start up your computer, the printer window will open automatically. All you have to do is click its taskbar button to look at the queue or cancel a print job.

When you have to share: printing on a network

What makes printing on a network different? Not much, except that you'll probably have to walk down the hall to get your job instead of reaching a few feet away from your desk. On your company's network, you can hook up a printer to any PC (even yours) and share it among everyone on the network. Here's how.

Setting up your system to use a network printer

If there's a printer out there that you want to use, it's easy to get connected. If your network administrator or another Windows user has given you the rights to use the printer, you just need to find its icon, point, and click. Here are step-by-step instructions:

1 Browse through the Network Neighborhood until you find the computer the printer is attached to; double-click on its icon and open the Printers folder on that machine.

2 Select the icon for the printer you want to use, and right-click to pop up the shortcut menu.

3 Choose Install to add the printer driver to your PC, and then follow the Wizard's instructions. Windows may ask you for the Windows NT CD to finish the installation process.

4 Now, you can print to this printer just as if it were hooked up to your own computer.

Sharing your printer with someone else

Before you can let other people use your printer, you have to agree to share it with them. Here's how:

Click the Start button and choose <u>S</u>ettings, <u>P</u>rinters to open the Printers folder. Right-click on the printer you want to let other people use, and choose S<u>h</u>aring. You'll see a dialog box like the one in Figure 15.13. To tell Windows who can and can't use the printer, click the Security tab and click the <u>P</u>ermissions button.

- Give the printer a **name** (make sure it's less than 32 characters long). You'll use this name plus the computer's name to identify it.

- Install **extra drivers**, if you expect that some of the people sharing your printer will use Windows 95 or an older version of Windows NT. When they connect to your shared printer, they can download these drivers directly from your computer.

- Click on the **Security** tab and click Permissions to adjust the permissions for each list of users. If you don't want Bob in Accounting sending his 200-page spreadsheets to your printer, just don't let him.

Fig. 15.13
Before you can let others send jobs to your printer, you have to tell Windows it's OK to share it with others. Right-click the printer's icon and choose S<u>h</u>aring to pop up this dialog box.

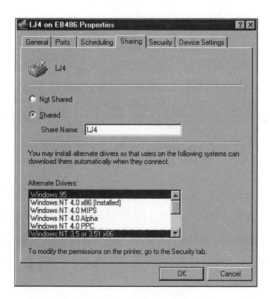

Click OK, and Windows adds a little outstretched hand to the bottom of the printer's icon. Now, other people can share your printer, although you can restrict access by only letting selected users have permission to use your printer.

TIP **If you want your assistant to be able to send jobs to your laser** printer but you really hate the idea of having other people share it, hide it! When Windows asks you to give the share a name, add a dollar sign to the end—LaserJet4$, for example. When Windows sees the dollar sign, it knows to hide the printer in the Network Neighborhood on other machines. Anyone who knows the secret name can still hook up to the printer by typing it in, but no one will be able to browse through the network and see it.

How do I tell which print job belongs to me?

You can tell Windows to add a **separator page** every time it starts a new print job. It wastes one sheet of paper for each job you send to the printer, but in a big office it can be the only way to make sure your print jobs don't wind up on someone else's desk by mistake.

TIP **You can only control the option for separator pages if the printer** is attached directly to your computer. If you want Windows to print a special page to help you spot the beginning of each new document you print on a shared printer, you'll have to ask the owner of the PC to which the printer is hooked up.

To turn this feature on, right-click the printer's icon, and look on the General properties tab. You'll find a selection of ready-made separator pages in the System32 folder, inside the Winnt folder.

Rushing a print job

There's a special variant of Murphy's Law that applies to shared printers. Let's say you're late for a meeting where you're supposed to present the sales results for the last quarter. You've sent the job to the printer, but it's not coming out. You check the print queue and discover that Bob in Accounting has 27 big jobs stacked up, and it might be hours before they all finish printing.

What do you do? Hey—it's time to cut in line in front of Bob. (Don't worry, he'll probably understand.)

1 Open the Printers folder.

2 Double-click the icon for the printer where your print job is waiting.

3 Select your print job, right-click, and choose Properties. Drag the priority slider to the right and click OK. Voilà! You're now next in line.

16

Making Text Stand Out with Fonts

● **In this chapter:**

● **Font? Typeface? Point size? What's that all about?**

● **Use fonts to make text easier to read**

● **I have some new fonts. What do I do now?**

● **How to keep track of which font is which**

● **I need to add special characters to my documents**

Need just the right look for that special document? Fonts let you dress up text so it looks great and is easy to read . . . . ⊙

Pick up any newspaper or magazine—or, for that matter, this book. Pay no attention to the words for now; instead, just look at the way those words are arranged on the page. You'll see a mixture of large and small letters, from big bold headlines to tiny footnotes. You might even see some fancy script that would be right at home on a wedding invitation.

If the designer was on the ball, those words aren't just randomly arranged on the page, either. Instead, the size and shape and placement of the letters have been carefully chosen to help guide your eye to the most important parts of the page. The big bold headlines signal the start of a new section, while the body of each story is displayed in type that's large enough for you to read without squinting.

You don't need to be a high-paid designer to perform the same typographic magic with your documents. Windows has all the tools you need to create documents that look like they were done by a desktop publishing genius. Each of those different typographic styles is called a **font**, and once you learn how fonts work, you're ready to put together your own front page.

What is a font, anyway, and why should I care?

Imagine how confusing the world would be if everyone dressed exactly alike. How would you tell the police officer from the butcher, or the auto mechanic from the baseball umpire? That's why, over the years, we've come up with uniforms that help us see at a glance what people do for a living. The police officer has a blue uniform, the butcher a white smock; the mechanic is dressed in greasy overalls, while the umpire is wearing a chest protector. Underneath all those outfits, of course, they're just people.

The words and letters you use in your documents operate exactly the same way. Letters, numbers, and characters all start as basic shapes—a capital A always looks like a tepee with a crossbar, for example—but you, as the type designer, can blow up a letter or shrink it, dress it in dark colors, or give it fancy decorations.

There's more to a font than just a pretty (type)face

There's plenty of technical jargon in every font, but it doesn't have to be confusing. The **font** is the complete description of the typed characters, including all the following attributes:

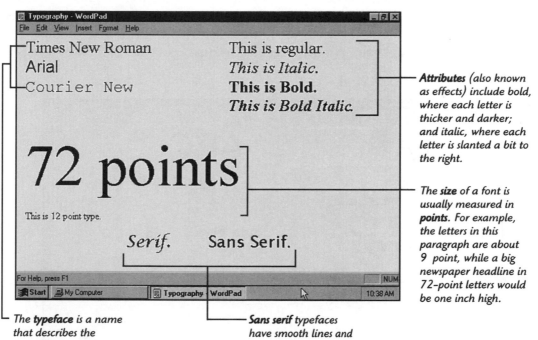

Attributes *(also known as effects) include bold, where each letter is thicker and darker; and italic, where each letter is slanted a bit to the right.*

The **size** *of a font is usually measured in* **points***. For example, the letters in this paragraph are about 9 point, while a big newspaper headline in 72-point letters would be one inch high.*

The **typeface** *is a name that describes the overall shape and detailed features of a set of characters. Times New Roman and Arial are the two most-used typefaces, because they come with Windows.*

Sans serif *typefaces have smooth lines and corners.* **Serif** *typefaces, on the other hand, have little decorations on the corners.*

❝ Plain English, please!

What's the difference between a font and a typeface? The font includes all the characters of a particular size, color, shape, and design. The typeface, on the other hand, is the detailed description of the shape of each letter, without regard to its size or other characteristics. Arial is a typeface, while 10 point Arial Italic is a font. Today, many people use the terms interchangeably, and in casual use there's no confusion. **❞**

For a quick illustration of how different typefaces can represent the same shapes, look at the letters in Figure 16.1. In every case, you can easily recognize the basic shape, but these examples illustrate the nearly infinite number of ways you can draw those same characters so that they have some personality.

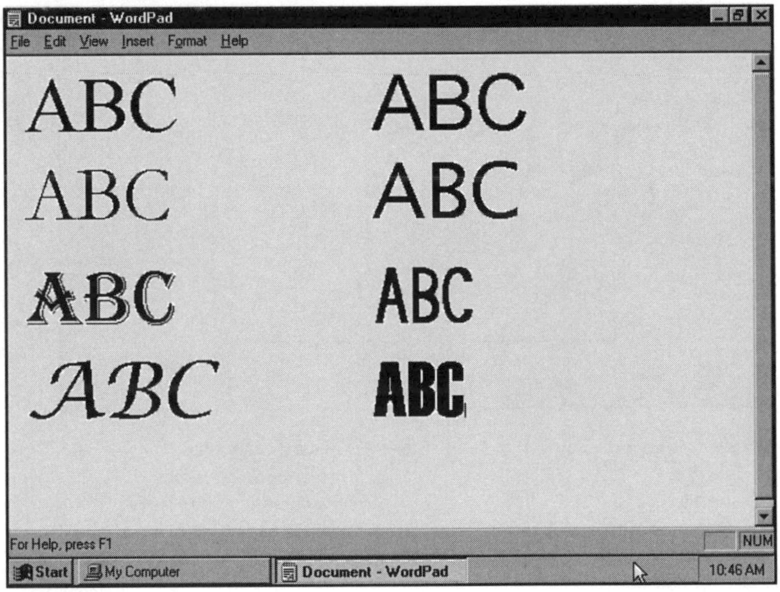

Fig. 16.1
The letters are the same, but the look is completely different. Different fonts can give your words some personality.

What can I do with fonts?

Every time you press a key—the letter A, let's say—on your computer's keyboard, it sends a message to Windows: "Hey! I'm sending up an *A*—put it on the screen!" The trouble is, because that letter has no uniform, you have no way of telling what it's supposed to do. So before Windows puts it on the screen, it looks for your instructions as to how you want it displayed.

- For a banner newspaper headline that you want readers to see from 10 feet away, you would probably use thick, dark letters with no fancy frills.

- For a wedding invitation, you might choose a script typeface that looks like it was written by hand.

- For the fine print at the bottom of a contract, you would use the thinnest, smallest type imaginable, so that only lawyers and bald eagles can read it without a magnifying glass.

In all three cases, the basic shapes of the letters are the same—you can tell the difference between a capital A and a small b, right?—but the thickness of the lines, the decorations on the corners of each letter, the slant of the letters, and so on, are all different.

How do I tell Windows which font to use?

Most Windows programs that use text let you specify the exact look you want for those words. You can simply make a word a bit bigger, or you can change everything about it so that it takes on a completely different look. With most applications, you'll find the font choices grouped under a menu call Format.

66 *Plain English, please!*

Formatting is a catch-all word for the way you tell Windows exactly how you want a document to look when it's printed or displayed on the screen. The name of the font determines one type of formatting; other kinds of formatting define the spaces around and between the words. Other common formatting questions: Is there extra space between lines? How much room do you want for the page margins? Is there a page number on every sheet? 99

To specify a font in WordPad, for example, choose Format, Font. You'll see a dialog box like the one in Figure 16.2.

To give your text a makeover, follow these steps. (Make sure you have some text selected first!)

1 Choose a typeface (WordPad calls this the font). In this example, you get a handy preview area that shows you what the typeface looks like.

2 Pick an attribute (WordPad calls them styles). Some typefaces offer four or more styles, while others give you only two to choose from

3 Set the size. As a rule of thumb, 10 or 12 points is appropriate for body text, while headlines can be as big as Windows will allow you to make them.

4 If you want any special effects attached to the text, like strikeout or underline formatting, this is the place to check. It's also where you can specify a color. (Please, no lime green or fluorescent pink!)

5 Ignore the Script box unless you're using a special keyboard designed to produce foreign characters.

Fig. 16.2

Give your words and letters a little personality by adjusting the formatting of each character. This is how WordPad arranges your Font options.

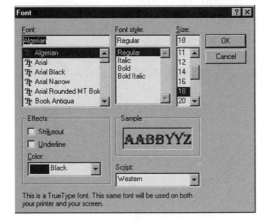

Q&A *I changed the font formatting, but my document still looks the same. What happened?*

If you chose formatting without having any text selected, you won't see the results until you type some new characters. WordPad and many other Windows programs add the formatting information at the insertion point, so it affects whatever you type from that point on. If you want to format text in the existing document, go back and try it again, but this time select the words you want to see changed.

Which fonts do I get with Windows NT?

Windows is incredibly stingy with fonts. When you first install any version of Windows, including Windows NT, you get just a handful of fonts—Arial, Times New Roman, and Courier New (which looks like an old-fashioned typewriter). You also get a couple of useful fonts that include interesting and sometimes strange characters you can use in headlines, or as bullets for the beginning of each item in a list. The Symbol font includes a few boring examples, but the font called WingDings has the best little surprises of all (see Fig. 16.3).

What's TrueType?

Johannes Gutenberg (who invented the printing press) would be amazed if he could see what's happened to type since the days he was carving pieces of wood into letters. For years, Windows has included a bit of technological wizardry called **TrueType** that lets anyone work with typography in ways that used to be reserved exclusively for professional typesetters.

Why is TrueType important? Because thanks to TrueType, what you see on the screen is really what you get out of the printer. If that doesn't seem like such a big deal, consider the alternative: From Gutenberg's day until as recently as 30 years ago, when you wanted to typeset your company's annual report, you had to pay a printer to pick pieces of hot metal type out of a humongous drawer and arrange them in heavy racks. Every different size, weight, and typeface had its own drawer full of metal.

Now that's a lot of metal, so it's not surprising that most typesetters, even if they had a huge selection of typefaces, only offered a limited

selection of sizes. "You want 24 point? Sorry, we have 18 and 36—pick one."

Because TrueType is digital, it gets rid of all that metal and substitutes some mental gymnastics instead. Each typeface is stored in your computer as a set of instructions that Windows uses to draw a letter on the screen. These instructions are completely **scalable**, so they work at every size from 4 points to 128 points. When you ask for 24 point Times New Roman, Windows first reads the instructions for putting that letter on the screen. Then it gets out its internal calculator and figures out how big to make each line and serif on each letter.

TrueType fonts can scale up to enormous sizes without using up extra space on your hard disk. They can be rotated at any angle, so you can do clever typographic tricks for logos and headlines. And best of all, they work on any printer that works with Windows, so you can be certain that what will pop out of the printer will be the same as what you see on the screen.

You can simply switch to the WingDings font, start typing, and see what you get. But the faster way, as we'll see shortly, is to use the built-in Windows Character Map applet instead.

Fig. 16.3
When you choose the WingDings font and start typing, your letters turn into these strange and interesting symbols instead.

What are those other fonts? And why do they look so ugly at 23 points?

To see all the fonts installed on your system, look in the Fonts folder; open the Control Panel and double-click the Fonts icon. When you open the Fonts folder, you'll see two different types of icons. One has a blue and gray TT for a label. The other has a big red A for an icon.

It's easy to figure out that the ones with TT on the label are TrueType fonts. The other fonts in the Fonts folder are called **raster** fonts. What's the difference? Let's try blowing up a few letters from each and see what happens.

Yuck. The problem with the raster fonts is that they're not scalable the way TrueType fonts are. Instead, they're specifically designed to look good on the screen at a small number of sizes.

Think of how a photograph works and you'll see the difference. TrueType fonts work like a photographic negative. When you ask Windows to blow up a TrueType font, it goes back to the original, and creates a new image just for that size. All the features are crisp and clear; in fact, just as with a photographic blowup, you can see more detail as the type gets bigger. When you blow up a raster font, though, it's like enlarging a photograph from a newspaper. As it gets larger, you begin seeing the dots instead of the picture.

Fig. 16.4
TrueType fonts (top) keep their nice, smooth edges as they get larger. Raster fonts (bottom) look great at some sizes, but get downright ugly when they're blown up.

Most Windows systems include at least a few raster fonts, including Courier and Symbol (cousins of the similarly named TrueType fonts), MS Sans Serif and MS Serif. These raster fonts are useful because they work quickly and look good on-screen in common sizes. But they won't necessarily look good when they come out of the printer, especially when you use them at sizes other than what they're designed for.

 TIP **You can tell Windows that you don't want to see those ugly raster** fonts anymore. In the Control Panel, open the Fonts folder and choose <u>V</u>iew, <u>O</u>ptions. On the last tab, there's a check box that tells Windows to show you only TrueType fonts.

When you look on the Fonts list of a program, you might also see printer fonts, which have a printer icon next to them. With these fonts you have the opposite problem: They're built into your printer, so when you format text using these typefaces it comes out of your printer looking letter-perfect. But Windows has no way of knowing how to display those fonts on the screen, so it matches the printer font with whatever it thinks is the closest match among the TrueType fonts you're using. If you depend on a set of printer fonts, ask your system administrator or the printer manufacturer how you can get matching TrueType screen fonts.

Font management

The best part about the way Windows works with fonts is that you don't really need to think about them unless you want to. Windows does the work of managing fonts, and whenever you use a Windows program, you automatically have access to all those fonts.

In fact, the only time you need to open the Fonts folder is when you want to add a new font, remove one, or figure out what a certain font looks like.

 TIP   **The fastest way to open the Fonts folder without using Cascading** menus is to pop up the Start menu, open the Run box, type Fonts in the box labeled <u>O</u>pen, and then press Enter.

How do I add a new font?

Some Windows programs automatically add new fonts to your system as part of their installation. You can also buy fonts or download them from the Internet and from online services like CompuServe or America Online. To start using a new font (or a bunch of them) in Windows, here's what to do:

 1 Open the Control Panel and double-click the Fonts icon to open the Fonts folder.

2 Choose <u>F</u>ile, <u>I</u>nstall New Font. You'll see the dialog box shown in Figure 16.5.

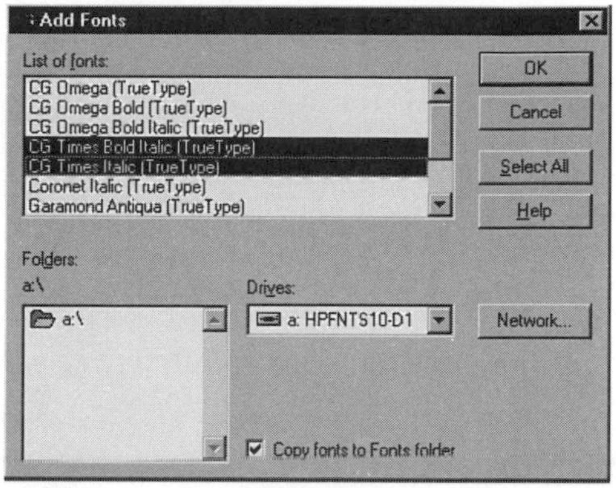

Fig. 16.5

When you open the Fonts folder and choose File, Install New Font, you'll see this dialog box.

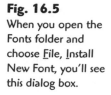

3 Browse through drives and folders until you find the one that contains the fonts you want to add. If the new fonts came on a floppy disk, for example, select A: here.

4 Select the fonts you want to add from the list of fonts. (If you have a disk full of fonts, save time by clicking the Select All button.)

5 Make sure to check the box labeled Copy fonts to Fonts folder. That way Windows will let you use those fonts next time you need them.

6 Click OK. Your hard drive will whir for a while, and when it's done your new fonts are installed. Now, when you select a font from within any Windows program, you'll see your new fonts.

TIP **There used to be a limit to the number of fonts you could install** under Windows. Not with Windows NT. As long as you have room on your hard disk, you can have a thousand fonts or more. Of course, you might have trouble keeping track of them all, but that's a different problem...

I wonder what *that* font looks like?

OK, so you've installed a few hundred fonts, and now you're working on a new WordPad document. You know the typeface you want is out there, but you can't remember whether it's Algerian or Braggadocio, or Caslon Bold. How can you pick the right one?

Well, if your application offers a preview window like the one in WordPad, it's easy: Just pick the font name in the dialog box and you can see a small sample of the typeface. If your application isn't so considerate, or you want to see a larger preview, try looking at the entire font.

In the Control Panel, open the Fonts folder and double-click the font you're curious about. You'll see a box like the one in Figure 16.6.

You get all sorts of interesting information when you open a font this way:

- Who made the font?

- What does each letter look like?

- How does this font look at different sizes?

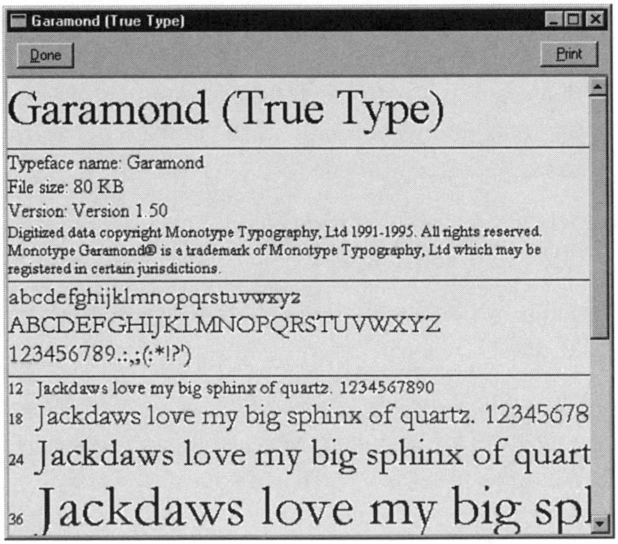

Fig. 16.6
Double-click a font icon for a detailed preview of what it looks like at a variety of sizes.

To see what this font looks like on paper, just click the Print button and Windows will send a detailed type sample to your printer.

To close the dialog box and get back to work, click the Done button.

That's *almost* the right font...

What happens if you know the right font is there, but you can't remember its name? If you can find a font that's close to the one you want, Windows will find other fonts that are similar in characteristics.

To track down a font this way, open the Fonts folder and right-click an empty space in the window. From the popup menu, choose View, List Fonts by Similarity. This looks a little like the Details view you'll see in other folders, but this window's a little different, as Figure 16.7 shows.

To use this view, simply choose the font you want to match in the list box at the top of the window. When you do, Windows will instantly re-sort the fonts in your list, and tell you whether they're very similar, fairly similar, or not similar at all. Double-click the entries at the top of the list to see if you've found the right one.

fonts
File Edit View Help
fonts
List fonts by similarity to: Arial
Name
Similarity to Arial
Arial Very similar
Arial Bold Very similar
Century Gothic Fairly similar
Arial Italic Fairly similar
Lucida Sans Regular Fairly similar
Lucida Sans Unicode Fairly similar
Arial Black Fairly similar
Lucida Sans Demibold Roman Fairly similar
Arial Bold Italic Fairly similar
Arial Narrow Fairly similar
Britannic Bold Fairly similar
Lucida Sans Italic Fairly similar
Arial Rounded MT Bold Not similar
Bookman Old Style Not similar
Century Schoolbook Not similar
1 font(s) selected

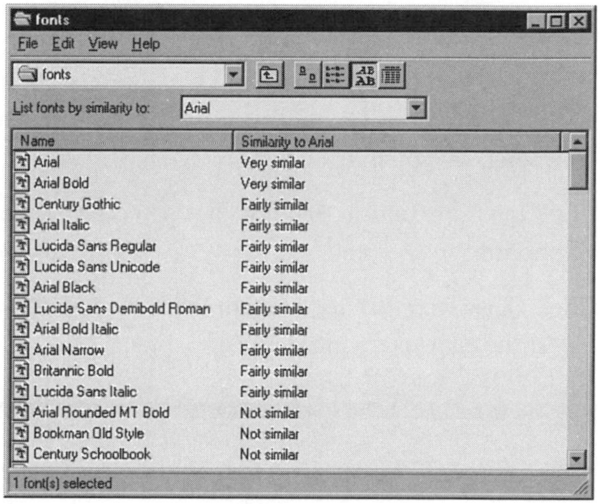

Fig. 16.7
Can't find that font? If you can find one that's close to what you want, Windows will sort the rest of your fonts by similarity.

I want to use a special character

There's more to life than letters and numbers. If you want to use a WingDings character to insert a Flying Fickle Finger of Fate before every important paragraph in your report, you have two choices.

The hard way is to memorize the secret Windows code for that character. For the finger WingDing, you can simply choose the WingDings font and type a capital **F**. That's fine if you want to memorize that detail. But you don't need to.

The easy way is to use the Windows Character Map applet. If you installed this program, you'll find it on the Start menu under Programs, Accessories. When you fire it up, you'll see a window like the one in figure 16.8.

TIP **If the Character Map applet isn't available on your menu,** you'll have to install it from the original Windows disks. Open Control Panel, choose Add/Remove Programs, and use the Windows NT Setup program to add this accessory.

The Character Map accessory is fairly easy to use.

1 Pick the typeface you want to use from the list box at the top. In this case, we'll choose WingDings.

2 Pick a character from the following list. Can't see those tiny characters? Point to any one of them, click the left mouse button, and hold it down as you slide the pointer across.

3 When you find the character you like, double-click to add it to the Characters to copy box at the top right. Continue adding as many characters as you like.

4 Click the Copy button to copy your selected characters to the Windows Clipboard.

5 Click Close to return to your application, and use the Paste command to insert the characters into your document.

Using fonts the smart way

Design experts have a clever phrase for documents that use too many fonts. The messy result is called **ransom-note typography**, because these documents look like what kidnappers produce when they chop letters out of a newspaper and paste them on the page.

It's not hard to avoid ransom-note typography. Just follow these simple rules:

- Try not to use more than four fonts on a page. If you do, your readers will get confused.

- Pick a serif face for headlines and a sans serif face for body type, or vice versa. The contrast helps readers easily see which is which.

- Use a simple typeface for body text. Intricate fonts are harder to read, especially at small sizes.

- Make sure there's a noticeable difference between different levels of information. If your headlines are 18 point and the subheads are 14 point, readers might not notice the distinction. Try 24 point and 14 point instead.

- If you really want to produce a ransom note, look for a Microsoft TrueType font called Ransom, which actually produces the silly look you're usually trying to avoid. It's fun for invitations and notes with friends, although you won't want to use it for a memo to the boss.

I have too many fonts!

Confused by all those fonts? Get rid of some. Deleting a font is as easy as right-clicking and choosing <u>D</u>elete.

CAUTION **It's OK to delete fonts you've added, but don't delete any of the** raster fonts that come with your system, like MS Sans Serif and MS Serif. All sorts of programs depend on them. Likewise, don't delete the Times New Roman, Arial, or Courier New TrueType fonts.

Part VI: Beyond the Basic PC

17

The Amazing, Talking, Singing, Exploding PC

● In this chapter:

- *Multimedia?* What is it, anyway?

- How to coax sound out of your PC

- Adding sound to your startup (and other system events)

- This thing is too loud!

- Use the Windows sounds—or record your own

- What about video?

Your personal computer might wear a gray flannel suit most of the time, but it can do more than crunch numbers and fiddle with fonts . . . . **>**

f your computer has the right hardware, it can handle just about anything your eyes and ears can recognize—from simple sound bytes to CD-quality songs, from full-size, symphony-style orchestrations to full-motion, Hollywood-style video.

Multimedia isn't just for game players, either. Even the most boring business task can benefit from the judicious use of sound and video. For example, you can record a brief message to your coworkers and plop it into an e-mail to add a personal touch to the latest budget numbers. It's not difficult to record or play back multimedia files, either; in fact, if your PC is relatively new, your most pressing multimedia challenge will be figuring out how to turn down the volume.

What is multimedia, anyway?

That's a good question... The funny thing about multimedia is that no two people can agree on exactly what it is. But most of us know it when we see or hear it. Generally, here's what you can expect to find when talk turns to **multimedia**:

- **Digital audio**—play back CD-quality sound, and even record your own.

- **Full-motion video**—not as sharp as what you're used to seeing on your TV, but good enough for even some demanding applications.

- **Hypermedia links**, like those found on the Internet's World Wide Web, where you click on buttons, pictures, and other "hot spots" to make multimedia events happen.

- **Software** to keep sound and pictures properly synchronized.

- **More software** to let you *edit* multimedia data files—snipping the relevant 10 seconds out of a two-minute sound clip, for example.

> **TIP** Data files for some of these multimedia types are huge. A 10-second sound clip, for example, might take up 100K of disk space, while a single four-minute video file could consume more than 40 megabytes of disk space! That's why CD-ROMs (which can hold more than 600M) are so popular for multimedia software.

Do you have the right hardware?

If you're lucky, your PC left the factory with its own sound card and speakers, and it was ready for multimedia the first time you turned it on. If not, you'll need to add some pieces inside and outside your PC.

CAUTION **Upgrading a PC is a job best left to experts. There's enough** voltage inside your PC to knock you out cold (or worse), and even if you follow all the precautions to ensure your own safety, you could damage the hardware itself with an accidental static discharge. Besides, you won't be able to install new drivers and finish the upgrade unless you have administrator privileges.

Squeezing speech and melodies out of your PC requires a few pieces of specialized hardware; if you want to be able to record your own sounds and store them on your PC, you'll need an additional gizmo.

- The **sound card** is the collection of electronic circuitry that converts the digital information in your sound files into analog signals that your speakers can understand. On some newer PCs, sound capabilities are built into the computer motherboard instead of being contained on an add-in card.

- Those signals have to go somewhere, which is why a multimedia PC needs **speakers** (for stereo sound, you'll need two). The speakers might sit on your desk, or they might be built into the computer itself; some designs even incorporate the speakers into your monitor. Regardless of design, they'll need to be connected to the appropriate jack on the back of the computer.

- To record your voice and other sounds, you'll need a **microphone**. They come in all shapes and sizes, and they plug into a jack right next to the one reserved for the speakers.

Where are the knobs and buttons?

There's a volume control on the taskbar; otherwise there are very few options. Double-click the Multimedia icon in the Windows Control Panel to pop up the full set of controls, as shown in Figure 17.1. For example, this is the place to tell Windows how you prefer to record sounds. Radio Quality doesn't sound as good as CD Quality, but the files are much smaller. You'll have to balance the sensitivity of your ears against the free space on your hard disk to decide which setting is right for you.

Fig. 17.1
If your coworkers sometimes plead with you to turn down that racket, use the volume control on your taskbar for quick access.

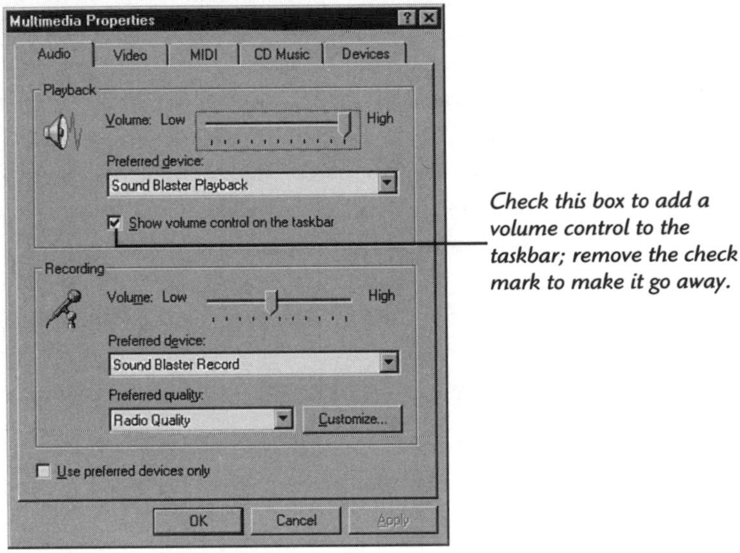

Check this box to add a volume control to the taskbar; remove the check mark to make it go away.

Begin annoying everyone within earshot

With a sound card and a pair of speakers, you can make a mighty racket. You'll find sample sounds and videos in the Media folder. Many of them are associated with particular sets of system sounds, but there are a few surprises (including a small collection of Beethoven and Mozart tunes) if you look deeply enough.

Before you start clicking, though, let's explain the difference between the two different types of sound files that Windows can handle:

- **Wave-form audio sounds** are simple recordings, just like the ones you make on a portable cassette player. If you hold a microphone up to the TV speaker when the Simpsons are on TV, for example, you can record a file that consists of Homer saying "Doh!" Wave files typically have the extension .WAV.

- **MIDI sequences**, on the other hand, behave more like sheet music than cassette tapes. Where a wave file always sounds the same when you play it back, a MIDI file will play back differently, depending on which instruments are in your MIDI "orchestra." Typically, MIDI files carry the .MID extension.

66 *Plain English, please!*

MIDI? WAV? Excuse me? **MIDI** is an acronym that stands for **Musical Instrument Digital Interface**. (Pronounce it *mid*-ee.) The name comes from the way these sounds are created and played back, by combining digital definitions of different "instruments" in a computerized orchestra. **Wave-form audio** (WAV), on the other hand, is simply a descriptive name for the file format. 99

MIDI files are much more compact than wave files, typically compressing down by as much as 30 times. But wave files are the only way to capture voices and other real-world sounds. In most applications, you'll find MIDI used for background music, while wave files are used for speech and vocal music. And as you probably guessed, you can find a wealth of extra information about audio files by right-clicking and poking around in the Properties sheets, as in Figure 17.2.

Fig. 17.2
What's in that MIDI file? Just right-click to see all the details. The properties sheet even contains a Preview tab from which you can play a media file without running Media Player.

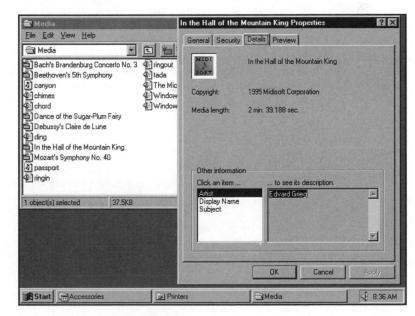

So what can I *do* with these sounds?

You can embed sound clips in mail and in reports, but the most common use of sound clips today is to make your computer beep and tweet in clever, distinctive ways. Windows lets you control this process by associating specific sound files with things that happen when you use Windows (it calls these **events**). There are dozens of Windows events that you can embellish with sounds. Here are some suggestions:

System Event	Sound
Start Windows	Jim Carrey bellowing "All righty, then!!!!"
Empty Recycle Bin	*Star Trek* transporter room noises
Program Error	HAL (the psycho computer in *2001: A Space Odyssey*) saying, "I'm sorry, Dave. I'm afraid I can't do that."
Exit Windows	Arnold Schwarzenegger snarling, "I'll be ba-a-a-a-ck!"

TIP **A sound clip is just another data file, so it's easy to send it to** someone else. Just open a folder window containing the sound file, and drag it into a document or a mail message. As long as the recipient has a sound card, he can simply double-click the embedded sound icon to hear your message.

Using the Sounds icon in Control Panel, you can tell Windows you want it to play your favorite *Star Trek* sound every time a window opens. If you can find the clip, Windows can make the association. Here's how it works:

1 Double-click the Control Panel Sounds icon to see the dialog box shown in Figure 17.3.

2 On this computer, Windows plays something called the Windows NT Logon Sound every time it starts up.

3 Not sure what you'll hear when you play that file? Click the VCR-style Play button in the Preview box to quickly listen.

4 To change the sound, just pick a different file from the drop-down list (the topmost entry is None). Use the <u>B</u>rowse button to search other folders for interesting sound clips.

Fig. 17.3
Match the sound with
the Windows event
to personalize your
working environment.

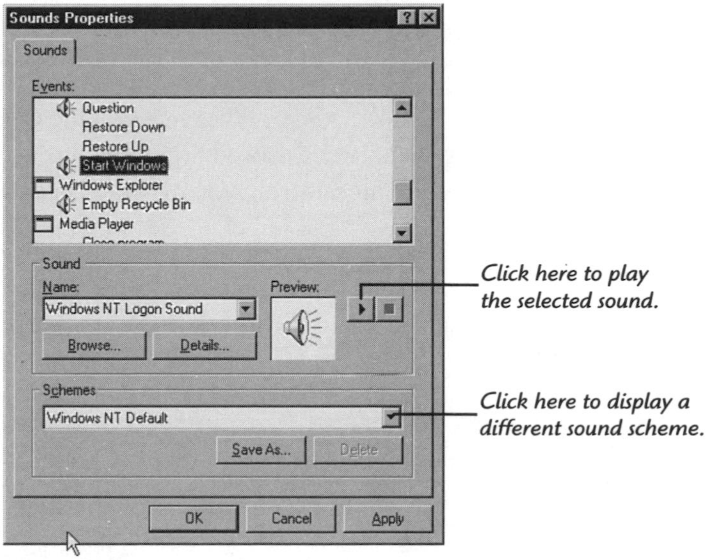

Sounds Properties

Sounds

E*v*ents:

Question
Restore Down
Restore Up
Start Windows
Windows Explorer
Empty Recycle Bin
Media Player
Close program

Sound

*N*ame:
Windows NT Logon Sound

Preview:

*Click here to play
the selected sound.*

Browse... | Details...

S*c*hemes
Windows NT Default

*Click here to display a
different sound scheme.*

Save As... | Delete

OK | Cancel | Apply

5 Click OK to apply the new sound to your desktop.

CAUTION **Sounds can drive you crazy! It may seem hip right now to have** Homer Simpson saying "Doh!" every time you see a dialog box, but how funny will it sound the 1,000th time? Really, a few sounds go a long way.

Like that mix of sounds? Save them!

In the bottom of the Sounds dialog box, you might have noticed a section called S<u>c</u>hemes. Windows NT includes a handful of ready-made **sound schemes**, loosely organized around themes like Robotz and the Jungle. But you can make your own just as easily. Let's say you've finished tinkering with the sounds. Maybe you've downloaded a few megabytes of clips from your favorite movies. You've matched the sounds you want to hear with your favorite system events. How do you save it?

Simple. Just open the Sounds dialog box, click <u>S</u>ave As, then type the name under which you want to save your killer sounds.

TIP **You can remove or change sounds for a single event in a scheme** you like... I've done that with the Utopia theme, in which I like almost all the system sounds except the whoosh that blasts out of the speakers every time a menu pulls down. After attaching No Sound to the menu pull-down event, I like the results much more.

Hey, turn it down!

When the guy in the next cubicle begins to complain, it's time to adjust the volume control. On most PCs, you'll have a Volume Control icon (a tiny speaker) on the right side of the taskbar, in the notification area next to the clock. To use this volume control, point at the icon and click.

In fact, this simple volume control offers one of Windows' best multimedia features—an instant mute button. To shut off all sounds in a flash, click the taskbar volume control, then check the Mute button, as shown in Figure 17.4.

Fig. 17.4

Just like the mute button on your TV, this option lets you answer the telephone and actually hear what the caller is saying.

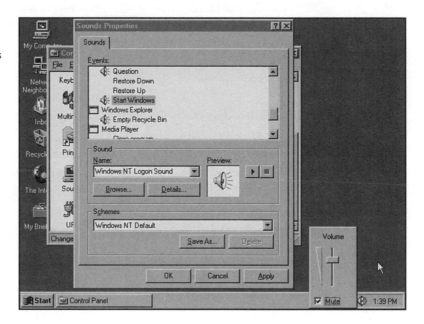

Windows also has a more sophisticated volume control that you can access by simply double-clicking the taskbar icon for the volume control. With the help of this audio control panel, you can adjust the volume and other settings for every different type of incoming and outgoing sound! (See Fig. 17.5 for this small wonder.)

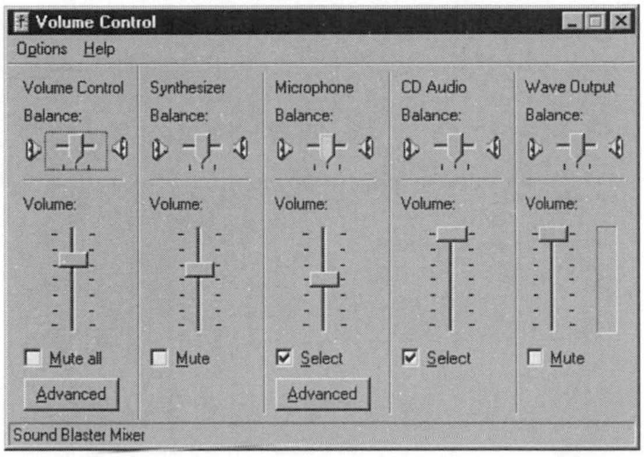

Fig. 17.5
I like my CDs and wave files to be just right: not too loud, not too soft. If your tastes run differently, adjust the volume controls accordingly.

What to do with all those multimedia files

You might already have an entire folder full of sound and video files. Look in the Winnt folder for another folder called Media, and use the Start menu Find, Files or Folders command to search for Wave Sounds, Video Clips, and other multimedia files. (If the Media folder isn't there, it's because whoever installed Windows NT on your system chose not to put it there.) By default, Windows associates those files with its own all-purpose playback device called Media Player. To find it, follow the cascading menus from the Start menu through Programs and Accessories, ending up in the Multimedia folder. This simple applet may look like a 98-pound weakling, but it can kick sand in the face of multimedia applications twice its size and weight.

What does Media Player do?

It provides a **common interface** for all sorts of media files, including sound and video.

Properties and options change to match the type of file. For example, you can tell Windows to let video clips take over the entire screen when they play, or you can specify that they run in a small window instead.

It lets you **cut and paste** data to and from any application that supports Object Linking and Embedding (OLE). Is that important? Mark my words: Before you know it you'll be storing voice clips inside mail messages on your computer, and you won't be able to tell where voice mail ends and e-mail begins!

The Media Player uses controls that are remarkably like those found on your CD player or VCR at home. Table 17.1 shows the buttons in the Media Player window; see Figure 17.6 and follow along.

Fig. 17.6

Want to play a snippet of sound or a video clip? Use Windows' built-in Media Player, which changes personality to match the data you feed it.

Table 17.1 Media Player buttons

What the button looks like	What it does
 ▶	**Play** starts a clip. (If you double-click a media file, however, it begins playing instantly.)
 ≜	**Pause** temporarily stops playing. (When you click the Play button, it changes to Pause. When you click Pause, it changes back to Play.)
 ■	**Stop** instantly shuts down the media file you're playing.
 ⏮	**Previous Mark** skips back to a spot you marked previously.
 ⏪	**Rewind** lets you move backward through a video or sound clip.
 ⏩	Click the **Fast Forward** button to jump ahead a few seconds. You can also drag the slider to rewind or fast forward the clip visually.
 ⏭	**Next Mark** jumps ahead to the next spot you've selected.
 ⬇	**Start Selection** puts a "begin here" mark in the current file.
 ⬆	**End Selection** tells Windows where your selection ends. Once you've marked a beginning and an end, you can copy the selected area to the Windows Clipboard and paste it into a new file.
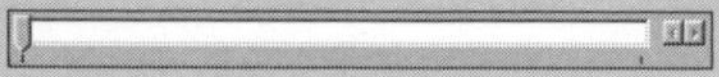 ▭	The **scale** lets you quickly move around in a lengthy media clip by simply dragging the slider control.

Play it again, Sam!

You want to reuse a media file? No problem. Choose Edit, Options and you can automatically rewind a clip when it reaches the end; that way, all you have to do is push the Play button. Or, in the same Options dialog box (shown in Fig. 17.7), check the Auto Repeat box to make sure the background music continues to play until you say, "Enough already!"

Fig. 17.7
Want to have a continuous sound or video background for your next electronic slide show? Open a MIDI sequence file or video clip and check the Auto Repeat box.

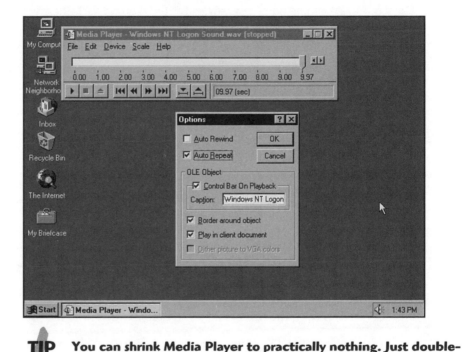

> **TIP**   **You can shrink Media Player to practically nothing. Just double-click the title bar to make all its menus, toolbars, and other distractions vanish completely. Double-click the title bar again to bring the player back.**

Recording your own sounds with Sound Recorder

Most modern multimedia PCs include a microphone and a jack on the back of the card, so that you can record your own voice memos or interesting sounds. To take advantage of this technology, follow the Start menu through Programs and Accessories to the Multimedia folder; you'll find the Sound Recorder applet there (it's illustrated in Fig. 17.8).

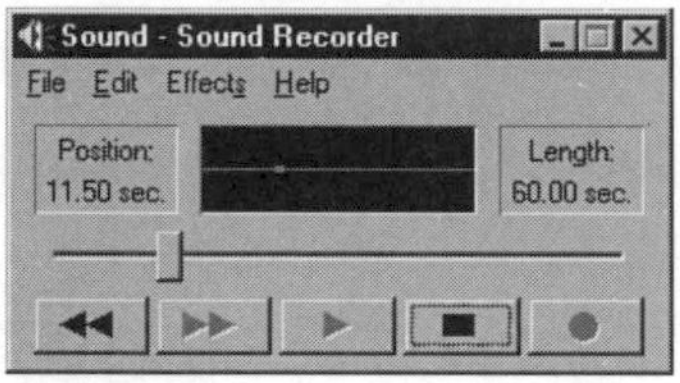

Fig. 17.8
Record your own sounds and use them in other documents. All you need is a sound card and a micro-phone, plus this mini-program.

Recording a sound couldn't be simpler:

1 Open the Sound Recorder applet.

2 Click the red, round Record button to start recording. You'll get a chance to give your recording a meaningful name later.

3 Click the Stop button when you've said your piece.

4 Use the Effects menu to tinker with the quality of the sound.

5 Click OK when you're satisfied with the new sound.

Q&A *My sounds don't sound right. Most are tinny, and some won't play at all. What 's wrong?*

You might have an old sound card that simply isn't capable of handling high-fidelity sound files. Or it might be configured incorrectly. Ask your system administrator to look at the driver settings and adjust them if necessary. If the problem only occurs with sounds you've recorded, you might have inadvertently told windows to use Telephone Quality instead of Radio or CD Quality. To adjust this setting, open Control Panel and double-click the Multimedia icon, then look at the drop-down list labeled Preferred quality.

Video for Windows

A lot of video clips get played automatically as part of a program. Microsoft's nifty **Encarta** encyclopedia, for example (shown in Fig. 17.9), has dozens of video clips and sound files. You don't need to use Media Player in those cases. Instead, the program does the work.

Fig. 17.9
Most of the video clips you'll find will be on CD-ROMs like this one, Microsoft's award-winning Encarta encyclopedia.

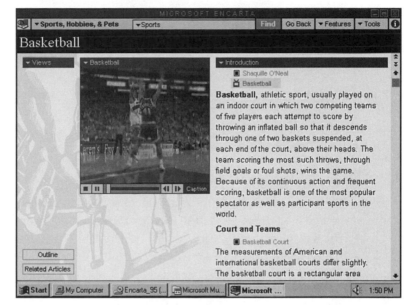

But what do you do when you just want to look at a video file? For Microsoft Video for Windows files (they have the extension .AVI) Media Player is perfect. For starters, choose <u>D</u>evice, <u>P</u>roperties to tell Windows whether you want the video to stretch to fit the entire screen, or whether you can settle for a small window (see Fig. 17.10). You'll get a sharper picture in a smaller window, but you might choose to settle for some fuzziness so that people standing a few feet away can see the clip more easily.

There's an amazing amount of techno-babble associated with multimedia. Behind the scenes, Windows has to deal with **codecs,** for example, which are compression-decompression routines that take those enormous video files and make them a little less huge. There are frame rates and sampling rates and audio formats and…well, you get the idea.

Fig. 17.10
You probably won't be happy viewing most video clips at full-screen resolution. To make the image larger, try moving up a little at a time.

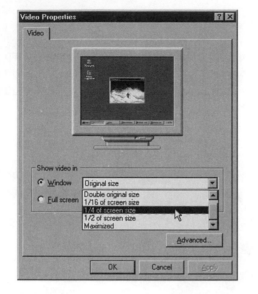

Most of the time, you'll find video clips on CD-ROMs (try browsing through the Windows NT CD, for example, to see which videos are included). You might find that some CD-ROMs don't use Media Player; instead, they depend on a different application to play back video. The most popular is Apple's QuickTime for Windows. You won't find it listed in the Windows Help files, but the basic principles for this player (and others like it) are the same.

Q&A *Why does this video look so jerky?*

You don't have enough hardware. Video is incredibly demanding, hardware-wise. If you don't have a fast CD-ROM and a Pentium, you can expect to see some problems with your video. What kind? Dropped frames, jerky motion, sound that doesn't keep up with the picture. There's no real cure, unfortunately, short of getting a new PC.

18

CD-ROMs

● **In this chapter:**

- **What's on the menu?**

- **What is a CD-ROM, anyway?**

- **Getting your CD-ROM installed**

- **You can even play music CDs on your computer**

- **Giving your CD-ROM a drive letter**

- **The CD started playing by itself—what gives?**

It looks like something that should hold Pavarotti or Pearl Jam. It holds as much data as a regular hard disk. What is it?. . . . . ▸

I'm talking about a CD-ROM, of course. It's practically impossible these days to buy a PC that doesn't include a special drive designed to read these shiny discs. If your PC doesn't have one, you'll find it next to impossible to install most new software programs, including Windows NT. You're also missing out on a world of useful information and great entertainment, including ability to play music CDs on your multimedia PC.

What is a CD-ROM, anyway?

As far as Windows is concerned, a CD-ROM is just another way to store and retrieve data. As far as we're concerned, though, a CD-ROM is a special kind of compact disc—it looks exactly like the musical variety, but works exclusively with PCs. So what makes these discs different from the ones with music on them?

- The acronym stands for **C**ompact **D**isc, **R**ead-**O**nly **M**emory. As the name implies, you can only read data from a CD-ROM disc—you can't use it to store your own files. (Drives that record CD-ROM discs are expensive and hard to find.)

- You need a special CD player to read the data from a CD-ROM disc. (Sorry, your Walkman can't do the job, even if you can figure a way to hook it up to your PC.)

- CD-ROMs hold a lot of data. You would need about 450 floppy disks to match the capacity of a CD-ROM, and a single CD-ROM can hold more data than most hard drives.

- Compared to floppy disks, a CD-ROM is practically indestructible.

- Compared to hard drives, a CD-ROM reader is relatively slow. When you ask a CD-ROM reader to track down a few bits of data, it takes about 10 to 20 times as long as it would for a hard drive, on average.

- There's no limit to the number of CD-ROMs you can keep in your collection—simply load the proper disc into the CD-ROM player when you want to use it.

" Plain English, please!

Is it **disc** or **disk**? That depends. Virtually all the storage devices that you normally associate with a computer end in K—hard disk, floppy disk, optical disk, and so on. But because CD-ROMs evolved from the audio industry, they follow a different standard spelling—compact disc. **"**

CD-ROMs are useful

CD-ROMs are perfect for passing around big programs—like Windows 95 and Windows NT— and big data files, like encyclopedias, phone directories, games, and collections of video clips. Two or three years ago, you had to have the sleuthing abilities of Sherlock Holmes to hunt down a CD-ROM. Today, you can find them practically anywhere.

Here are a few of the things you can do with CD-ROMs.

Install a new program

These days, buying a new program on floppy disks is like buying the stripped-down model of a new car. Yes, it'll get you where you want to go, but you won't get any of the optional features, like power windows and cup holders.

The same is true of software, and one excellent example is Microsoft Office, a collection of three or four big application programs, including Word and Excel. A recent version of Office uses more than 40 floppy disks! If you've ever installed one of these monster programs you know how tiring it can get: `Please insert disk 37 into drive A: and click OK...` Even worse, the version on floppy disks leaves out some of the useful features and bonuses you'll find on the CD-ROM version.

CAUTION **Just because it comes on a shiny disc instead of a pile of floppies,** there's no reason to treat software any differently. Software on CD-ROMs is licensed just like the kind you get on floppies, and making unauthorized copies is equally illegal. Before you install a new program, you must have the rights to do so. If Windows won't let you, you'll have to ask your network administrator for help.

Like me, you probably have better things to do with your time, which is why I recommend buying software that comes on CD-ROMs whenever you have the option. If you have a new CD, open the Windows Control Panel (click the Start button, then choose Settings, Control Panel) and let the Add/Remove Programs Wizard automatically search your CD for a setup file. If it finds one, it offers to install the software for you, as you can see in Figure 18.1.

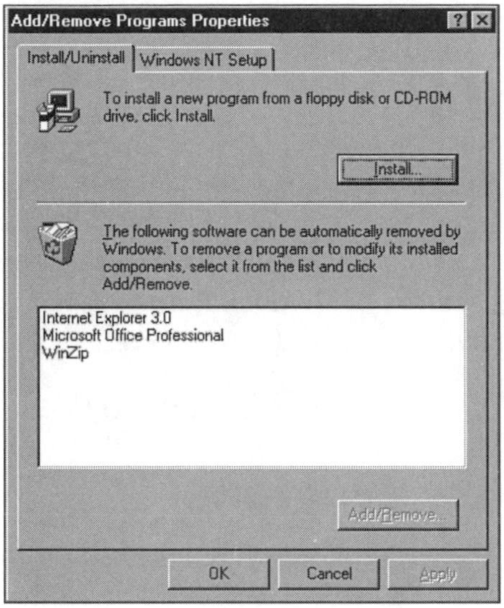

Fig. 18.1
What could be easier? Well, actually, there *is* an easier way, called Autoplay—but we'll get to that in a minute.

Run programs (okay, slowly)

You can actually run some programs directly from a CD-ROM. Most of the time, you won't want to. Why? Because running a program this way makes a turtle race look like a flying finish at the Indy 500. Even the fastest CD-ROM reader crawls compared to your hard disk.

Some programs will give you the option of setting up to run directly from the CD-ROM. Most of the time, you should just say no. There are three exceptions:

- When you're so pressed for space that you literally don't have enough room to install the program.

- When you just want to try out the new program, and you're not concerned with actually getting any real work done. If you don't like the program, pop out the CD-ROM and send it back; you haven't cluttered up your hard disk. If you do like it, though, go back and install it properly on your hard disk.

- When the program is specifically designed to be run from a CD-ROM, as is the case with most encyclopedias and other data-intensive programs. In these cases, you'll often be given the option to install certain program files on your system for faster performance, while leaving the data on the CD-ROM.

Play a multimedia game or a video clip

Why would you want to use a CD-ROM for fun and games? Because video files are huge—a three-minute music video, for example, can take up nearly 30 megabytes of hard disk space. (See Fig. 18.2 for a graphic example.) At that rate, one or two half-hour videos would take over your hard drive faster than a swarm of termites chomping through a log cabin.

Fig. 18.2
This video clip from *Rob Roy* runs only two-and-a-half minutes, but it gobbles up nearly 30MB of disk space. That's fine for the Windows 95 CD-ROM, where we found this clip, but you wouldn't want to use your hard disk this way.

Play a music CD

Yes, there's a big difference between music CDs and CD-ROMs. Put a CD-ROM in a typical music CD player and nothing will happen. But I'll bet you didn't know you can put a music CD in a CD-ROM player and get results!

If your sound card and CD-ROM reader are properly connected, you can slip in a music CD and have it play through your computer's speakers. It's an easy and convenient way to have some relaxing (or energetic) background music while you work.

How do you coax tunes from your computer? On most multimedia PCs, it happens automatically. When you insert a music CD, Windows senses the new disc and automatically launches the CD Player program. If that doesn't work, you can start the CD Player yourself by clicking the Start button and following the menus from <u>P</u>rograms to Accessories to Multimedia. When you start the CD Player mini-program, you'll see a screen like the one in Figure 18.3.

Fig. 18.3
Use the Windows CD Player to temporarily turn your PC into a giant Walkman.

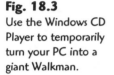

Use the toolbar for one-click access

Like most Windows programs, the CD Player has its own toolbar, which gives you one-click access to the functions you'll want to use most often. It also has a status bar at the bottom of the window and an elapsed-time indicator smack in the middle. If you can't see the toolbar or any of the other pieces, look under the <u>V</u>iew menu for the choices that turn them on.

Here's what the CD Player toolbar lets you do:

- Create and edit a **play list** that includes the artist, title, and songs on the CD.

- Display the **track time elapsed**—how long the current song has been playing.

- Display the **track time remaining**—how long before the current song ends.

- Show the **disc time remaining**—how much longer before you reach the end of the disc or playlist.

- Play the songs on the CD in **random order**.

- Play **continuously**—when the disc reaches the end, start over again.

- Play just the **song intros**—a snippet of 10 seconds or so from the beginning of each song. Handy when trying to find that song whose name you just can't remember.

TIP **Can't remember what any of the CD Player controls do? Look for** the ToolTips. Let the mouse pointer rest over any button, including the play controls to the right of the elapsed-time display, and a helpful label will pop up to tell you what the button does.

Build your own Play List

One of the coolest features in the Windows NT CD Player is its ability to keep track of the details of every music CD in your collection, including the artist's name, the title of the CD, and the names of each song on the disc. Unfortunately, it's not automatic—you have to enter the information yourself. But you only have to do it once. Each time you insert a music CD, Windows scans the disc for a special identification code, then looks in the list of titles you've entered. When it finds a match, it puts up a list like the one in Figure 18.4.

Fig. 18.4
You can drag titles from the right window to the left to create a custom Play List of just the songs you want to hear, in just the order you want to hear them.

Building your own playlist is a snap. Choose Disc, Edit Play List from the pull-down menus, then follow these steps:

- **To add information about a new CD...** press the Tab key to move from field to field. Use the CD's liner notes to enter the title and artist's name, then start entering the titles of each track. After you've entered a song title, just press Enter to move to the next entry.

- **To change CD information you've already entered...** click the appropriate field and start typing. Click the song titles in the right window to correct a typing mistake.

- **To move from track to track...** use the VCR-style buttons to play, pause, or skip to a different track.

- **To play songs in a specific order**... click the Edit Play List button at the far left of the toolbar, then drag the titles from the Available Tracks window on the right and drop them in the Play List window on the left. Click the Clear All button to start from scratch.

- **To turn down the volume**... choose View, Volume Control. You'll have to use the pull-down menus—no toolbar button here.

- **To eject the CD**... click the Eject button at the bottom right of the CD controls.

Where does Windows keep all the information about music CDs that you type in? You'll find it, usually in your WinNt folder, in a little file called CDPLAYER.INI. (Click Find, Files or Folders and search for that name if you can't find it in that location on your computer.) If you've painstakingly entered lots of information about the CDs you play regularly, it's a good idea to make a backup copy of this file. That way, if anything ever happens to it you can simply restore your backup instead of retyping all those entries.

Q&A   ***The CD Player program says it's playing just fine, but I don't hear any music. What's wrong?***

You need to make a special connection between your CD player and your sound card before you can hear the sound from a music CD. If you have an external CD-ROM reader—one that sits on your desktop outside your PC—there will be a cable that runs from the back of the CD reader to a jack on the sound card. Internal CD-ROM players—those that are installed directly in your computer's case—use a special wire that is connected inside the PC. Talk to your company's hardware expert for details on how your drive works.

Which drive letter does your CD-ROM get?

As I noted in Chapter 5, every drive in your system uses a letter of the alphabet, followed by a colon, for its name. Your first floppy drive is always A:, your main hard drive is always C:, and so on. Which letter gets assigned to your CD-ROM? That depends. Windows usually takes the next available letter when you start up, but that isn't always D:. If you have two hard drives, for example, or if you're on a network and you've assigned drive letters to various folders on different file servers, your next available drive letter could be anything between E: and Z:. And it could change from one day to the next, depending on your network setup.

That can play havoc with programs that expect to see the same drive letter every time you start them up. So Windows lets you permanently assign a drive letter to your CD. On my system, for example, I've set the CD-ROM reader up so it always appears as drive E:. This option requires the Disk Administrator program, which is only available to system administrators. So if you want to permanently reassign your CD-ROM drive letter you'll have to ask your administrator to do it for you.

Hey, that CD's playing itself!

If you slip a CD-ROM in your CD-ROM reader and your computer instantly starts up a program, don't get spooked—that's just a feature called **AutoPlay**.

The idea is that some CD-ROMs—especially games and educational software—should act just like a video cassette or a music CD instead of a disk filled with files and folders. AutoPlay discs contain a couple of extra files that Windows looks for every time it notices you've inserted a new CD. If it finds those files, it launches its main program automatically.

The CD-ROM version of Windows NT demonstrates AutoPlay in action. Just slip the disc into your drive, and (assuming you've already installed Windows), you'll see a screen like the one in Figure 18.5.

Fig. 18.5
Whenever you insert this disc into the CD-ROM reader, Windows automatically starts up this program.

In search of super CD-ROMs

Wondering what you can do with a CD-ROM? Well, besides Windows NT, there are literally thousands of titles you can put in a CD-ROM drive to jazz up your computer. Picking a few at random means leaving out some excellent CD-ROMs, so don't take these as recommendations but rather as starting points.

I read Stephen Hawking's book, **A Brief History of Time**, and was thoroughly lost in the dense discussions of relativity and space-time continuums. Then I saw this CD-ROM, and now I know why the universe is expanding.

Microsoft's **Cinemania '96** is an amazing collection of movie reviews, film clips, biographies, etc., that no movie buff should be without. And you can keep it up to date with monthly downloads from the World Wide Web.

Bookshelf '96 is an encyclopedia, thesaurus, dictionary, atlas, and more, all in one. Extremely useful in business and at home, it's included free with CD-ROM versions of Microsoft Office.

And then there's **Myst**, which is the strangest, most mysterious game you'll ever see. Even if you don't like games, you might like this spooky, eerie adventure.

What if you don't want your AutoPlay CD to start automatically? Hold down the Shift key as you insert the CD-ROM, and Windows will ignore the AutoPlay instructions. Now you can open the My Computer window, right-click the CD-ROM icon, and use other options like <u>O</u>pen to see the files on the CD-ROM.

19

Mobile Computing: Taking Your Show on the Road

● In this chapter:

- What are these PC Card slots for?

- How to dock your notebook

- Use the Briefcase to keep files in sync

- He's dead, Jim—why Windows NT and your notebook battery can't cooperate

Planning to run Windows NT on a portable PC? You'll have to learn a few special techniques—things don't always work the way you expect . . . . >

Unlike desktop PCs, notebook computers are not all the same. Notebook PCs are more like snowflakes, because no two notebooks are exactly alike. Besides the obvious differences in size and shape, there are subtle differences in the way the keyboard is laid out, how the mouse works, and what happens when you start running on batteries instead of AC power.

Because notebook computers are so different, it's impossible to offer too much specific advice for making them work properly. But there are four areas where you'll need to configure Windows NT carefully for use on a notebook computer.

TIP   **One of the four Windows setup options is designed especially for** portable computers. If you have a notebook, make sure you and your system administrator choose this option when you set up Windows, so that all the right files are copied to your notebook. And if you didn't (because you didn't know then what you know now)? Find the Windows NT CD–ROM (and your system administrator) and run Setup again. Windows is smart enough to add just the pieces you need.

Making sense of your PC Card slots

The engineers who design portable computers go to a lot of trouble to make them as small and light as possible. So it's no surprise that inside a notebook PC, actual physical space is a rare and precious commodity. On your desktop computer, you can add all sorts of useful devices by plugging them into add-in slots. Notebooks use add-in slots, too, but they're considerably smaller, and although they work differently, they allow you to add extra functions to your computer when you need them.

These slots go by two names—**PCMCIA** (the old name) and **PC Card** (the newer version). Your notebook computer probably has at least one and maybe two PC Card slots, usually located on one or both sides. The PC Cards themselves are about the size of a credit card, and come in varying thicknesses. In all cases, they're designed to be small enough to fit in a shirt pocket.

66 *Plain English, please!*

PCMCIA (to pronounce it, just rattle off the letters, one after another) originally stood for the industry association that developed the PC Card standard, the **Personal Computer Memory Card Interface Association**. But anyone who had to remember this tongue-twister knows what it must *really* stand for: *People Can't Memorize Computer Industry Acronyms....* 99

What kind of devices can be packed onto a PC Card? You name it. I've seen modems (the most popular choice by far), network interface cards, and hard drives of 500M and more. There are connectors for portable CD-ROM drives, sound cards that hook into external speakers, and even digital cameras that let your $3,000 computer do what a $300 camera can do. The reason PC Cards are so useful is that you can simply pop them in and out of your PC. If you decide you need a faster modem or a connector for your CD-ROM drive, you don't need to buy a whole new computer; just get a PC Card and plug it in.

Here's what you need to know about PC Cards.

- Like many kinds of hardware in Windows, *they need software drivers*. To check that your PC Card driver is properly installed, open Control Panel and double-click the PC Card (PCMCIA) icon. You'll see a screen like the one in Figure 19.1. If Windows says that it can't find a PCMCIA controller, you'll need to ask your system administrator for help.

Fig. 19.1
This notebook computer has two PC Card sockets. The one in use now has a 3Com network card, and its drivers are properly configured.

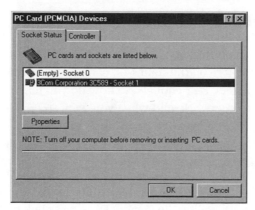

- *To use a PC Card,* you'll first have to shut down Windows NT. Then just insert the card firmly into the slot and restart Windows NT. (Make sure the card is inserted in the right direction and with the right side up. You may also need to fuss with specialized cables if you're using a device like a modem or network adapter.) If the card's drivers have been properly installed, it should just work. If not…you'll need to call the system administrator again.

- *To remove a PC Card,* you first have to shut down Windows NT. Why? Because some programs may depend on that card, and Windows NT can't notify them in advance before you slice the lifeline. When you restart Windows NT after removing the PC Card, you may see an error message like the one in Figure 19.2. That tells you that Windows tried and failed to load the driver for the PC Card it expected to find in that slot. It's a harmless error message, but you can prevent it from appearing by using hardware profiles, which we'll get to shortly.

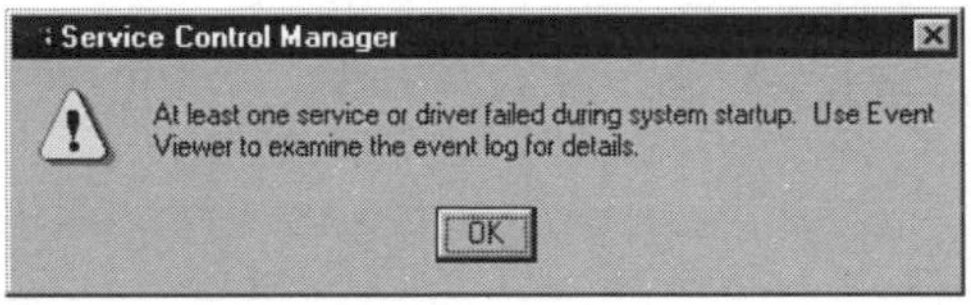

Fig. 19.2
Oops! Windows expected to find a PC Card in the slot. If you see this message often, it's time to set up special hardware profiles to match the configurations you use.

: Service Control Manager   ✕

⚠ At least one service or driver failed during system startup. Use Event Viewer to examine the event log for details.

[OK]

To network, or not to network?

When you're in the office, you plug in a PC Card to connect to the company network. When you're on the road, you can't find a wire long enough to reach back to headquarters. Fair enough. So how do you tell Windows when you want it to load the network, and when you want to be alone? Use a special system option called **hardware profiles**. You can create as many profiles as you want, but the most common use is to tell Windows how to handle your network connections.

By default, there's only one hardware profile. To add a new one, open Control Panel, double-click the System icon, and click the Hardware Profiles tab. You'll see a dialog box like the one in Figure 19.3. Click the Copy button to create a new profile; give it a descriptive name that will help you choose the right profile each time you start the computer.

After creating a new profile, you need to tell Windows a few facts about each one. Highlight the entry in the Available Hardware Profiles list and click the Properties button. Choose the Network tab (see Fig. 19.4) and check the only box there.

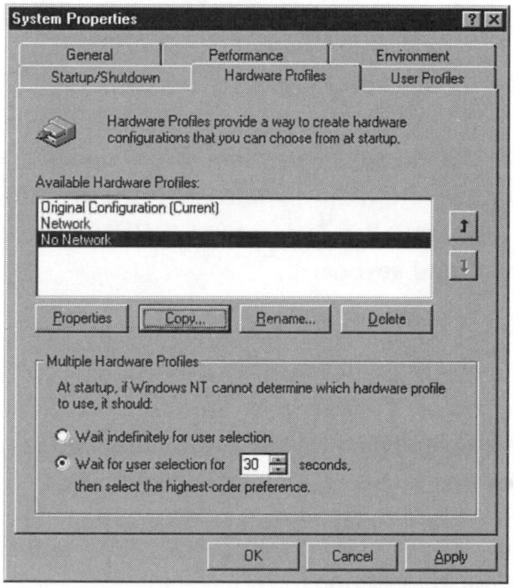

Fig. 19.3

Create a separate hardware profile for those times when you're not connected to the network. With these descriptive names, the purpose of each profile is hard to miss.

Fig. 19.4

Sometimes you need a network; sometimes you don't. Check this box to tell Windows that this is a no-network profile.

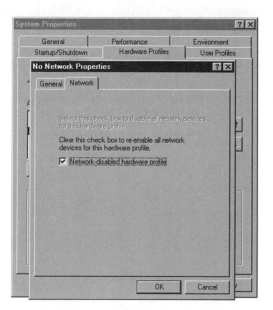

Now, each time you start up Windows, you'll first see a text-only menu that offers you a choice of hardware profiles. Choose the one that matches your current hardware setup.

What do I do with this docking station?

Some notebooks come with an optional accessory called a **docking station**. It's a slick idea: When you're on the road, you use the hardware that's installed in your PC and its PC Card slots. But when you get back to the office, you slip the notebook into the docking station and it automatically hooks up to your company network, to a desktop CD-ROM drive, even to a separate full-sized monitor and keyboard.

Every time you switch between "notebook in the docking station" and "notebook on its own," Windows does a quick check of the environment to see what has changed. To make sure Windows has enough notice to handle these changes gracefully, always follow the notebook maker's instructions for docking and undocking. Typically, this means:

- Shut down Windows NT before inserting the computer or removing it from the docking station.

- Use the computer's "eject" button to remove the notebook. Don't just start disconnecting wires!

To set up a docking station with its own hardware profile, follow the steps outlined in the previous section to create a new hardware profile, and click its Properties button. This time, choose the General tab (see Fig. 19.5). Check the box labeled This is a portable computer, then choose the proper setting for each profile.

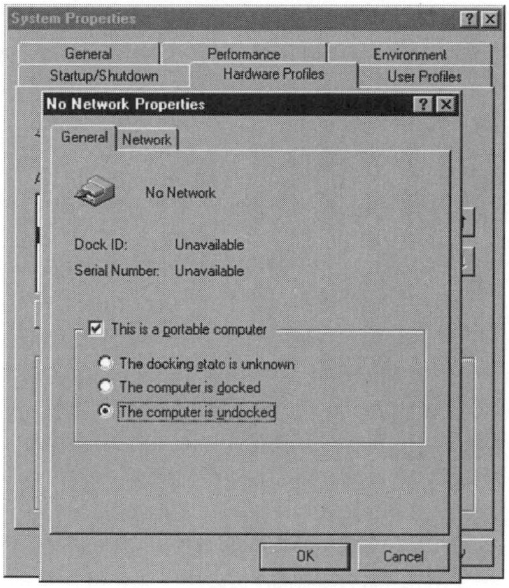

Fig. 19.5
Windows can configure your notebook computer correctly when you're hooked up to a docking station, but first you have to create a hardware profile and check the right boxes.

Bringing it all back home (and then back to the office)

Some people use a notebook PC as their one and only PC. If that's you, skip this section. But what if you have a notebook *and* a desktop PC? How do you make sure that the files you've worked with on the desktop PC are the same ones you take on the road? Well, you have two options.

The hard way: use a floppy disk

The old-fashioned technique for moving files from one place to another is to do it in two steps: copy the files from the first machine onto a floppy disk, then stick that disk into the second machine and copy the same files to the other hard disk.

Besides being slow and cumbersome, this technique has plenty of room for error. You have to be extra careful that you never accidentally replace the new file you just edited with the older file on the other machine. Murphy's Law says you'll only do this when the file you're working with is valuable and irreplaceable (at least that's the way it works for me).

TIP **Do you know the definition of an oh-no! second? That's the** interval between the moment you press the Enter key to irretrievably delete the files you worked on all week and the moment you realize (too late) what you just did. "Oh no!"

The one-button way: Use the Briefcase

Both Windows 95 and Windows NT incorporate a special utility designed just for notebook users. It's called the **Briefcase**, and it works much like a smart version of the fancy leather briefcase you use to carry paperwork to and from the office. Here's how it works:

You tell Windows to create a special briefcase folder on your notebook PC (which may be running Windows 95 or Windows NT 4.0), and then you drag data files from your desktop PC into the Briefcase. Every time you're ready to leave on a trip, you ask Windows to rummage through the Briefcase and compare its contents with the originals. If it finds different versions of the same file, it offers to replace the older version with the newer one. If it finds files you've created in either place since you last updated the Briefcase, it offers to create them in the other location as well. And if it notices that you've deleted files in one place, it asks if you want to delete them in the other location as well.

Set up your Briefcase

If you installed Windows using the Portable option, you should already have a Briefcase right on the Windows desktop, alongside the My Computer icon. To add a new Briefcase after the fact, just click the desktop and choose New, Briefcase. The first time you open this window, you'll see the Welcome message (shown in Fig. 19.6). Follow these instructions to get started.

I have two desktop PCs (one at the office and another at home) plus a notebook PC, and I can't imagine keeping my computer files organized without the Briefcase. Here are some useful Briefcase-management techniques I've learned that aren't in the manual or the Help screens:

- Try to connect the notebook and desktop PCs using a network connection if you can. Managing a Briefcase on a floppy diskette is annoyingly slow and usually more trouble than it's worth.

- You can create more than one Briefcase. I have separate Briefcase folders I use for synchronizing different types of data on different computers.

- Put the Briefcase where you want it. It doesn't have to go on the desktop. You can always create a shortcut to the Briefcase and put that icon on the desktop.

- Rename the Briefcase if you want to. My Briefcase is a pretty dopey name. Instead, I recommend giving the Briefcase on your notebook PC the same name as the folder where you store all your data files on your desktop PC.

- Drag entire folders into a Briefcase. When you do, Windows will keep track of all the files you create and delete in the Briefcase and in the original folder.

Fig. 19.6
Can't remember how a Briefcase works? Don't worry—the first time you use a new Briefcase, you'll see this helpful message.

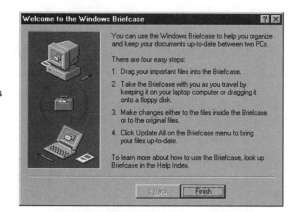

Keeping the Briefcase in sync with the original

Once you've copied the files from your desktop to the notebook Briefcase, work with them by opening the Briefcase and double-clicking the files you want to edit. Windows knows where the original is located and whether the two files are up to date. If you want to quickly check on the status of your files, just open the Briefcase and choose View, Details. You'll see all the extra information in a window like the one shown in Figure 19.7.

To tell Windows you want your files updated, choose Briefcase, Update All. (If you just want to update a file or two, highlight those entries and use Update Selection, instead.) Windows will compare dates, times, and sizes of each file in the original location and in the Briefcase, then show you what it found in a window like the one shown in Figure 19.8. The name and status of the original files appear on the left; the information for the Briefcase copy is on the right.

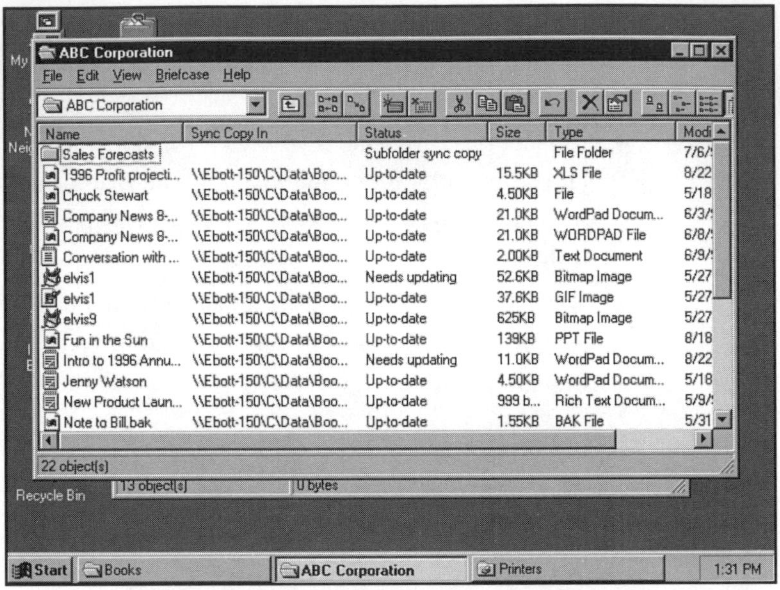

Fig. 19.7
The Status column tells you all you need to know about the files in the Briefcase. Click the column heading to bring all the "needs updating" files together.

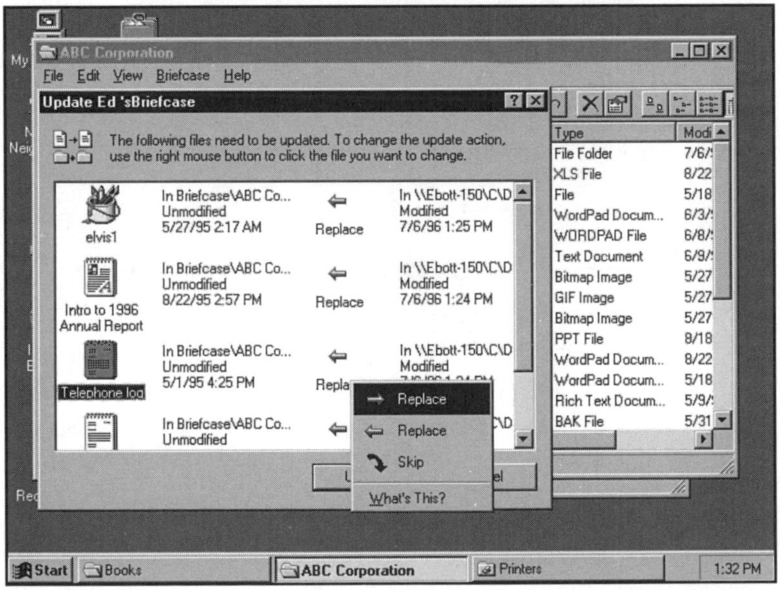

Fig. 19.8
When you're ready to compare the Briefcase files against the originals, choose Update All. You can override the suggested updates by right-clicking.

After it's finished its check, Windows offers to replace older files with newer versions, in either direction. If it sees that both files have changed, Windows offers to Skip the exchange. You can override either action by right-clicking on the action icon and choosing a different action. When you're ready to bring the Briefcase up to date, click the Update button.

CAUTION   **Make sure that the system clock on each PC is set correctly.** The Briefcase uses date and time stamps to decide which direction your files should move. If the date is incorrect, you might accidentally replace a newer file with an older one.

How long will this battery last?

On your desktop PC, you rarely think about power, but it's a huge issue with notebook PCs. When you're flying from Los Angeles to New York, and you absolutely, positively have to have your work finished by the time the plane touches down, you'll want Windows' help to squeeze every last ounce of life from your notebook's internal batteries.

Every notebook maker gives you its own power-management utilities; they continually monitor the hard disk, the keyboard, and the mouse to see what you're up to, and when they sense that you're concentrating on the in-flight movie instead of your work, they shut down the power to those pieces of your PC until you send a wake-up call by tapping the keyboard or clicking the mouse again.

Unfortunately, Windows NT wasn't designed to work well with power-management utilities. In fact, if you try to use them together you could lose data. The companies that make notebook computers know this is a big problem for busy people who spend a lot of time in planes, trains, and automobiles, and they're working on solutions. So, if you own a notebook computer and you plan to use it with Windows NT, your best bet is to ask the company that made the computer when it will have a compatible power-management program.

Part VII:

Communicating with the Rest of the World

20

Other People, Other Computers: Working with a Network

● **In this chapter:**

- **What's a network, anyway?**

- **Why you have to type a password when you start Windows**

- **Safely share files and printers with other people**

- **How to connect to a file server**

- **The ins and outs of NetWare**

Think networking is difficult to understand? Think again.
After all, it's just sharing. . . . . ⬤

I n the office, you probably share documents all the time. So how can you send your version of a file to someone else for her comments? One way is to copy your file to a floppy disk, stick it in a manila envelope, put it in your outbasket, and wait a few days for the revisions to work their way back to you. Not a very practical solution, is it? Wouldn't it make more sense if you could somehow hook your computers together so you could both work with the same file whenever you need to?

That's the idea behind computer networks. With the help of a little bit of extra hardware (and a lot of wire), you can extend the reach of your computer to share files, folders, and printers—instantly. Computer networks can stretch around the world, or they can be as small as two PCs sitting side by side on the same table. No matter how big or small your network is, you can work with it easily once you learn the basics.

Network basics

In general, networks help you and your company get more productive use out of the hardware you own. Networks also let you and your coworkers keep data locked up by assigning passwords and defining permissions so that only the right people can get to it. There are slightly different techniques for sharing (and securing) files and printers on different kinds of networks.

Nearly every kind of network lets you share files on a central computer called a **file server**. As long as you know the name of the file server, and your **network administrator** (the person who runs your network) has set up the network to allow you to access it, you can read and write files on folders on the file server. Depending on the kind of network your company uses, you may also belong to a **workgroup**—a (usually) smaller assortment of users connected to one file server on the network. A bank, for example, might choose to create workgroups called Admin, Mortgage, and Collections, each with its own file server.

Finally, if your company uses Windows NT on its file servers, too, you'll probably belong to a **domain,** which is a (usually) larger collection of workgroups and servers. Grouping users this way makes it easier for administrators to manage all those computers. Because all the user names and passwords in the domain are stored in a central location, domains also make life easier for you if you move from office to office as part of your job—you can log on from any computer and know that the Windows network will recognize you.

How do networks work?

Have you ever used interoffice mail? Then you already know the fundamental principles behind computer networking. When you want to send a printed report to someone else, you slip it into an envelope, write the recipient's name on the To: line, put your own name on the From: line, and put it in your outbox. The next time the mailroom guy passes by on his rounds, he picks up the envelope and delivers it.

Your company's computer network handles files in much the same way.

Each PC on the network uses a piece of software called a **network client** to chop files into small pieces called **packets**. (You might have to do the same thing with a thousand-page printed report if your envelopes can only hold 100 pages at a time.) The client software on the sending end stuffs each packet into the electronic equivalent of a manila envelope and adds the To and From information, plus details about how to put the file back together ("This is packet #6 of 32"); the client on the receiving end opens all the envelopes and reassembles the pieces into a file that looks just like the one that was sent. (This all happens quickly and invisibly, of course.)

Every computer on the network has a plug-in card called a **network adapter**. It's easy to spot the

adapter—that's where the network cable is plugged into your PC. It functions something like a combination in- and out-basket, since every packet that comes into or out of the computer has to go through this piece of hardware.

For your computer to successfully send envelopes full of information across the network, it has to use the same **protocol** as the rest of the computers on the network. No, it has nothing to do with which fork you use at a formal dinner party; a protocol is simply the language that your network speaks. Protocols generally have tongue-twisting acronyms like IPX/SPX or TCP/IP instead of plain-English names. (Puzzled about how to pronounce these catchy acronyms? There's nothing fancy involved. Just ignore the slashes and pronounce each letter in turn.)

Finally, your network may allow you to add **services** such as file and printer sharing. With the right service installed on your networked computer, for example, you can give someone else permission to send documents through his network adapter, across the cable, into your network adapter, and ultimately to your printer or onto your hard drive. Needless to say, you'll want to think carefully about the consequences before you let someone share your PC or printer!

66 *Plain English, please!*

You'll sometimes hear people refer to their network as a LAN or WAN. What's that all about? **LAN** stands for **Local Area Network**. As the name implies, a LAN is usually concentrated in a single location, and most of the machines are connected with wires. A **WAN**, which is short for **Wide Area Network**, consists of two or more LANs, usually joined together by high-speed telephone lines. In big companies, it's not surprising to see WANs that tie together people in different states and even different continents. **99**

The same is true for printers. Instead of buying an expensive laser printer for every employee, your company can buy one fast, powerful printer for each department, hook all the printers to a network, and let the employees in each department use the one that's closest to them.

On some networks, you can let other people share a folder on your own computer's hard drive so you can both get to the files anytime. And Windows NT even includes a program called Chat, which lets you converse with your coworkers by typing messages into a shared window; you can use Chat to carry on the equivalent of a conference call, or just to goof off while everyone around you *thinks* you're working hard.

 TIP   **Some of the techniques described in this chapter won't work on** your network. It all depends on how much trust the person who set up your network had in you and your fellow workers. If you work for the CIA, security will surely be a lot tighter than if you work for a real estate agency.

What's in the Network Neighborhood?

 If you're connected to a network, you'll find an extra icon on your Windows desktop. Just as My Computer contains everything that's inside your personal PC, the Network Neighborhood is filled with icons representing everything your computer is connected to. Figure 20.1 is a representation of what I see when I double-click on this icon.

Here's what you'll find inside:

- An icon for the Entire Network. Double-click here to see all the resources (printers, shared folders, file servers, and so on) in all the workgroups and domains on your network.

- Other computers in your local workgroup (they have to be running either Windows NT or a compatible version of Windows, such as Windows 95 or Windows for Workgroups 3.11).

- File servers. These may be running the server edition of Windows NT, or they may be part of a NetWare or UNIX network.

Fig. 20.1

You and your immediate neighbors show up in the Network Neighborhood. If you want to see everything that's available on your network, double-click on the Entire Network icon.

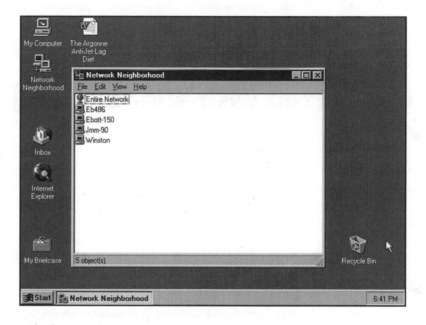

66 *Plain English, please!*

NetWare is a popular network operating system sold by Novell Corp. of Salt Lake City, Utah. If your company has a network today, chances are good that there's at least one NetWare file server somewhere on it, because this has been the standard operating system for corporate networks for many years. **UNIX**, which comes in dozens of varieties from all sorts of different companies, is the operating system of the Internet. It is widely used in universities and on high-powered graphic workstations. Windows NT was specifically designed to cooperate with these and other popular networks. 99

Some or all of the PCs on your network get their own icons in the Network Neighborhood. Dig a little deeper and you can see whether the owner of that PC has put the Windows equivalent of a "Share Me" sign on any of his folders or printers. For example, if Bob in Accounting wants you to look over this month's payroll report, he could put the report in a folder, call it Payroll Reports, and tell Windows that it's OK if you look at it. Now, when you explore the icon for Bob's PC in the Network Neighborhood, you'll see that shared folder as well.

CAUTION **Be prepared to wait when you double-click on the Entire Network icon.** If you're part of a big network, it can take a few minutes, literally, for Windows to track down all those pieces and put together the list of icons to show you.

Getting started with Windows on your network

If you're on a network, you have to identify yourself to the network every time you turn on your PC and start Windows. There are a variety of Windows logon screens, depending on which kind of network your company uses. (See Fig. 20.2 for an example of one such dialog box.)

Q&A ***Ctrl+Alt+Del? Isn't that how you reboot a computer?***

In many operating systems it is. In fact, the designers of Windows NT chose this key combination as a way of keeping hackers from faking a Windows NT logon screen and capturing your password as you type it in. If you press Ctrl+Alt+Del and you see the Windows NT logon screen, you can be sure that Windows NT's security is working.

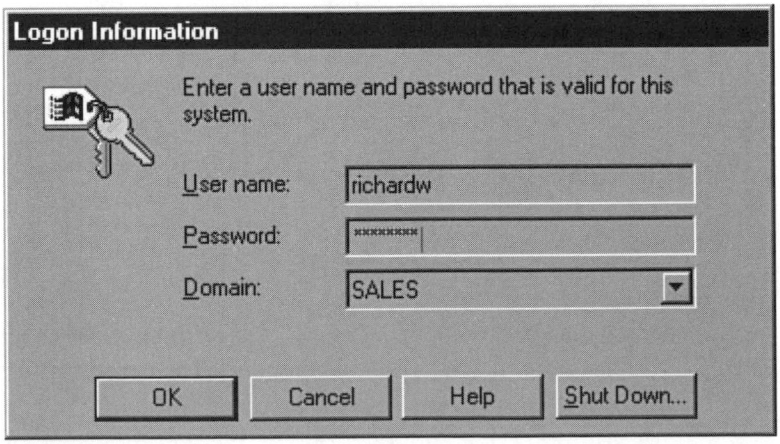

Fig. 20.2
Every time you turn on your computer, Windows asks you to log on by entering your user name and password.

Logon Information
Enter a user name and password that is valid for this system.
User name: richardw
Password: ********
Domain: SALES
OK   Cancel   Help   Shut Down...

Why do I have to log on?

Logging on does two things. The process sends your user name and password to any file servers on your network so that you can have access to files stored there. It also tells Windows which **user profile** belongs to you.

As you'll recall, your system administrator originally set up your PC so that more than one person can use it; at a minimum, there's an account for the system administrator and for you. User profiles keep track of the different settings for each user. For example, you can arrange the icons and wallpaper on your Windows desktop and the choices on your Start menu exactly the way you want, without being concerned that someone else who uses the same PC will rearrange things. User profiles also set aside completely separate areas on the computer where you and other users can store private files without worrying whether someone else will read them or, worse, delete them.

Q&A *Help! I forgot my password! What should I do?*

Call your network administrator. It takes special management tools to erase your old password and give you a new one when you've forgotten the original password. Why the runaround? Well, the whole point of passwords is to offer security. If you forget your password, there's no way Windows can tell that it's really *you* instead of some snoop trying to steal your files.

Hate your password? Change it!

You can change your Windows NT password by pressing Ctrl-Alt-Del. Everything on your screen will disappear (don't worry; it will all come back when you're done) and you'll see the Windows NT Security dialog box (Fig. 20.3). Windows asks you to enter your original password (to prove you are who you say you are) and then enter the new password. If you want to change your password for another network, such as NetWare, ask your network administrator for help.

How does Windows know who I am?

Easy. Whoever set up your network account entered some information in a dialog box like the one in Figure 20.3.

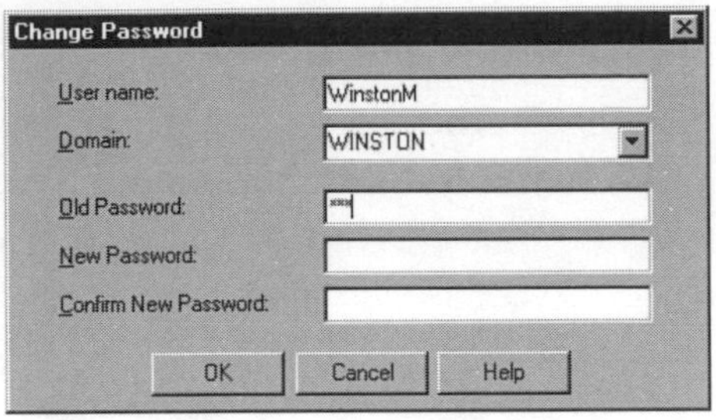

Fig. 20.3
Use this dialog box to change your password. Make sure you pick something that a stranger won't guess easily.

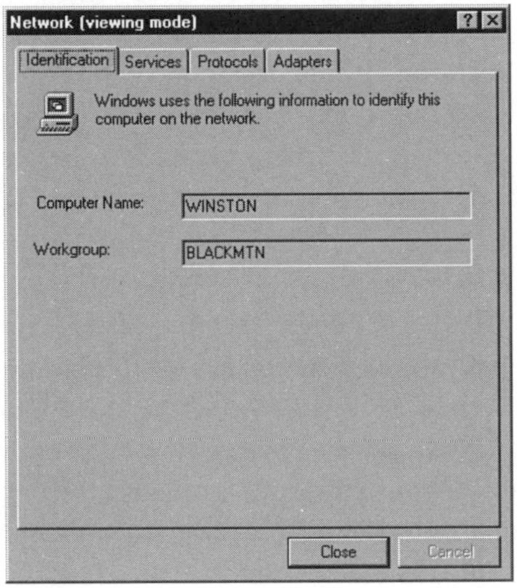

Fig. 20.4
Name, rank, and serial number? The Network properties dialog box tells Windows your computer's name and the name of your workgroup or domain.

You already entered your **user name** when you logged on to the network. (The user name is usually some variant of your first and last name, although it can be any name or even a string of letters and numbers that looks like nonsense.) Windows uses this information to look up your network rights and desktop preferences.

Your computer also has a name that other people need to use when they connect to any folders or printers you've set up for sharing. The system administrator defined this name when he or she first set up Windows on your computer.

Why one name for you and one for your computer? Well, there's no reason why two or more people can't use one computer, with different mailboxes and desktops and other personal preferences. But no matter who's using the computer, its resources—such as hard disks, CD-ROM drives, and attached printers—will always remain the same. Identifying users by user name guarantees that mail will get to the right place. Identifying computers by computer name makes it easy for anyone who wants to share a resource to find it quickly, regardless of who's using it.

Do you want to change the name of your computer or your user account? Sorry, you can't do it yourself, unless you can log on as a system administrator. There's a good reason for this restriction: If either name changes without warning, other people on the network may not be able to find the resources they're looking for, when they need them.

Connecting with NetWare file servers

Networking gets more complicated (but not necessarily more difficult) when you mix and match different network operating systems. At my office, for example, we have a mix of Windows NT and NetWare file servers, all of them used by different workgroups for different tasks. In some cases, my Windows user name and password are sufficient to grant me access to the files and folders and printers connected to the NetWare server. In other cases, I need to remember a separate user name and password to log on.

It's no different from the way the security system in my office building works. My electronic card key lets me unlock doors on my floor, but on other floors, run by other companies, I need a different key (and special permission) before they'll let me in the door.

Setting up your NetWare connection

On networks that include NetWare file servers, you (or your network administrator) will need to use the Client Service for NetWare, found in the Control Panel. When you double-click this icon, you'll see a dialog box like the one in Figure 20.5. The most important setting here is the one for your **preferred server**. That setting tells Windows where to send the user name and password you enter, so that you can have permission to use Netware resources.

Fig. 20.5

If your company uses NetWare file servers, you (or your network administrator) need to tell Windows which server has your logon information.

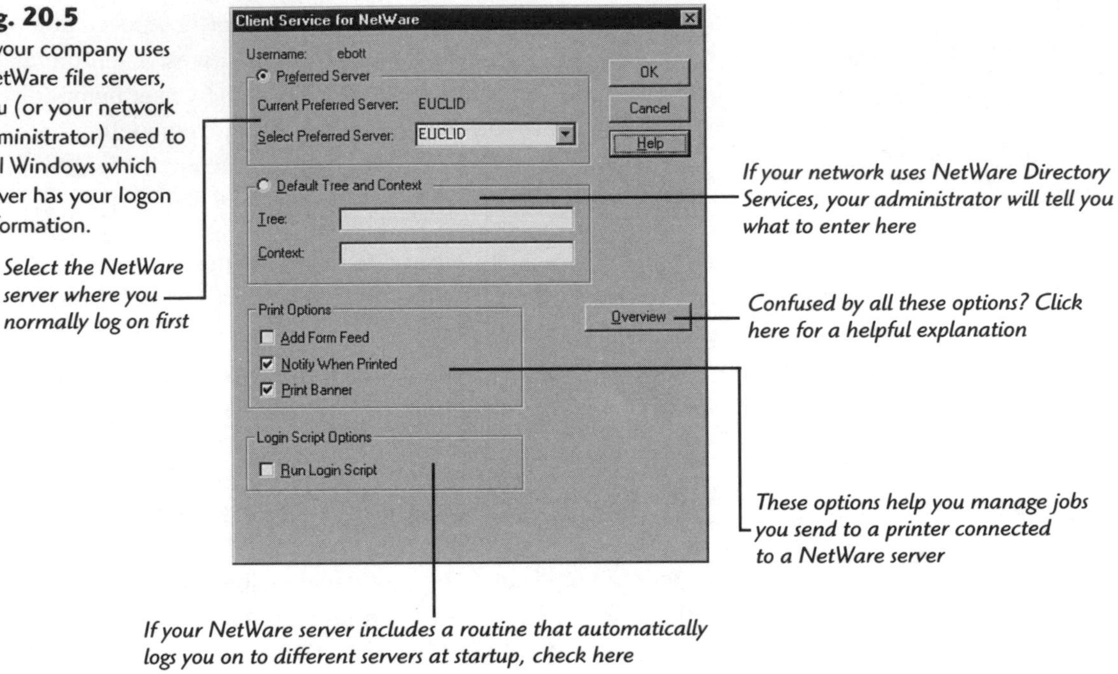

Select the NetWare server where you normally log on first

If your network uses NetWare Directory Services, your administrator will tell you what to enter here

Confused by all these options? Click here for a helpful explanation

These options help you manage jobs you send to a printer connected to a NetWare server

If your NetWare server includes a routine that automatically logs you on to different servers at startup, check here

Logging on and logging off

Before you can use files and folders on a NetWare server, you first have to **attach** to the server—that's NetWare's term for what Windows calls logging on. If the server is your preferred server, this happened automatically when you logged on to Windows NT. If you need to use another NetWare server, just browse through the Network Neighborhood, find the appropriate server, and double-click on its icon. You'll see a dialog box like the one in Figure 20.6.

Why enter a user name? Doesn't Windows remember your user name? Well, yes, but when you connect to a new file server you may be expected to use a different name. For example, my company uses a NetWare server to give every employee access to a collection of CD-ROMs stored on a big jukebox-style drive. There are no sensitive files stored here, and because CDs are a read-only medium, there's no risk that someone will accidentally delete a file. So, to log in to this server, every user enters the same user name and password. That way, the network administrator doesn't have to manage a long list of users.

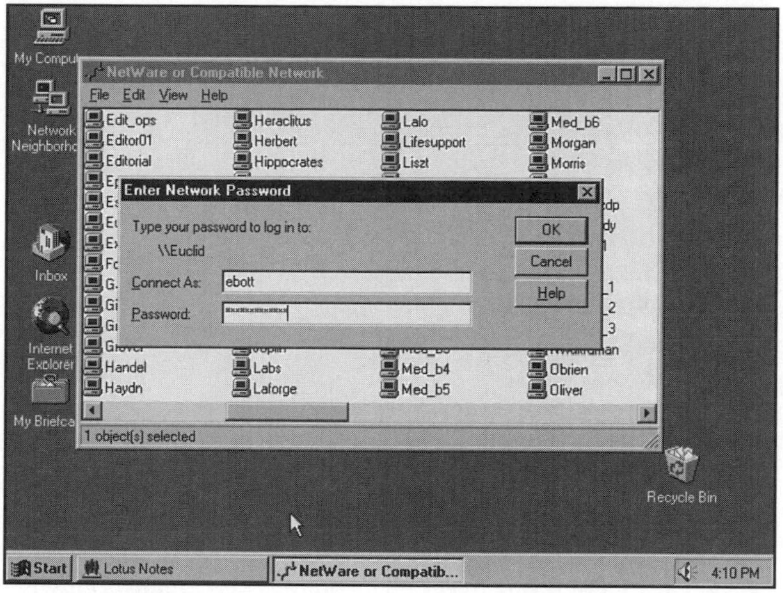

Fig. 20.6
When you double-click on a NetWare server, you may be asked to enter a user name and password.

![Screenshot of NetWare or Compatible Network window with Enter Network Password dialog]

✔ **TIP**

Are you tired of waiting (and waiting and waiting and waiting) while browsing through the Network Neighborhood to find a file server you use frequently? Try dragging the server's icon onto your desktop. Windows will offer to create a shortcut to the server for you. Say yes, and from now on you can bypass the 'Hood and go directly to your network destination.

What should you do when you're finished using resources on a NetWare server that isn't your preferred server? Your network administrator would be very grateful if you logged out. You see, the total number of connections to a file server is limited, and if you remain attached to the server after you've completed your task, you may lock out another user who needs access to the same resources.

To disconnect from a NetWare server and free the connection for another user, right-click the server's icon and choose Log Out. As you can see from Figure 20.7, Windows will warn you that you're about to lose contact with the shared resources on it. If you're sure this is what you want to do, click OK.

Fig. 20.7
When you right-click
on the icon for a
NetWare server, you
have the option to
log out and free the
connection for another
user.

Who am I, anyway?

I'm not trying to get philosophical here, really. But when you want to find out
which NetWare servers you're attached to, under which user names, just
right-click the Network Neighborhood and choose Who Am I from the pop-up
menu. The NetWare Client Service will respond with a dialog box like the one
in Figure 20.8, telling you the name of your preferred server, along with the
user names you've used to attach to any additional servers.

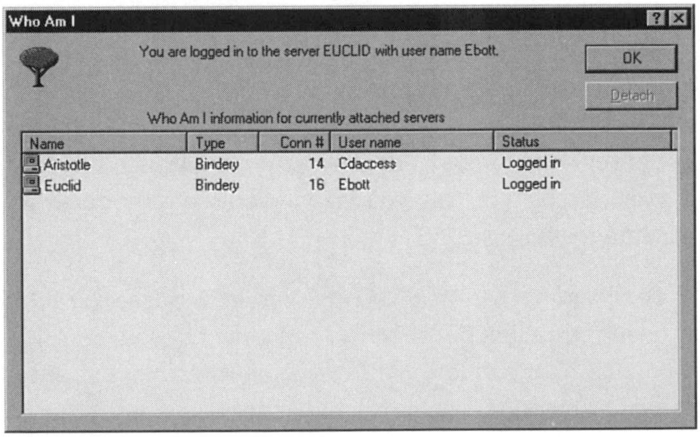

Fig. 20.8
It's not exactly the
Meaning of Life,
but the Who Am I
command will at least
tell you who the
NetWare Client Service
thinks you are.

How to use the files on a file server

 There are lots of good reasons to store your work on a file server. Most of the time, you'll store data files on the network because it makes it easier for a group of people to share the workload—an annual report that you and a team of coworkers are updating, for example, or a consolidated budget spreadsheet with a different manager responsible for each page.

 TIP **You can also install programs on a file server and run them on** your own computer. That's an ideal solution for programs you don't use that often, or when you're running low on disk space on your own PC. But there are pitfalls to this approach. Some programs expect to keep track of personalized configuration information, and they get thoroughly confused if they can't find a local folder to store this information in. Your best bet, if you plan to run programs directly from a file server, is to ask your network administrator to help you set up the program.

 To use files your own computer, you double-click the My Computer icon. To use files on another computer, you have to go through one extra step.

The easy way: browse through the Network Neighborhood

Just as on your own computer, you can open or save files on any computer to which you're networked—just point and click. Start in the Network Neighborhood, double-clicking the name of the computer you want to use, and then work your way through the shared folders until you find the place and name you want. You can even do this using the File Open and File Save As dialog boxes when you save a document, as shown in Figure 20.9.

The hard way: Mapping to a drive letter

On your own computer, you're used to referring to disk drives by letter, such as A: and C:, for your main floppy and hard drives. With some programs, drive letters are the only way to use files; these programs (mostly older DOS and Windows programs) won't let you point and click your way through the Network Neighborhood. Instead, you have to fool Windows into using a drive letter for one of these shared folders. The process is called **drive mapping**— as the phrase suggests, you're creating a "map" of network locations, each one labeled with a drive letter, that Windows can refer to when you use one of the mapped drive letters. Here's how:

Fig. 20.9
Use the drop-down list in the File Open and File Save As dialog boxes to work with a file on another computer somewhere in the Network Neighborhood.

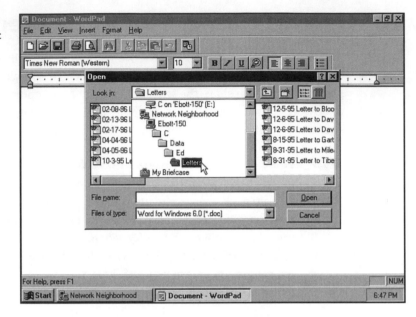

Browse through the Network Neighborhood until you reach the folder you want to use. Right-click the shared folder, and choose <u>M</u>ap Network Drive. (Fig. 20.10 shows the dialog box.) Notice that the computer name and folder name are already filled in. You'll see a slightly different version of the same dialog box if you right-click the My Computer icon and choose the <u>M</u>ap Network Drive command.)

Pick a drive letter from the drop-down list.

Fig. 20.10
Use this dialog box to tell Windows where in the Network Neighborhood to look when you use a specific drive letter.

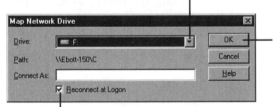

Click OK to tell Windows about the mapping. The mapped drive (E:, for example) will appear in the My Computer folder.

Check the Reconnect at logon box if you want to make the drive-letter mapping permanent; leave this box empty if you just want to use this folder one time.

What do all those slashes mean?

The complicated strings of text in the drive-mapping boxes are called **UNC names**. Just as you can refer to locations on your computer with a drive letter, a colon, a backslash, and a folder name, you can refer to locations on another computer by typing its full name. A UNC name starts with two backslashes, followed by the computer name, another backslash, the name of the shared folder or volume, another backslash, and so on.

Here's how it works: Let's say your company has a file server named Calvin on which the network administrator has defined a shared folder named Data. The Data folder in turn contains a folder called Letters. You can get to the Letters folder (in a File Save As dialog box, say) by typing its full UNC name:

\\Calvin\Data\Letters

66 *Plain English, please!*

UNC means **Universal Naming Convention**. That's a fancy designation for an agreement between different network software makers. UNC names allow you to connect to any file server, even when you don't know exactly what kind of network operating system the file server is using. 99

Share information (and your printer, too!) with other people

When you're working in an office as part of a team, you'll find plenty of productive ways to use Windows' built-in sharing features. On a Windows network, you can set aside a portion of your hard drive (or all of it, for that matter) as a sort of lending library. Anyone else on the network can stop by and browse through the contents at their leisure.

If security's an issue, you can have Windows assign a librarian to monitor the shared area and demand some ID, in the form of a password, before letting a stranger in. Windows lets you share printers and CD-ROM drives, too.

You might share your entire hard drive with a trusted administrative assistant; that way, every time either of you wanted to use the files on your hard disk, they'd be right there. Or you could give a coworker the rights to look at just one folder filled with documents you're collaborating on. The documents themselves remain on your hard disk while Windows' messengers shuttle them across the network wire on demand.

How do I share files and folders?

Before you can share anything on your PC with other users on your company's network (or stop sharing it), your administrator has to grant you that permission. If you've been assigned to the built-in Windows NT Power Users group, you already have this right. If, on the other hand, you've been assigned to the less privileged Users group, you'll be able to see access restrictions on files you create, but you won't be able to change them. For more information about users and groups, see Chapter 3.

Assuming you have the right permissions, sharing files and folders with others on your network is a simple process:

1 To share an entire drive, right-click the icon for the drive you want in the My Computer window. To share a folder, right-click the folder icon. Choose Sharing from the shortcut menu. You'll see a dialog box like the one in Figure 20.11.

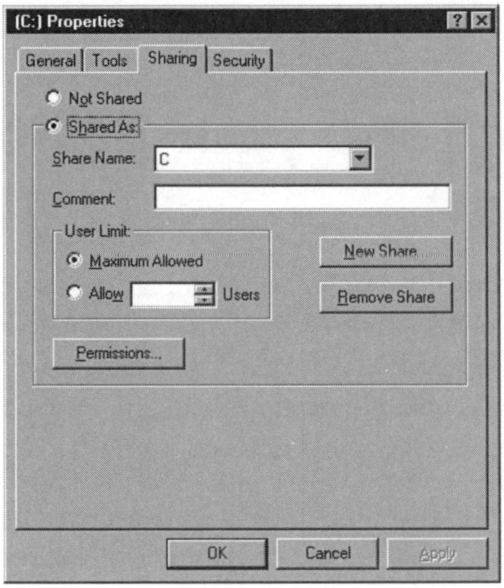

Fig. 20.11
Right-click a drive or folder and choose Sharing to reveal this dialog box. Click Permissions to fine-tune who gets access to what.

2 Check the Shared As button, and give the shared drive or folder a name. You can call it anything, but it helps to use a descriptive name, since this is the name other people will see when they browse through the Network Neighborhood.

3 Do you want to limit the number of connections that people can make to your hard disk? If the shared files are popular and you find that all that activity is slowing down your work, try setting this number to 2 or 3.

4 If you want to restrict access to the shared folder, click the Permissions button. You can carefully tailor what each user can do, so that different people have different levels of access to your files. Or you can assign permission to groups of users on your network.

5 Click OK to make the changes effective. Note the hand that appears under the folder or drive icon to indicate that it is shared.

When you click the Permissions button, you'll see one of the most confusing dialog boxes in Windows NT. (To follow along, look at Fig. 20.12.) Believe it or not, NT assumes, when you share a drive or a folder, that you want to give everyone in your entire network full control over that file. They can read it, change it, rename it, even delete it completely!

If that's not what you intended, change the options in the Access Through Share Permissions dialog box.

• **To remove a user or group,** highlight the name in the list and click the Remove button.

• **To add a user or group,** click the Add button. (The list of groups appears first; users' names appear only if you click the Show Users button.)

• **To change a permission,** highlight the name of the user or group and click the drop-down list labeled Type of Access. Change and Full Control allow users to delete, edit, or rename files. Read allows users only to look at the data in a file.

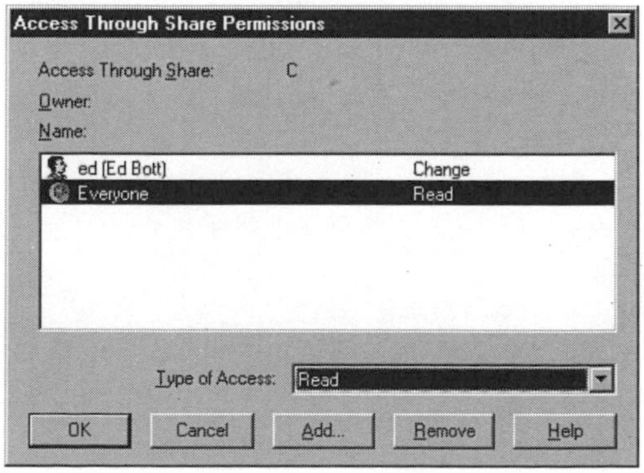

Fig. 20.12
Do you want anyone to be able to poke around in your files—and even rename or delete them? If not, then change the Type of Access for the Everyone group from Full Control to Read.

To share a printer, open the My Computer folder, double-click on the Printers icon, highlight the name of a printer, and follow the same steps.

When you browse through the Network Neighborhood and double-click on the icon for a PC, you'll see an icon for each shared folder and printer that's available. To open the shared folder, just double-click. If the owner of that computer has assigned a password, you'll have to enter it here before you can see what's available.

21

Sending and Receiving E-Mail

● **In this chapter:**

● **Sending a message to someone you love (or hate)**

● **Reading messages you get from others**

● **Sorting (and organizing) the mail**

● **Faxes and voice mail on my PC? How?**

With Windows Messaging, the e-mail Inbox for Windows NT, you can keep in touch with friends and coworkers without ever having to lick a stamp. . . . . ▶

Windows includes an all-in-one program to make sure you stay in touch with anyone in your company or the outside world—especially if they also use Windows. Windows Messaging lets you send and retrieve electronic mail, as well as keep track of names, addresses, and other important information for coworkers, business contacts, family, and friends.

You can say just about anything in e-mail, from a simple "Hello" to a long explanation of why fourth-quarter expenses went through the roof. (But before you send your first e-mail, look over the essentials of e-mail etiquette later in this chapter.) With the help of Windows Messaging, you can send and receive mail automatically, organize it into folders, and find a particular message weeks or even months after you received it.

E-mail essentials

If you understand how the postman gets mail and packages to your door, you've already mastered the basic concepts of electronic mail. You create messages, add attachments, fill out an envelope, and drop it in the Windows Messaging mailbox, where the Windows postal agent picks it up at the same time it drops off any mail that other people have sent to you. Best of all, you don't have to lick a single stamp!

Where do I start?

Before you can use Windows Messaging, you have to set it up on your PC. If it isn't installed on your system, use the Add/Remove Programs icon in Control Panel to add it to your system. (You'll probably need to ask for help from your system administrator, especially if you intend to connect to a Microsoft Mail post office or an Internet mail server.) Windows includes a wizard to help you set up Windows Messaging the first time.

 If you want to change any of the Windows Messaging options, double-click the Mail icon in Control Panel to pop up the Settings dialog box for Windows Messaging. Click any item in the list and then click the Properties button. You'll see a dialog box like the one in Figure 21.1.

A guided tour of the Inbox on the desktop

E-mail to anywhere: Use Microsoft Windows Messaging to send and receive electronic mail—not just on a local network, but anywhere in the world.

Folder list
Organize your messages into folders. You can add as many new folders as you like, and even put folders inside of other folders.

Toolbar
One-click access to frequently used mail functions. Push the button to create a new message, reply to mail, manage your Address Book, and more. Windows Messaging lets you add new buttons or delete existing ones.

Column headings
Click any heading to sort your messages. Click again to sort in reverse order.

Status bar
Look here for helpful messages about the current task.

Message window
The contents of the selected folder show up here. The default view shows the message subject, the sender's name, and other details, but you can create a different view of each folder, if you prefer. For example, you can group all your messages by sender or by subject.

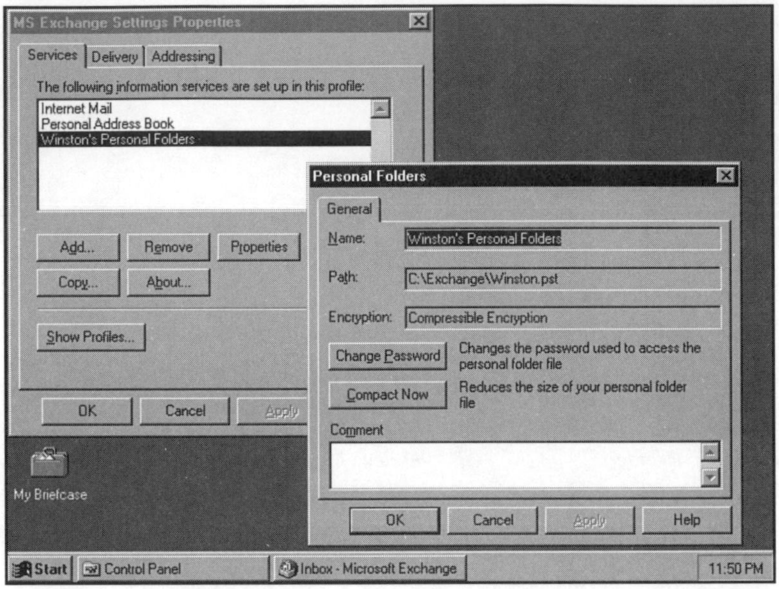

Fig. 21.1
Double-click the
Mail icon in Control
Panel to pop up this
configuration dialog
box, then click
Properties to see more
details about each
item. Confused by all
these options? Ask your
network administrator
to make sure you're set
up correctly.

Fig. 21.1
Double-click the Mail icon in Control Panel to pop up this configuration dialog box, then click Properties to see more details about each item. Confused by all these options? Ask your network administrator to make sure you're set up correctly.

Some of the options are self-explanatory, but most of them are technical and absolutely baffling. If you're not sure how to configure Windows Messaging, ask your network administrator for help. (If you're not on a network, most of the really difficult settings don't apply to you anyway.)

What can I do with Windows Messaging?

After Windows Messaging is successfully installed on your PC, just click the Inbox icon on your desktop or choose Windows Messaging from the Programs section of the Start menu. After the Windows Messaging window opens, you can do one of four things:

- **Send a simple message** as e-mail. It might be the electronic equivalent of a postcard ("Having a wonderful time. Wish you were online.") or as heavy as a package from the IRS. You can send it just about anywhere: to someone on your local network, if you're on one—or to a friend or business associate with an e-mail account on the Internet.

- **Send a file** (or a whole bunch of files) as an e-mail attachment. The attachment might be a file you've created with a word processor or a spreadsheet; all the recipient has to do is double-click its icon to see (and edit) the file.

66 *Plain English, please!*

An **attachment** is a file that rides along with an e-mail message, just as you sometimes receive a package with a letter taped to the outside. Almost all mail systems can exchange attachments with each other these days, thanks to the standardization of mailing methods. (You don't really need to know about all the standards, but in case someone asks you, Windows Messaging is "MIME-compatible." That's a standard.)

Attachments are tricky things—if the person on the other end of the mail connection is using a mail program other than Windows Messaging, there's no guarantee the standard attachment-handling formats will work properly. The package might get lost or damaged in transit. If you plan to exchange an important attachment with someone, your best bet is to first try a test with a small WordPad file, to make sure the two mail systems can handle the package properly. 99

- Finally, you can **receive messages** from anyone who knows your e-mail address.

Who can I send a message to?

When you address a letter to your next-door neighbor and drop it in your local mailbox, you can be reasonably sure that your local mail carrier will deliver it. After all, it's on his route. What if you send a postcard to Moscow? It'll get there, too, as long as the Postal Service and its counterparts in Russia have an agreement to exchange mail. But if you try to send a package to Mr. Floyd on the dark side of the Moon, it'll probably come back marked "Undeliverable."

E-mail works the same way. Windows Messaging has its own local delivery route, plus agreements with foreign e-mail systems to swap mail. Depending on how you and your network administrator have it set up, Windows Messaging lets you communicate with other Windows users on your company's network, or with anyone who has an e-mail account on the Internet.

For more information about the Internet, see Chapters 22 and 23.

I want to send an e-mail message...

To send an old-fashioned paper letter, you'll need a piece of paper, an envelope, an address book, and a stamp. To compose an e-mail message, you'll need the electronic equivalent of everything but the stamp. Fortunately, all of this is usually just a click or two away.

Here's how to get started:

1 **Click** the new message button (you can also press Ctrl+N). You'll see the New Message form shown in Figure 21.2.

A mail program by any other name...

Windows has included electronic-mail software for years. Windows for Workgroups offered Microsoft Mail, Windows 95 included the Microsoft Exchange Inbox, and Windows NT 4.0 has Windows Messaging. Microsoft has even developed a couple of e-mail programs that never made it into the same box as Windows.

Why does Microsoft sell all these e-mail programs? And more importantly, do you need to know the differences between them?

The answers are "Who knows?" and "Not really." If you insist, though, here's a quick summary:

- **Microsoft Mail** is an old-fashioned e-mail system that works well on small networks and not so well on the Internet.

- **Microsoft Exchange Inbox** and **Windows Messaging** are nearly identical versions of the same all-in-one e-mail program. The name changed in Windows NT to avoid causing confusion with...

- **Microsoft Exchange** which is a big, expensive, and very complicated e-mail program designed for big companies to use. It requires a server version that runs on the network, and client versions that users run on their PCs to send and receive mail. This client program looks a lot like Windows Messaging, with several additional features.

- And there's more. Microsoft also makes a simple mail program called **Internet Mail and News**, and Microsoft Office 97 will include yet another e-mail program, called **Outlook**.

Which e-mail program should you use? Your network administrator probably already decided for you and everyone else in your company. If that decision was Windows Messaging or Microsoft Exchange, pay close attention to this chapter.

Click here to **Send** your
message to the Outbox.

Want to send a data file along with your message?
Click the **Insert file** button to attach it to your
message.

Fig. 21.2
The electronic letter,
complete with
envelope.

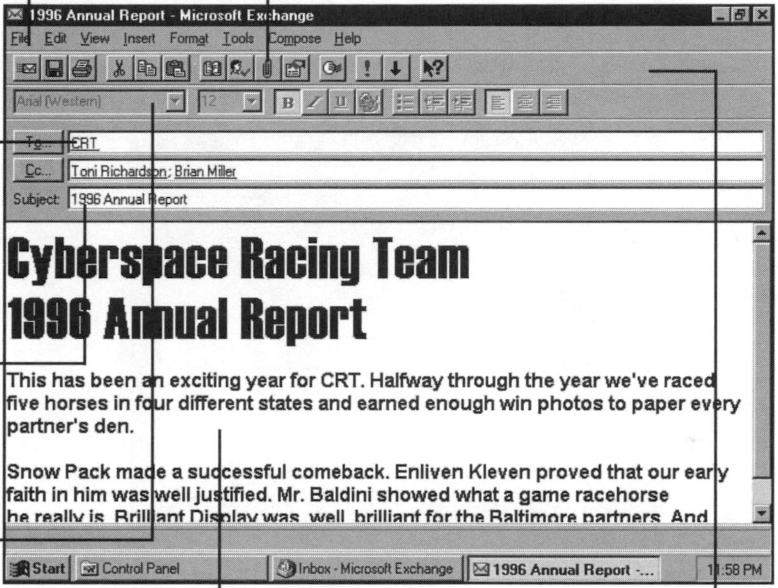

The **envelope**.
Click the To and
Cc buttons to tell
Windows Messaging
where to deliver
your message.

Put a short
summary
of the message in
the **Subject** line.

Use the **format-
ting toolbar** to
quickly change
fonts, add bullets,
or adjust the
text alignment.

1996 Annual Report - Microsoft Exchange

File Edit View Insert Format Tools Compose Help

Arial (Western)   12   B I U

To... CRT
Cc... Toni Richardson; Brian Miller
Subject: 1996 Annual Report

Cyberspace Racing Team
1996 Annual Report

This has been an exciting year for CRT. Halfway through the year we've raced
five horses in four different states and earned enough win photos to paper every
partner's den.

Snow Pack made a successful comeback. Enliven Kleven proved that our early
faith in him was well justified. Mr. Baldini showed what a game racehorse
he really is. Brilliant Display was, well, brilliant for the Baltimore partners. And

Start Control Panel   Inbox - Microsoft Exchange   1996 Annual Report -...   11:58 PM

Enter the **message text** in this window.
You can use fancy fonts, bold and italic
formatting, even colors. If your recipients
are also Windows Messaging or Microsoft
Exchange users, they'll see exactly what you
sent.

Not sure what the buttons on
the **toolbar** do? Aim the
mouse pointer at a button
and leave it there for a few
seconds to see a helpful
ToolTip.

66 *Plain English, please!*

When you use Windows Messaging, you may occasionally see a reference
to **MAPI**. The acronym, pronounced "mappy," stands for the Messaging
Application Programming Interface, a common set of software widgets that
let different e-mail programs communicate reliably with one another.
Thanks to MAPI, you can use Windows Messaging to swap e-mail with a
coworker who uses Lotus Development's cc:Mail or Notes, or Novell's
GroupWise. 99

2 Enter one or more addresses for the primary recipients. Press the To
button to search through the Address Book (see Fig. 21.3). Highlight the
name you want to add, then press the To button to add the name to the
Recipients list. If you want to send copies to other people, add their
names by clicking the Cc button here, too. (You can even add a new
name to your address book here—just click New.)

TIP **Every message needs at least one primary receiver, whose name** goes in the To box. If you want someone to receive a copy of the message, put his or her name in the Cc box. Want to send a secret copy to someone? Use Bcc, for blind carbon copy. As you're composing a message, select Bcc Box from the View menu to add this capability.

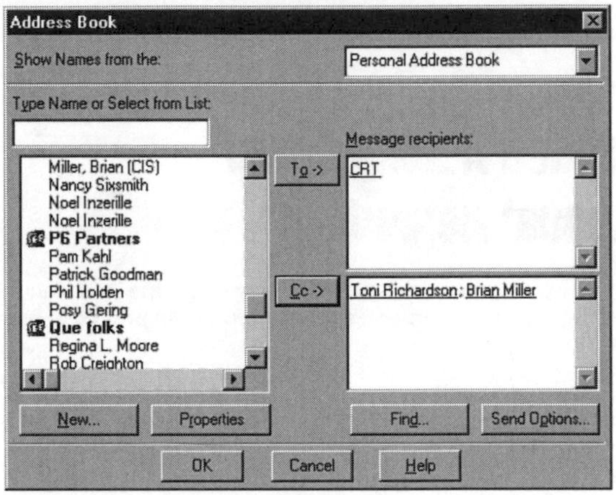

Fig. 21.3
Your Address Book contains the details you need to send a message to anyone that Windows Messaging can reach.

TIP **You don't have to enter the full name of a recipient, as long as** there's an entry in your Address Book. Just enter some or all of the name, and Windows Messaging will search for the nearest matching name. For example, if there's only one Bill in your Address Book—the entry for Bill Gates—you can type **Bill** in the address field and Windows Messaging will automatically fill in the rest of the name when you press the Send button. If there's more than one Bill, Windows Messaging will show you a list of possible addressees and let you pick the right one.

3 Enter a Subject. Be as clear and detailed as possible. For example, Copy machine is broken! is a better Subject line than Big problem!!!

4 Attach any files, if necessary.

CAUTION **Be careful when sending files to other people who aren't using** Windows Messaging. You have no guarantee that the program they use to receive mail will correctly receive the attachment you send. Try a test run before you send a crucial file.

5 To select additional options, choose File, Properties and click the appropriate buttons and boxes. For example, if you want to be notified when the person at the other end reads your message, click the Read Receipt button.

6 Click Send or press Ctrl+S. Your message goes into the Outbox and will be sent the next time Windows Messaging checks for mail.

What are those funny-looking symbols I see in some e-mail messages?

It's hard to be humorous in e-mail. Subtle humor is the worst of all. When you're face-to-face, you signal a joke with a smile and a wink. So how do you pass the same message along in an e-mail message?

I sometimes add **<g>** (for "grin") after a remark that might leave the reader wondering what I meant. You can do the same. But if you want to really be creative, try using an **emoticon**—a clever word that packs emotion and icon into the same space. The most common of all is the **smiley**, a little grinning face turned on its side to suggest that that last remark was not meant to be taken seriously.

There are literally thousands of smileys. Here's a sampling of some of the more useful ones. (If you can't figure them out, try turning your head 90 degrees to the left...)

:-) or :)   Plain ol' smiley. "Just kidding."

;-)   Winky smiley. Used for slightly more sarcastic remarks. "Just kidding. Really!"

:-(Frowning smiley. "I didn't like that last remark." Also used to express unhappiness.

>:->   Devilish smiley. For really caustic comments.

:*)   Drunk smiley.

:-{)   Smiley with moustache.

{:-)   Wearing bad toupee.

:'-(Crying.

:-@   Screaming

O :-)   Angel smiley (see the halo?)

:-D   Laughing (at you!)

:-/   Skeptical smiley

:-o   Uh-oh!

X-(Dead smiley

—<—{(@   Long-stemmed rose (for when you're feeling romantic)

E-mail etiquette

Once you've used e-mail for a while, you'll wonder how you ever got along without it. You'll get rid of those stupid pink "While You Were Out" message slips. When you come back from lunch, you'll find easy-to-read electronic messages instead of indecipherable scribblings on yellow sticky notes all over your computer screen. Maybe you'll even use e-mail to send love letters to your sweetheart or instant expressions of outrage to your Congressman.

After awhile, you may think the e in e-mail stands for easy, and there's the problem. E-mail is so effortless that it's easy to send the wrong kind of message, and once you've hit the Send button, there's no way to bring it back.

Want to avoid the most common e-mail boo-boos? Memorize these helpful tips:

- Be extra clear when you write e-mail. If you're responding to someone else's message, include a snippet of the original message so the person at the other end knows what you're talking about. Don't just send a message saying "Great idea. Go for it!" You're likely to get a message back—"Go for what?"

- Include a meaningful Subject line. Your message is more likely to get read if the Subject line gives a strong clue about the message contents.

- Avoid sarcasm and subtle humor unless you're positive the recipient will get your joke. If you must, at least add a "Just

kidding!" afterwards. Better yet, pick your favorite smiley icon and tack it onto the message.

- Never, ever send a message when you're angry. Mad at your boss? Go ahead and write that memo telling him what you really think, but don't send it. You'll probably feel a lot cooler in the morning, so go home, get a good night's sleep, and when you get to work the next day delete the message without re-reading it. Start a new message and send it instead. Remember: E-mail is forever. Especially when it's embarrassing.

- Don't put people on the Cc: list unless they really need to see a copy of your message. Electronic junk mail is just as irritating as the paper variety.

- Be extra careful when you use the Reply To All button. One infamous e-mail writer at a large computer company accidentally sent a steamy love letter intended for his sweetheart to all 5,000 employees at his company. People still whisper behind his back when they see him in the hallways.

- When you use e-mail at work, your employer has a right to read any message you send or receive, and other people may even have a right to demand copies of your mail—if they subpoena your employer as part of a lawsuit, for example. A good rule of thumb: Don't say anything in e-mail that you wouldn't want to explain in court.

How do I send mail to people on different services?

Good question. The answer depends on several factors.

If you're sending and receiving mail through an Internet connection, you can address mail to any online service using the standard Internet addressing scheme: *name@location.location.etc.* For instance, the developer on this book was lgentry@que.mcp.com—e-mail her and tell her what you thought of the book! Addresses at online services look like this:

> *IDnumber*@compuserve.com, *IDnumber*@prodigy.com,
> *nickname*@aol.com.

If you're on a local area network, your e-mail administrator may have set up mail "gateways" to connect to various services, such as CompuServe. Ask about this—there may be a special way that messages need to be addressed.

TIP **What's the best way to find someone's e-mail address? If they're** not on your network, call them on the phone and ask! Seriously. There's no comprehensive Yellow Pages or Directory Assistance for e-mail. Not yet.

What do I do with these messages?

Sooner or later (usually sooner), your Windows Messaging mailbox will start overflowing with messages, and you'll have trouble keeping up with your mail. The solution? Create a filing system, and move related messages into folders so you can find them easily later.

To read a message, just double-click it.

To reply to a message, click the Reply to Sender button. To reply to everyone on the list for the original message, use the Reply to All button.

To delete a message, click the Delete button. Windows Messaging doesn't actually delete the message; it just moves it to the Deleted Items folder, where you'll need to delete it again to really get rid of it.

To store a message in a folder, drag the message from the right-hand pane and drop it on a folder icon in the Folders list on the left side of the Windows Messaging window.

Q&A   ***I don't see the Folders list. Is Windows Messaging broken?***

No, it's just not set up to show that view when you click on the Inbox icon on the desktop. To reveal the Folders list, click the Show/Hide Folder List button on the Windows Messaging toolbar.

CAUTION   **If you use Windows Messaging for your regular e-mail, you'll** quickly fill it with irreplaceable messages. Don't run the risk of losing them forever! Keep backup copies of your mail file. Use the Find, Files or Folders option to search for files called *.PST, then copy the results to a safe place.

What do these default folders do?

When you first use Windows Messaging, it has only four folders. Here's what they're used for:

The **Inbox** is the place where incoming mail is delivered.

When you send a message, it goes into the **Outbox** until Windows Messaging is ready to deliver it. (It'll deliver the message the next time you connect to the network or service that's supposed to carry it. When's that? It depends on how you've got Windows Messaging configured.) Windows Messaging must be running to send or receive messages.

Sent Items keeps a copy of each message that you send. You can tell Windows Messaging not to save these messages by choosing Tools, Options and checking the appropriate box.

Deleted Items is the Windows Messaging equivalent of the Recycle Bin. Messages you delete go here. When you select a message in this folder and delete it, Windows Messaging gets rid of it permanently. If you're pressed for space on your hard disk, it's a good idea to get in the habit of deleting unimportant messages as soon as you've read them.

Can Windows Messaging handle anything besides e-mail?

Microsoft calls Windows Messaging a "universal inbox," because theoretically you can fill your inbox with e-mail, documents, even faxes and voice-mail messages. You'll need special software to handle these other types of messages, though, and that software isn't included with Windows NT.

When you set up Windows Messaging to handle faxes, Windows turns your fax modem into the full-fledged equivalent of a fax machine. You can receive any fax, anytime, from anyone, anywhere. You can send faxes, too—if you can print a document, you can fax it. Check Microsoft's site on the World Wide Web (www.microsoft.com) to download the fax software when it's available.

With the right modem and still more software, you can even store voice-mail messages in your Windows Messaging Inbox. Of course, to pull off this trick you'll need a modem that includes voice-mail features, along with the software to control it. Creative Labs makes a product called Phone Blaster that does both of these things.

22

Exploring the Internet and the World Wide Web

● **In this chapter:**

- **What is the Internet, anyway, and what can I do there?**

- **Connecting Windows NT to the Internet**

- **How the World Wide Web works**

- **Find what you need on the Web—fast!**

- **Keep a list of your favorite Web sites**

There are more pages on the World Wide Web than any human can count. To start exploring, just follow the links . . . . ▶

Douglas Adams, the author of *The Hitchhiker's Guide to the Galaxy* and all its sequels, said it better than I can: "The Internet is big. Really big. It gives the idea of infinity much better than infinity itself."

With that kind of introduction, it seems a bit presumptuous to try to explain the Internet in one small chapter of this book. So let's start with a general disclaimer: If you want to know everything about the Internet, you'll have to read several big books (including some excellent ones published by the people who brought you this one). You'll also have to master some hard technical terms, because there's very little plain English to be found when you start talking about the Internet!

Fortunately, it's all worth the effort. Thanks to its best-known destination, the World Wide Web, the Internet is a very cool and useful place, and this chapter can help get you moving in the right direction.

What is the Internet?

Today, all those original rocket scientists are still using the Internet, but they have to share the space with ordinary people like you and me. And where commercial activity was once strictly forbidden, today it's the single most important force driving the growth of the Net. No one knows exactly how many people use the Internet for business or pleasure each day, but the number is surely in the tens of millions.

TIP **Does your company have an intranet? That's not a typo—instead,** it's a way to refer to a new trend in corporate networks, which use the same techniques as the World Wide Web to share information among employees only. If your company has created an intranet, you'll be able to share files and read Web pages using Internet Explorer. The only difference will be that you'll open files on your company network instead of finding them on the World Wide Web.

How does the Internet work?

I'd rather answer a month's worth of Final Jeopardy questions than try to explain the Internet in 50 words or less. But OK, here goes...

On the Internet, every computer is connected to every other computer—directly or indirectly, using a networking protocol called **TCP/IP**, a "common language" computers use to communicate with each other via the Internet.

Every computer that is connected to the Internet has a unique address (called an **IP address**) that consists of one long number broken into four groups of up to three digits. Like your Social Security number (if you live in the United States) or your passport number, it's associated with one and only one individual. For example, the main machine at Macmillan Computer Publishing, the company that produced this book, is called 198.70.48.1.

Connecting the dots

What's in a name? On the Internet, the answer is: a lot of dots.

Internet names typically consist of two parts: a **host name** and a **domain name**. Individual pieces of both the host and domain names are separated by dots, or periods. Internet e-mail addresses usually consist of the host name and the name of a mail server, separated by an at sign (@).

The domain name helps narrow the group of computers and people I'm associated with. If I work for a big company like Macmillan Computer Publishing, for example, my domain name might be mcp.com (pronounced *m c p dot com*). The *com* tells other people that this group is a company. If the extension were *edu* or *org* or *gov*, they'd know that mcp was affiliated with an educational institution, a nonprofit organization, or the government, respectively.

Large domains can be broken into **subdomains** to make life easier on the people who have to keep track of all these computers. So if I ran

mcp.com, I might create a subgroup called que.mcp.com (remember, you pronounce each of the periods between the parts of a domain name as *dot*).

Finally, all the people who have individual access to computers in the organization would get their own unique **host name**. There's no rule that says you have to use your real name, either: You could call yourself jean-luc.picard@que.mcp.com if you wanted, and that would be a perfectly legal Internet name. (When you say your Internet address out loud, remember to pronounce the at sign as "at.") Generally, though, your host name will be some combination of your first and last name or initials.

There might be another jean-luc.picard elsewhere on the Net, but the unique combination of a host name and domain name, separated by an at sign, guarantees that you can always reach people, as long as you know the name they use on the Internet.

> 66 *Plain English, please!*
>
> TCP stands for **Transmission Control Protocol**. IP stands for **Internet Protocol**. Together, they form the standard language that different computers use to exchange information on the Internet. (Don't worry, there will *not* be a test on all these acronyms!) 99

That's all fine and dandy if you're a computer, but human beings are more comfortable with words than with numbers. So all those Internet addresses also have corresponding names. Instead of having to remember my up-to-12-digit Internet ID number, all you have to know is that my machine's Internet name is ed.bott.com and my Internet e-mail address is ed@bott.com. Special machines called **domain name servers** make sure that the computers they work for can translate names to numbers, and vice versa.

OK, how do I get hooked up?

The Internet is not a company or organization—when you get on the Net, you're pretty much on your own. However, one way or another, you have to find a set of wires that can carry information between you and all those other computers:

- If your company already has an Internet connection, it's easy. The same cable that carries information around your company's local network can also connect you to the Internet. Your network administrator probably set up your Internet connection at the same time he or she installed Windows NT.

- If you don't have a company connection, or you want to hook up to the Internet from home or a hotel room, you'll need a modem and a place where you can call and establish a connection to the rest of the Internet. Companies that sell this service are called **service providers**. We'll talk more about dial-up networking in the next chapter.

Getting Windows NT ready for the Internet

Before you can sample the wide variety of information on the largest network in the known universe, your computer has to be configured to be part of the Internet. And as soon as you start talking about networking, things get just a little...well, complicated.

Even if you understand every technical detail of the process, you'll probably still need to get help from the network administrator, because Windows NT won't let an ordinary user tamper with the networking software (in fact, all the buttons in the Network Control Panel dialog box are grayed out for all but administrators). Regardless of who does it, though, here's what needs to be done:

1 First, **set up a network adapter**. If you already have a network card in your computer, you probably don't need to worry about this step. Double-click the Control Panel's Network icon and click the Adapters tab to pop up a dialog box like the one in Figure 22.1.

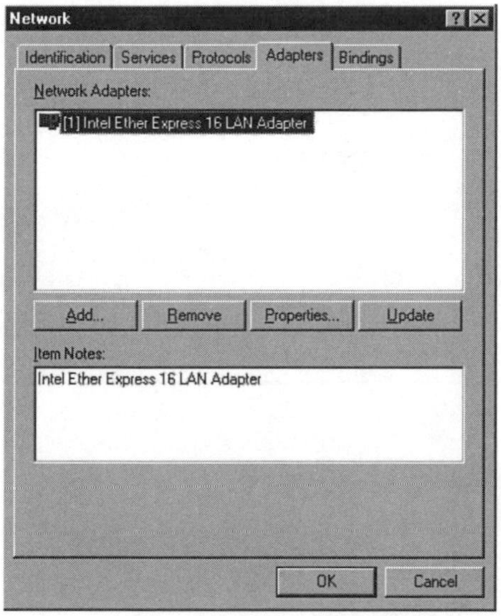

Fig. 22.1
Check here to see that Windows NT knows about the network adapter inside your PC.

Network	? X

Identification | Services | Protocols | Adapters | Bindings

Network Adapters:

[1] Intel Ether Express 16 LAN Adapter

Add...　Remove　Properties...　Update

Item Notes:

Intel Ether Express 16 LAN Adapter

OK　Cancel

2 Next, **install the TCP/IP software**. Think of this as a graduate course in Internet-speak for your PC. Use the Control Panel's Network utility again. TCP/IP is a protocol, so click that tab. If it's not on the list, click the Add button (see Fig. 22.2). If it is, keep going.

3 Highlight the TCP/IP Protocol entry in the Network dialog box, click the Properties button, and **enter your configuration information**. Whoever runs your network should have already set up an account for you; ask him or her for a "cheat sheet" with all the right settings printed on it.

At a minimum, you'll have to check two of the four tabs in the TCP/IP Properties dialog box: IP address and DNS (see Fig. 22.3). Don't worry if you don't understand precisely what these settings do; concentrate on entering the names and numbers correctly, and you'll be fine.

Fig. 22.2
Before your computer can talk to other computers on the Internet, it has to learn to speak TCP/IP, the universal language of the Internet.

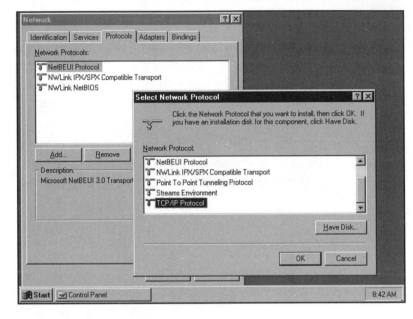

Fig. 22.3
Do you speak TCP/IP? Of course you don't, but if you expect your computer to communicate on the Internet, you'll have to make sure that this dialog box is filled out flawlessly.

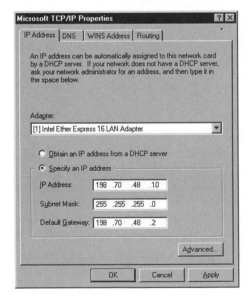

When you finish all this clicking and configuring, Windows should remind you that you'll have to restart your computer before your new software can kick into gear. Go ahead—restart now. After you've shut down and logged on fresh, your TCP/IP connection should be ready to go. If you've got a direct Internet connection over your company network, you'll now be able to go anywhere on the Internet without doing anything else.

> ❝ *Plain English, please!*
>
> Occasionally, you'll see a reference to something called **Winsock**. That's the technical term for the **Windows Sockets standard**. As the name implies, this is the software that Windows programs use to "plug into" the Internet. There are dozens of different versions of the Winsock software floating around, but the one that comes with Windows NT is the only one you need to be concerned about. If you start getting Winsock error messages, it's time to call for technical support! ❞

What's out there?

You could fill a book with all the great things you can do with an Internet connection. There's an excellent book filled with worthwhile information from the same people who created this one. If you want to know more about the Internet, get *Using the Internet*, available from Que Corporation.

Meanwhile, here's a sampling of the things you can do once you're connected to the Net.

Web pages, Web pages, and more Web pages

The hottest of all Internet destinations is the **World Wide Web** (AKA the WWW or just "the Web"). There are literally more pages of information on the WWW than anyone can count, ranging from the extremely silly to the enormously valuable. Depending on the skill and budget of the designer, Web pages can be dull, one-font lists or visually dramatic presentations with text, graphics, sound, and animation. (See Fig. 22.4 for one of my favorite pages, **www.pccomputing.com**.) In either case, the thing that makes the Web unlike printed pages and televised images is the presence of **hypertext links,** where you can click to jump instantly to other related Web pages.

Fig. 22.4
The hottest ticket on the Internet? No doubt about it—the World Wide Web, with its dazzling graphics and sheer volume of information, is the place to see.

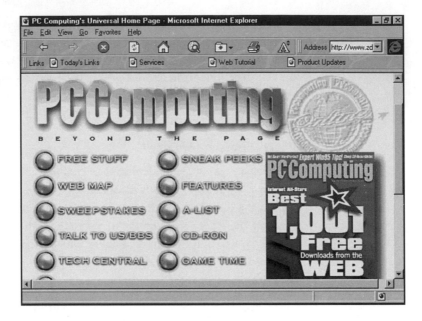

Information

If there's a stray fact or figure in the world, it's probably available somewhere on the Internet. I regularly use the Internet to answer questions for business and fun—everything from computer support to TV trivia. And sometimes the Web is literally a lifesaver: When a friend of mine discovered that his son had been diagnosed with a rare disease, he used the Net to track down more information. Within two hours, he had found an exhaustive collection of relevant articles, including detailed descriptions of the symptoms and treatments, plus names of the world's top specialists. (His son's doing just fine now, by the way.)

New programs, shareware, and freebies (FTP)

The Internet is stuffed to bursting with software. Look for **FTP servers**— those are central storehouses that use the Internet's **File Transfer Protocol** to exchange files with computers like yours. One of the most useful collections of software—for Windows users, anyway—is the one at www.microsoft. com. Internet Explorer handles FTP tasks automatically; all you have to do is point and click.

Mail and Newsgroups

You can drop in on discussions of every imaginable topic, from championship dog breeding to astrophysics, on public bulletin boards called **UseNet newsgroups**. You don't have to say a word; you can just **lurk** (watch without participating) and learn. Or you can chime in and add your own comments to a news group.

Shopping

Some people think we'll do all of our shopping on the Internet someday. Of course, those are the same people who said computers would eliminate paper in the office, too, so let's not believe it too quickly. Still, there are an impressive number of products you can buy on the Net today—flowers, movie tickets, CDs, software, and much more. Even if you plan to purchase a new product in person, you can gather information about it in advance, as I did recently when I was in the market for a new car. (Try www.edmunds.com for advice on how to get the best price for new or used cars.)

Is the Internet safe for credit cards?

By its very nature, the Internet is an insecure place. When you fill in a Web form and send data to someone on the Internet, it consists of plain, easy-to-read text, and it's sent from machine to machine in routes that are practically random. So how do you keep hackers from intercepting, reading, and even altering your data as it flashes through cyberspace? Fortunately, a pair of time-tested technologies make it possible for anyone to add the digital equivalent of notarized signatures and sealed envelopes to information exchanges over the Internet.

Authentication provides a way of establishing that you are who you say you are. The simplest form of authentication requires you to enter your user name and password before you can even look at a given Web page. More sophisticated authentication schemes use special pieces of software called digital signatures and certificates to guarantee that your credit card number gets safely from your PC to your favorite Internet florist.

How do you make sure your password isn't captured as it floats across the Internet? With the second security technique, **encryption**. Like the secret codes that spies use, Internet Explorer and other Web browsers can scramble data so that no one can read it except the intended recipient.

Of course, all Internet security schemes depend on sensible behavior and physical security as well. Even the best security is useless if your password is written on a yellow sticky note pasted to your monitor.

How the Web works

The basic building block of the World Wide Web is the **HTML page**. Like the pages in this book or in a magazine, a typical Web page might include headlines and body text, bulleted lists, photos, drawings, icons, and tables filled with information. Unlike its paper-based cousins, though, Web pages can also include links and buttons that let you jump to other Web pages with a single click. And it's all put together using a special language called **HyperText Markup Language**, or HTML.

They may look dazzling on your monitor, but each Web page is actually just a simple text file, filled with hidden codes that tell your Web browser—in this case, Internet Explorer—how the screen is supposed to be arranged, which fonts to use, and which graphics files need to be displayed. See Figure 22.5 for a close-up look at the HTML **source code** for the PC Computing Web page we saw a few pages ago.

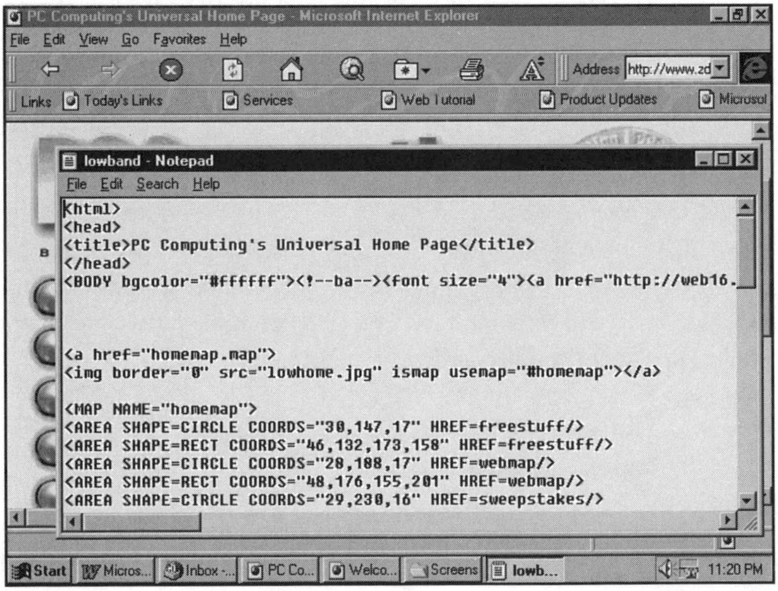

Fig. 22.5
HyperText Markup Language, or HTML, looks like plain English (well, mostly), but your Web browser can transform these files into dazzling displays.

You don't need to know what's inside a Web page, as long as you know its full name and address, known as a **Universal Resource Locator**, or URL. The URL for a file called **index.htm** in a folder called **home** on a machine called **www.myserver.com** would be www.myserver.com/home/index.htm. (By the way, notice that those are slashes, not the backslashes you see elsewhere in Windows.)

Graphics page: Internet Explorer

If you're interested in the Internet and the World Wide Web, you'll need a program called a browser. The Internet Explorer was designed especially for Windows. Watch what happens to the tools on the toolbar as the mouse pointer passes over them!

Use the Back and Forward buttons to flip quickly through the pages you've already seen.

You can go home again—or at least to the home page, where your journey through the Web begins.

When you see a page you think you'll want to visit again, click to add it to your Favorites folder.

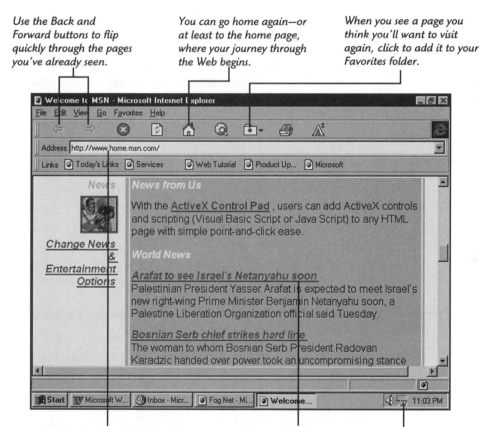

Every Web page has its own address, called a Universal Resource Locator, or URL. Type it here, or click a link to enter it automatically.

The underlined entries are hypertext links to other interesting pages on the Web. Click to jump straight there.

Worried about sending your credit card over the Internet? When you see a padlock icon here, you know it's safe.

TIP **Remember, every computer on the Internet has a name *and* a** number. So, for example, the Microsoft Network is www.msn.com as well as 204.255.247.121. If your Web browser shows a number instead of a name, don't be alarmed—it's almost certainly the page you asked for.

Every time you click a link or type in a URL, you're asking your Web browser to go out on the Internet, find the file that goes by that name, and copy the file to your computer using **HyperText Transfer Protocol**, or HTTP. Even though the entire file may take a while to arrive, Internet Explorer starts displaying the top of the page as soon as it can figure out what goes there.

TIP **You don't need to type http:// to retrieve a Web page. When you** type a recognizable Web address and hit Enter, Internet Explorer will automatically fill in the first part.

Introducing Internet Explorer

To get started with Internet Explorer, double-click the icon on the desktop. (If you hook up to the Internet through a dial-up connection and you're not currently connected, Windows will ask you if you want to dial now.) That opens your home page, the launching pad for your Web search. To jump to another page, click a link, or type an Address here and then press Enter. When you click a link, its URL appears in the Address line automatically.

- **Back** and **Forward** quickly flip through saved copies of pages you've looked at recently.

- Your favorite Web page isn't responding? It happens. Click **Stop** to tell Internet Explorer to quit trying and move on.

- If the page doesn't look quite right, press **Reload** and let Internet Explorer try once more.

- You can use any page, anywhere, as your **Home**. The Microsoft Network (www.msn.com) can help you build a personalized Web page filled with links to your favorite sites.

- Click the **Search** button to pop up Microsoft's all-in-one search page. Or change it to your preferred search page, if you like.

Fig. 22.6
Ready, set, double-click! Internet Explorer includes a collection of buttons that let you manage common activities easily.

- The **Favorites** folder stores shortcuts to interesting Web pages. You can add folders within this folder if you really want to get organized.

- Click the **Print** button to put your Web pages on paper.

You can rearrange the gizmos at the top of the Internet Explorer window. Grab the left edge of the toolbar, Quick Links, and Address box and move them up or down. If you put two or more items on the same line, use the same handle to make each one wider or narrower.

Getting started

If you have access to the Internet at work, chances are good that the icon for Internet Explorer is already on your desktop. If it's not, you'll need the system administrator's help to get the Internet Explorer software onto your system.

On the Internet, software has a life span that's measured in months, or even weeks. When there's a new version of Internet Explorer, it's easy to download the updated file and double-click its icon. So if the version of Internet Explorer on your screen doesn't look exactly like the one here, don't be surprised. A menu or two may have changed, but it should work just about the same as the one I describe in this book.

Making Internet Explorer work your way

The basic operation of Internet Explorer is pretty simple: just click and scroll until you find the information you're looking for. For most people, the default settings will work fine. To change the basic look and feel of Internet Explorer, choose View, Options. You'll see a dialog box with tabs like the two shown in Figure 22.7.

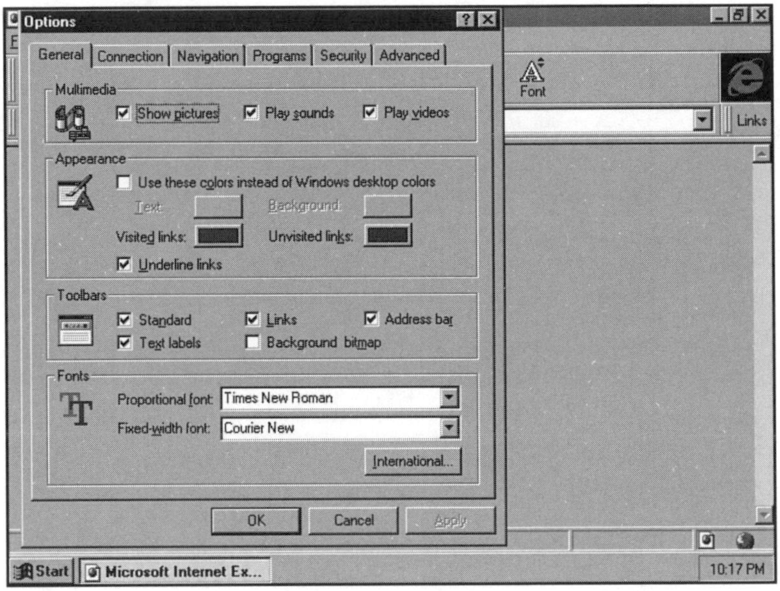

Fig. 22.7
These options can make browsing the Web faster, and if your vision is less than 20-20, they can also make Web pages easier to read.

Here are a handful of changes you might want to make to the default Internet Explorer settings:

- Does the Web feel too slow? Turn off the display of **pictures**, **sounds**, and **video** to make Web pages pop onto the screen faster (although you'll lose some potentially useful information this way).

- Don't like the colors that Internet Explorer uses to **highlight links**? Change 'em.

- Likewise for the default colors for **text** and **backgrounds** (although it's not a good idea to change these to anything too wild, because you might not be able to read some Web pages).

- Internet Explorer lets you change **fonts**, too. But because most people who design Web pages have those default fonts in mind, you probably won't be happy with the results if you switch fonts.

TIP   **Is it just me getting older, or is the world getting fuzzier?**
Whatever the explanation, I appreciate the Font button on the Internet
Explorer toolbar. Each time I click that button, Internet Explorer reformats
the text on the page I'm looking at, using a different set of fonts. There are
five choices in all, with the largest being big enough to read from across the
room. Try it!

Java and other exotic brews

These days it seems like you can't go five clicks without stumbling over a
Web page that's Java-enabled. Don't worry—this Java won't keep you up late
at night. That's the snappy trademark for a programming language that Web
developers can use to create programs that let your Web browser do some
cool tricks. There's only one thing you need to know about Java: It's built
into Internet Explorer, so you should be able to view any page, even a Java-
enabled one, if you've installed this browser.

CAUTION   **Actually, there's a second thing you should know, but only if you**
have at least a slight streak of paranoia. In theory, Java **applets** (the small
programs that run on Web servers) can carry viruses or attempt to damage
data on a computer. If you're worried about this risk, choose View, Options,
click the Security tab, and remove the checkbox from the Enable Java
programs box.

Blocking the naughty bits

The Internet is worldwide, and although many people enforce rules and
regulations in their corner of the Net, no one really controls it. As a result,
freedom of speech has flourished in cyberspace, bringing in the digital
equivalent of dirty magazines and hate mail. Despite the sensational stories
you might read in the papers, pornography and extreme politics occupy only
a tiny back alley of the Net. In fact, it's unlikely you'll stumble across the ugly
side of the Internet unless you go looking for it.

But there's also a way to prevent objectionable material (most of it, anyway)
from ever getting to your screen. Internet Explorer lets you turn on a rating
system called Content Advisor, which monitors sex, violence, and strong
language on the Net and lets you specify what you don't want to see. This
feature is intended mainly for households with children, but a business might
also find it a useful way to keep employees from peeking at playboy.com
during working hours.

To begin using Content Advisor, choose View, Options and then click the Advanced tab. The first time you use Ratings, you'll need to register a supervisor password; later, you'll use that password to turn the feature on or off. Click the Properties button to adjust your preferred ratings (see Fig. 22.8). Slide the levers to the right to make the system less restrictive. Slide all the levers to the left and you'll be lucky to be allowed into disney.com!

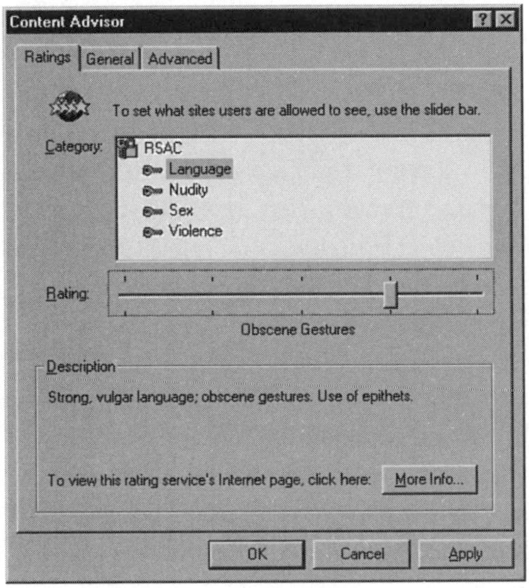

Fig. 22.8
These ratings can help screen some (but not all) the objectionable elements on the Web.

Finding what you want on the Web (and remembering where you found it!)

Wandering through the World Wide Web sometimes feels a little like channel-surfing on the world's largest cable network. Everything is interconnected, which makes for some fascinating (and potentially frustrating) wrong turns and detours. So how do you cope with 16 million channels when you don't have a TV Guide? If it's after hours, and you're exploring for the sheer pleasure of it, go ahead: Follow those interesting links and see where they take you. But if you have work to do, and you need answers *now*, here are some strategies for using your online time wisely.

There's no place like your home page

Every time you double-click on the Internet Explorer icon, it goes out on the net and finds your home page. If you find yourself continually navigating to the same spot on the Web, why not make that your home page? With that page showing in your Web browser, choose View, Options, and click the Navigation tab (Fig. 22.9). Make sure Start Page is showing in the drop-down list labeled Page, then click the Use Current button. Now, whenever you start Internet Explorer or click the Home button, you'll jump straight to that page.

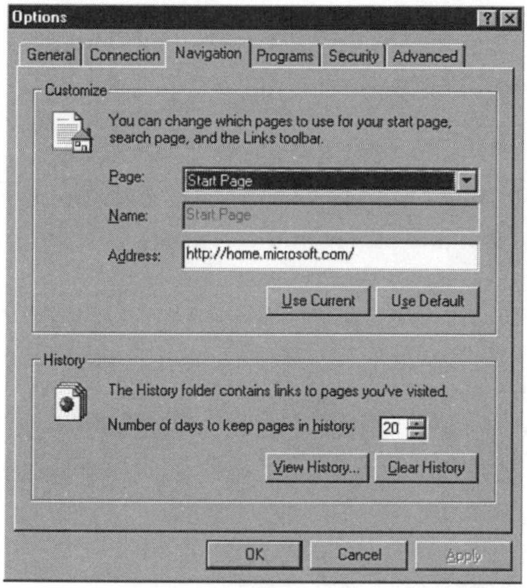

Fig. 22.9

Set up your Start Page here. While you're at it, reset the destinations for your search page and the Quick Links, too.

The same dialog box lets you reset the addresses that pop up when you click the Quick Links buttons, too. One of the default links, for example, is a Web tutorial, which you don't need after you've learned your way around. Go ahead and replace it with another favorite page if you prefer (don't forget to give the page a new name, too).

Using Favorites (didn't I see that last week?)

As you browse the Web, you'll run across all sorts of interesting pages. Sometimes they're relevant to your current search, while other times they represent an opportunity to take a time-wasting detour. Either way, the best thing you can do is to make a note of the page and its address, so you can come back to it later.

There's no need to write the address on a sticky note and slap it on your monitor, either. A much better way to keep track of Web sites you want to visit again is with the help of the Favorites folder:

1 Load the page you want Internet Explorer to keep track of.

2 Click the Favorites button and look at the drop-down list.

3 Click the first choice on the list, Add to Favorites. Internet Explorer will offer to create a shortcut to the page.

4 Give the shortcut a new name, if you like.

5 Click OK. The next time you click the Favorites button, you'll see that shortcut (and any others you've created) on the Favorites menu.

After a while, the Favorites menu has a way of getting stuffed with too many shortcuts. The solution? Organize it! Click the Favorites button again, but this time choose the second menu option, Organize Favorites. The Favorites folder will open in a dialog box like the one in Figure 22.10.

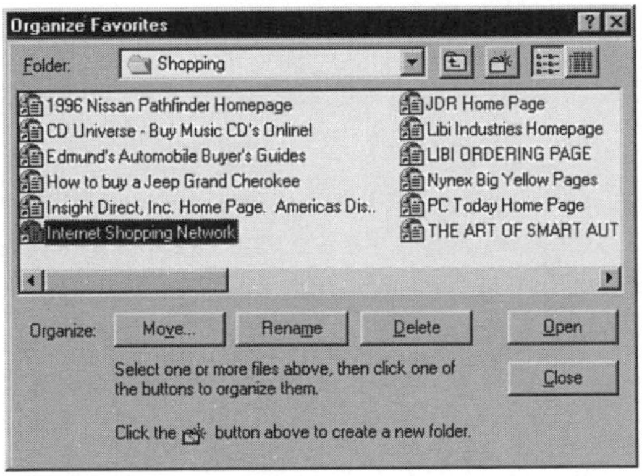

Fig. 22.10

When the Favorites folder starts to get too full, reorganize your shortcuts into new folders (like this one for Shopping), and delete the ones you no longer need.

If there are shortcuts you no longer need, delete them. You can also rename Internet shortcuts here. To organize a group of favorite pages into a new folder, first click the Create New Folder button and give your new folder a name. Select one or more shortcuts, then click the Move button to drop them into the folder you just created. Click the Close button to go back to your Web browser. Now, when you look at the Favorites list you'll see the folders on the list as well, with their contents cascading out to the right when you click each one.

Search pages (I know it's out there somewhere)

Where do you begin searching when you haven't got the slightest idea where the information you're looking for is stored? That's where **search pages** come in handy. There are dozens of different Web pages that offer to do the searching for you—Yahoo (www.yahoo.com), AltaVista (www.altavista.digital.com), and Excite (www.excite.com) are three popular ones. (See Fig. 22.11 to see what AltaVista looks like.) You enter the word or phrase you're looking for, click a button, and wait (usually only a few seconds) while the search engine chugs away to find links that you might find useful.

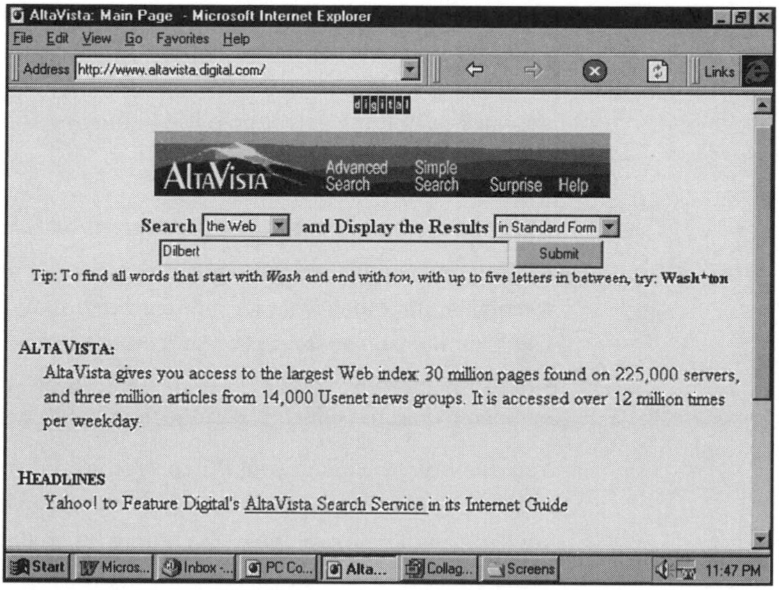

Fig. 22.11
To follow the adventures of my favorite comic character, try this search, using Digital's AltaVista page.

Saving, printing, and downloading Web pages

Although Internet Explorer is the best place to view Web pages, you can save the data you see there and use it elsewhere as well. Here's how:

- **To save a Web page as a file**, choose File, Save As File. Use HTML format if you plan to view the pages using Internet Explorer. Choose text format if you just want to save the text.

- **To copy text from a Web page**, select the text, right-click, and choose Copy. You can now paste the selected text into any other Windows document.

- **To copy a graphic from a Web page**, point to the graphic and right-click, then choose Save Picture As. You can give the file a new name and location, if you like.

- **To print a Web page**, just click the Print button.

Downloading files

Sometimes, when you click a link, Internet Explorer will pop up a dialog box instead of displaying a page. When that happens, it means you've clicked a link for a file rather than a Web page. This will certainly be the case if you're downloading an update to a software program, for example. To save the file so you can work with it later, just give it a name and location on your hard disk.

Q&A   *Do I need to worry about computer viruses?*

A computer virus is a renegade piece of computer software that does something other than what it's supposed to do, usually without any warning. Like their human counterparts, computer viruses are transmitted through contact, most often by infected disks and programs. If you ever contract a computer virus, the effects can range from mildly annoying to catastrophic.

You don't run any risk of your PC contracting a computer virus through the Internet, as long as you don't download any programs. Follow that rule, and you'll be absolutely safe. What if you do want to download programs? Well, make one of your first downloads a virus-checking and removal program, or bite the bullet and go buy a commercial virus-detection-and-repair program such as Norton Antivirus.

23

Dial-Up Networking

● **In this chapter:**

● **Add a modem for instant access to the network**

● **How Dial-Up Networking can help telecommuters**

● **Dialing for data...automatically**

● **Making an Internet connection over the phone**

If you have a modem and a phone line, Windows NT lets you log on to your office network or the Internet from anywhere, as though you were just down the hall . . . . ➤

Most of the time, when you think of networking, you think of the cables that snake through your office walls, physically connecting all the computers and file servers in your organization. But you can be part of a network even if you're miles from the nearest computer, without a network cable in sight. No, it's not magic—as long as you have a modem and a phone line, you can use the Windows NT feature called Dial-Up Networking to log on to a distant network as if it were just down the hall. Once you've successfully established a Dial-Up Networking connection, you can browse files on a server, print documents, send e-mail—even connect to the Internet.

Who needs Dial-Up Networking?

There are at least three situations in which Dial-Up Networking comes in handy:

- **To dial from home** into a computer on your company's network. You might only want to use this capability on the rare occasions when you take work home. Or your company might encourage you and other workers to telecommute. If that's the case, you can use the phone to do everything you'd do in the office—except trade gossip around the water cooler.

- **To connect to the Internet.** These days, it's rare to find a company that doesn't have its own full-time Internet connection, complete with World Wide Web server. But if your company hasn't connected the office network to the Internet, you can still browse the Web and explore other parts of the Internet. As long as you have an account with an Internet service provider, you can use Dial-Up Networking and Windows NT's TCP/IP protocol to connect your computer to the Internet.

- **To connect to a different network** that isn't normally part of your office network. Let's say you work in the Milwaukee branch of a Really Big Corporation. Once a week, you share files with the folks in the Chicago branch office. You don't need to pay for an expensive full-time connection between the two networks; just set up a modem and a dial-up server in each office, and you can connect to each other's networks for only as long as it takes to exchange your shared files.

Using Dial-Up Networking

Before you can even think of getting started with Dial-Up Networking, you'll need to run through a preflight checklist:

- First, of course, you'll need a modem, which in turn needs to be plugged into a phone line.

- You'll also need a special piece of networking software called **Remote Access Service**. (Only an administrator can install this software on your PC.)

- Naturally, you'll need to have a server to dial into.

- Finally, it's essential that you have a user name and password already established on the dial-up server.

How fast is your phone line?

Telecommuters get to stay off the freeways, but that doesn't mean they can avoid traffic jams on the Information Superhighway.

The data files you work with at the office can be surprisingly big. And the most useful part of the Internet, the World Wide Web, is stuffed with enormous graphics files that practically crawl across your screen if you try to use a modem that's too slow. If you plan to use Dial-Up Networking regularly, get the fastest modem you can.

Do you have an older modem that transmits and receives at 14,400 bps or less? Then you're driving the digital equivalent of a Yugo—old, slow, and definitely not capable of coping with life in the fast lane.

Today's standard modems can send and receive 28,800 bits per second (and a few specialized designs can run even faster, at least in theory). The numbers indicate transmission speeds; the higher the number, the faster those bits will move across the phone wire and into your computer and down your screen. Of course, make sure the modem at the other end is running at the same speed!

If that's not fast enough for you, talk to your local phone company and your system administrator about installing an ISDN connection. ISDN stands for Integrated Services Digital Network, a super-fast phone line that can pump data in and out of your PC at four times the speed of a standard phone line. ISDN lines are expensive, and they require special hardware. But if your job depends on getting information as fast as possible, it might be worth the extra cost.

To open the Dial-Up Networking program, double-click on its icon in the My Computer window. If this is the first time you've used Dial-Up Networking, Windows will offer to create a new phonebook entry for you. But we'll assume your system administrator has already created that essential data file for everyone on your network, in which case you'll see a dialog box like the one in Figure 23.1.

All your dial-up connections are stored in a phonebook. Use the drop-down list to select the one you want to use.

Click here to start the wizard that creates a new entry in the phonebook.

Fig. 23.1
The Dial-Up Net-working dialog box is Mission Control for all your remote connections—to the company network or the Internet.

If you're using Dial-Up Networking from a notebook with telephony options installed, you can choose a location.

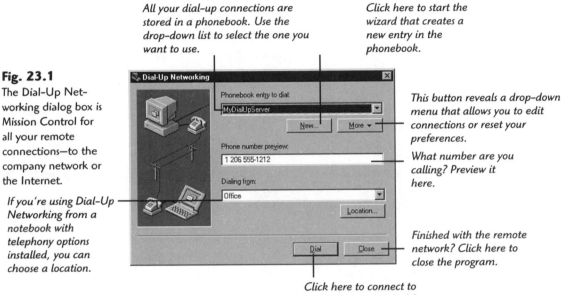

This button reveals a drop-down menu that allows you to edit connections or reset your preferences.

What number are you calling? Preview it here.

Finished with the remote network? Click here to close the program.

Click here to connect to the remote network. After you've logged on, this button's label changes to Hang Up.

Creating and editing phonebook entries

Dial-Up Networking stores all your connection information in a phonebook, with each entry consisting of a phone number and other options that help your computer and the remote server successfully connect. If you're a networking wizard, you can set up a connection by checking boxes and typing numbers in a complicated set of dialog boxes.

If you're not a wizard (and who is?), don't worry—Windows includes its own Wizard, consisting of a series of simple dialog boxes that you fill out. Use the Wizard to create each new entry in your Dial-Up Networking phonebook. If you're dialing in to a Windows NT server, using the Wizard is a simple, three-step process.

Step 1: Start the Wizard.

To begin creating a new phonebook entry, double-click the Dial-Up Networking icon (you'll find it in the My Computer window, or you can click the Start button, then follow the cascading menus from Programs to Accessories to Dial-Up Networking). Click the New button. The New Phonebook Entry Wizard, shown in Figure 23.2, takes over here. The default name, MyDialUp-Server, isn't that useful, is it? Instead, give your connection a name that describes it more accurately, such as Office Server.

Fig. 23.2

Use the Wizard to create a new Dial-Up Networking connection. Depending on which boxes you check, you can connect to another computer or to the Internet.

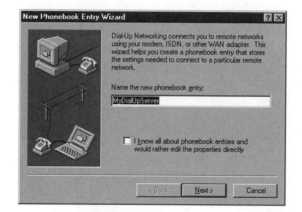

Step 2: Tell Windows what kind of server you're calling.

After you've given the connection a name, the Wizard needs to know what kind of server you plan to call (see Fig. 23.3). If you're dialing into an Internet service provider, you'll need to ask their technical support staff which boxes are relevant here. But you can safely click the Next button to connect to a Windows NT server.

Step 3: Number, please.

Of course, your modem won't be able to make the call until it knows what number to dial, and this is the place to enter that crucial bit of data. If you'll always call from the same computer, you can enter the exact phone number, complete with prefixes and area or country codes. On a notebook computer, where the dialing options need to change depending on where you call from, check the Telephony dialing properties box (see Fig. 23.4).

Fig. 23.3
Pick a server, any server. If you're dialing a Windows NT Remote Access Server, leave all three boxes unchecked.

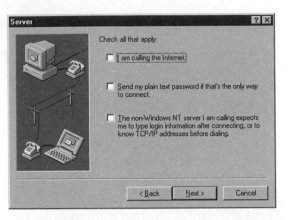

Fig. 23.4
Use the Telephony dialing properties if you expect to dial in from different locations. Otherwise, uncheck the box and enter the number exactly as you want it dialed.

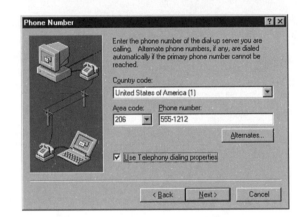

Some dial-up servers allow access through several phone numbers. If that's the case at your server location, click the Alternates button and enter the additional numbers here. Windows NT will use the main number as your preferred dial-up connection, calling the alternates only if you get a busy signal.

TIP To learn more about Telephony dialing properties, see Appendix B.

That's as complicated as it gets—as long as you're dialing into a Windows NT server. (There's a long list of additional options if you're dialing into an Internet service provider, but we'll get to that in a minute.)

Changing a phonebook entry

What happens if you need to change a phonebook entry after you've created it? Well, you *can* click the <u>M</u>ore button to reveal the unusual drop-down menu shown in Figure 23.5. The first choice on the menu, `Edit entry and modem properties`, pops up a large, complicated, multi-tabbed dialog box with all the connection properties available for your inspection. If all you need to do is change the name of the connection or its phone number, go ahead and choose this option. But if your changes are substantial, I recommend that you delete the entry (using the same menu) and rerun the Wizard.

Fig. 23.5
You can edit any dial-up connection by choosing this option from the More menu... but it's easier to just use the Wizard again.

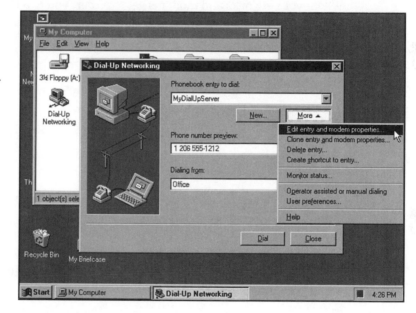

Making the connection

To use Dial-Up Networking, open the My Computer window, then double-click Dial-Up Networking. Choose the connection you want to dial from the drop-down list, then click the <u>D</u>ial button. Depending on how you've configured Dial-Up Networking, you'll see a succession of dialog boxes and messages as your computer attempts to connect with the remote computer. Once you've succeeded, you're ready to begin working with the network.

TIP   **If you find yourself dialing the same connection over and over** again, make a shortcut to it and put it in a convenient place. Double-click the Dial-Up Networking icon, select the connection, click the <u>M</u>ore button, and choose Create shortcut to entry. The default location is the desktop, but you can also put a Dial-Up Networking shortcut on the Start menu for easy access.

Dialing your own way

Whenever networks and modems get together, you can bet your bottom dollar that things will quickly get complicated. That's surely the case with Dial-Up Networking, where you have dozens of options designed to make your remote connections faster and easier to use:

- You can configure Windows NT to dial automatically whenever you request a file that's stored on the network.

- You can ask Windows to pop up informational boxes that tell you what's happening at each step of the process, or you can hide those boxes if they annoy you.

- You can even keep your phone bill down by telling Windows you want the remote server to call *you*.

Most of the options you can configure are found on a four-tab User Preferences dialog box. Open Dial-Up Networking, click the <u>M</u>ore button, and choose User pre<u>f</u>erences from the drop-down menu.

I want to get connected automatically...

The Dialing tab (see Fig. 23.6) helps you control how and when Windows dials the phone. Two settings, auto-dial and redial, can be particularly helpful.

- **Auto-dial** tells Windows to dial the default connection whenever you request access to a network resource—for example, when you start Internet Explorer, or when you ask Windows Messaging to check your e-mail. Auto-dial handles the process without demanding that you open a folder or click a button.

- **Redial** settings control what happens when your Dial-Up Networking attempt results in a busy signal. If you know that the line is likely to be free soon afterwards, tell Windows to keep trying, every 15, 30, or 60 seconds.

Fig. 23.6
When Dial-Up Networking encounters a busy signal, it surrenders. If you want Windows to keep dialing, tell it to try, try again.

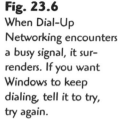

I want the server to call me back...

There are two reasons to use the account callback option, which tells a dial-up server to call you back whenever you dial in. One is financial—the computer equivalent of placing a collect call to yourself from overseas; your spouse refuses the charges and calls you back at an agreed-upon number, saving a ton of money in the process. When you allow the server to call you back, you shift the financial burden to that phone line.

The other motivation for using the callback option is tied to security. If the server is configured to always call you back at a predetermined telephone number—the line in your home office, for example—it's much harder for a would-be hacker to gain access to your company's network.

If your network administrator tells you to enable this option, go ahead. Otherwise, skip this tab.

I want to know what's happening...

The seven checkboxes on the tabbed dialog page labeled Appearance (see Fig. 23.7) give you pinpoint control over all the dialog boxes and messages that pop up when you use Dial-Up Networking.

Fig. 23.7
Most of these options are self–explanatory. If your only phone line handles voice and computer calls, be sure to check the last box!

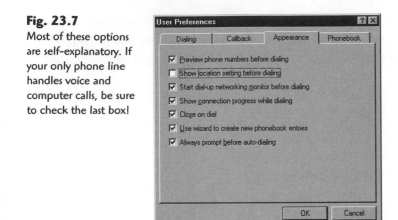

The first two options control what you see each time you make a dial-up connection. If you have only one entry in your phonebook and you always call from the same location, leave both boxes unchecked.

The next two boxes help you keep track of what's happening with your connection as you dial. With these boxes checked, you'll see a string of messages ("Dialing," "Verifying username and password," "Authenticating," and so on) as you dial.

The `Close on dial` option automatically closes Dial-Up Networking after you click the Dial button. I prefer to leave this option unchecked, so that I can have easy access to the matching Hang Up button!

Unless you're a communications genius, leave a checkmark next to the option labeled `Use wizard to create new phonebook entries`.

The last entry controls auto-dial. On my home system, where I have a separate phone line devoted to my modem, I leave this option unchecked so that Dial-Up Networking can do its thing without requiring my active intervention. If your voice and data calls share a single line, you'll want to leave this box checked so that Windows doesn't unexpectedly interrupt you when you're on the phone.

I want my own phonebook...

Your system administrator has the option to create a systemwide phonebook filled with connections all users of a given system can choose from. You also have the option, each time you create a phonebook entry, to store it in a personal phonebook. This tab lets you control whether you use the system phonebook, your personal phonebook, or a completely different phonebook.

What's happening with that connection?

Your last set of options is buried elsewhere, but that doesn't mean it's any less important. The Dial-Up Networking Monitor is a simple dialog box that tells you in precise detail what's going on with your remote networking connection. To make it appear, double-click the Dial-Up Networking icon, then click the More button and choose Monitor status. You'll see a dialog box like the one in Figure 23.8.

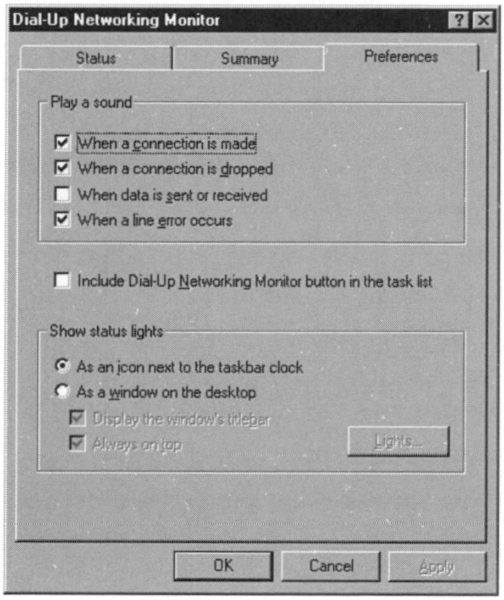

Fig. 23.8
Those first two tabs are strictly for propeller-heads, but the last tab lets you install this useful monitor as a Taskbar icon.

I recommend that you configure the monitor to appear as a Taskbar icon. When you do, you see a set of flashing lights that let you know the connection is working. You can double-click on the icon to pop up the status monitor at any time, or right-click on the icon to pop up a menu that lets you hang up or dial anytime.

Connecting to the Internet

Most people who use Windows NT do so in the office, where Internet access comes along with the network. But what do you do if that's not the case in your office? If you have a modem (or an ISDN adapter) connected to a phone line, you can use Dial-Up Networking to connect to the Internet.

Before you can use Dial-Up Networking for Internet access, you'll need to make sure you have the TCP/IP protocol and Remote Access Service installed, and of course you'll need a modem and phone line. (If not, you probably know who to call by now....) You'll also need a cheat sheet from your Internet service provider containing the information you need to make a proper TCP/IP connection. With those details out of the way, just open the Dial-Up Networking dialog box and click the New button to create a phonebook entry.

When you get to the Server portion of the Wizard, check all three boxes. Now, as you step through the Wizard's instructions, you'll encounter a slew of new dialog boxes asking you for TCP/IP addresses, logins, DNS server information, and more. Fill in all the details, then click OK. You now are one click away from connecting to the Internet.

Q&A   *Where do I find an Internet service provider?*

You can take your choice of service providers, from small companies in storefronts to huge organizations like CompuServe and Microsoft. You can find ads for service providers in the business section of most big-city newspapers. If you have a friend who's already connected to the Net, ask for a recommendation. In any case, it shouldn't cost more than about a dollar a day for all the access an average user needs.

Upgraders' Guide: So You've Used Windows Before?

● **In this chapter:**

● **What's new in Windows NT 4.0?**

● **Getting Around in Windows NT 4.0**

● **Where did my applications go? Will they still run?**

● **Finding familiar tools**

What kind of Windows user are you, anyway?. . . . . ❯

What's New in Windows NT 4.0?

If you've used Windows 95, you'll probably wonder why anyone's making a fuss over Windows NT 4.0. From the outside, at least, the two operating systems look remarkably similar. There are some significant differences beneath the surface, especially when you start talking about networks. But the mechanics of opening and closing windows, starting programs, and managing files are practically identical regardless of which operating system you use.

But if you're like many, many people who have used Windows 3.1 (or its Windows NT counterparts) for years and are just now switching to Windows NT 4.0, you're in for a treat. You're also in for a bit of confusion, because Windows NT 4.0 is different, inside and out, from the Windows you've become accustomed to using.

If you found it frustrating to work with files and programs in your old version of Windows, you're not alone. When Microsoft set out to design a brand-new look for Windows 95, it asked regular people to work with Windows, and it watched as they struggled to do even simple tasks.

Then it took those lessons to heart and designed a computer operating system that should be easier to use than anything you've ever seen before. That new look and feel appeared first in Windows 95, and now it's available as part of Windows NT.

What's new in Windows NT 4.0?

- Windows NT 4.0 is more consistent than previous versions of Windows. There are fewer layers of management in Windows NT 4.0. All those middle managers—Program Manager, File Manager, and Print Manager—got pink slips the day Microsoft retired Windows 3.1.

- It's a better-looking operating system, if that matters. It's faster, too. (That does matter.)

- You can forget about DOS and most of its confusing old rules. You don't have to worry about keeping track of complex directory paths anymore, for example, because Windows NT 4.0 replaces those directories with folders that open into windows with a double-click.

- You can also expect it to make your personal computer a little less personal, because Windows NT incorporates the kind of security features that you typically find only in Tom Clancy novels, and you'll need to get permission from a system administrator to do some tasks that you take for granted in Windows 3.1

- Eventually, you'll have a whole new class of application programs to choose from, although for now you'll probably keep using some of your old programs.

In short, if you've been using Windows 3.1 for any length of time, you should expect this new Windows to make life easier and make you more productive.

This section isn't intended to be a complete set of instructions for Windows NT 4.0. Instead, the idea is to introduce Windows NT 4.0 and show you how it's different from the Windows you already know how to use.

If you see something that catches your eye, look in the margin for a pointer to the chapter that covers that feature in more detail. Windows NT 4.0 is big and complicated, with a wealth of new features, but it's also extremely consistent.

How does it all work? I'm glad you asked...

Getting around in Windows NT 4.0

Sign in here...

If you're used to staring at a C:\> prompt and typing **WIN** to start Windows, it's time to learn a new daily routine. When you flip the big red switch each morning, Windows NT 4.0 bypasses the C:\> prompt completely. The only thing you'll have to type is your password. Windows expects you to log on each time you start up; if you're hooked up to a local area network, you can connect to everything with a single logon.

Logging on isn't just for networks, either. Windows NT 4.0 lets two or more people share a single PC. Because each user has a unique logon name and password, the system can keep their personal settings and files safe and completely separate.

Welcome to the Windows NT 4.0 desktop

No matter what you're looking for, you'll start the search here.

*Open up **My Computer** to see all the files and folders and disk drives on your system.*

*Look in the **Network Neighborhood** for other computers and printers that you can share.*

*Double–click on the **Inbox** to open Windows Messaging. If you have an e-mail account or a fax modem, all your messages will come here.*

***Internet Explorer** lets you browse through pages on the World Wide Web in search of information and entertainment.*

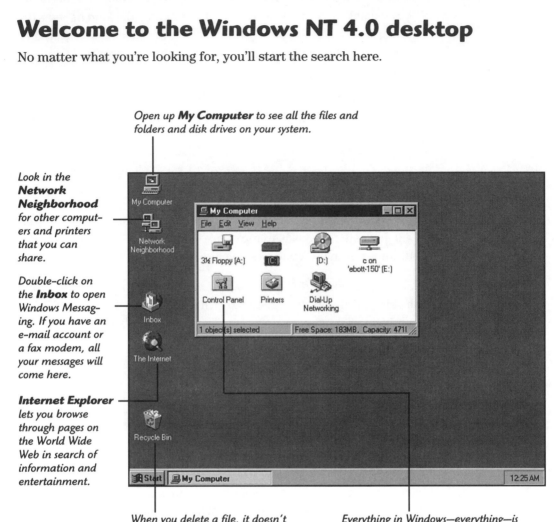

*When you delete a file, it doesn't actually go away. Windows saves it in the **Recycle Bin**, where you can easily reclaim it if you discover you made a mistake.*

*Everything in Windows—everything—is an icon, and groups of related icons are stored in **folders** like this one.*

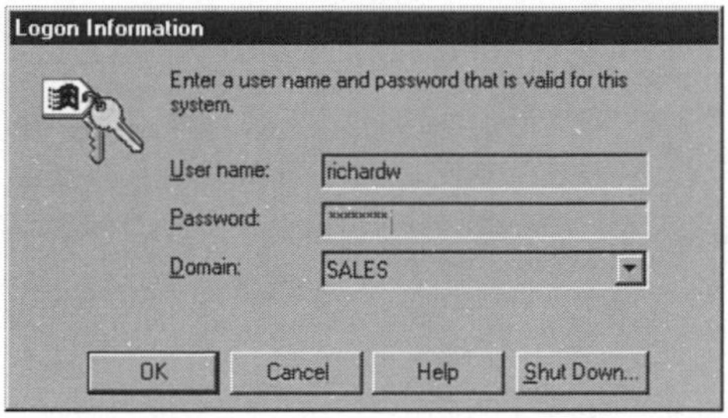

Fig. A.1

Every time you start up Windows, you'll have to log on. The dialog box you see may look a little different, depending on your network configuration.

TIP If you're on a Novell NetWare network, you may see a different logon box, including a box where you can enter the name of your logon server. There's no way to bypass the logon box.

What does the Start button do?

When you first start up Windows NT 4.0, your first question will probably be, "What happened to Program Manager?" (Don't worry—we'll get to that in a second.) Your second question will probably be, "What happens when I click the Start button?"

There are only seven options on the Start menu, but it's hard to think of a thing you *can't* do when you click here. Think of the Start menu as Windows' central business district. From here, every side road leads to another interesting destination packed with surprises.

How to use the mouse

If you've used Windows for any length of time, you already know how to use the mouse. With this version of Windows, your mouse learns a new set of tricks.

- **Selecting** a group of files is easier. When you need to select a bunch of things, use the mouse to throw an imaginary lasso around everything you need.

- You probably never used the right mouse button in Windows 3.1, but it gets a full aerobic workout in Windows NT 4.0. Whenever you're not sure what to do next, point to an unfamiliar object and right-click to pop up **shortcut menus** like the one in Figure A.4.

*The **Programs** menu replaces the Windows 3.1 Program Manager. Click here, and your program groups cascade off in a series of new menus that open to the right.*

*Windows remembers the **Documents** you've opened recently. To pick up where you left off yesterday, just look on this menu.*

Fig. A.2
The Start menu. You can get nearly anywhere from here, although it may take a few clicks...

*If something in Windows isn't working exactly the way you'd like, click on the **Settings** menu to twiddle knobs and dials until you've got it right. The Control Panel is here, as are any printers you have access to.*

*Need **Help?** The built-in Windows instruction book lets you find step-by-step instructions and explanations for every common task.*

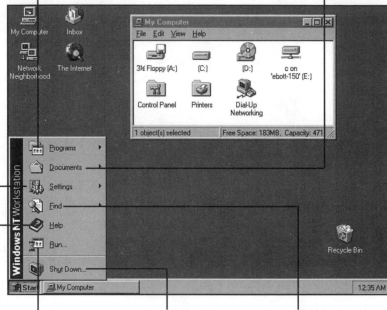

*The **Run** dialog box lets you type in the name of a program or a folder to open it instantly. Handy for the mouse-phobic.*

*Don't just push that big red switch to turn off your PC! Use the **Shut Down** command to make sure all your data is safe.*

*Can't track down that file? Even if you don't remember the name, the **Find** menu can help you narrow your search. All you have to know is a stray fact or two about the file (if you're positive it contained the word "asparagus," for example, and you know you saved it last April, you'll find it in seconds).*

Fig. A.3
What's the opposite of "Open Sesame?" The last option on the Start menu lets you shut down Windows quickly and safely.

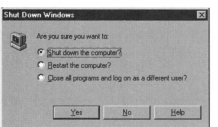

Fig. A.4

When in doubt, point and click the *right* mouse button. Practically every object you can think of has one of these useful shortcut menus attached to it.

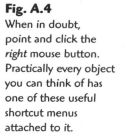

• **Dragging and dropping** is the preferred way to get work done. Drag files from one folder to another to move or copy them, and drop file icons on top of a printer icon to put them on paper with the least amount of fuss. If you use the right mouse button to drag an icon around, you'll get a shortcut menu like the one in Figure A.5.

Fig. A.5

Drag an icon from here to there, and you can't be sure exactly what's going to happen. Use the right mouse button instead, and this pop-up menu lets you tell Windows exactly what you want it to do.

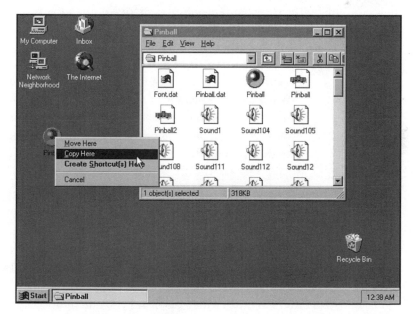

Switch programs with the Taskbar

Attention, couch potatoes! If you can switch channels with your television's remote control, you can switch between all the Windows programs you have running at any given time.The Taskbar stays anchored at the bottom of the desktop, where it's always visible. Every program that's running right now, and every folder that's open, gets its own button on the Taskbar.

With Windows 3.1, you had to clear windows out of the way before you could find the one you were looking for, and you were never quite sure where all those windows hid when you needed them most. With Windows NT 4.0, it doesn't matter how many windows you have open: Look for any window's name on the Taskbar, click the button, and watch as it floats to the top of the stack.

Fig. A.6
Every running program appears on the Taskbar, which is always visible at the bottom of the desktop. Click on any button to bring that window to the top of the pile.

| Start | Pinball | Microsoft Inte... | Network Nei | Phone Dialer | 12:40 AM |

Don't overlook one of the coolest features of all on the Taskbar. At the far right, just to the left of the clock, you'll occasionally see a tiny status icon for part of your system: a printer, a modem, perhaps the volume control on your sound card. Right-click on any of these icons and you'll usually be surprised by the results. Use the volume control to turn off your multimedia speakers instantly, for example, before someone in the next room begins complaining about the racket.

TIP **If you learned to switch between applications using the keyboard** shortcut Alt+Tab, you'll be happy to know it works in Windows NT 4.0, too. When you have more than one program running or folder open, hold down the Alt key and keep holding it down as you Tab from one program to the next. When you find the one you're looking for, release both keys to switch to that window.

Icons and folders: Windows' building blocks

If you've used Windows 3.1 for any length of time, you've learned that icons are small pictures you click to start a program. You've also learned that you can arrange icons into groups within Program Manager. In Windows 3.1, you won't find icons anywhere else, and you can't put one group inside another to keep your desktop neat.

Windows NT 4.0 is completely different. For starters, *everything* is an icon. Every file, every program, every printer, every computer on your company's local area network. To keep all those files neatly organized, Windows arranges them into folders. You can organize your data files the same way, even creating new folders inside folders. When you've learned how to work with one icon and one folder, you've mastered the most essential Windows skill of all.

What's inside that icon?

In Windows 3.1, you could learn a few basic facts about a file by looking at it: the name, when it was created, how big it is, that sort of thing. Windows NT 4.0 lets you do the same thing (and a whole lot more) with properties sheets. When you point to any icon and click the right mouse button, a fact-packed box like the one in Figure A.7 pops up.

Fig. A.7
The Properties menu always brings up a sheet of information like this one. The exact details you'll see change from icon to icon, depending on the type of object you're pointing to.

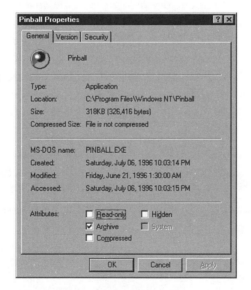

One of the most useful choices on the right-mouse menu is the Quick Viewer. When you see Quick View on the shortcut menu of a document, you can ask Windows to show you the document itself, even if you don't have a copy of the program that created the document.

Why is there an arrow in the corner of some icons?

Let's say one of your favorite programs is buried in a folder inside a folder inside another folder inside three more folders. Every time you want to start that program, you double-click so many times you're thinking of applying for an index-finger transplant. To make things easier, you could move the program to a more convenient location, but that's not necessary. The better solution is to create a **shortcut** to the program and put it right on your desktop.

Shortcuts are tremendously useful things, and they're everywhere in Windows NT 4.0. To get a feeling for how a shortcut works, think of how you might organize a library for maximum efficiency. Would you shelve the new John Grisham novel in the fiction section? With the law books? Or in the action-adventure aisle? If you were willing to pay for three copies, you could put one in each section, but that would be wasteful. Instead, you could keep one copy in the fiction section, and place a cross-reference in the other two sections telling patrons to ask a clerk to bring them Grisham's latest.

When you put a shortcut on your desktop, it looks just like the original, except for a small arrow in the lower left corner. But it's actually only a pointer to another icon, and no matter how big the original file is, a shortcut occupies only a tiny piece of your hard disk. When you double-click on the shortcut, Windows goes searching for the original (the **target** is the official name) and calls it up, just as though you'd clicked on the original.

Folders

There's nothing complicated about folders. Just as you use manila folders to keep related pieces of paper together, you use Windows folders to keep related icons together. Folders always act the same, although you can take your choice of four different ways to view the icons inside, as you can see in Figure A.8.

Fig. A.8
One folder, four views. Anytime you see a window filled with icons, you can have your choice of four icon arrangements. The toolbar is optional.

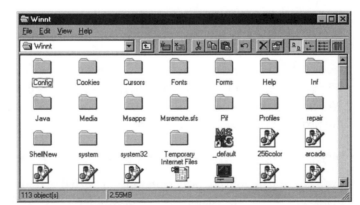

Fig. A.8
Continued

TIP   **If you're used to File Manager, you'll like the Details view best of** all. With this arrangement of icons, you can click on the column headings to sort by the values in that column. Click again to sort in reverse order.

Closing and resizing windows with the new buttons

It's OK to keep lots of windows open, especially given how easy it is switch between windows using the Taskbar. But you will occasionally want to clear windows out of the way or close them completely. With Windows 3.1, closing a window is a big hassle. With Windows NT 4.0, it's a snap to shrink a window to an icon, expand it to its full size, or shut it down completely. Just look in the top right corner of the window for one of these four buttons:

 The Close button is shaped like an X, as in "Cross this off the list, please."

 To keep the window running but remove all traces of it from the desktop, use the Minimize button. This has the same effect as stuffing the entire contents of the window into its Taskbar button. When you need the window again, just click on the Taskbar.

 On the other hand, if you want to devote all your attention to a window, click its Maximize button. That tells Windows to expand the window to fill every square inch of space on your monitor

 When you want the maximized application to return to a normal window, click the Restore button.

Where did my applications go? Will they still run?

When you upgrade your old copy of Windows 3.1 to Windows NT 4.0, your old Windows software (sometimes referred to as 16-bit Windows programs) should keep working just as they always did. There are a few exceptions, such as utility programs intended to make your hard disk run faster, but most people shouldn't have to worry about them.

Your older programs will probably work, but that doesn't mean they'll behave exactly the same as new Windows NT 4.0 programs. In fact, if you don't recognize the difference between old Windows programs and new ones, you might run into problems. Here's what to watch out for.

What's the difference between new Windows programs and old ones?

New 32-bit Windows programs are generally designed to run with both Windows 95 and Windows NT 4.0. If you're paying close attention, you'll notice subtle differences in the way new Windows programs look. Dialog boxes, for example, are likely to have tabbed pages on them, just like the ones in Windows itself.

Not only do they look different, these new Windows programs also act differenly than their predecessors.

You can use long filenames

When you open or save a file using a new Windows program like WordPad (the word processor that comes with Windows), you can enter a long file name that helps you (or anyone else) see at a glance exactly what's inside the file. Older Windows programs don't know how to read those long file names; they're still stuck with the old DOS file-naming rules: With these old programs your file name has to be eight characters or less, not counting an optional three-letter extension tacked onto the end.

So what happens if you've created a file with a long name and then you open it with an older program that doesn't speak that language? If your long file name was a WordPad document called "Letter to my accountant, 8-24-96" the old program will chop off all but the first six characters of the name and then tack on two extra characters of its own, making the name "LETTER~1.DOC." Not very informative, is it?

Why did the old program add the DOC extension to the end of the file name? Actually, it was there all along, but Windows NT 4.0 hides those extensions when it knows what type of file you're working with. Because it knows that files ending in DOC can be opened with WordPad, it simply shows you the name.

New and improved dialog boxes

Every time you open or save a file with a new Windows NT 4.0 program, you'll use a slick dialog box like the one shown in Figure A.10. If you think it looks a lot like Explorer, you're right. In fact, when one of these dialog boxes is open, you can do all sorts of cool things with the icons inside it.

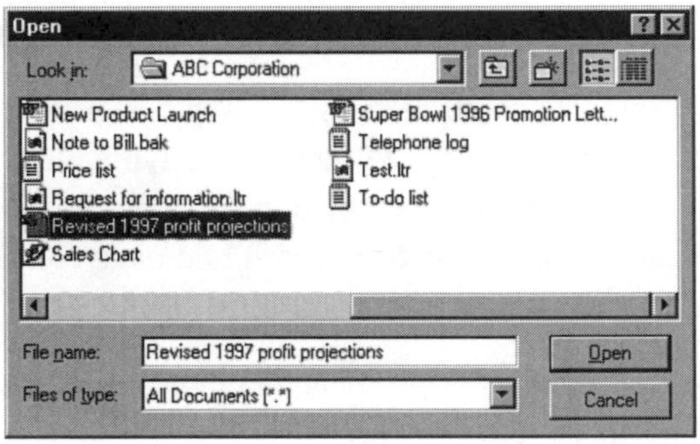

Fig. A.9

These new dialog boxes appear when you open or save a file using a Windows NT 4.0 program. If you want to add a new folder or rename a file, you can do it here.

- **To add a new folder**, right-click and choose New, Folder.

- **To delete a file**, right-click on its icon and choose Delete.

- **To give a file a different name** (perhaps so you can save your new file under that name instead), select the file and then click on its name and start typing.

In short, anything you can do in a folder window or with the Windows NT Explorer, you can do in one of these dialog boxes.

More about dragging and dropping

New 32-bit Windows programs typically let you drag and drop icons in much more flexible ways than older programs do. They also take better advantage of shortcuts, which means you can mail a shortcut to a coworker using Windows Messaging and know that they'll be able to open it.

Extra crash protection

New Windows programs use 32 bits at a time instead of 16 bits. In theory at least, they're less likely to crash than older programs. With either type of program, though, if a bug causes your computer to stop responding, you can recover by pressing Ctrl+Alt+Del; click the <u>T</u>ask Manager button, and look in the list for a program that has stopped responding (see Fig. A.10), then shut it down without harming the rest of your open programs and data files.

Fig. A.10
No kidding—when you press Ctrl+Alt+Del, you can see a list of all the programs you're running right now. If one is misbehaving, you can make it go away with one click.

Installing (and uninstalling) new Windows programs

Finally, new Windows programs should be easier to install—and easier to remove later if you decide you don't need them anymore. To take care of either task, open Control Panel and double-click on the Add/Remove Programs item.

What about my DOS programs?

Windows NT 4.0 doesn't go through MS-DOS (the old Microsoft operating system) when you start it up, but that doesn't mean it's clueless about DOS programs. On the contrary, some of your old DOS programs that refused to run gracefully under Windows 3.1 may actually perform better under Windows NT 4.0.

If you know how to fine-tune the settings of an old DOS program, you can tweak it under Windows NT 4.0, too. Just right-click on the program's icon, then choose Properties to see a box like the one in Figure A.12.

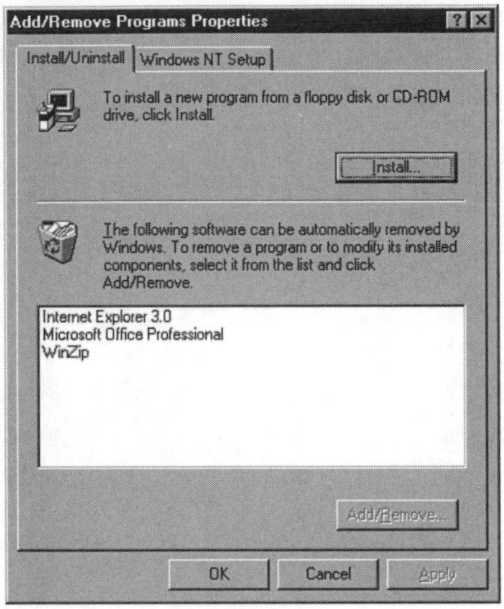

Fig. A.11
Use this dialog box
to add or remove
programs. New
programs can even
include a way for you
to uninstall them later.

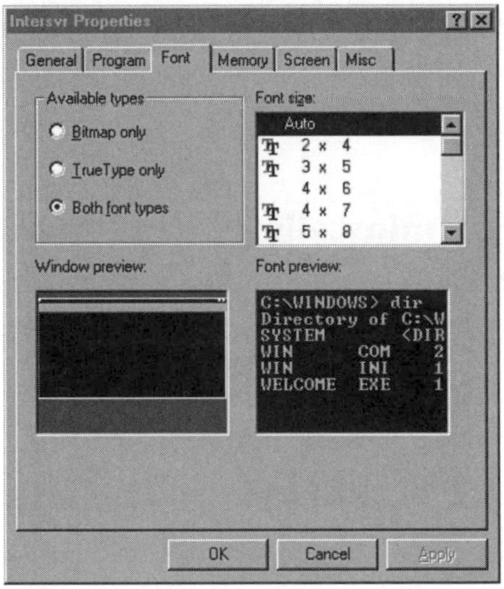

Fig. A.12
Most of the stuff in this
dialog box is strictly for
DOS experts. Still, it's
nice to know all your
old MS-DOS programs
will run in a window.

Finding familiar tools

All those middle managers you learned how to deal with in Windows 3.1 are gone in Windows NT 4.0. There's no more Program Manager, no File Manager, no Print Manager. What happened to them? They got their pink slips because they weren't needed anymore; the jobs they used to do are now handled by other parts of Windows: the Start button replaced Program

Manager, and the Windows NT Explorer replaced File Manager. (There's still a print manager of sorts, although it's not called that anymore—it's just a window with the printer's name.)

What happened to Program Manager?

Click the Start button to pop up the Start menu, and then rest the mouse pointer on the Programs choice. After a second or so, a new menu will cascade off to the right. That's where all your Program Manager groups went

When you install a new program, instead of creating a Program Manager group, it will create a new folder containing shortcuts for all the new programs it wants you to know about, then arrange the new folder on one of the cascading menus.

Unlike Program Manager, you can rearrange these folders so that you have groups inside of groups. That makes it easier to stay organized. (The easy way to do it: Right-click on the Start button. Remember, when you're not sure what to do next, point and right-click.)

I used to have 40 program groups fighting for space in my Program Manager window, and it was occasionally impossible to find anything. With Windows NT 4.0, I've rearranged all the folders the way I like them. Now, when I call up the Start menu and click on Programs, I see a short, easy-to-follow list of the programs I use all the time (see Fig. A.13).

Fig. A.13
Windows NT 4.0 turned the old Program Manager sideways and rear-ranged your groups. Click here to start up any program you've installed.

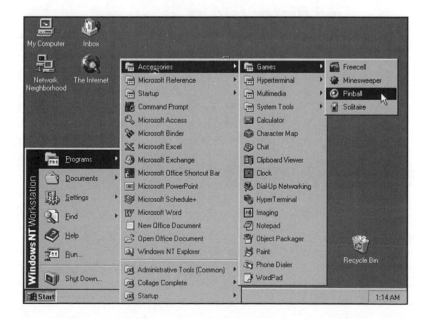

Where's File Manager?

You probably learned how to use the Windows 3.1 File Manager, but I'll bet you never learned to like it. Besides, with those cramped eight-character file names, what could you really do with it?

When Microsoft finished Windows NT 4.0, File Manager got a gold watch, a hearty handshake, and a one-way ticket to the retirement home. Now, when you want to move, copy, delete or rename files in Windows NT 4.0, you have a lot of choices.

The Windows NT Explorer: Seeing everything at once

The Windows NT Explorer is about the closest thing Windows NT 4.0 offers to the old File Manager. To start it up, click the Start button, choose Programs, and look for Windows NT Explorer on the first cascading menu. When you first start it up, it will probably look something like the window in Figure A.14.

Folder windows: one at a time

Folder windows work just like the right pane of the Windows NT Explorer. If you find the Explorer view confusing, this arrangement might be easier to work with. To open a folder window, double-click on My Computer and then just keep double-clicking. A typical folder window appears in Figure A.15.

Find files or folders

Windows NT 4.0 includes an amazingly powerful way to track down any object anywhere on your PC, or even across a network. All you need to know is a little bit of information about the thing you're looking for.

When you choose Find from the Start menu, you'll pop up a dialog box like the one in Figure A.16. Enter a part of the name if you know it. If you don't know that much, try clicking on the Advanced tab and entering a word or phrase that you're certain is in the file you're looking for. You can also tell Windows you want it to restrict its search to files in a certain location (like your Windows folder) or to files created in a certain time period, such as during the month of April, 1996.

Fig. A.14

The Windows NT Explorer is the replacement for File Manager. Click on any drive or folder on the left side and the right side shows you its contents.

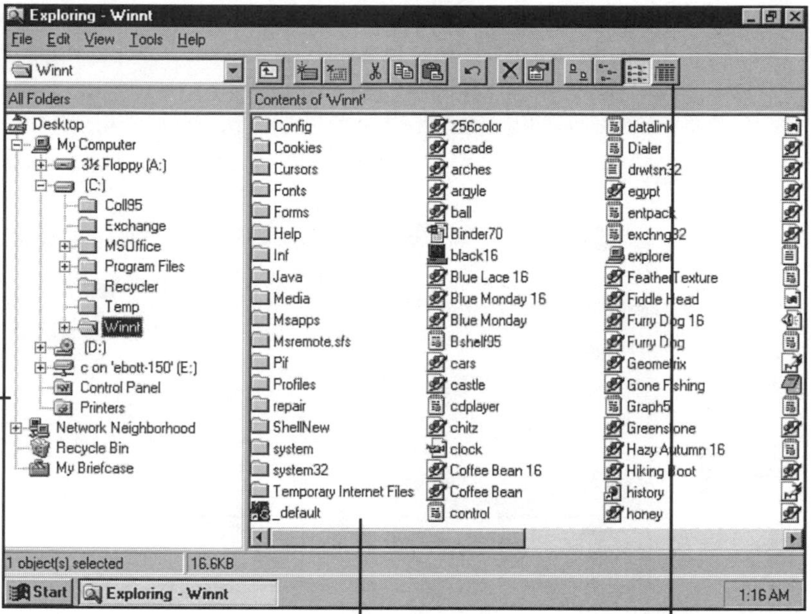

You can scroll up and down through a tree-style listing that includes everything on your computer and on any networks you're attached to. Click on the plus signs to see more detail; click on the minus signs to put all that confusing detail away.

Windows displays the contents of the folder (or other object) that's currently selected in the tree pane. As you choose new items on the left, the display on the right changes to match.

Just as with a folder window, you can change the view of the items in the right pane to large icons, small icons, list, or details.

Fig. A.15

The no-frills version of Explorer. When you double-click on a drive in the My Computer window, you get one of these windows.

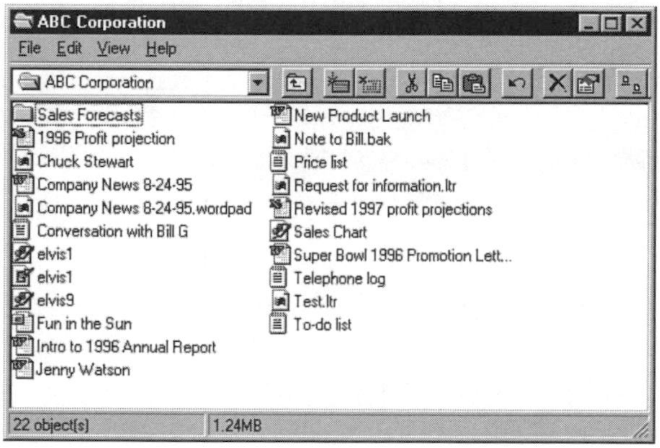

After you click the Find Now button. Windows goes to work, poring through files in search of the ones you described. The search results list at the bottom of the Find window works just like—you guessed it—the Windows NT Explorer. You can change the view to large or small icons, sort the files by any column, even rename, copy, or delete files you see here.

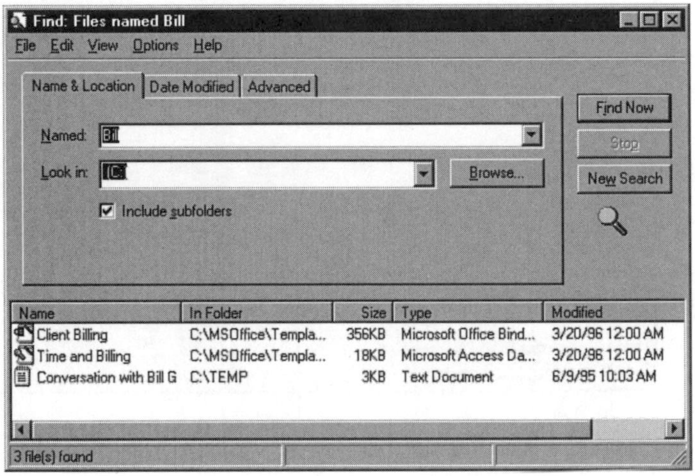

Fig. A.16
What happened to that file? Choose Find from the Start menu and you can find nearly anything, nearly anywhere, even if you can only remember a few sketchy details about it.

Is there still a Control Panel?

Yes, Virginia, there is still a Control Panel, and it still looks a lot like its Windows 3.1 counterpart. As a cursory glance at the icons in Figure A.17 shows, you can adjust anything on, in, or around your computer with a few clicks.

Fig. A.17
The new and improved Control Panel lets you pop the hood on Windows and fiddle with your computer's innards.

Figure A.18 shows one of the dialog boxes that appears when you double-click on a Control Panel icon. In this case, you see the Mouse program.

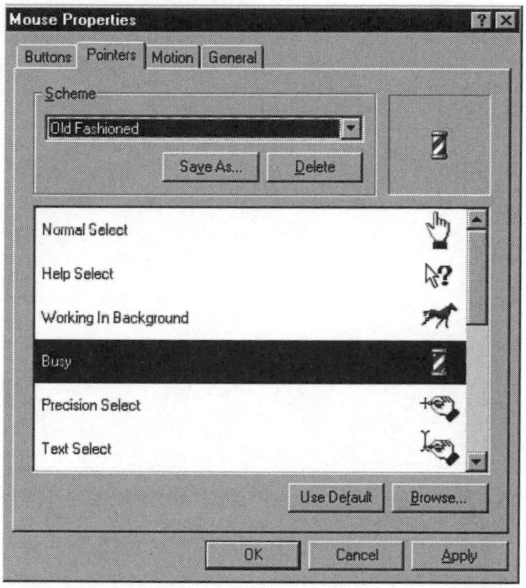

Fig. A.18
What can you do with the Control Panel? This mini-program lets you replace the boring old hourglass with one that does cartwheels.

How do I set up a printer?

As far as Windows is concerned, a new printer can be anywhere—connected to your computer, or out on the network somewhere. Regardless of where it's located, here's how you tell Windows you want to make a new printer available: Click on the Start button and choose Settings, Printers to open the Printers folder. Double-click on the Add Printer icon to add a new printer from the lengthy list included with Windows NT 4.0; after you're done, Windows volunteers to print a test page to make sure that everything's working.

Once the printer is installed, it gets its own icon in the Printers folder, and you can check the status of the printer and any jobs by simply double-clicking on it (see Fig. A.19).

How do I add new fonts?

Adding a new font under Windows 3.1 is complicated. Under Windows NT 4.0, all you have to do is open the Fonts folder in the Control Panel, then choose File, Install New Font from the pull-down menus. Once the fonts are in place, you can use the same folder to print out font samples or to sort your fonts into groups of typefaces that resemble one another (see Fig. A.20).

Fig. A.19
Double-click the Add
Printer icon to set up a
new printer, then use
this window to check
on the status of your
print jobs.

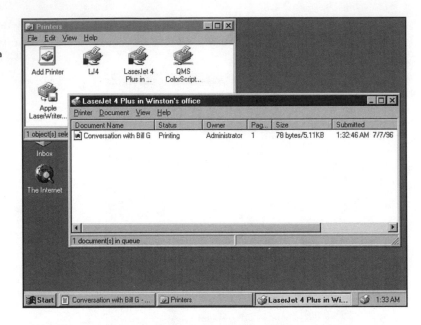

Fig. A.20
Look inside the Fonts
folder for a detailed
look at every font
installed on your
computer. (So *that's*
what Haettenschweiler
looks like!)

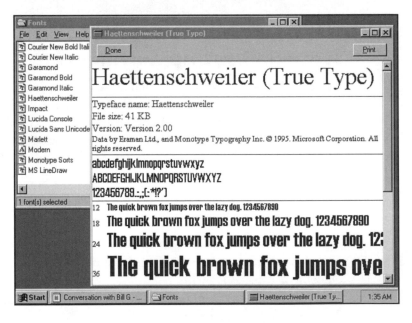

How do I change the look and feel of Windows?

Maybe you changed your Windows 3.1 wallpaper into something flashy or fun. Maybe you even added a screen saver. But there's no comparison with the sheer number of things you can do to make your system look and feel different with the help of Windows NT 4.0.

When you right-click on any empty spot on the desktop and choose Properties, Windows pops up the Display properties dialog box (see Fig. A.21 for an example of what it might look like).

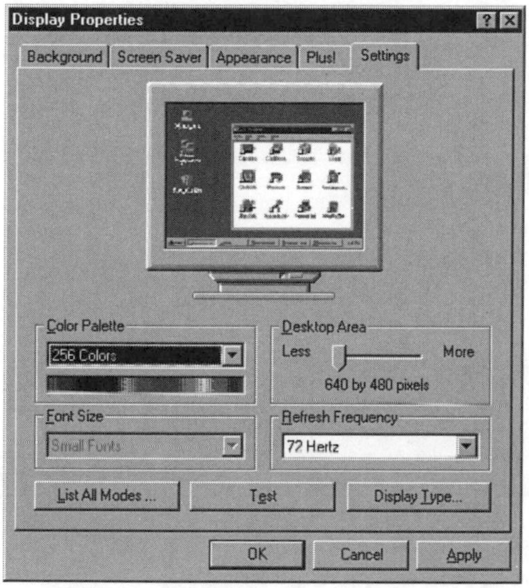

Fig. A.21
Put some personality in your PC! Right-click on an empty spot on the desktop, then choose Properties to adjust every detail of the desktop's look and feel.

Screen savers keep snoops from reading whatever you're working on if they walk by when you're not around.

Wallpaper lets you place an image on the desktop.

You can switch **resolution**—the number of objects you can see on the screen at one time—and **color depth**, which is the number of simultaneous colors you can see. Some of the changes don't require you to even restart Windows, in dramatic contrast to the way these things worked under older versions.

If you don't like the colors, fonts, and size of everything on the desktop, you can change it here by clicking on the **Appearance** tab.

Where do I go for Help?

There's an impressive set of instructions available right on the Start menu. Stumped? Click here and search for a word (see Fig. A.22). You might just find the answer you're looking for.

Fig. A.22
Help! There's an amazing amount of information in the Windows NT 4.0 Help system, including buttons that let you jump straight to the dialog box you're looking for.

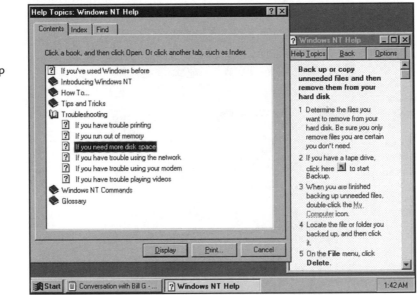

What about those little programs?

Some of the old familiar Windows 3.1 accessories are gone. If you'd like, we can now observe a moment of silence for the Calendar, the Windows Anti-Virus program, and the Cardfile list manager. (If you installed Windows NT over the top of Windows 3.1, those programs may be hanging around, but there aren't new versions of them.)

But the new Windows includes enough new and genuinely useful programs and accessories that you'll probably forgive Microsoft for dropping those old programs.

The list of accessories that come free with Windows NT 4.0 includes:

- **WordPad**, a simple word processing program.

- **Paint**, which lets you indulge your artistic tendencies.

- **Phone Dialer**, dials and tracks phone calls for you.

- **HyperTerminal**, a basic communication package.

- The **CD Player** lets you blast rock and roll (or Bach and Mozart) from your CD-ROM and multimedia speakers.

- The **Volume Control** keeps the neighbors from getting upset at the rock and roll part.

- **Imaging** lets you view and annotate image files (including faxes).

- There's even a **Backup** program that helps you copy important files to a safe place.

Figure A.23 shows a sampling of the programs you're likely to find in the Accessories folder.

Fig. A.23
Play a CD, write a memo, dial your phone. The Windows NT 4.0 accessories are small, free programs that handle a variety of odd jobs for you.

Connecting to the outside world

No computer is an island. When you feel like sharing anything from files to ideas, here's where to turn.

Networking

If you've got a network adapter in your computer, you can easily share files and printers with others. To see what's out there, look in the Network Neighborhood for any other computers or file servers that might be available.

Sharing files, folders, and printers is considerably different from anything you've ever experienced in Windows. When you right-click on the icon for a drive, folder, or file and choose Properties, you'll find a Security tab that allows you to tell Windows who can and can't have access to your system. You can set things up so that some people can only read files, others can change files, and still others won't even know there are any files there.

E-mail from anywhere

Once the network is up and running, take advantage of it by using the built-in mail program, called Windows Messaging. It can take your mail, from other Windows users or from the Internet, and store it in a single, well-organized Inbox.

The Internet

Chances are your company network already offers you access to the Internet. If that's the case, you don't need any software other than what's in Windows NT. The most interesting application of all is Internet Explorer, a browser program that lets you find information and entertainment on the World Wide Web.

B

Modems, Monitors, and More

● In this chapter:

● What do those pieces inside your PC do?

● My system is too slow!

● Why your computer can sometimes make you feel lousy

● How to set up and use a modem—it's not that hard

● Why does Windows NT want to know where I'm calling from?

Your PC is really a collection of small pieces of hardware (plus a few big ones), strung together with cables and wires. Here's what all those pieces do . . . . ▶

Y ou don't need to know every little detail about your PC, like who made the floppy disk drive. You don't need to know who made your car's spark plugs, either, as long as it has a full set. But you should know whether your car has an automatic or manual transmission. And if you know some basic facts about your PC, you'll have a lot easier time when you need to talk with other people about your hardware. Here are some fast facts about common types of hardware:

What's inside your PC?

When they say...	They really mean...	What Windows uses it for...
CPU	The central processing unit, found on a teensy silicon chip inside your computer. Today's most popular chips are the Pentium and the 486; you can't run Windows NT on older chips like the 386, 286, or 8088.	This is your PC's brain—the boss that tells all the other pieces what to do every time you press a key or move a mouse. If your CPU is too slow, you'll get to see the Windows hourglass all the time.
RAM (pronounce it like the sheep)	**Random-access memory**, short-term storage area for data. Anything that's stored here will vanish—poof!—as soon as you turn the power off, unless you save it on a hard floppy disk. some windows.	Windows carves out a chunk of RAM for everything you do—no matter how big or small. Try to do too much at once and Windows will tell you it's time to add more RAM or close
Hard disk	Long-term storage, where your computer can remember things, even after you turn the power off. All your files, folders, and programs are stored here, the same way TV programs are stored on videotape.	When you double-click on an icon, Windows has to find the icon's data on your hard drive, then copy it into RAM so you can work with it. Even the fastest hard disk is slow compared to the rest of your PC.
Monitor (also called display, or screen, or sometimes CRT)	The part of your PC that looks like a TV screen. Under a powerful magnifying class, you can see that the picture is actually made up of thousands of tiny red, green, and blue dots, called pixels.	This is the place where you see your work. Without a monitor, Windows would be useless. A bigger monitor lets you see more at once; a sharper monitor is easier on your eyes.

When they say...	They really mean...	What Windows uses it for...
Video adapter	The hardware that actually puts the things you see on-screen. If you have **20/20 vision and the right monitor,** you can use some video cards to shrink windows and icons so you see even more things at once.	Hey, drawing all those boxes and buttons is hard work. Plain old **video cards** are called **VGA**; fancy video cards are called **Super VGA**. Really expensive video cards get slick brand names.

What does all this hardware *do?*

Microsoft will gladly tell you that Windows NT requires a **minimum hardware configuration,** and it also has a **recommended configuration.** If your PC doesn't measure up to the minimum standards, you can't run Windows NT at all. If it falls short of the recommended level, it will run, but it might be painfully slow. Does Windows work OK for you? Then you shouldn't need to worry about it!

66 *Plain English, please!*

Because there are so many choices between different components, PCs are almost like snowflakes—no two are exactly alike. **Configuration** is the catch-all word that refers to the unique combination of parts in your PC. 99

Does my PC have enough horsepower?

If your PC had an engine, the CPU chip and memory would be it. To run Windows NT, you'll need at least a 486 chip and 12M of RAM. But most people will need more computer muscle than that to get their work done.

How do you know how much CPU and memory you have? Watch your PC's screen when you first turn it on; most computers introduce the CPU and inventory memory here. The only trick is converting kilobytes (K) into megabytes (M), and vice versa. There are roughly a thousand kilobytes in one megabyte, so if your PC counts to 12288K when you start it up, you really have 12M. That's the bare minimum you need for Windows NT—16M is better.

Q&A *My PC is getting really slow. What could be wrong?*

You might be running low on memory. When Windows runs out of RAM, it first tries to use the hard disk to simulate extra memory. Windows takes the chunk of RAM your first program is using and swaps it from memory onto the hard disk (which is about a thousand times slower than RAM). That frees up a chunk of RAM for your second program to use, but when you switch back to the first program, Windows has to swap both chunks of data. Add another program, and pretty soon Windows is spending all its time swapping data onto your hard drive and back again instead of running programs. The result is a lot of noise from your hard disk, and a PC that's running in super-slo-mo.

It's a clever fake, but anyone who's ever seen an Elvis impersonator knows there's nothing like the real thing. If your system slows to a crawl too often, you need more memory.

TIP **CPU speed is measured in megahertz, which stands for one million** cycles-per-second. (Each cycle is one little two-step for your CPU; it's not a very complicated move, but since some CPUs can do 200 million of these hokey-pokeys every second, it looks like it's dancing up a storm.) The more megahertz you have, the more muscles your PC can flex: In Windows terms, 20 is slower than a bottle of Heinz ketchup; 200 is faster than a Roger Clemens fastball. If your CPU clocks in at 66MHz or more, you can run Windows NT just fine.

Sometimes the image seems blurry

To run Windows, you need a color monitor and a video card. Windows can usually recognize your video card and set things up so it works properly. Like TVs, monitor screens are measured diagonally. And they're never, ever as big as they claim to be.

CAUTION **There's one place where I draw the line when it comes to saving** money on hardware. I won't settle for a crummy monitor, and you shouldn't, either. We're talking about your *eyes*, for heaven's sake. You're not likely to go blind from using an undersized monitor with a blurry image, but you'll probably go home with a headache every day. If you have to cut corners with a slower PC, that's one thing. But make sure your monitor isn't going to hurt your eyes.

Is my hard disk big enough?

Hard drives are measured in **megabytes,** unless you have more than one thousand or them, which equals a **gigabyte** (pronounce it GIG-uh-bite). To run Windows and one additional program, you'll need *at least* a 200M hard drive, and that won't leave a lot of room for your work. Depending on the kind of software you use and the type of data files you create, you may need 500M or more to hold it all.

How much room is left on your hard disk? Look in Chapter 5 for step-by-step instructions on how to find out.

 TIP If you think you've run out of disk space, you might be surprised: You can use Windows NT's built-in disk-compression features to pack nearly twice as much data into the same space. For more details, see Chapter 5.

Don't forget about the floppy disk!

Some older PCs only have one drive, designed to use 5.25-inch disks (you can spot these because they're big and soft—you can literally bend them in half). These days, most computers use the smaller 3.5-inch disks, and Windows NT won't even recognize the old variety. It's almost impossible to find new software on the larger disks, and the smaller ones are more reliable and durable anyway.

And, of course, the mouse and keyboard

It may seem obvious, but to run Windows you have to have a mouse and a keyboard.

Unless you spill a Diet Coke on your keyboard there's no real reason to replace it, although these days there are all sorts of wacky keyboard designs to choose from. Most of them look like they survived a 7.1 earthquake, with the keyboard split into two pieces. The theory is that you'll be less likely to get carpal tunnel syndrome if you hold your hands sideways while you type. I have a hard enough time making my two fingers hit the keys when I can see them, so I'll stick with the traditional design, thank you very much.

66 *Plain English, please!*

And, now that I've made my opinion clear, let me add a brief note about the Microsoft Natural Keyboard. My editor insists that switching to this keyboard helped her get off of the therapist's schedule and back to work, with a tremendous decrease in pain in her wrists from tendonitis. 99

As for **mice** (which is the plural of mouse, although some people say **mouses** and a few wackos say **meeses,** as in "I hate those meeses to pieces"), you have two basic choices. The dull, conventional mouse that comes with most PCs looks like a bar of soap with a long wire dangling out the back. If you don't like sliding the mouse around on your desktop, with or without a mouse pad, try a **trackball**. Unlike the bar-of-soap mouse, which has a roller on the bottom, the trackball has a roller in the top; the whole thing stays in one place while you twiddle the roller with your thumb.

Trackballs are most popular on notebook PCs, where a long dangling cord is likely to get under the wheels of the drink cart as the flight attendant rolls by. Some notebooks have bizarre mouse substitutes that look like pencil erasers or little pads. Not to worry—the point is still to move the pointer on the screen. As long as there's a left and right button, you're in business.

How to put your work on paper

Printers help you dazzle other people with your brilliant ideas, even if you can't convince them to come around and look over your shoulder at whatever's on your screen. We'll cover printers and how to use 'em with Windows in Chapter 15. Plenty of info there.

Connecting with other computers

Modems let you hook your PC to a telephone line and do all sorts of cool things—send e-mail, find files on your PC at the office without leaving your living room, and cruise up and down the Information Superhighway. We'll talk about modems later in this chapter.

Network adapters connect your PC to other PCs so that all the computers on the network can share files, folders, printers, and so on. Setting up a network is best left to experts, but using them with Windows is really pretty easy. For the details, see Chapter 20.

Do you need a multimedia PC?

If you're the one using it, a **multimedia PC** is a powerful tool for adding lifelike sound and video clips to presentations and important documents. If the guy in the next cubicle is using it, though, multimedia is a big waste of money, and if I hear that stupid Homer Simpson sound clip one more time, I'll rip those speakers out of the back of his PC.

Ahem. Multimedia *is* controversial. For most people, it's unnecessary but fun. Typical multimedia PCs include a CD-ROM player, a sound card, a pair of speakers, and perhaps a microphone. We'll cover multimedia in more detail in Chapters 17 and 18.

Let's talk for a second about ergonomics

Maybe the most important parts of your PC aren't parts of your PC at all. If you use a computer regularly, you owe it to yourself (and your body) to pay attention to the way you sit in front of your computer.

The human body wasn't designed to handle the stress of nonstop typing. When you twist your body up like a pretzel and pound on a keyboard for hours at a time, the results can be painful, and you can even permanently damage your back, neck, or wrists if you don't use your PC properly.

The most infamous disorder attributed to the stress of computing is called **carpal tunnel syndrome**, a specific kind of repetitive stress injury—the symptoms include debilitating pain in the wrists and, in severe cases, permanent nerve damage. How do you avoid this and other unpleasant PC problems? Ask an expert in **ergonomics**—the science of designing human-friendly working environments.

Among other things, an ergonomic expert will tell you the following:

- Use a chair that gives you good back support, and make sure it's the right height.

- Give your wrists a rest, literally, with a padded cushion that sits in front of your keyboard. That way, your wrist muscles won't stretch into unnatural, potentially damaging positions.

- Make sure your monitor is at least two feet away from your face, and that you don't have to stretch your neck to view it properly.

- And take a break at least every half hour. There are even computer programs that will pop up a message every so often to remind you that you've been typing too long.

Using a modem (and setting it up)

A **modem** (pronounce it *moe*-dem) is a specialized piece of hardware that converts data from digital form—bits and bytes on your hard disk or your computer's memory—into analog form, that high-pitched warbling sound you hear when two modems meet. What sounds like horrible screeching is actually the very precise language that two modems use to transfer information back and forth.

With the right software, you can use your modem to exchange just about any form of information. Depending on what you're trying to accomplish, the communications part may work in the **background**, shuffling data into and out of your computer while you work on something else. Or it may run as a **terminal program**—a sort of all-purpose communications window in which you type commands to tell the computer on the other end of the connection what you want to do.

> ## 66 *Plain English, please!*
>
> Why are they called modems? The mo is short for modulate (pronounce it mahd-juh-late), which is the process of converting the digital data on your PC into analog sound patterns that can travel over a telephone wire. The dem, as you might have guessed, is short for demodulate (same as before, but add dee on the front), which is the process of reassembling the sounds into bits at the other end of the line. Put it together and you get mo(dulator)-dem(odulator), an extremely formal term for the nearly magical devices that convert data between digital and analog forms. 99

How to install a modem

Windows NT doesn't recognize every modem ever made, but sometimes it feels that way. As part of its installation process, Windows can "talk" directly with your modem, ask it to identify itself using information stored on a chip inside the modem, and then automatically install the right software driver and communication settings for any of several hundred types of modems.

Before you can install a new modem, you'll need to log on as an administrator. If you don't, you'll see a dialog box like the one in Figure 24.1. You may need to enlist your system administrator's help to get the new modem installed. Fortunately, the whole process usually takes just a few minutes.

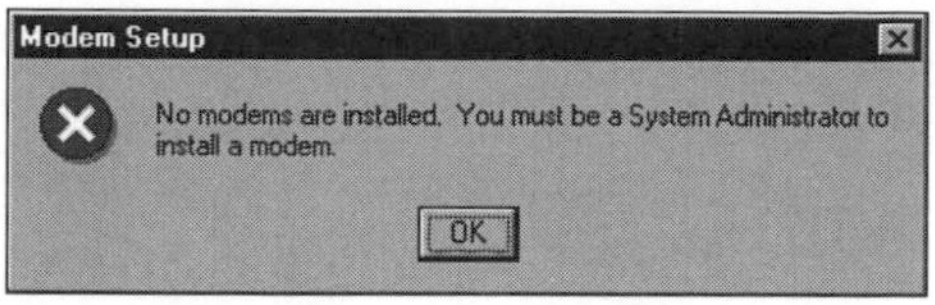

Fig. 24.1
Installing a new modem doesn't take long—as long as you have the help of a system administrator.

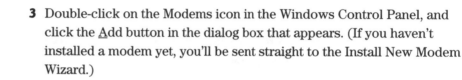

When you add a new modem to your computer, the best strategy is to let Windows figure out on its own what brand it is. Most of the time, Windows will get it right, and most of the time, the process won't take long. To let Windows take a stab at it, follow these steps:

1 Plug the modem into your PC and make sure both are powered up and ready to go.

2 Connect your telephone line to the modem.

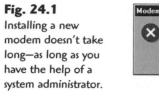 3  Double-click on the Modems icon in the Windows Control Panel, and click the <u>A</u>dd button in the dialog box that appears. (If you haven't installed a modem yet, you'll be sent straight to the Install New Modem Wizard.)

The Install New Modem Wizard (shown in Fig. 24.2) pops up. Follow the instructions, and you should be done within a few clicks.

Fig. 24.2
The Install New Modem Wizard walks you through the process of introducing a new modem to Windows.

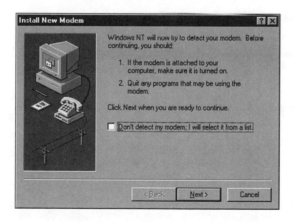

TIP **Should you use an *internal modem* that sits inside your PC? Or are** you better off with an **external modem**, which plugs into the back of your PC and sits on your desktop? The internal species cost less and save space. External modems are easier to turn off when you run into troubles, and they give you a (sometimes) useful set of blinking lights and LED displays to watch as you connect. Personally, I prefer external modems, but you can't go wrong with either choice.

Making connections

After you've successfully set up the hardware part of your modem, it's sometimes necessary to configure the software side so that other modems can understand your modem when it starts squalling. Click the Connection tab of the Properties dialog box for the modem you're using (see Fig. 24.3) to see which options are available.

Q&A *What should you do with that button labeled Advanced?*

Ignore it. Most of the options there will thoroughly scramble your attempts to communicate with the outside world. Don't mess with these settings unless a modem expert tells you to. And even then, tread carefully.

Never overlook the obvious when your equipment isn't working

I once mobilized an entire technical support department to diagnose a serious communication problem. It turned out that I, um, well... OK, I had forgotten to connect the modem to my phone line. (The tech support guy had a good sense of humor, fortunately.) I learned that day to always check the obvious. Before you ask for help, ask yourself these questions:

- Is the modem plugged in?
- Is the power turned on?
- Is the modem connected to the phone line?

- Have I checked the connections carefully? Any loose wires?
- Is my modem dialing the right phone number?

Oh, and this advice applies to more than just modems. Try running through an equivalent checklist any time you have a problem with your PC or printer. Unless, of course, you *like* having a tech support expert tell you to turn on the power before you call next time.

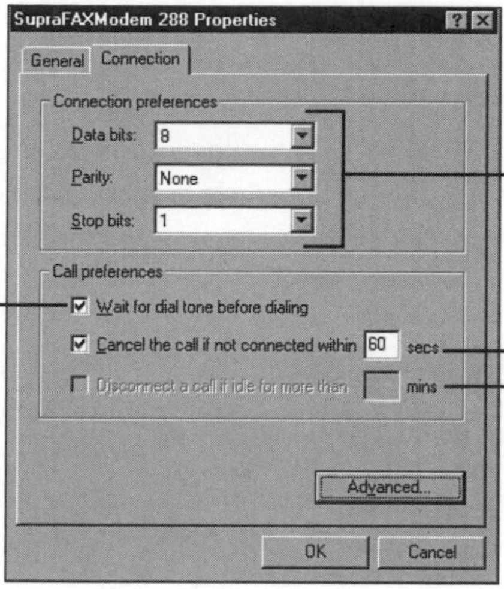

Fig. 24.3
Here's where you adjust the fine points of your online connection.

Having trouble connecting because Windows starts punching out tones before the dial tone is ready? Make sure this box is checked.

The default connection assumes you'll use the settings 8-None-1. If you see a screen full of garbage when you first connect, try resetting these boxes to 7-Even-1 instead.

Tell Windows that if the phone rings for too long, it's probably time to hang up and try later. The default is 60 seconds.

Tell Windows that you want it to hang up automatically if you forget to disconnect on your own. This feature is very handy when you're paying for online time by the minute.

Why does Windows care where you are?

In communications, just as in real estate, location is everything. Does the phone at your office work the same as the one at home? Probably not. And what about hotels? If you're in the office, you might need to dial 9 to get an outside line. At some hotels, you dial 8 to access long distance lines. At home, you just dial the number. Windows lets you define and save different locations as part of your communication profile. When you move from one location to another, just let Windows know, and it will handle the dialing details flawlessly.

Dialing for data with HyperTerminal

Once you've got the modem properly configured and all the settings just so, it's time to connect to the outside world. You may have a communications program that automatically hooks up to an online service. (If you use America Online or CompuServe, for example, the software these companies provide does everything for you.) But you can also use a terminal program to control the remote computer directly. This procedure is always more difficult, because you actually have to type commands at a prompt. But for some systems, it's the only option for getting connected.

How to set up a new location

To switch locations, double-click on the Modems icon in Control Panel, then click the button labeled Dialing Properties. You'll see a dialog box much like this one. Set up the location as desired. Then click OK to save your changes, Cancel to back out without saving.

TIP **You might choose to set up several locations on a single computer, even if** you never leave your desk. This trick can be useful if you want to dial some calls direct and charge others to a telephone calling card or an alternate long-distance carrier. Just set up a new "location" for each billing option, give it a descriptive name like "MCI Calling Card," and enter the appropriate details.

The drop-down list contains all the locations you've defined. Click New to begin a brand-new location; click Remove to get rid of a location you don't plan to use again.

Want to charge the call to a telephone credit card instead of the phone you're using? Check this box and follow the instructions.

Enter the area code and country of the location. Windows will compare these items against the numbers in your address book or connection document to decide whether a call is local or long distance.

Dialing Properties

My Locations

I am dialing from: Hyatt Bellevue   New...   Remove

Where I am:

The area code is: 206

I am in: United States of America

How I dial from this location:

To access an outside line, 1st dial: 9 for local, 8 for long dist.

☐ Dial using Calling Card: None (Direct Dial)   Change...

☐ This location has call waiting. To disable it, dial:

The phone system at this location uses: ⦿ Tone dialing ○ Pulse dialing

OK   Cancel   Apply

Finally, if you're traveling in a place where they still haven't switched to touch-tone phones, change this option.

Do you need to dial a special prefix to get an outside line? Enter local and long-distance options here.

*If you have Call Waiting, the beeping tones can thoroughly befuddle a modem. Check here to disable call waiting. On many phone systems, you can punch *70 to turn off this feature.*

TIP **What's the difference between Dial-Up Networking and HyperTerminal?** Although both use a modem and a phone line to connect your computer with the outside world, their goals are different. Use HyperTerminal to call another computer and access its menus—as you might with a telephone banking service. Use Dial-Up Networking and your modem to connect to your company's network or the Internet over a telephone line.

HyperTerminal is the Windows NT and Windows 95 replacement for the old Terminal program that came with older versions of Windows. To use HyperTerminal, you create and save a connection document that contains all the settings for the number you want to call. Later, you just double-click on the icon for your connection to dial up again. Here's how it works.

To open the HyperTerminal folder, click on the Start button and follow the cascading menus from Programs to Accessories, then open the HyperTerminal folder. See the icon labeled Hypertrm? Double-click here to start a new document with all the information you need to connect to another computer.

The process couldn't be simpler. Give your connection a name, pick an icon from the list that the setup wizard offers, and click OK. You'll see a dialog box like the one in Figure 24.4. Fill in the blanks and click OK.

Fig. 24.4
Setting up a HyperTerminal connection is simple: Enter an area code and a phone number, and tell Windows which modem you expect to use.

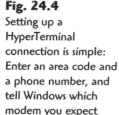

You're finished. HyperTerminal assumes you're ready to dial right now and pops up the dialog box shown in Figure 24.5. Pick a new location if you need to, then click the Dial button to establish your connection.

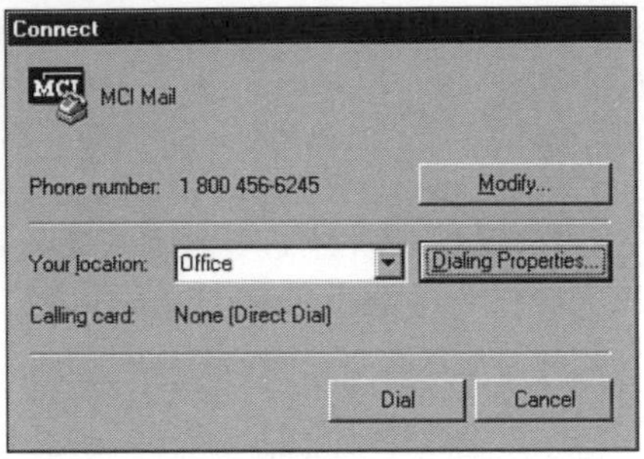

Fig. 24.5
Use a HyperTerminal connection to dial into another computer or an online service. You can tell Windows to use a different location so you don't have to worry about dialing the right numbers first.

There isn't enough space here to cover all the things you can do with HyperTerminal. For that, you should check out the online help files. But here's a sample of some things worth trying:

- Every time you make a connection, the program saves the data that passed by on your screen. As long as you save the connection, you can open it again and review the text from the last session.

- To save any of the text that scrolls through the HyperTerminal window, select it with the mouse and copy it to the Clipboard, then paste it into Notepad or another text editor.

- To make a connection or disconnect immediately, use the icons on the HyperTerminal toolbar.

- You can send and receive files of all sorts when you've connected to another modem. Pull down the <u>T</u>ransfer menu and look for the <u>S</u>end File and <u>R</u>eceive File options.

 TIP **If the typeface that HyperTerminal uses is too small to see** comfortably, or too large to fit properly in your window, change it! Choose <u>V</u>iew, <u>F</u>ont to pick a different typeface and size. Don't expect too many choices, though: HyperTerminal will only use a handful of fixed-size fonts that make sense in a terminal window

Setting up the Windows Phone Dialer

Thanks to one last Windows accessory, you can actually use your modem as a sort of personal assistant to place phone calls for you. (Of course, this only works if your phone and modem are properly hooked together. Make sure there's a phone line running from your wall jack to the line jack of your modem, and another wire running between your telephone and the phone jack on your modem.) Here's how.

 Look in the Accessories folder for the Phone Dialer icon (if it's not there, you may have to install it using your original Windows NT CD-ROM). Click to pop up a window like the one in Figure 24.6.

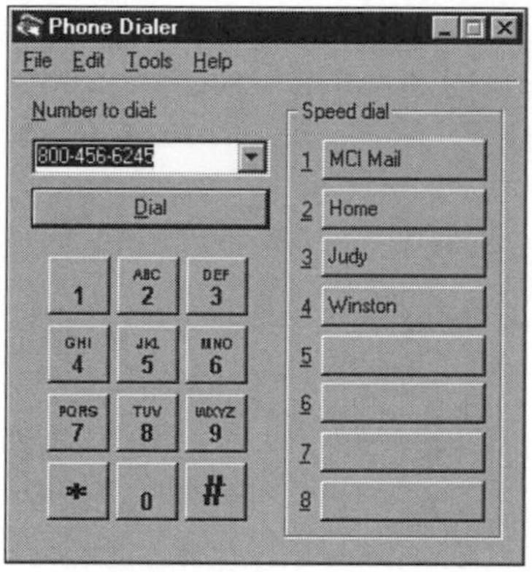

Fig. 24.6
The Windows Phone Dialer uses your modem to place phone calls. Once you hear the ringing phone, it's OK to pick up the line and prepare to start talking.

To dial a number, click in the box at the top left and enter your number. You can also click on the keypad buttons to enter the phone number. If you use a program like Schedule+ (included with Microsoft Office) or the Windows Messaging Inbox, you can click a button in your phone book to automatically start up the Phone Dialer and punch in the numbers.

When you hear the phone ringing, pick up the receiver and prepare to start talking.

To program one of the Speed dial buttons at right, just click on the button and fill in the dialog box shown in Figure 24.7. Add a name and telephone number, then click one of the Save options. Now you can dial that number simply by clicking the Speed dial button.

 I programmed a speed dial button, but I got it wrong. How do I start over?

Choose Edit, Speed Dial, then click the button you want to change.

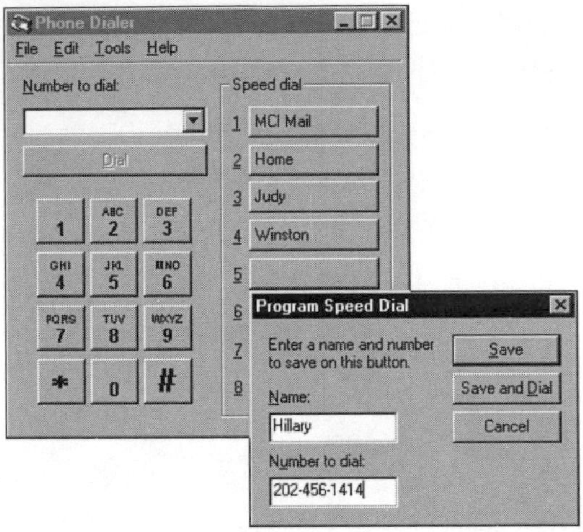

Fig. 24.7
Always calling the same numbers? Add the number for your best friend or your best customer to one of these speed dial buttons.

This @%&#!! modem doesn't work!

Murphy has a special book of "Murphy's laws" reserved just for modems and communications issues. It's a thick book, too. The best starting place for fixing modem problems is the Windows online help system. Search for `Troubleshooting` and find the page shown in Figure 24.8. Virtually all the tough modem problems are explained well here, with helpful step-by-step instructions.

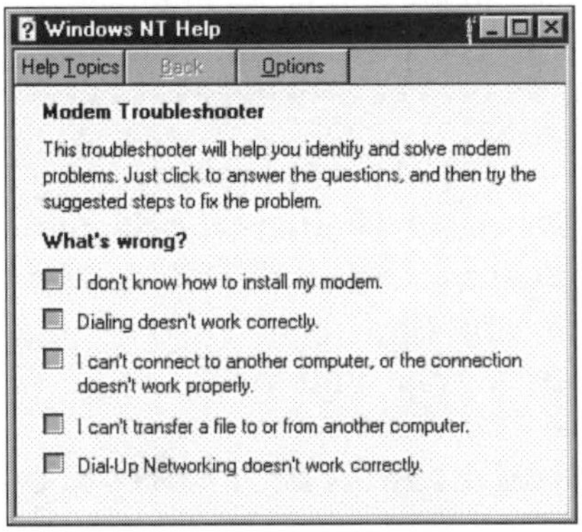

Fig. 24.8
Use the Windows online help to track down trouble with your modem.

How fast is fast enough?

If you were sending nothing but one-line messages to the people on your electronic mailing list, you probably wouldn't care how fast your modem is. But when you start sending around complicated messages with attached files, you soon discover that time really is money. If you can send twice as many bits across the wire every minute, you can send the same file in half the time.

Modem speeds are a moving target, but today the fastest conventional (analog) modems transmit data at a maximum speed of 28,800 bits per second, or bps. The previous generation of modems, many of them still in use today, operate at half that speed, or 14,400 bps. (Just say "twenty-eight-eight" or "fourteen-four" if you want to impress other people as a computer expert.) Still older models work at 9,600 bps.

For some jobs, such as transferring e-mail or accessing a text-based bulletin board system, a modem that runs at 14,400 bps is sufficient. If you intend to browse the World Wide Web or transmit other large graphics and sound files, you'll want a 28,800 bps modem.

Want to go faster than that? Sorry, no can do—at least not with this technology. You'll have to switch to a different telephone standard called ISDN (Integrated Services Digital Network). Windows NT works well with ISDN adapters, but that's a topic for another book. For now, just stick with POTS (Plain Old Telephone Service).

Index

X - Y - Z

A VIACOM SERVICE

The Information SuperLibrary™

Bookstore	Search	What's New	Reference	Software	Newsletter	Company Overviews
Yellow Pages	Internet Starter Kit	HTML Workshop	Win a Free T-Shirt!	Macmillan Computer Publishing	Site Map	Talk to Us

CHECK OUT THE BOOKS IN THIS LIBRARY.

You'll find thousands of shareware files and over 1600 computer books designed for both technowizards and technophobes. You can browse through 700 sample chapters, get the latest news on the Net, and find just about anything using our massive search directories.

All Macmillan Computer Publishing books are available at your local bookstore.

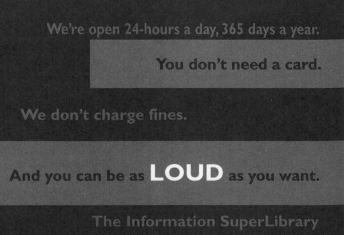

We're open 24-hours a day, 365 days a year.

You don't need a card.

We don't charge fines.

And you can be as **LOUD** as you want.

The Information SuperLibrary
http://www.mcp.com/mcp/   ftp.mcp.com